Management and Expenditure on Higher Education

Management and Expenditure on Higher Education

Editors

Dr Gedam Kamalakar
&
Dr Rupavath Chandru

KALPAZ

ISBN: 978-93-5324-963-2 (HB)

First Published, 2023

Published by

Kalpaz Publications
C-30, Satyawati Nagar,
Delhi – 110052
Ph.: 011-47034999, 9811692060
www.kalpazpublications.com
E-mail: kalpaz@hotmail.com

Printed at: **Gyan Press, Delhi.**

Contents

Foreword 11
Preface 13
Acknowledgement 15
List of Contributors 17

1. Use of Technology in Classrooms 21
Dr Kurapati Suresh Kumar

2. Individual Demand for Technical/Professional Education versus General Higher Education in Tamil Nadu 29
Dr Annamalai Jegan

3. Efficacy of a Customised English Language Learning Google Site: Scope for Blended Learning in the Post-Covid Times 43
Roopna Ravindran

4. Causes of Pedagogical Issues and its Effect on Student Centric Learning and Leadership - A Study of Teaching Approach in Covid Times 51
Mrs Phebi Priyadarsini & Ms Syeda Maryam

5. How to 'Future-Proof' The Utilisation of Space in Universities by Integrating New Digital Technologies 56
Madan Mohan Laddunuri

6. A Study of the Higher Education Sector in Telangana on the Impact of Teaching Resources in Online Teaching 66
Samala Anjaneyulu

7. A study on Undergraduation Student's Perception towards Entrepreneurship Education in Telangana 75
Swetha Konatham

8. National Educational Policy 2020: Some Insights 83
Dr P. Venugopal

9. NEP 2020: A Review in Post Covid Scenario 90
Dr C. Rama Mohan Reddy

10. Higher Education at Cross Roads: Post Covid-19 Scenario in India 98
Dr T. Sasikanth Reddy

11. UGC and Higher Education in India 105
Dr K.S.C. Rangarao & Dr V. Govindu

12. Emerging Trends in Higher Education Union Industry Government Partnership 115
Aditya Sharma

13. Impact of Covid-19 on the Higher Education System of Rural Areas in Telangana 121
Tula Ravikumar

14. Covid-19: Implications for Equity and Inclusion in Higher Education 129
Ananya Behera and Abbas Mohammad

15. Higher Education in India: Contemporary Issues and Remedies .. 139
Dr M. Sriramulu

16. Adoption of Foreign Policies and Practices in Promoting Equality and Inclusiveness in the Education 145
Nooreen Gowher

17. Impact of Technology on Education after Covid-19 153
Dr Ratna G. Chandak

18. Liberalising India's Private Vision of the National Education Policy 2020 163
Ch. Bikshapathi

19. Holistic, Multidisciplinary and Futuristic Aspects of Education in the Light of NEP-2020 169
Dr Asit Mantry

20. Promoting Critical Thinking Skills in Students 174
Dr B. Prathima

21. Teaching Learning Strategies in Higher Education 183
Dr Ch. Prasad

22. Higher Education Access and Equity in Dalit in India 190
Dr Enapa Upender Rao

23. Teaching, Learning and Evaluation (TLE) in Higher Education Institutions during Covid-19 Havoc: Some empirical findings and amicable suggestions 201
Dr Gopala Sudarshanam

24. India Joining the Mainstream of Global Standard Higher Education: A Review 217
Dr K. Krishna Murthy

25. Impact of Covid-19 on Higher Education in India : A Critical Review 221
Dr Mahesh Kumar Ganwar

26. Modernisation of Higher Education towards Achieving Equity 229
Dr Mohanraj N. Pattar & Dr Premchand Chavan

27. Collaborative Learning Assessment 234
Dr Mrunali N. Deshpande (Lilhare)

28. Role of Technology in Education Role in Media and Society 241
Dr N. Manikyarao

29. Evaluation Assessment of Choice Based Credit System - A Critical Review 248
Dr Padala Thirupathi

30. Mobile-phone based Activities Programme for Teacher Educators 263
Dr Pagare Prashant

31. New Education Policy -2020: Impact on Social Sciences 269
Dr ParvatamVenkateshwar

32. Flipped Classrooms as a Source of Advancing the Process of Teaching and Learning 277
Dr Rafic Taj. V

33. Life Skills, Skill Development and Personality Development 288
Dr Sathyanarayana G.

34. Foreign Direct Investment and Role of Indian Higher Education System 2020 298
Dr Jaisheela. B

35. Evaluation and Assessment Teacher Education in India - A Critical Review 307
Kola Kiran Kumar

36. Higher Education in the Wake of Covid-19 Pandemic: Challenges for the Higher Education in Hill areas in Uttarakhand and Himachal Pradesh 316
Dr Veerababu & Mahesh Naamani

37. Equity and Inclusion in Higher Education 324
Monika

38. New Dimension in Higher Education in India 330
Dr Kandi Kamala

39. Status of Higher Education in India: E-Governance and Challenges 342
Dr M. Ramana

40. New Education Policy 2020 Major Challenges 347
Dr. A. Madhuri

41. Emerging Trends in Highere Education Technology Drive the Future of Education 355
Prof. C. R. Reddy

Index 361

Telangana State Council Of Higher Education
(A Statutory Body of the Government of Telangana)
Opp : Mahavir Hospital, Mahavir Marg, Masabtank, Hyderabad - 500 028.
Ph. 040-23311879, 040-23331118
Website : www.tsche.ac.in, E-mail : chairmantsche@gmail.com

MESSAGE

Higher Education is an important sector for the development and growth of individuals that contributes to the development of a country. There is a close link between education and employment. At any time, society and nation expect and desire that higher education is to contribute to the creation of new knowledge through research and diffusion of knowledge through effective learning processes. In contemporary times governments are aiming at that the knowledge created to achieve desired outcomes. Education system has evolved over centuries in response to social, economic and technological conditions which in turn impacted the education system. In the twenty first century the higher education ecosystem has undergone a dramatic and undeniable change. All societies, nations, individuals and institutions irrespective of ideology and value system are forced to accept the role, proliferation and impact of digital tools and technology platforms on higher education system. They have restructured not only the academic aspects but also the administrative frontiers of Higher Educational Institutions (HEIs).

The education sector is one among many to bear the brunt of the SARS CoV2 Virus (COVID-19) lockdowns. During the months followed the HEIs have suddenly moved into an online mode of delivery to attenuate the challenge by creating and establishing a "new normal" to evolve in to a new future. The New Education Policy envisions restructuring the current eco-system of education with long lasting results. It provides a lot of flexibility for all the stakeholders in meeting the challenges of the twenty first century. Proper implementation of ideas incorporated in the NEP document and the policy herald a new and bright future for the coming generations. A few components -of the policy are already adapted as mitigation measures to overcome the challenges thrown by the COVID 19. The volume covers a few aspects of the emerging ecosystem and challenges with which all the stakeholders are to be aware of. I appreciate the efforts made by the Department of Political Science, Government Degree College for Women, Begumpet, for organising an International Conference and publishing the proceedings of the conference. I also congratulate the editors, and Dr. Gedam Kamalakar, Dr Rupavath Chandru and paper writers, for their unstinted support to the cause of higher education and endeavour.

22.10.2022

Prof. R. Limbadri
Chairman

PROF.C. GANESH
Principal.

Office: 8331041300

UNIVERSITY COLLEGE OF ARTS & SOCIAL SCIENCES
Osmania University, Hyderabad – 500 007 (TS)
principal.ucass@gmail.com

Foreword

The world has realised that the economic success of the states is determined by their education systems. Education is a Nation's Strength. A developed nation is inevitably an educated nation. Indian higher education system is the third largest in the world, next to the United States and China. Since independence, India as a develop-ing nation is contentiously progressing in the education field. In today's day and age, the premise that quality higher education is crucial for sustainable human development is undeniable. Higher education leads to acquiring analytical and problem-solving skills, ultimately helping humans to develop intellectual curiosity and character. It pushes the students to identify and set career goals that make them ready for professional setups. Therefore, a refined higher education enables economic, physical and social well-being to a student. In 2022, the higher education ecosystem has undergone a dramatic and undeniable makeover. This volume is an attempt to analyze issues relating to privatisation, emergence of foreign education providers and issues of foreign direct investment in higher education in the Indian context. The level of practices of various providers has appeared on the scene due to high demand for higher education; however, there is no policy framework to deal with the changing phenomenon. There may be a scope for developing an imbalance in the growth of basic and applied disciplines. Hence regulations have to be made in order to deal with these issues and they are to be considered.

The volume covers a number of Issues related to the teachers formed the main component of the studies on the quality of higher education.

The other issues related to academic reform, privatisation of higher education and financing of higher education. The higher education in India has witnessed many fold increase beyond institutional capacity since independence.

Prof. Chinta Ganesh
Principal
University College of Arts and Social Sciences
Osmania University, Hyderabad.

Dr. B. R. Ambedkar Open University

Prof. G. Ram Reddy Marg, Road No. 46, Jubilee Hills
Hyderabad 500 033

Grams : "OPVARSITY"
Fax : 040-2354 4830
Tel: 040-2368 0466
Mobile: 09912 319439
E-mail: dresudharani@gmail.com

Preface

Higher education in India, recently, pitchforked into policy significance. The volume provides an overview of various aspects of India's higher education policy and dwells into the wider context of change. India as a rising economy has to orient its policies, strategies and perspectives' to the global challenges. At the same time, it has to be sensitive to its local, grassroots realities of equity and inclusive character. The quintessence of Higher Education Institutions (HEI), as envisioned in the National Education Policy 2020, aims at building vibrant community of scholars and researchers, breaking down silos between disciplines to enable students well-rounded in meeting challenges of the future. To a great extent a substantial number of HEIs in the country are offering either single stream courses or multidisciplinary courses with rigid disciplinary boundaries.

The volume discusses the present state of higher education in India. It analyses the broad structure of education and the way structure has been evolving. Higher education sector has in recent years been attracting increasing attention, largely due to its contribution to improving productivity, increasing economic growth, and enhancing innovation and technological capability. However, the pressure to expand, coupled with the Social constraints of the state, has compelled many governments to adopt market-friendly reforms to support the growing sector, which are more or less autonomous with respect to curriculum and financesThe volume is a compendium on various issues related to higher education in the context of internationalisation. We hope that academic administrators, policy makers, education instructors and researches will find insights on various issues.

Prof. E. Sudha Rani

Director (Academic) & I/C Dean

Acknowledgement

The Department of Political Science, Government Degree College for Women, Begumpet, Hyderabad has organized an International conference on "**New Dimensions in Higher Education in the Post Covid-19: Global Perspective**" on 24th & 25th March 2022 in Collaboration with ICSSR, New Delhi, TSCHE & NAAC. The Chief Guest of the conference Shri. Navin Mittal, IAS, Commissioner of Collegiate Education. Prof. D. Ravinder, Vice Chancellor, Osmania University, Hyderabad, Prof. Prof. R. Limbadri, Chairman, Telangana State Council of Higher Education (TSCHE), Prof T. Tirupati Rao, Chancellor of Manipur Central University. The conference has received 122 full papers and selected papers has been published in UGC Care listed journal in two volume 1 & 2 August 2022 ISSN No. 2347-7180 and remaining articles will be published ISBN Publication. I am very thankful to International speakers of USA, Singapore, Hong Kong & China and the scholars who have participated the conference from 15 states. I express my special thanks to Prof. Jandhyala B.G Tilak, Former Vice Chancellor, National Institute of Educational Planning and Administration, New Delhi for delivering keynote address. I feel highly honored and greatly indebted to Prof JLN Rao who has been a constant source of inspiration and for sparing his valuable time to guide this work and motivation which enhanced me to complete the conference proceedings in the form of kalpaz publication edited book. Eminent Professor Hara Gopal discussed on NAAC upgradation and quality enhancement, Prof. Kancha Ilaiah, Prof. T. Mrunalini, Ajay Gudavarthy, Associate Professor and Shri. Chiranjeevulu, IAS, participated in the conference. I express my heartfelt gratitude to Dr. K..Kamala, Asst. Professor of Political Science, Convener of International Conference who has given an opportunity and motivation to be an editor and proofreader of this volume.

Dr. G. Kamalakar
Dept. of Political Science
Osmania University Hyderabad

List of Contributors

Dr. Suresh Kumar Kurapati, Lecturer in Political Science, Prakasam, Andhra Pradesh, India

Dr. Annamalai Jegan, Assistant Professor, Department of Economics, Kanchi Mamunivar Government Institute for Post-graduate Studies and Research (Autonomous), Puducherry, India

Roopna Ravindran, Assistant Professor, Dept. of English, GDC, Chevella, Telangana India

Mrs Phebi Priyadarsini, Research Scholar- NIT AP, Assistant Professor, Department of Business Administration, Loyola Academy, Secunderabad, Telangana State. 500010.

Ms Syeda Maryam, BBA Student, Department of Business Administration, Loyola Academy, Secunderabad, Telangana, India

Madan Mohan Laddunuri, Affiliation: Mallareddy University Hyderabad Telangana India

Samala Anjaneyulu, Assistant Professor P.V. Ram Reddy P.G. College, Hyderabad, Telangana, India

Swetha Konatham, Assistant Professor, Princeton Degree and PG College, Ramathapur Hyderabad, Telangana, India

Dr. P. Venugopal, Asst. Professor, Dept. of Commerce, Govt. Degree College Nagari, Chittoor Dist, A.P India

Dr. C. Rama Mohan Reddy, Lecturer Political Science, Govt. Degree CollegeYerraguntla Town, YSR Kadapa Dist, A.P India

Dr. T. Sasikanth Reddy, Lecturer in English, S.C.N.R Govt. Degree College, Proddatur Town, YSR Dist, A.P. India

Dr. K.S.V. Rangarao, Lecturer In Political Science, Sri. D.N.R. Govt. Degree College For Women Palakol W.G.Dt. AP. India

Dr. V. Govindu, Faculty, Department Of Political Science And Public Adminis-tration, Vikrama Simhapuri university, Nellore, Andhra Pradesh, India

Aditya Sharma Loyola academy, Old alwal, Secunderabad Telangana India

Dr Tula Ravi Kumar, Dept. of Political Science, Osmania University, Hyderabad, Telangana, India

Ananya Behera, Former Senior Research Fellow, Department of Sociology, Utkal University, Bhubaneswar

Abbas Mohammad, Guest Faculty, Karnataka State Law University, Hubbali

Dr. M. Sriramulu, Lecturer In Commerce, Andhra Pradesh, India

Nooreen Gowher, Student Pursuing M.Ed, Hyderabad, Telangana, India

Dr Ratna Ghanshyam Chandak Principal, Akola, India

Ch. Bikshapathi, Associate Professor In Political Science, Hyderabad, India

Dr. Asit Mantry, Assistant Professor,

Dr B. Prathima a, Assistant Professor, Dept of Commerce, A.P, India

Dr. Ch. Prasad, Principal, Siddipet, Telangana, India

Dr. Enapa Upender Rao, Assistant Professor Contract, Dept. of English, Hyderabad, India

Dr. Gopala Sudarshanam, Senior Assistant Professor Of Commerce, Siddipet, Telangana, India

Dr. K. Krishna Murthy, Assistant Professor, Department Of Telugu, Hyderabad, Telangana

Dr. Mahesh Kumar Ganwar Assistant Professor, Dept Of Sociology, Kalburgi, India

Dr. Mohanraj N. Pattar Assistant Professor Of Physics, Kalaburagi, India

Dr. Premchand Chavan Assistant Professor Of Physics, Kalaburagi, India

Dr. Mrunali N. Deshpande (Lilhare), Gondia, India

Dr. N. Manikyarao, Faculty Member, Dept. Of Journalism And Mass Communication, Nagarjuna University, Andhra Pradesh, India

Dr. Padala Thirupathi, Assistant Professor, Department Of Botany, Jagtial, Telangana, India

Pagare Prashant, Department Of Education, Aurangabad, India

Dr. Parvatam Venkateshwar, Lecturer In Political Science, Hyderabad. Telangana, India

Dr. Rafic Taj. **V** Assistant Professor, Department Of Education, Karnataka, India

Dr. Sathyanarayana G. Principal , Hyderabad, Telangana, India

Dr. Jaisheela. B H.O.D. Department Telangana Of Commerce And Management, Karnataka, India

Kola Kiran Kumar, Research Scholar, Department of Education, Madhya Pradesh, India

Dr Veerababu Asst Professor Department Of Political Science, Hyderabad, India

Mahesh Naamani, Phd Research Scholar, Hyderabad, Telangana, India

Monika Research Scholar, Department Of Educational Studies, Jammu, India

Dr. Kandi Kamala, Assistant Professor, Dept. of Political Science, Government Degree University for Women (Autonomous) Begumpet, (Affiliation) of Osmania University, Hyderabad, Telangana State, India. 500016

Dr M.Ramana, Assistant professor, Department of Political Science, Hyderabad, Telangana, India

Dr. A. Madhuri, Asst Professor, Dept. of Microbiology

Prof. C. R. Reddy, UGC Emeritus of Commerce Sri Krishnadevaraya University

1

Use of Technology in Classrooms

Dr Kurapati Suresh Kumar

Abstract

Technology has modified the method of learning and teaching. Many learning theories can be used to apply and integrate this technology more effectively. Learning happens in situations, while technology focuses on the settings and programme which make learners be involved. The world is constantly changing and the ways in which we function at home, work, and school are also changing. The speed at which technology has developed plays a major role in these changes. Various types of technologies are used at present in the classroom. Technology in the classroom is manifested through the use of computers. The use of tech is a great help for teachers since they can already enhance their teaching skills and strategies every time they are facing their class. This technology is very essential in the classroom but there are some instances wherein this technology has been to be disadvantageous. The present paper focuses on the Advantages and Disadvantages of technology in the classroom.

Keywords: Technology, classroom, computer, teaching skill, teachers.

Introduction

Technology slowly seems to be taking over many aspects of human society. Education has gradually evolved to incorporate technology in the dissemination of information. This advancement has revolutionised the classroom environment leading to improved grades and learning experiences. The main argument for incorporating technology in the classroom is students should be able to apply classroom concepts to daily life with ease. Understanding the role technology plays in the classrooms and work among other areas is of vital importance. Staying competitive in the twenty-first century dictates the need for technological finesse. However, one of the biggest problems facing the radical change in the centuries-old pedagogical methods used in education is that no parent wants their children to be the initial case study.

Educators have seen first-hand the benefits of technology in the classroom. According to a study by the IT Trade Association CompTIA released, around 75 percent of educators think that technology has a positive impact on the education process. While many education experts tout the advantages of incorporating technology into the school curriculum and the classroom, technology can sometimes hinder learning and the educational process. Because schools occasionally purchase technology before their systems and educators are adequately equipped for and trained to use it effectively, technology sometimes goes unused or prevents students learning. Becoming aware of some of the disadvantages in utilising technology in the classrooms can allow schools to better prepare for the widespread use of computers and devices by their student and teacher populations. Nevertheless, using technology in the classrooms as a means of instruction would be useful by the teachers if they are supported by appropriate educational theories and models. Many researchers have investigated the effect of constructivism on classroom practices to know how technology usage and application in the classrooms can potentially increase the process of teaching and learning (Richards, 1998; Brush & Saye, 2009). According to Schunk (2000), constructivism is a "philosophical and psychological approach" which is built upon social cognitive proposes that individuals, conducts and the atmosphere is in mutual interaction. States that learning happens in situations where learners form what they have learned mostly and consider it as a task of their experience in situations. The learning settings are like atmospheres where tools of knowledge-building are provided to produce and influence the art of understanding through which students have teamwork and support one another as they utilise different tools and learning resources in their search for learning aims and activities for solving problems (Hannfin & Hill, 2002).

Objective

- Importance of technology in education.
- To know the types of technology used in the classroom.
- To know the advantages and disadvantages of technology in the classroom.

Importance of Technology in Education

The role of technology in the field of education is fourfold: it is included as a part of the curriculum, as an instructional delivery system, as a means of aiding instructions, and also as a tool to enhance the entire learning process. Thanks to technology; education has gone from passive and reactive to interactive and aggressive.

Education is essential in corporate and academic settings. In the former, education or training is used to help workers do things differently than they did before. In the latter; education is geared towards creating curiosity in the minds of students. In either case, the use of technology can help students understand and retain concepts better.

Factors affecting technology in education

Jung talks about the enormous challenge teachers are facing in our society due to the rapid expansion of knowledge. Modern technologies are demanding that teachers learn how to use these technologies in their teaching. Hence these new technologies increase the teachers' training needs. Gressard and Loyd (1985) asserted that teachers' attitudes toward computers are a key factor in the successful implementation of ICT in education. They pointed out that teachers do not always have positive attitudes towards computers and their poor attitudes may lead to a failure of the computer-based projects.

Types of Technology used in the classroom

1. *Use of computers in the classroom*: Computers have evolved and they have changed the way they look and the way they function. Nowadays we have both desktop computers and portable computers commonly known as notebooks or laptops. New technologies have also emerged and birthed some new computer-related gadgets like the iPod or galaxy tablet. These computers can be used by teachers to assign work to students and study groups in a classroom. Also, teachers can use computers to illustrate visually related subjects which helps students to learn easily. Modern computers come with installed applications which can help students study well.
2. *Creating class websites and blogs*: It is very easy to create a website or blog using word press or any other content management software. Teachers can create class blogs where they post assignments. If the school has no website sever to host these class blogs, the teacher can use free website hosting services like word press, blogger.com. Via these platforms, the teacher will create a blog under a subdomain of that host. Students will find all academic assignments via that blog.
3. *Use of mobile devices*: Teachers and students can use smartphones for academic purposes in the classroom. Mobile learning is becoming so popular, it is similar to e-learning or long-distance education.

4. *Use of digital microphones in the classroom*: Big classrooms are characterised by endless noise, so teachers can resort to these wireless digital microphones. The microphone will transmit the voice to the loudspeakers and every student will hear their teacher clearly. This helps the teacher not to strain their voice while trying to explain points to their students. These digital microphones are not too expensive so even a small income-generating school can manage to buy a wireless microphone for every classroom.
5. *Use of online media*: Teachers and students can both use online streaming media to learn in the classroom. With the aid of a projector, computer, internet, and a whiteboard, a teacher displays real-time examples using sites like youtube.com. This website has videos that can be used for academic reference.

Advantages and Disadvantages of Technology in the Classroom

1. Students can practice collaboration skills by working in teams on projects using shared documents or conferencing technologies. This allows collaboration to happen outside of the classroom or between classrooms in different locations.
2. Technology allows teachers to engage and motivate students in new ways, like taking students on a virtual field trip to other parts of the world.
3. Using technology can make classroom practice more interactive (if you have something like a smart board in your room) and can encourage kids to continue their learning at home (looking up something online from a lesson during the day). The teacher can provide links that may be useful for students.
4. Technology allows more communication for students and parents-kids who are too nervous to ask questions in class can email a teacher or ask for extra feedback on an essay.
5. Makes teaching efficient, in that there is less paper and organising and collating of notes. This helps the school work towards environmental sustainability and consciousness. Fewer photocopies and more online/USB exchanges.
6. Teachers can design student-centered lessons by allowing students to take an active part in the lesson. Classroom time can be spent with students asking critical questions and engaging in creative problem-solving.
7. While technology can be a great addition to the classroom, it also can be a source of frustration for both the teacher and the student.

Unless the teacher is well trained in technology and can support the hardware in the classroom, a technology expert will be needed to troubleshoot problems. If schools cannot support the purchased technology, it essentially renders it useless in times of crisis or disrepair. Additionally, technology often needs frequent maintenance to keep it in good condition for use.

8. Connection problems, downloading issues, policing software, and other difficulties can cause roadblocks when implementing a lesson in the technology-based classroom, teachers sometimes shy away from using it simply because of lack of time.
9. A lot of families cannot afford to continue updating their technological purchases (computers, laptops). Providing the technology themselves can be costly. On the other hand, some schools receive such little funding that technology in the classroom is a non-essential luxury.
10. Technology can have unexpected breakdowns. Power failures, low batteries, viruses, and broken equipment are all excuses students love to use.
11. Most students engage in multiple forms of communication online, this has led to a decrease in verbal and written literacy as students use short-hand expressions and do very little editing themselves.
12. Many experts and experienced people say that, due to such technology in education, student's imagination is affected, their thinking ability is reduced.
13. There can be health issues too when used over the limit.

Successful Technology Integration into the Classroom

Gorder (2008) stated that successful technology integration is what makes a difference in reforming a classroom. Integrating technology is not easy, it is a three-step process that involves the teacher learning the technology and using the technology in teaching and learning so that student learning is enhanced.

According to Hew (2007), teachers need specific technical information and know-how to use computer-based technologies in teaching. It is not enough for specialised progress to stress the method of operating a specific programme but additionally, there needs to be guided in how to use the programme to increase student learning. Emphasis also needs to be placed on classroom management as it relates to computer-based technologies. Additional rules and procedures need to be incorporated once computers, printers, and other electronics are added to the classroom mix.

Factors Contributing to Teacher's Use of Technology

According to Oblinger (2003), the millennial generation or the students who were born after 1982, is different from their former generation in noticeable features. The new ones are inclined to approach group activity and are interested in new technologies. They are actively fascinated by playing online video games and chatting. This is what is opposite to the traditional lecture style that the older generation of teachers believes in most classrooms. The method of learning for the new generation is centered on group work, empirical and multitasking activities, and using technology. For the new generation of learners, technology is regarded as an integral part of their daily lives in their environments.

There is a positive relationship between a teacher's computer self-efficacy and technology integration in the classroom (Koh & Frick, 2009). In a study conducted by Hernandez-Ramos (2005) he notes that since technology is frequently used by youth these days, sometimes student knowledge of technology can trump teacher knowledge. In these cases, the teacher's roles as the skillful and students as the amateur can often be exchanged and may cause some teachers to feel uncomfortable by this condition because most of the teachers tend to have mastery over the students in using technology in their classrooms.

Other important factors that help teachers use technology in teaching include modeling by colleagues, expectations by the administration of academic institutions, positive experiences with computers in teaching, and teacher beliefs and attitudes about technology in teaching. Researchers have shown that a key factor in encouraging teachers to introduce and sustain the use of multimedia in classroom instruction is modeling (Alvine, 2000; Becker, 2000; Bowman, 2000; Bullock, 2004; Aust *et al.,* 2005).

Constructivism as a Framework for Educational Technology

In a study conducted by Hernandez-Ramos (2005), the participants of the study who were teachers in the Silicon Valley in California were asked about the factors that affected their use of technology in the classroom. Results of the study proved that there are three main factors that affected teacher's technology incorporation practices:

1. If teachers had been prone to technology in their teacher training programmes, technology was utilised more often by both teachers and learners than in other classes.
2. The teachers who had an understanding of software usage used technology more often in their classes.

3. Teachers believing in constructivism used technology more often in their classrooms. Their students also used technology more often than those teachers and students who did not utilise technology. Constructivist teachers use their teaching methodology inspiring from the old Chinese saying: "Tell me and I will forget; show me, and I may remember; involve me and I will understand". This statement stresses that student's engagement in the learning is the best strategy.

Conclusion

The advantages discussed concerning computer technology in the classroom outweigh the disadvantages. Computer technology is a positive supplement to bridge the gap between education and the technological world in which we live. Effective teaching is possible while various types of technology will be integrated. Computer-assisted technologies in schools offer students greater access to information, and eager motivation to learn, a jump-start on marketable job skills, and an enhanced quality of classwork. Just adding a technology tool to a traditional teaching approach does not produce more effective instruction and makes the process harder and more complex without providing many benefits. For technology to be used effectively in the classroom, teachers have to make sure that they are using it as part of an approach that involves the students in the activity. Utilising technology does not necessarily mean that one should firmly be a supporter of constructivism, since it is essentially not persuasive for the group of teachers who still believe in traditional methods of teaching, and these two approaches are inclined to enhance the other and give the best results from both utilisation and a theoretical approach. As technology assists the teachers to plan their teaching materials in a way that supports their theoretical approach, they get less reluctant to utilise technology. The better application is that both constructivist theory and technology are integrated into the classrooms effectively since it prepares the tools which are vital for teachers to plan a teaching model that satisfies the requirements of a learner-oriented spotlight.

References

1. Brush, T., & Saye, J. W. (2009). Strategies for preparing preservice social studies teachers to integrate technology effectively: Model and practices. Contemporary Issues in Technology and Teacher Education, 9(1), 46-59.
2. Drayton, B., Falk, J. K., Stroud, R., Hobbs, K., & Hammerman, J. (2010). After installation: Ubiquitous computing and high school science in three experienced, high-technology schools. Journal of Technology, Learning, and Assessment, 9(3).

3. Gorder, L. M. (2008). A study of teacher perceptions of instructional technology integration in the classroom. Delta PI Epsilon Journal, 2, 63-76.
4. Hernandez-Ramos, P. (2005). If Not Herc, Where? Understanding Teachers' Use of Technology in Silicon Valley Schools.
5. Journal of Research on Technology in Education, (38)1, 39-64.
6. Hew, K. F. (2007). Integrating technology into k-12 teaching and learning: Current knowledge gaps and recommendations for future research. Educational Technology, Research, and Development, 55, 223-252.
7. Means, B. (2010). Technology and education change: Focus on student learning. Journal of Research on Technology in Education, 42(3), 285-307.
8. Richards, R. T. (1998). Infusing technology and literacy into the undergraduate teacher education curriculum through the use of electronic portfolios. T.H.E. Journal, 25(9), 46-50.
9. Schunk, D. H. (2000). Learning theories: an educational perspective. New Jersey: Prentice-Hall.
10. Bennett, F.(1999). Computers as tutors: solving the crisis in education. (p.3). sarasota, FL: Faben Inc. publishers.
11. Boyle, F.T. (1998).IBM taking head's and our classrooms. College English, 55(6), pp. 618-626.

2

Individual Demand for Technical/ Professional Education versus General Higher Education in Tamil Nadu

Dr Annamalai Jegan

Abstract

Increasing social demand for higher education is fuelled by a desire for higher education from large sections of people of India in the hope of attaining better quality of life and greater social equity. People demand more for technical/professional education than general education. Professional education gives more job opportunities, higher returns and social benefits. The demand for technical/professionals is more than general education degree holders. Professional/technical courses are comparatively more expensive than general education due to higher demand and supply constraints. On the other hand, Economic reforms and liberal education policies have encouraged private sector in providing higher education. Existence of privatisation has been working as de-facto commercialism. In this situation, who can affordable the high cost of higher education. This study is focuses on determinants of demand for higher education in Tamil Nadu in general and also estimating individual demand for technical/professional higher education and general higher education in particular. The study consists of both secondary and primary data analysis. For Secondary data, the study has been taken data from 1980-81 – 2006-07. To estimating the aggregate demand function for higher education used Multivariate regression method through Ordinary Least Square Method. The study reveals that the percentage of people living below poverty line and availability of higher education facilities influence aggregate demand function of higher education. For primary data analysis, the study has been taken sample area of Villupuram district in Tamil Nadu. The study made the logit model to estimate the individual enrolment choice between technical/professional education and general higher education. It reveals that gender, income group, board of examination, percentage of marks in class

12, type of management, income group and getting student loan influencing on individual demand function for higher education.

Key words: General higher education, Professioal, technical education, demand.

Introduction

In this study is to understand the student's enrollment choice between professional/technical higher education and general higher education examined. Technical/Professional education consists of medicine, medical auxiliaries, engineering and technology, law and others which include those courses which do not come under the board category like catering and hotel management, etc. General higher education consists of arts, science, commerce, and other subjects in humanities. People demand more for professional education than general education. Professional education gives more job opportunities, higher returns and social benefits. Secondly, in modern world, everything is technology based and high technologies are used in day-to-day life. So society needs more technical man power and resource persons. This is the reason why professional degree holders are shining in job market than other degree holders. The demand for professionals is more than general education degree holders. On the other hand, professional courses are comparatively more expensive than general education due to higher demand and supply constraints. In this situation, all students are unable to go for professional education. We need to understand that socio-economic factors and non-economic factors are influencing students go to enroll in professional/technical education.

Methodology and Source of Data

To examine this objective, the study has adopted both Secondary and primary data analysis. For Secondary data analysis, the study period is covered from 1980-81 – 2006-07. The data collected from various official documents and reports such as Tamil Nadu Development Report, UGC Annual Report, Selected Education Statistics (SES), Analysis of Budget Expenditure on Education and Indian Economic Survey. To estimating the aggregate demand function for higher education in Tamil Nadu used Multivariate regression method through Ordinary Least Square Method.

To understand the choice behaviour of an individual student the primary data was collected. The study traced the passed out students from the graduated higher secondary school. Primary data were collected through well-planned survey in the sample district of Villupuram in Tamil Nadu. Tracer method was adopted to find out whether students enrolled for higher education or not. Proportionate simple random sampling is used at different stages of sample design for selected sample schools, sample students and by gender and specific groups in each sample school. A structured questionnaire survey schedule was used for data collection from two percent of sample higher secondary graduate students in Villupuram district in the academic year 2008-09. Logistic regression is to identify the relationship between the independent variables and the probability of occurrence. This function is the logit function also called as log-odds function Demand for higher education in sample district, analyzed in this chapter, consists of two parts. First, the logit models have been used to estimate the factors that decide demand for higher education and the second part has predicted the probability of demand (enrollment) for higher education.

Aggregate Demand Function for Higher Education in Tamil Nadu during 1980-81 to 2006-07

Tamil Nadu is one of the major states of India and a progressive state in the status of growth and performance of education in general and higher education in particular. It is high in achievement of school education at different levels such as primary, secondary and higher secondary schooling. As a result upstream higher education is expected to do better in terms of enrollment (higher demand) growth. It is a high literacy state and people in the state are aware of the value of education. It is significant to note that public policy and public spending of the state is high when compared to other states. The emphasis on policy is on access and equity. There is a policy for reservations which provides 69 percent to Schedule Castes, Schedule Tribes and Other Backward Classes. It allows greater opportunities to the people from socially and economically backward groups. This context is necessary to study demand for higher education in Tamil Nadu. Purpose of the study is to derive the aggregate demand function for higher education in Tamil Nadu through time series data for the period 1980-81 to 2006-07.

In the model, aggregate demand function for Tamil Nadu during 1980-81 to 2006-07 is given below:

$$Y = 9.060^{*} - 0.111^{*}\,\text{Perbpl} + 0.162^{*}\,\text{Heispl}$$

$$(0.098) \quad (-6.661) \quad (3.033)$$

R^2=0.956, Adjusted R^2= 0.953, F = 262.557, No. of Obs. = 27 (1980-81-2006-07)

The result of linear regression shows that the percentage of people living below poverty line and availability of higher education facilities influence aggregate demand function of higher education. The value of R^2 indicates that 98 percent of variation in demand for higher education in Tamil Nadu is explained by percentage of people living below poverty line and availability of higher education facilities.

Percentage of people living below poverty line (BPL) is negatively impacting demand for higher education at one percent level of significance. The result shows that a unit fall in percentage of people below poverty line leads to increase in GER by 0.111. As a result of affirmative action policy by the state, the economic opportunities to the poor people have been increasing and there is a resultant decline in the proportion of people below poverty line and this has resulted in higher demand for higher education in Tamil Nadu.

Secondly, availability of higher education facilities shows a positive sign with one percent significance influencing aggregate demand function for higher education in Tamil Nadu. The result depict that more the number of higher educational institutions in the system, higher the students enrollment. It is true in the case of Tamil Nadu, it is having 17 state universities, 20 deemed universities, 3 institutions of national importance and 1345 colleges, in addition to the recently opened Central University at Thiruvarur. It has tremendously increased the growth of student enrollment for higher education.

Coefficient for availability of higher education is positive with enrollment. It shows that more number of higher education institutions in Tamil Nadu the more number of students enrolled in higher education. This indeed is true in Tamil Nadu. The aspiration effect that we witnessed in case of India led to large number of educational institutions in the state accommodating the aspirations of youth to join higher education. The result testifies that proportion of population below poverty line has declined in Tamil Nadu. The reduction which may be due to increase in income per capita and the effect of interventions to reduce the below poverty line people has added to the aspirations to study in higher education institutions.

Student's Enrolment Choice between Professional/Technical Education and General Higher Education in Tamil Nadu

In this model out of the 283 students who opted to join degree courses, 181 students are enrolled in general degree courses and the remaining 102 in technical and professional degree courses, (63.95 percent and 36.1 percent respectively). It would be worth examining why students chose technical and professional degree courses and not the general degree courses. The model thus looks like:

ENROL_TPHE = 1 if the student has enrolled in various technical and professional courses such as Engineering/Technology, Medicine, Alternative medicine, Medical assistance, and Computer

Applications in various kind of higher education like central/ state universities, affiliated colleges and autonomous institutions and

= 0, otherwise (Enrolled in general course in higher education like humanities, social science, physical science, commerce and management)

With the set of explanatory variables used in this model are individual characteristics, socio-economic background of household, academic background and ability factors-I and II and current enrollment factors of students.

Table 1.2: Variable description and Coding Pattern

Variables (Notation)	Description
Binary Response	
Student choice between enrolled in technical/professional HE and general HE. **(ENROl_TECH/PRO)**	Dummy variable that takes the value 0 = students enrolled in general degree courses in higher education and the value 1 = students enrolled in technical/professional degree courses in higher education.
Explanatory variables	
Individual factor	
Gender **(GENDER)**	(0-1) dummy variable, the value 0 corresponding to female and the value 1 corresponding to male
Socio-Economic characteristics of the household	
Religion **(RELIGION)**	(0-1) dummy variable, the value 0 corresponding to Hindu and the value 1 corresponding Non-Hindu.
Social groups **(CASTE)**	(1-3) Discrete variables that takes the value of 1 if the students belongs to Backward Class (BC), 2 if the students belongs to Most Backward Class (MBC) and 3 if the students belonging to Schedule Castes/Schedule Tribes (SCs/STs)
Father's Education **(FAT_EDN)**	(0-2) Discrete variables that takes the value of 0 if the level of father's education is up to elementary level, 1 if the level of father's education is between secondary to higher secondary level and 2 if the level is graduate and above.
Mother's Education **(MOT_EDN)**	(0-2) Discrete variables that take the value of 0 if the level of mother's education is up to elementary level, 1 if the level is from secondary to higher secondary level and 2 if the level is graduate and above.
Father's Occupation **(FAT_OCC)**	(0-1) Dummy variable that the takes the value of 1 if the father's occupation is salaried in either public or private sector and 0 if otherwise.

(*Contd...*)

Mother's Occupation **(MOT_OCC)**	(0-1) Dummy variable that the takes the value of 1 if the mother's occupation is salary employed in either public or private sector and 0 otherwise
Income groups of the families **(INCOME_GROUP)**	(1-5) Discrete variables that take the value of 1if the families belong to very poor, 2 if the families belonging to poor, 3 if the families belong to middle, 4 if the families belong to upper middle and the value 5 if the families belong to rich groups.
Annual Income of the family by groups **(INCOM_DUMMY)**	(0-1) Dummy variable that takes the value of 1 if middle, upper middle and rich income (proportion of annual income of the family more than .60 percent) and 0 if otherwise (less than .40)
Saving habits in the family **(SAVE_FAM)**	(0-1) dummy variable, the value 1 corresponding to the family is having saving habits and 0 otherwise
Cultivation Land **(CULTI_LAND)**	(0-1) dummy variable, the value 1 corresponding to family having cultivation land and 0 if otherwise
Number of Siblings **(SIBS_FAM)**	Continuous variable showing the number of siblings in the family
No. of earning persons in the family **(EARNERS_FAM)**	Continuous variable measuring the number of earning persons in the family
Dependent of the family **(DEPEND_FAM)**	Continuous variable measuring the number of earning persons in the family
No. of siblings studying at present both at school and college level **(NSIB_EDN)**	Continuous variable measuring the number of siblings are obtaining education both at school and college
Previous education background and Scholastic ability-I	
Management of school by class 10 **(MAN_SCH10)**	(0-2) Discrete variables that takes value 0 if the students studied in Govt. school, 1 for Aided school and 2 for Private (unaided) school
Board of Examination in Class 10 **(BOARD_EXAM10)**	(0-1) dummy variable, the value of 1 corresponding to students who passed from Non-state board (Matriculation board, CBSE/Anglo-Indians Board) and 0 if otherwise (state board)
Percentage of Mark in Class **(PERCENT_MARK10)**	Continuous variable referring to the percentage of aggregate marks scored in secondary (Class 10) level
Previous education background and Scholastic ability-II	
Management of School by Class 12 **(MAN_SCH12)**	(0-1) Dummy variable, the value 1 corresponding to medium of instruction by English and 0 if otherwise (Tamil -mother tongue)
Percentage of Mark in Class **(PERCENT_MARK12)**	Continuous variable referring to percentage of aggregate marks scored in Higher Secondary school

(*Contd...*)

Student Current Enrolment Status	
Type of Management(current) **(TYPE_MAN)**	(0-1)Dummy variable that takes the value 0 = students enrolled in government and aided higher education at institutions and the value 0, if otherwise
Financing pattern for education expenditure of the household	
Spending through family income only **(FIN_INCOM)**	(0-1) Dummy variable, the value 1 is equal to the household spending through family income only and 0 if otherwise
Getting student loan for Education **(STUDENT_LOAN)**	(0-1) Dummy variable, the value 1 if the student is getting student loan for current educational expenditure and 0, if otherwise

Result and Interpretation: Determinants of Demand for Technical/ Professional Higher Education versus Genera Higher Education

Logistic regression for student's enrollment choice between technical/ professional degree courses and general degree courses reveals significant predictors for determinants of demand for technical/professional higher education. The result reveals that there are six significant variables determining demand for technical/professional courses in higher education such as gender, income group, board of examination at matric level, stream of higher secondary subject, percentage of marks in class 12 (scholastic ability-II), type of management (current enrollment), income group and getting student loan. All these variables are found to be positive and they are significant at 1 percent level, explaining the likelihood of student's enrollment in technical/professional courses. The result by using the odds ratio is given in table 1.2 and briefly discussed below.

Table: 1.2 Result of Binary Logistic Regression for Student's Enrollment Choice between Technical and Professional Education and General Higher Education

Significant Variables	B	S.E.	Wald	df	Sig.	Exp(B)
GEN_DER	1.234	.361	11.647	1	.001	3.434
BOARD_EXAM10	1.352	.438	9.520	1	.002	3.866
PCENT_MARK12	.070	.018	15.697	1	.000	1.072
INCOMQ_GROUP	.852	.378	5.076	1	.024	2.344
TOMGMNT_ENROL	1.881	.530	12.575	1	.000	6.557
STUD_LOAN	2.709	.541	25.055	1	.000	15.011
CONSTANT	-8.388	1.375	37.197	1	.000	.000

Gender

There is gender disparity in student enrollment in different levels of education here more specifically in higher education. This variable is coded as dummy variable, 1 for male and 0 for female students. Comparatively, more male students are enrolled in higher education than female students. The results of the study shows that regression coefficient of gender is 1.234 that results in an odds ratio equal to 3.434. The regression coefficient has a positive sign (1.234) and corresponding odds ratio (3.434) suggests that for each unit of increase in male students, there will be an increase in the odds of those enrolled in technical/professional degree courses as against students enrolled in general degree courses by more than three times.

Board of Examination

In the case of Tamil Nadu, four boards exist at the secondary levels which conduct the class 10 board exams. They are State board, Matriculation, Central Board of School Education and Anglo-Indian School. The study has coded the value 1 for non-state board like matriculation, central board of school education and Anglo-Indian school and the value 0 for state board based on medium of instruction. The regression coefficient of board of examination has the positive sign (1.352) which indicates that the students graduating from Non-state board leads to an increase in the likelihood of students enrolled in technical/professional courses. The corresponding odds ratio (3.866) suggests that for each one unit increase in students graduating from non-state board examinations, there will be increase in the odds of student enrolling into in technical/ profession education as compared to students who enrolled into general education by about four times.

Scholastic ability-II

Scholastic ability-II is an important factor in students choosing specific degree courses either technical /profession both in public and private higher educational institutions. The estimated â coefficient of percentage of marks at higher secondary level is 0.070 with a positive sign. The odds ratio corresponding to â coefficient of percentage of mark in higher secondary level is 1.072. It means for a one percent increase in marks in 12th (scholastic ability), there will be an increase in the odds of students enrollment in technical and profession education as compared to students' enrollment into general education by 1.072 times.

Income group

Income is a pre-determined factor influencing demand for goods and services market as well education market. Income variable has been formulated by different income groups like income quintile 1 to income quintile 5. These five income groups are named as very poor, poor, middle, upper middle and rich. It is used as dummy variable, the value 1 for income quintile 3, 4 & 5 and the value 0 for income quintile 1and 2. This income variable is not even significant at 5 percent level in models 1 and 2. It means that students irrespective of income groups enrolled for higher education. When we check out the income variable as student's enrollment choice between technical/professional higher education and general higher education in model-3, the income variable was significant at 5 percent level. It is explicit that students from high income groups only enrolled in high cost technical/professional courses both public and private higher education institutions.

The estimated â coefficient of income group here is 0.852 that resulted in an odds ratio equal to 2.344. The regression coefficient showed a positive sign (0.852) which indicates that students from rich and upper middle income groups will increase the likelihood of enrollment into technical and professional courses in higher education. The corresponding odds ratio is 2.344 which suggests that for each one unit of increase in students belonging to rich and upper middle income group, there will be an increase in the odds of enrollment into technical and profession courses as compared to student's enrollment into general education by more than two times.

Type of Management (Current Enrollment)

Type of management determines the cost of education in pursuing higher education in the present situation. It varies from government and aided institutions to private institutions and within private institutions, it varies from one to another institution. Here, the variable is used as dummy variable, the value 0 for students enrolled in government institutions and 1 for students enrolled in private institutions. More students prefer government institutions than private institutions due to cost of education. In practice, usually more number of technical and profession courses are run by private institutions. Therefore, ultimately, students are forced to go to private institutions. The regression co-efffficient of this variable is 1.881 and corresponding odds ratio 6.557 which suggests that for each one unit of increase in private institutions there will be an increase in the odds of students enrolled in technical and professional education as compared to students' enrollment in general education by more than six times.

Student Loan

Student loan fulfils the dream of students from different income groups to go for high cost of technical/professional courses. It could reduce the immediate burden of household education expenditure. It has been used as dummy variable, the value 0 for students not getting student loans and 1 for students getting student loans. It was not significant at 5 percent level in models 1 and 2. In the case of model-3, student highly influenced demand for technical/professional courses on and it's significant at 5 percent level. It means that student's demand student loan is due to cost burden. Even banks have loan schemes for providing student loans for technical/ professional courses. The result shows that the regression coefficient of student loan showed a positive sign (2.709) which indicates that the availability of student loan for the students will increase the likelihood of student's enrollment into technical/professional degree courses. The odds ratio is = Exp (â) = 15.011 which explains that for each student taking loan there will be an increase into the odds of students enrollment in higher technical and profession education as compared to students' enrollment in general education by about fifteen times. As this thesis is being submitted the Finance Minister of India, Mr Chidambaram makes a statement on his visit to the state of Tamil Nadu that one in four student loan (education loan) is availed by the state of Tamil Nadu at the national level (dated October 27, 2013).

Predict the Probability of Students' Enrollment into Technical/ Professional Education versus General (higher) education

In Figure 1.1, student's enrollment choice for technical/professional education is considered for males without student loan in Government institutions. It can be noted that whether poor (Q0) or rich (Q1) the probability to join professional courses increased with percentage of marks in higher secondary board examination. In the case of Tamil Nadu state board (EB=0) as well as for Central Board of Secondary Education (EB=1)

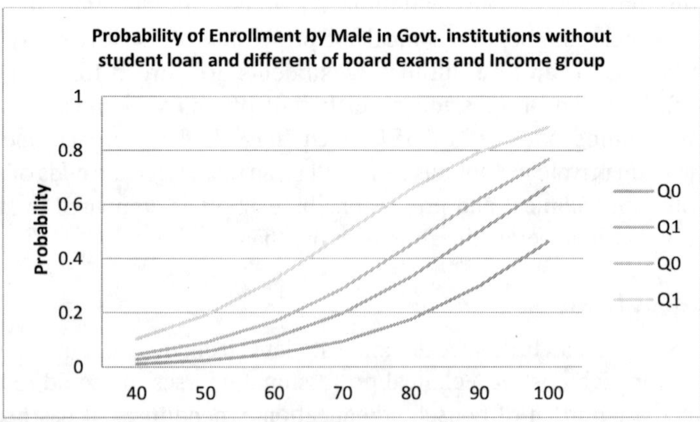

Fig. 1.1.

the above relationship holds. It is important to note that students of CBSE exam at secondary level have higher probability to join technical/ professional courses as compared to students passing out of Tamil Nadu board in all the income groups (Q0 and Q1).

In Figure 1.2, student's enrollment choice for technical/professional education courses is considered for females without student loan in the Government institutions. It can be noted that whether poor (Q0) or rich (Q1) the probability to join professional courses increased with percentage of marks in higher secondary board examination. In the case of Tamil Nadu state board (EB=0) as well as Central board of secondary education (EB=1) the above relationship holds. It is important to note that a student's of CBSE exam at secondary level have higher probability to join technical/ professional courses as compared to students passing out of Tamil Nadu board in all income groups (Q0 and Q1).

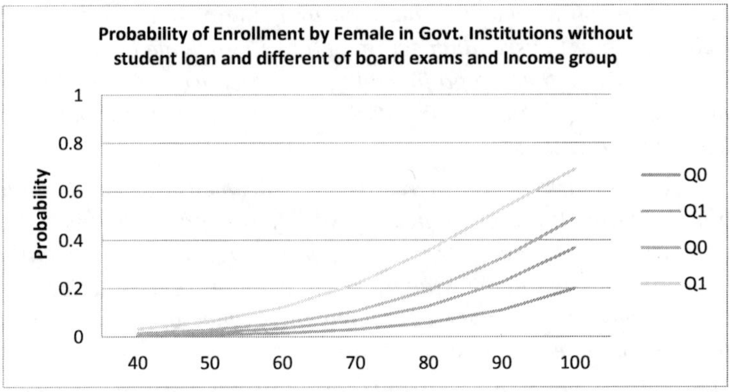

Fig. 1.2

Summary and Conclusion

To conclude, the study made an attempt to estimate demand for higher education both at macro and micro levels. At macro level, the study understands the determinants of aggregate demand for higher education in the state of Tamil Nadu. The study found that percentage of people living below poverty line is negatively and availability of higher education facilities is positively influence on aggregate demand for higher education in Tamil Nadu.

Further, the study explained that the model explores the student's choice between technical/professional higher education and general higher education and its determinants on demand for technical/profession education at micro level. There are six variables influencing on demand for technical/professional higher education such as gender, board of examination at class 10, percentage of marks in class 12, income group, type of management (in currently enrollment) and student loan. All these variables are positively associated with student's enrollment choice on technical/professional courses and they are significant at one percent level except among income-group variable. Income group is also showed expected positive sign and it's significant at five percent level.

Gender is positively associated with enrollment. It means that more number of male students is accessing technical/professional higher education. It seems that female students are discriminated in enrolling in high cost technical/professional courses by family/household. Board of examination at class 10 positively influences students to enroll (choice) in technical/profession courses. It is a different content but still valid about students who graduated in class 10 from non-state boards like Matriculation, Central board of secondary education and Anglo-Indian school. They studied in different curriculum set up and in English medium. These two aspects encourage them to go for going higher education. Thus, board of examination is highly influencing student's enrollment choice in technical/professional education.

Percent of marks is considered as proxy for measurement of student's scholastic ability. It has evaluated at two different points in this study i.e. class 10 and class 12 levels. In model-3, percentage of marks is significant and positively influencing student's choice. It reveals that better the percentage of marks in class 12, higher the chance of getting technical/professional courses where competitions were high.

Income group plays a significant role in students enrolled into technical/profession courses. It has been explored in model-3. Income groups are positively significant on student's enrollment choice into technical/professional education. It means that higher the income, higher the students enrolled in technical professional courses. It seems that students from well to do families can afford the high cost of technical/profession education on the contrary, students from poor economic (low income) groups, could not afford hence opted for low cost general higher courses in public institutions.

Private sector plays an important role in providing higher education to the masses. It is explicit that type of management (current enrolment) is positive and significant at one percent level. It means that more number of students enrolled into technical/professional courses in private institutions. It shows that an increase in the number of private institutions increases the student's enrollment into technical/professional courses.

Student loan is an important reason for students moving into mainstreams of higher education. Results of logit model show that student loan is significant and has a positive influence on student's enrollment choice into technical/professional courses. It shows that student's loan is more supportive to students enrolling in high cost technical/profession courses. It also helps to students from lower economic strata (lower income group) to access the high cost of technical/professional education. As discussed above, it has helped them in understanding the choice between technical/professional higher education and general courses in higher education.

References

Albert, C. (2000). 'Higher Education Demand in Spain: The Influence of Labour Market Signals and Family Background', *Higher Education*, 40 (2), 147-162.

Analysis of Budget Expenditure on Education (Year) Ministry of Human Resources Development, (Department of Secondary and Higher Education) Planning and Monitoring Unit, New Delhi (India) http://education.nic.in/planbudget/ABE-2007.pdf

Becker, W.E. and Lewis, D.R. (1993). Higher Education and Economic Growth. Kluwer Academic Publisher, USA.

Beneito et al (2001). *Determinants of the Demand for Education in Spain*, *Applied Economics*, Vol.33 (12), 1541-1551.

Berger and Kostal (2002). Financial Resource, Regulation and Enrollment in US public higher education, *Economics of Education Review.*21 (2002) pp.101-110.

Bhushan, Sudhanshu (2005). *Knowledge Economy and Higher Education*, *Indian Journal of Labour Economics* (IJLE) Vol.48 (4), Oct-Dec, pp.869-880.

Bishop, John (1978). The Effect of Public Policies on the Demand for Higher Education. *The Journal of Human Resource*, 12, 1978, 285-307.

Blaug, M. (1966). An Economic Interpretation of the Private Demand for Education, *Economica*, 33(1) 166-182, 1966.

Blaug, M. (1976). The Empirical Status of Human Capital Theory: A Slightly Jaundiced Survey, *Journal of Economic Literature*, 14 (3) 1976, 827-855.

Chang and Hsing (1996). A study of Demand for Higher Education at Private Institutions in the US: A Dynamic and General Specification, *Education Economics*, 4(3), 267-278.

Campbell, and Siegel (1967). The demand for Higher Education in the United States, 1919-1964, *American Economic Review, (June*) 1967, 57, 482-494

Canton and Jong (2005). The Demand for Higher in the Netherlands, 1950-1999, Economics of Education Review, 24 (2005) 651-663.

Cohn, Elhanan, (1978). *Higher Education Enrollment Projections,* Review of Higher Education1 (Winter *1978*): 18-30.

Charles, T. Clofelter and Michael Rothschild (1993). Studies *of Supply and Demand in Higher Education,* University of Chicago Press.

Duchesne, I and W. Nonneman, (1998). The demand for higher Education in Belgium, *Economics of Education Review* 17, no. 2:211-218.

Feldman, P. and Hoenack, S. A. (1969). Private demand for Higher Education in the United States. In *The Economics and Financing of Higher Education in the United States*. Washington, D.C.: The Joint Economic Committee, 1969.

Galper and Dunn (1969). A short-run demand function for Higher Education in the United States, *The Journal of Political Economy*. 77 (5) 1969, 765-777.

Handa, M.L. and Skolnik, M.L. (1975). Unemployment, Expected Returns, and the Demand for University Education in Ontario: Some Empirical Results, *Higher Education*, 4 (1), 27- 43.

Hoenack, S.A. and Weiler, W.C. (1975). Individual demand for higher education. *Journal of Higher Education*, 1975, 46, 623-652.

Hopkins, T.D. (1974). 'Higher Education Enrollment Demand', *Economic Enquiry*, 12 (1), 53- 65.

Jackson, G.A. and Weathersby, G.B. (1975), 'Individual Demand for Higher Education', *Journal of Higher education*, 66 (6), 623-651

King, Jonathan (1993) Demand for Higher Education in Puerto Rico, *Economics of Education Review,* 12 (3) 1993, 257-265.

Kodde and Ritzen, (1994). Integrating Consumption and Investment Motives in a Neo-Classical Model of Demand for Higher Education, KYKLOS, 37(4),1984, 598-608.

Kothari V. N. & Panchamuki, P. R. (1975). A Survey Of Research in Economics of Education in India, survey sponsored by the Indian Council of Social Research, New Delhi, August 1975.

Li, Wenli (2007). Family Background, Financial Constraint and Higher Education attendance in China *Economics of Education Review,26,2007, 725-735.*

Mueller and Rockerbie (2005). Determining Demand for University Education in Ontario by type of Student, *Economics of Education Review*, 24. 2005, 469-483.

Nicholls (1984). The Demand for Tertiary Education: An Australian Study, *Higher Education,* 13 (4). 1984, 369-377.

Philip, Altbach, G (1993). The Dilemma of Change in Indian Higher Education, *Vol.26(1), Perspectives on Higher Education in India,* (Jul., 1993), pp. 3-20.

Psacharopoulos, George (1979). A Quantitative Analysis of Demand for Higher Education, *Higher Education*, 1979, 159-177.

Radner, R. and Miller, L.S. (1970). Demand and Supply in U.S. Higher Education: A Progress Report, *The American Economic Review*, 60(2) 326-334.

Schaafsma, Joseph(1976). The Consumption and Investment Aspects of the Demand for education, *The Journal of Human Resources*, Vol.2, 1976, 233-242.

Schultz (1963). Investment in Human Capital- A Conceptual Analysis, *Meenakshi Mudranalaya, Meerut, New Delhi*.

Srinivasan, J. (2010). *Demand for Education in India: A Sub Regional Study*. New Delhi: Book Well Publishers.

Thorat, Sukhadeo (2006). Higher Education in India, Emerging issues Relates to Access, Inclusiveness and Quality, Nehru Memorial Lecture, University of Mumbai, Mumbai, Nov, 24, 2006.

Tilak, J.B.G (2005). Higher Education: A Public Good or A Commodity For Trade? Commitment to Higher Education or Commitment of Higher Education to Trade, 2nd Nobel Laureates Meeting in Barcelona, Friday,2, December 2005.

Vaizey, John. (1962). Education as a Public or Private Good? Education, London, Faber and Faber, ltd., pp. 28-36.

Yang, Yung (1998). Estimating the Demand for Higher Education in the United States of America 1965-95. Available at www.cscy.edn/indiv/yangy.

3

Efficacy of a Customised English Language Learning Google Site: Scope for Blended Learning in the Post-Covid Times

Roopna Ravindran

Abstract

One of the driving questions during the Covid time was how Higher Educational institutions, educationists or teachers could provide learning opportunities to support digital equity and inclusive English Language education. An immediate answer to this question proves to be a customised English Language Learning Website developed by an English teacher working in a Degree College for the UG students of Telangana. It was then the need of the hour as many of the students did not have means to learn during the Covid-19 lock down. The Google site created out of zero budgets has numerous resources selected by an experienced teacher. Apart from the PDFs of all the lessons in the English text book prescribed by Osmania University, the website offers Navigation Support Documents on each lesson, grammar and vocabulary topics. Video Lectures, Speeches, Activities, Stories, Audio books, Songs etc. also are available in the site. There are separate webpages mainly aimed at developing Listening, Speaking, Reading and Writing Skills. Post-Covid-19, the website stands supplementing the face-to-face English classes. This is a paper that has emerged from an action research. The faculty members of English and students of various Degree Colleges in Telangana were asked to provide their feedback on the reach, usefulness and impact made by the website during and Post-Covid times. This paper aims to find out the efficacy of the website in the context of a blended learning approach.

Introduction

This paper aims to study the efficacy of an English Language Learning Website created by a teacher in one of the Government Degree Colleges of Telangana during the Covid times. An acceptable introduction into blended learning is discussed and the transition from online to blended learning is marked in this article. The Google site can be used by English Language teachers, both in and outside the classroom, to facilitate independent, engaging and motivational learning.

The unprecedented times of Covid-19 have been a blessing in disguise considering the use of technology in education. Web 2.0 tools have been put to ultimatum during these strenuous times. Google provides many free interfaces and Google meet, Google classroom, Google site were put to optimum use during the pandemic. Google site provides myriad opportunities for content management, while teaching English to Undergraduate Students.

Google site has been beneficial in offering visually appealing website templates with ease of content creation even for a layperson. The English Language Learning website has reaped its benefits in Tertiary Level English Language Education during the pandemic. The website was created with a view to provide free learning resources to undergraduate students from all strata of the society. The user friendly, simple outlook for the website makes it easy to use for the digital immigrant students. Google sites can be easily created and managed. It does not require any programmeming language. The interface ensures sustainability at minimum cost. It offers storage of lecture materials virtually. From the perspective of students, it is a visually engaging platform for students. A simple interface and by default all pages appear in the navigation unless they are hidden. The website can be conveniently used to display the creativity of students.

The website has been categorised into different subpages for the ease of content management and access. Every lesson, grammar and vocabulary topic in the General English textbook has been converted into PDF form and uploaded into the website. The presentation of the content follows Communicative Language Teaching method with pre-reading and post-reading questions and activities. Navigation Support Documents of each lesson, grammar and vocabulary topics are also given along with the PDF. This NSD provides all information related to the particular topic. It has links to video lessons, biography of the author, audio lesson, poem recitation, and discussion of vocabulary, comprehension questions, and language learning activities and so on. Questions related to competitive exams are included in the NSD of every topic is Apart from the topics in the curriculum, the website also has numerous authentic content segregated into Listening, Speaking, Reading and Writing webpages. The Listening webpage has numerous listening comprehension activities compiled and presented by an English teacher working in one of the Degree Colleges of Telangana. Speaking webpage has countless conversation building activities. There are opportunities for students to create dialogue which are relevant in their real life scenario. Reading section has comprehension activities with numerous worksheets. Writing webpage has insights into writing paragraphs, Formal and Informal Letters, Stories, Essays, etc. The Google site has a section "Learn English" specifically devoted to Communicative Language activities and games. Google site as a whole provides innumerable opportunities for the development of customised repository of information relevant to the particular category of students.

What, Why and How of the Customised English Language Learning Website

Google site have not been put to optimum use for English Language Learning in Telangana. And Pandemic proved to be the best time to adapt to the contemporary learning needs and utilise this resource for the benefit of undergraduate students in the Government Degree Colleges of Telangana. Colleges with minimal infrastructure and funds can make use of this less complex platform to connect their students to the virtual world. It is quite different from other established websites as it is created by an experienced teacher who knows the needs of the students.

Digital divide is a reality and it is the responsibility of the society to minimize this divide in every possible way. The creation of this Language Learning website is a positive move in this direction. The motive is to ensure equity in Higher Education and create a feeling of inclusiveness in the students.

Lev Vygotsky, Social constructivist, talked about scaffolding. Teachers who are introducing new material to their students can usually determine when some students need more guidance in order to comprehend the material. Vygotsky scaffolding is a theory that focuses on a student's ability to learn information through the help of a more informed individual. When used effectively, scaffolding can help a student learn content they wouldn't have been able to process on their own.

Pandemic created a kind of 'left out' feeling for the digital aliens. Paulo Freire, develops the distinction between the banking model of education and a critical pedagogy in his *Pedagogy of the Oppressed.* Friere remarked that "As a humanist, Freire defended the theses that it is every person's ontological vocation to become more human… ultimately the oppressed will be able to authentically change their circumstances only if their intentions and actions are consistent with their goal." The students who belong to the lower socio-economic backgrounds missed out many opportunities to learn as they did not have infrastructural support during the Covid lock down. It is the moral responsibility of teachers to psychologically empower these students and provide equal opportunities for them to learn. Synchronous classes were not successful from the perspective of these students. They could not attend all the classes as they did not own a phone. Every student has the right to education, whatever are the circumstances. Phones were available with most of the students or their family members. There was no chance for them to visit the library during the lock down. Books were not available. Students and academicians were not initially prepared. However, with the technological advancements, the Government and Educationists were able to find out ways to sort the situation. Teachers also have been thinking out of the box and coming up with creative and practical oriented solutions.

Relevance of the ELL Website during the Covid-19

English Language Learning website proved to be an ideal Content management system during the pandemic. Lesson plans, PPTs, worksheets, videos, everything related to the topics to be taught were available at one source. Required information could be brought to light and the remaining could be kept hidden until it is required to be brought into highlight. Interaction is a key in Language Learning classes and that is how students learn to use English language. However, the students were not very comfortable interacting through the Google site. They used the websites mostly to download PDFs, watch videos and listen to audio books. Students were comfortable interacting in the WhatsApp Groups and Google Meet. However, the students who turned up in the real time Google Meet classes were low.

The pandemic also opened up opportunities for students to develop their digital skills out of necessity. Students who had minimum knowledge about internet, websites etc. received a direction to pool out relevant data. Maximising the student's exposure to English is important. The following surveys conducted proved the efficacy of the website during and post-Covid times.

The Website and Post-Covid Times

Now that Pandemic is slowing evading and students are adapting to the face-to-face classes. Should the classes go back to the earlier conventional modes? It is certainly an absolute No. The Higher Educational scenario has evolved through the difficult times of pandemic and its learning are not to be warded off. Coming out of the pandemic, it is not advisable to leave off the online learning. The students of the Government Degree Colleges are quite comfortable with the offline classes. However, they wish to incorporate technology minimally. The English Language Learning Website can be used to supplement the regular curriculum. Information is readily available to students and peer teachers. The interaction, discussion and communicative language pedagogy within the class can enliven the language learning experience. In addition to these face-to-face learning experience, use of the website provides scope to venture further into the topics individually giving way to self-learning and autonomy in their later stages of language learning.

Blended Learning with Google Site

Against this backdrop, the researcher thought of adopting blended learning approach to teach English language skills to her students and to prepare them for their prospective professional skills. Blended learning is an approach to learning in which different learning methods are combined. It is the combination of multiple approaches to pedagogy or teaching. Further, the term has evolved as "a thoughtful integration of classroom face-to-face learning experiences with online learning experiences" (Garrison and Kanuka, 97). It includes traditional face-to-face (F2F) classroom interaction and different forms of technology-based learning.

The turn of the century has witnessed a profound impact of technology on education and English Language Teaching (ELT) is not an exception. With the advent of the Internet and its new means of communication facilitating collaboration between groups and individuals all over the world, the time has come to introduce this newness into the language learning courses also.

There is an effective transition from Online to Blend. Identifying how online and face-to-face mode of teaching and learning can support each other is the key to finding an apt tool for students. Blended learning was desirable due to the limitation in the campus.

It is worthwhile to look at the following before one studies the efficacy of the site in the post-Covid context. What is blended learning? What are the function and features of Google site when implemented as a blended learning tool? What is blended? How much blend is required?

The term "blended learning" first appeared in around 2000.The term Blended learning originated in the Business world in connection with corporate training and then was employed in Higher Education and lastly it appeared in Language Teaching and Learning.

It is a flexible term, used to describe any and all varieties of teaching where there is integration of both face-to-face and online delivery methods. The practice of blending learning is, therefore, not a new way of teaching, nor is it a single method of learning. So, new are the opportunities offered by the Internet and Web 2.0 tools and the range of components that can be encompassed in the blend surely may give novelty to the teaching of English Language.

In ELT blended learning is the term most commonly used to refer to any combination of face-to-face teaching with computer technology.

Blended learning imbibes the values of traditional classroom teaching along with the use of technology which helps to improve the effectiveness in the performance among English Teachers by deriving experiences.

How best to integrate technology into the curriculum appears to confirm the viewpoints

There is no single perfect blend

Blend must be context dependent

Further research is required to improve the quality of the content

Face-to-face with blend of Google site. Ever changing innovations in technology to meet the needs of digital learners.

A face-to-face language learning course with additional online materials where online tools are used to support and extend face-to-face lessons. It can ideally be used as a complementary to the real classroom. Blended learning is used to create a new hybrid technology. Sharma and Barret (2007) present four key principles to be followed for adopting a blended learning approach in the classroom. These are as follows:

1. Separate the role of the teacher and the role of technology.
2. Teach in a principled way.
3. Use technology to complement and enhance F2F teaching.
4. It's not so much the programme, more what you do with it.

Content management system, data repositories and function primarily like websites. These systems focus on managing various content from electronic documents to audio and visual files and providing access to them.

Ultilising synchronous and asynchronous technologies for the purpose of delivering educational content. Teachers can share and distribute the right content to the right learner at the right time. Google site is great for blended learning. Teachers can access anytime. Students also have the possibility of learning at their convenience. Everything is delivered through a standard Google Chrome Web browser anytime and from anywhere. Percentage of online content should be less as the students have only smart phones. Google sites support the teachers of undergraduate courses to motivate their students' learning and empower them with interactive course materials. Students who do not attend classes regularly can also make use of this. This is a study of the effect of the blended strategies on learning and attitude of tertiary students. Learning to utilise the student learning environment to the maximum. Authentic material is provided by a credible individual who has experience teaching students for quite number of years. The website is student centered. The teacher controls the choice of texts for discussion and discusses questions for the reading selection.

Student Survey during and post-Covid

Sampling was collected from 195 students so as to ascertain the background by administering online self-regulatory learning questionnaire so as to measure the performance as an outcome. Utilisation of Google sites as a Course Management System in a blended learning in English Language Context.

The students gave a positive response. They used the words, interesting, helpful to describe the website. In the survey students have mentioned that they are quite eager to utilise the resources available in the website.

In this investigation of 195 undergraduate students, the investigation inferred that more number of students have moderate level of perception towards blended learning. Student teachers do not differ each other in their perception towards blended learning with respect to their gender and there is no significant difference in perception.

A survey conducted among 200 UG students from varied backgrounds revealed that 60 percent of them preferred the "Learn English" section of the website which had exciting learning materials in it.

Teacher Survey during the Covid

Eleven faculty members who were familiar with the website were selected to give feedback on the impact of website on their teaching learning process. These tools can spark teacher's imagination and creativity with examples of innovative ways of teaching and learning as well as of sharing ideas more quickly and getting things done more effectively. Multiple resources and materials are available on the website. It is a one stop shop for resources. Time management as they do not have to search for content in different websites. But they were apprehensive about the student's ability to read textbooks, lessons, documents online. In their opinion, students need physical textbooks. However, Audio books, Audio lessons, NSDs are novel and innovative. Teachers wanted to create their own websites rather than utilising the already created one.

Pitfalls to be sorted out for better outcome

Key word search is a limitation of Google site. Search Engine Optimisation is not favourable to the Google site. The website does not show on the top in the google search. Performance testing is not there. Google site cannot compete with the new generation private technologies. However, Colleges without much resource can excellently make use of this site to impart quality education. Students need to be given training to utilize the website. This Google site is not interactive. Interaction is crucial for language classes even during Covid times, students preferred to interact via WhatsApp, mails, etc. It is important to look for additional channels for interaction and opportunities for collaboration. Promoting discussion online is a tough task. Whats-app group is supporting. Students need to be constantly motivated to utilise the websites. It is not easy to read books online from a smart phone. Students get diverted. The site does not provide any provision to keep a track of the students visiting on a daily basis. They use it with an initial curiosity and then leave it. Teacher needs to continuously monitor the progress, direct the students to check a particular page and generate discussion in face-to-face mode. Teacher's strong role as facilitator is seen in this blended mode of learning. Students however are not very comfortable to read continuously. They are used to reading from the photo copies of text used to be distributed in class.

Conclusion

Inherent advantages of both the methods. Constantly evaluate, reflect and learn. Open content. The blended learning is using freely available technology. Encourage learner autonomy and reflection. This is a solution to the hazards caused in learning by inadequate classroom spaces, lack of teaching learning facilities. Students read and discuss a variety of materials. They free write on the topic and discuss with their peers what they have written. Sufficient scaffolding and close monitoring of student activity as technology is integrated into classroom activities. Induction for students on website is essential. Explain students the advantages of using Google site in addition to their regular printed study materials. Familiarise them with all the features of a Google site. Improves retention, learning effectiveness and cost effectiveness. Increased attention span. Flexible approach to learning. A lot of brainstorming and research have gone into the creation of this website. Pandemic will slowly fade, but blended learning is here to stay.

References

Driscoll, M. Blended Learning: Let's get beyond the hype. LTI Magazine. (2002). Retrieved March 7, 2011, from http://ltinewsline.com/ltimagazine/article/articledetail.jsp?id=11755

Garrison, R. and Kanuka, H. "Blended learning: Uncovering its transformative potential in higher education". *Internet and Higher Education*. 7(2004): 95-105.

Garrison, R., and Vaughan, N. D. "Blended Learning in Higher Education: Framework, Principles, and Guidelines". *The Jossey-Bass higher and adult education series*. San Francisco: Jossey-Bass, 2008.

Sharma, Pete and Barney Barrett. *Blended Learning*. Oxford: Macmillan Publishers Ltd., 2007.

4

Causes of Pedagogical Issues and its Effect on Student Centric Learning and Leadership - A Study of Teaching Approach in Covid Times

Mrs Phebi Priyadarsini & Ms Syeda Maryam

Abstract

Coronavirus pandemic has affected several sectors with its harsh blow but it was most challenging for educators and students. The education sector experienced several changes as the crisis has left its mark on student learning and development. It was the most devastating crisis that occurred in the history of education. It is very essential to look into the frame of reference that can help to modify the education system. The current study focuses on practical and enriched learning for students to make education more fun, interesting, interactive, critical, philosophical and empowering for the students so that each student is capable of success after higher studies. The purpose of study is to spread awareness for the need for change in teacher's role, to move away from a narrow definition of academic success. The confined thinking and reluctance of teachers' is leading to loss of students' interest, unfinished studies, and gap of knowledge. The right action is to let teachers' think beyond cultural cobwebs and engage in activities involving virtual teaching and learning methods.

Keywords : Pedagogy, Students, Teachers, Education, Learning, Studies.

Introduction

Pedagogy simply means the occurrence and approach to teaching. 'It is the art and science of how something is taught and how students learn it'. Online teaching proved to be the rescuer when the covid year was almost declared to be a zero academic year by the government. Later, the students critisized that teachers' are reluctant to adapt to technology and to innovate and showcasing no interest in online studies. But have we ever perceived why this happened? There are reasons these pedagogy issues were faced and affected the student centric learning and leadership. The unanticipated shift brought some vital challenges for teachers as well as students. The teachers accustomed of traditional teaching were asked to shift to online platforms without any prior information, training, facilities, or platforms. Even if the teacher wanted to practice student centric learning and make the sessions interesting, that couldn't, because of lack of technical knowledge. The teachers were given no time to adjust with the modified teaching practices and there were no prospects of resistance to change and were forced to adapt the status quo which increased their stress and workload sequentially affecting their performance. Teachers have faced the problem of environment dissuading and family issues which have kept them from giving full attention towards teaching. Immediate shift also emphasised more on student centric learning which emphasis on youth choice and voice. The pedagogy issues stated above also reduced the student teacher communication and interaction to a major extent.

Besides, students in higher education institutions were not interested in attending online classes because they felt that there was no much substance taught in classes. Due to financial crisis, most of the students in higher education, could not afford to pay high fees which resulted in students to dropout leading to unfinished studies and gap in knowledge. The teachers were not being able to bring into action the student centric learning due to the disinterest from the student group. It not only effected the student learning but also the student centric leadership as they were not able to interact properly and students were not able to open up and express themselves, and also were in lack of guidance.

Objective of the Study

The primary objective of the study is to evaluate the causes of pedagogical issues in Covid times and analyse the interconnection of pedagogical issues with student centric learning and leadership in higher education.

Review of Literature

The impact of coronavirus on higher education over the last two years, was the most challenging because the students entering and about to complete higher education are ones who will be entering to professionalise themselves or entering into the real world. According to a recent study by Mckinsey[1], majority of students completed schooling without behaviours, skills, and requisite mind-sets to become successful at workplace or higher education institutions. The study states that students who were tested in 2021, were almost ten and nine points behind in math and reading, respectively, as compared with the students in the pre-Covid years.

As unfinished learning was real during the Covid time, there require a shift from a traditional face-to-face controlled environment to an online learning environment, and it does require some pieces of training[2] and the teaching staff should be encouraged to have the right attitude in embracing the new paradigm[3].

Good pedagogical approach focuses on student centric learning. Maryellen Weimer, in her work, 'Learner Centered Teaching' compares the student-centered and teacher-centered practices of higher education institutions towards the role of student/teacher, the process/purpose of evaluation, the course content, classroom management, and the learning responsibility from students' end. These five elements can be used to identify the challenges faced by teachers and seek to attempt more student-centered approach in the classrooms.

The student centric learning paves a way for student centric leadership. Peter De Witt, in his book, instructional leadership, specifies that, 'when school leaders reflect on what keeps them in a highly challenging job, they typically describe the difference they make to the lives of children and the difference children make to their own lives'.

All these above concepts focus on student hardships and improvement of online pedagogy but this paper focuses on issues faced by teachers on shift of learning pattern and its effects on student centric learning and leadership.

Methodology

A total of sixty teachers both male and female from Loyola Academy and Johnson Grammar ISC, Hyderabad, were selected for the study. Non-probability sampling was used. A questionnaire was designed with questions on pedagogical issues they faced and what effects it had on the student learning and academic leadership. The age group of teachers was from 35 to 55 years. The teachers of age group 40 to 55 years were more in the sample collected.

Teachers of age group of 35-40 years were able to adapt to the shift from traditional learning to online learning in one week to fourteen days and said there was no much increase in workload for them. They all have a positive response about the teaching process but prefer teaching offline or offline with ICT tools as the student interaction had gone down. All of these teachers prefer teaching to be student centric rather than teacher-centred. They believe that student centric leadership is about developing knowledge and leadership qualities in students.

Teachers of age group 40-55 faced difficulty in adapting to shift to online teaching and it took them 30 to 75 days to adapt to online method. They also complained about the increase in workload and the interaction being reduced in classes. They preferred offline over online. They were definitely agreeing with student centric learning because it focuses on student needs. They felt student presentation and participation will help students learn and open up which is good for student leadership.

Pedagogical Issues and Student Centric Learning and Leadership

Pedagogy is an approach to teaching it can be improvised as per the needs with proper advice and guidance. If there are problems in teaching it will affect the students learning and their interest in education. Students are the co-creators of education and involvement of them in what, when and how they learn often provides them flexibility in their learning. It helps students pursuing higher education not only with academic knowledge but also with skills for directing self and fellow students, heightening their curiosity and inculcating collaboration which are basic foundation for student leadership.

The student should be trained to be unique, noticeable and effective intellectually and academically. To let students take active role in education system through leadership is very important with changing employment specifications. To make them doers and unlock their potential and develop valuable executive qualities, should be one of the priorities of the teachers. Providing opportunities and rights for students and teachers to communicate, collaborate and reflect freely is important in the changing times. Putting students in shoes of teachers and teachers in shoes of students for creating positive and synergistic environment is much needed. These practices and approaches can help students to be future earners and employers instead of job contenders. This academic student centric leadership will develop future industry leaders. Furthermore, this kind of education system produce man and woman of action. These techniques make approach to teach more realistic, practical, enriching and customised learning. This strategic study is most crucial for success of education in these times and future as children and youth nowadays require more than just teaching inside the classroom. They require learning and development which is unbounded and enhanced.

Thus, the pedagogical issues can be solved through proper training of teachers, giving them time to adjust, asking support from students that can help teachers in adapting which they most often will do because of the importance given by teachers to students' interest. This can be done so that both sides can grow beyond classrooms.

Conclusion

The sample which constitutes 80 percent of teachers from the age group of 40 -55 years faced issues during online teaching in Covid times which could have been resolved if given some training and time to adjust. Most of the complaints were about less student interaction and participation as teachers were facing difficulties to implement student centric learning method due to technical constraints which made students less responsive and dull. Furthermore, it brought out no prospects of leadership from the students' end. If these pedagogical issues are solved it will automatically improve the student centric learning and leadership approach.

References

1. https://www.mckinsey.com/industries/education/our-insights/covid-19-and-education-the-lingering-effects-of-unfinished-learning
2. Investigating self-directed learning and technology readiness in blending learning environment, Geng et al. International Journal of Educational Technology in Higher Education (2019) 16:17 https://doi.org/10.1186/s41239-019-0147-0
3. Hassan Mirzajani Rosnaini Mahmud Ahmad Fauzi Mohd Ayub Su Luan Wong, (2016), "Teachers' acceptance of ICT and its integration in the classroom", Quality Assurance in Education, Vol. 24, Iss 1, pp. 26-40.
4. https://unesdoc.unesco.org/ark:/48223/pf0000375693
5. https://www.google.com/url?q=https://www.edweek.org/education/opinion-the-five-dimensions-of-student-centered-leadership/2014/02&usg=AOvVaw0MEwwoRkRskGdPYrnnlUga
6. https://www.teachhub.com/teaching-strategies/2020/07/student-centered-learning-strategies/
7. https://www.theeducatoronline.com/k12/news/ten-ways-teachers-are-adapting-to-remote-classrooms/271071
8. https://eric.ed.gov/?id=EJ938583
9. https://www.sciencedirect.com/science/article/pii/S2590291120300905
10. https://www.bristol.ac.uk/education/research/networks/mobile/events/iaswshop1notes/pedagogical.html

5

How to 'Future-Proof' The Utilisation of Space in Universities by Integrating New Digital Technologies

Madan Mohan Laddunuri

Abstract

There is a very narrow definition of 'space' that refers to the physical elements of a university campus, that is, its buildings and surrounding areas. However, according to Goodyear conceptualisations of various learning spaces, they specialise in 'material spaces and their virtual/digital counterparts'.

Among the contributing factors to this evolution are the increasing functionality and affordability of mobile devices, the greater penetration of broadband networks, as well as the increased access to (free) Wi-Fi networks (Australian Communications and Media Authority 2015; Deloitte 2016). Higher education is impacted by three different changes, all of which have been influenced by other changes in the sector:

1. The impact on pedagogies:

The rise of new technologies has created new ways to create and work with knowledge. Students can use digital media to 'discover and construct knowledge that is meaningful to them' (Ellis and Goodyear, 2016) even though their levels of digital literacy and learning styles may vary.

2. The impact on facilities:

Technology demands that the university facilities keep up with student needs. Students expect wider, perhaps even ubiquitous, access to educational resources through the Internet.

3. The impact on students:

Technology enables students to take a significant proportion of their learning off-campus. As the student body becomes more diverse, partly as a result of widening participation initiatives (Shah, Bennett, and Southgate, 2015), many students today enter university with a wide range of expectations. This may include being able to juggle other aspects their lives in the context of studying (Crozier *et al.* 2008; Reay, Ball, and David, 2002)

To maximize the potential of new technologies, universities must reconsider how they use space. I examine how digital technologies shape the organisation of space in universities, with a particular focus on organisational level.

This includes addressing the impact of latest technologies on pedagogies, on facilities and on students. This paper discusses five organisational consequences, with an aim to guide estate planning and strategic investment in campus buildings and facilities.

In this Perspective, I even propose that universities will need to reevaluate their use of 'space' in order to maximise the potential of digital technology. I've talked about the ramifications from an organisational standpoint, particularly the need to:

1. To create spaces that are flexible and can be reconfigured easily to suit different needs thereby allowing for changes in the patterns of use;
2. To facilitate connections between students and staff;
3. To integrate different elements of student life and university services;
4. To allocate sufficient resources to the development and maintenance of a wireless Internet network that is reliable, fast, and easy to connect to;
5. To deliver information and services in a variety of formats guaranteeing the students can know course information from mobiles and other devices from off-campus or any part of the world.

Introduction

Over the last decades, technology has radically changed the world, and indeed higher education. In particular, 'advances in wireless Internet and movable devices have allowed students to be more flexible as to the time and place of literacy in ways that were unconceivable ten years ago' (Shabha, 2000). This quotation, still, is from the time 2000 – before the rise of the iPod (launched in 2001), YouTube (created in 2005), e-book compendiums similar as Amazon's Kindle (2008), and ubiquitous Internet access through mobile broadband similar as 3G (first launched 2003).

To put these advances in perspective, in 1995 lower than one of the world's population had access to the Internet, today around 40 has (Internet Live Stats 2017). The number of Internet users has increased tenfold from 1999 to 2014, with the milestones of first billion users reached in 2005, the alternatives alternate billion in 2010, and the third billion in 2014 (Internet Live Stats 2017). Likewise, the use of mobile Internet has exceeded desktop use worldwide (Stat Counter 2016). This move towards mobile web access has accelerated since 2007 with the rise of smartphones (similar as the iPhone), and since 2010 with the rise of tablet computers (similar as the iPad).

The increased functionality and affordability of mobile devices, lesser broadband network penetration as well as increased access to (free)

Wi-Fi networks are all contributing factors to this elaboration (Australian Dispatches and Media Authority, 2015; Deloitte, 2016). The significance for advanced education is threefold, and partly influenced by other changes that have impacted the sector.

1. **The impact on pedagogies** this rise of new technologies allows for and creates new ways to work with knowledge.Students may use digital media to 'discover and construct knowledge that's meaningful to them' (Ellis and Goodyear, 2016) indeed though levels of digital knowledge and literacy styles may vary.
2. **The impact on installation facilities** available to students have to keep up with technological developments. Students are coming to university awaiting wider, maybe indeed ubiquitous, access to internet and educational resources.
3. **The impact on students** technology allows students to take a significant proportion of the literacy off-lot. With the composition of the student body getting more different, incompletely because of widening participation enterprise (Shah, Bennett, and Southgate, 2015) students may enter university with a broader range of requirements and prospects.

This may include a lesser inflexibility to fit other corridor of their lives similar as work and family commitments around study (Crozier *et al.* 2008; Reay, Ball, and David, 2002). These changes form the background to this Perspective, which will examine how digital technologies shape the use of space in universities with a particular focus on the implications on organisational position.

The use of space in universities

The narrowest description of space relates to the physical elements of a university, that is, its bulidings and grinding lot. Still, as Eliis and Goodyear argue,'the term "space" is used heavily in educational and social research, with a wide range of meanings' (2016).

In their conceptualisation of different models of learning spaces, they concentrate on 'material spaces and their virtual/ digital counterparts'. Utmost of the literature in this area doesn't distinguish between 'space'and 'place'and frequently these terms are used interchangeably.

A full appraisal of the distinction (and relationship) between these concepts goes beyond the purpose of this Perspective, but I consider it essential to point out that 'place', not 'space', is frequently used to describe people's experiences with (in) a physical environment, for illustration, in the fields of architecture, anthropology, (social) geography and civic studies.

Or, as in gold states – 'places are created, furnished, reconfigured, substantiated and made meaningful as people go on with their lives' (2009).

In his aptly named 'Against Space, Place, Movement, Knowledge' he argues that of all the terms we use to describe the world we inhabit, it (space) is the most abstract, the most empty, the most detached from the realities of life and experience. (…) When we're at home, we're outdoors, not in space, and when we go outside we're in the open, not in space. (…) Space is nothing, and because it's nothing it cannot truly be inhabited at all. (Ingold, 2009). Another view predicted in the daily reality of estate directors the daily reality of estate directors, considers 'space 'in terms of spatial criteria, similar as gross bottom areas residency rates and space morals (Boys, 2010; Temple, 2008). This view probably matters utmost to university leaders, trying to shape physical 'space' in pursuit of the educational, fiscal and strategic goals of the institution. This entails, amongst other effects, understanding 'how the affordances of available space chart onto educational requirements at task level, course level, programme level and faculty level (Ellis and Goodyear, 2016).

For the remainder of this perspective, I'll essay to combine this abstract understanding to of 'space' from a operation and planning perspective, with the ontologically relatively different nature of 'place' which cannot be left out since university spaces similar as lecture halls, cafes, services, libraries, laboratories take on important of their character from the presence and actions of the people within them (Temple, 2009). Without the staff and students inhabiting these buildings, they would be nothing but aesthetically pleasing structures of glass, concrete, steel and stone (Coulson, Roberts, and Taylor, 2015; Edwards, 2014).

How also is the use of space affected by the rise of new technologies, in terms of the impact on pedagogies, facilities and students?. The most extreme implication of new technologies is that they may render the university in its current form obsolete. Indeed, some observers have questioned the wisdom of father investment in the physical lot, considering the costs associated with maintaining the estate and being infrastructures (Shabha, 2000; O Donghue and Dorward, 2001). The online literacy (E-Learning) Hype around the turn of the century initiated debate in the sector; whether universities should be investing in'clicks' rather than'bricks' (Taylor, 2001; Selwyn, 2007).

Proponents of such a strategic re-direction predicted the rise of 'virtual universities'– individual organisations appearing only on the internet, with no physical locales away from executive units, which deliver courses solely through information and communication technologies. These have yet to materialise in any meaningful form –with the exception of institutions like the open university, but one could argue they've was long before the internet and are simply adopting new technologies to deliver courses they used to deliver by correspondence. Clearly, numerous further universities are now offering distance learning as a way to reach working grown-ups and increase profit.

In other countries, still, institutions similar as the Virtual University of Pakistan and the University of the People in the US have been established that brand themselves as being'online'yet rely on a network of physical locations to support with ultramodern computer lab and Internet access installations. Utmost bricks-and-mortar institutions give some form of online learning as part of their roster, either as courses that are incompletely delivered online (amalgamation learning), or as stage-online programmes (which would be more akin to distance education).

Arguments include the 'need to have hands-on experience with scarce, precious outfit and the 'value of interacting directly with leading scholars' as well as 'the serendipitous benefits of mixing with an arbitrary collection of peers in the social as well as the academic spaces of the university' (Ellis and Goodyear, 2016). It's worthwhile to note that still presumptive these arguments in favour of a physical university might appear, there's limited research to support them (Phipps and Merisotis, 1999). While a wholly digital university is indeed probable, albeit with distinct implications for managing similar learning processes, this Perspective represents simply a stage on the way towards simpler presumed fustiness of physical universities.

Universities continue to spend on new building structures (Morris, Adams, and Ratcliffe, 2016). For illustration, total investment in new building structures across the UK in 2016 increased 43 percent compared to former times (Financial Times, 2016). Now that we've established that universities will remain physical realities (at least for the foreseeable future), we can consider how to best "future-evidence" the estate to deal with technological advancements. I'll concentrate on the organisational consequences that decide from the three main implications stressed before; Pedagogies, facilities and students.

I. Impact of technology on pedagogies

Current best practice approaches to teaching and learning emphasise the significance of student engagement in the form of active, meaningful involvement in the learning process (Graetz, 2006). Simultaneously, physical environments 'are decreasingly honoured as the "holders" that give environment to group relations' (Milne, 2007). Traditional classrooms and lecture halls don't encourage engaged learning, with stationary seating arrangements, for illustration, that don't allow students to turn their seats around thereby limiting the success of ways for engagement similar as interactivity, discussion and group work. Long and Ehrmann argue that students who are in face-to-face lecture halls take up a'broadcast-model'of learning (Long and Ehrmann, 2005), pressing how 'the physical learning environment becomes an integral part the learning process and able of impacting students in important ways long the physical learning space has been left before' (Thomas, 2010).

With respects to the design of learning spaces, an influential report by the Joint Information Systems Committee (2006) states 'that the kind of learning that allows for active, meaningful involvement in the process requires learning spaces to promote innovative ways of allowing'.

The report states that upon entering a university lot, students should be filled with 'a sense of excitement about learning'. One way of achieving this, from an organisational perspective, is to honor the 'education of teaching as an integral part of the planning and use of similar spaces' (Long and Ehrmann, 2005).

But is the culture they sense one of a former period or one that meshes with their habits' (Lomas and Oblinger, 2006). Such a physical representation that's aligned with students' habits can be expressed by designing spaces that are flexible, to accommodate both current and evolving pedagogies, future-proofed, to enable space to be re-allocated and reconfigured, bold, to look beyond tried and tested pedagogies, creative, to energise and inspire learning and teachers, supportive, to develop the eventually of all learners, enterprising, to make each able of supporting different purposes. (Joint Information Systems Committee, 2006).

As early as 1978, Fawcett argued that lot of design needed inflexibility, in order to take in to account the uncertainty and insecurity of the relationship between activities and space 'the probability that a building won't come obsolete, and it's a private probability grounded on the state of knowledge about the activities that might do in the structural buildings' (1978).

One important point of the university of the (foreseeable) future is that the'spatial organisation of buildings can be altered to suit any unique conditions of its users to any particular point in time' (Ellis and Goodyear, 2016). For illustration, spaces with the capability to subdivide rooms or to rearrange furniture make it possible for the same space to be used in different ways, by different groups, at different times of the day. For illustration, a computer lab might be used for a games night, lecture halls can be used to host community functions and classrooms can be combined to come the point of a music concert or theatre performance (Lomas and Oblinger, 2006). Still, this might bear fresh storehouse and porterage. This inflexibility not only allows for customisation, letting students and faculty take increased control of their environment, it also fosters different tutoring and learning styles. Flexible spaces can accommodate different approaches to tutoring allowing teachers to tailor pedagogies to the subject, the learners and in the intended learning issues. For illustration, provisioning rooms with portable tables, chairpersons and whiteboards so that they can be reconfigured fluently between classes.

Impact of technology on facilities

Current views on pedagogy acknowledge that learning doesn't only do in formally designated learning spaces (still flexible they are), but in 'informal spaces not necessarily firstly imaged as learning spaces' similar as corridors and coffee shops (Cross, 2011). By extension, the lot as a total has the implicit to come a learning space, which has major consequences for the design of all lot areas, but in particular the design of informal spaces. Independent study is no longer rigorously confined to the library or computer rooms; inner and out of door areas can come spaces for learning as long as students and scholars can access the internet and power points. For illustration, combining food services with seating areas and wireless access enables both casual and learning conditions and encourages unexpected connections and encourages serendipitous connections and commerce among students and staff.

The main consequence from an organisational perspective, relates to the significance of designating spaces that facilities connections (Lomas and Oblinger, 2006). Another consequence that flows from this attention to social spaces is that of integration. Decreasingly, 'students' comfort with the Internet means it is not "technology" to them – 'it may be a way of life' (Lomas and Oblinger, 2006). Thus, students feel to quickly blend the physical and virtual world, 'moving seamlessly between living and learning surroundings' (Lomas and Oblinger, 2006). Universities can facilitate students by designing spaces where students can mix classes, group work, and study, with social conditioning, eating and sleeping. A furnishing multi-use space, which integrates services and brings together different elements of students life serve their requirements. Some institutions have copied business practice by appointing a Chief Technology Officer, or Chief Information Officer, at administrative position whose job it's to oversee the ICT strategy and policy.

Impact of technology on students

With laptops, mobile phones, tablets getting more affordable and power of these bais adding, institutions will have to find ways to deliver information and services in a variety of formats. Convenience is precedence for students, who are used to a wide range of services being accessible from anywhere, anytime, similar as food delivery, as food delivery, entertainment and online shopping. Students can use course information and library resources from outside and from mobiles, allows any space to come a learning space machine and even from bedroom.

Interweaving the material and virtual world opens up new possibilities for students to fit other aspects of their lives around study, similar as paid work and family liabilities. (Ellis and Goodyear, 2016). Also, shifting the emphasis of learning and studying down from the university and on to the home might be problematic for those students whose home environment isn't conducive to the learning process, e.g. because of family demands. Also there's a strike to these developments as adding reliance on IT for delivery of education or access to learning assets has the implicit to increase the fiscal burden and mobile. Also with changes in IT as rapid-fire as they presently are, people might need fresh training to catch up with the rear most developments. This might make it more delicate for certain groups (Low socioeconomic status, mature aged, those with learning disabilities) to enter and share in advanced education (Shah, Bennett, and Southgate, 2015).

From an organisational perspective, there might be a need to re-train staff and students to increase digital knowledge and comfort situations with new technologies in order to maximise the benefits in educational practice.

In this Perspective, I even propose that universities will need to reevaluate their use of 'space' in order to maximise the potential of digital technology. I've talked about the ramifications from an organisational standpoint, particularly the need to:

1. To create spaces that are flexible and can be reconfigured easily to suit different needs thereby allowing for changes in the patterns of use;
2. To facilitate connections between students and staff;
3. To integrate different elements of student life and university services;
4. To allocate sufficient resources to the development and maintenance of a wireless Internet network that is reliable, fast, and easy to connect to.
5. To deliver information and services in a variety of formats guaranteeing the students can know course information from mobiles and other devices from off- campus or any part of the world.

References

1. Australian Communications and Media Authority. 2015. "Australians Get Mobile." Web pages. June 9. http://www.acma.gov.au/theACMA/engage-blogs/engage-blogs/Research-snapshots/Australians-get-mobile. [Google Scholar]
2. Boys, Jos. 2010. *Towards Creative Learning Spaces: Re-thinking the Architecture of Post-compulsory Education*. London : Routledge . [Crossref], [Google Scholar]
3. Coulson, Jonathan, Paul Roberts, and Isabelle Taylor. 2015. *University Planning and Architecture:* The Search for Perfection. London: Routledge. [Crossref], [Google Scholar]
4. Cross, Jay. 2011. *Informal Learning: Rediscovering the Natural Pathways That Inspire Innovation and Performance*. San Francisco, CA: Pfeiffer. [Google Scholar]
5. Crozier, Gill, Diane Reay, John Clayton, Lori Colliander, and Jan Grinstead. 2008. "Different Strokes for Different Folks: Diverse Students in Diverse Institutions – Experiences of Higher Education." *Research Papers in Education* 23 (2): 167–177. doi: 10.1080/02671520802048703 [Taylor & Francis Online], [Web of Science ®], [Google Scholar]
6. Deloitte. 2016. *"Deloitte Mobile Consumer Report." Deloitte Global Mobile Consumer Survey 2016: UK Cut*. http://www.deloitte.co.uk/mobileuk/. [Google Scholar]
7. Edwards, Brian. 2014. *University Architecture*. London: Taylor & Francis. [Crossref], [Google Scholar]
8. Ellis, R. A., and P. Goodyear. 2016. "Models of Learning Space: Integrating Research on Space, Place and Learning in Higher Education." *Review of Education* 4 (2): 149–191. doi: 10.1002/rev3.3056 [Crossref], [Web of Science ®], [Google Scholar]
9. Fawcett, W. H. 1978. *A Mathematical Approach to Adaptability in Buildings*. Cambridge: University of Cambridge. [Google Scholar]
10. Financial Times. 2016. "Boom at UK Universities Sees Construction Rise 43% Year-on-Year." *Financial Times*. https://www.ft.com/content/03522a1c-4a9b-11e6-8d68-72e9211e86ab. [Google Scholar]
11. Graetz, Ken A. 2006. "The Psychology of Learning Environments." *EDUCAUSE Review* 41 (6): 60–75. [Google Scholar]
12. Ingold, Tim. 2009. "Against Space: Place, Movement, Knowledge." In Boundless Worlds: An Anthropological Approach to Movement, edited by Peter Kirby, 29–43. Oxford: Berghahn Books. [Google Scholar]
13. Internet Live Stats. 2017. "Number of Internet Users (2016) – Internet Live Stats." Accessed March 24. http://www.internetlivestats.com/internet-users/. [Google Scholar]
14. Joint Information Systems Committee. 2006. *Designing Spaces for Effective Learning:* A Guide to 21st Century Learning Space Design. Bristol : HEFCE. [Google Scholar]
15. Lomas, Cyprien, and Diane G. Oblinger. 2006. "Student Practices and Their Impact on Learning Spaces." In *Learning Spaces*, edited by Diana G. Oblinger. Educause. www.educause.edu/learningspaces. [Google Scholar]
16. Long, Phillip D., and Stephen C. Ehrmann. 2005. "The Future of the Learning Space: Breaking out of the Box." *EDUCAUSE Review* 40 (4): 42–58. [Google Scholar]
17. Maclure, Stuart. 1984. *Educational Development and School Building: Aspects of Public Policy, 1945–73*. London: Longman Publishing Group. [Google Scholar]

18. Milne, Andrew J. 2007. "Entering the Interaction Age: Implementing a Future Vision for Campus Learning Spaces … Today." *EDUCAUSE Review* 42 (1): 13. [Google Scholar]
19. Morris, Steven, Richard Adams, and Rebecca Ratcliffe. 2016. "How Universities Went on a Building Spree as Tuition Fees Pour in." *The Guardian*, September 22, sec. Education. https://www.theguardian.com/education/2016/sep/22/uk-universities-building-schemes-tuition-fees-new-students. [Google Scholar]
20. O'Donoghue, John, Gurmak Singh, and Lisa Dorward. 2001. "Virtual Education in Universities: A Technological Imperative." *British Journal of Educational Technology* 32 (5): 511–523. doi: 10.1111/1467-8535.00221 [Crossref], [Web of Science ®], [Google Scholar]
21. Phipps, Ronald, and Jamie Merisotis. 1999. "What's the Difference? A Review of Contemporary Research on the Effectiveness of Distance Learning in Higher Education." http://eric.ed.gov/?id=ED429524. [Google Scholar]
22. Reay, Diane, Stephen Ball, and Miriam David. 2002. "'It's Taking Me a Long Time but I'll Get There in the End': Mature Students on Access Courses and Higher Education Choice." *British Educational Research Journal* 28 (1): 5–19. doi: 10.1080/01411920120109711 [Taylor & Francis Online], [Web of Science ®], [Google Scholar]
23. Selwyn, Neil. 2007. "The Use of Computer Technology in University Teaching and Learning: A Critical Perspective." *Journal of Computer Assisted Learning* 23 (2): 83–94. doi: 10.1111/j.1365-2729.2006.00204.x [Crossref], [Web of Science ®], [Google Scholar]
24. Shabha, Ghasson. 2000. "Virtual Universities in the Third Millennium: An Assessment of the Implications of Teleworking on University Buildings and Space Planning." *Facilities* 18 (5/6): 235–244. doi: 10.1108/02632770010328108 [Crossref], [Google Scholar]
25. Shah, Mahsood, Anna Bennett, and Erica Southgate. 2015. *Widening Higher Education Participation: A Global Perspective*. Kidlington: Chandos Publishing. [Google Scholar]
26. StatCounter. 2016. "Mobile and Tablet Internet Usage Exceeds Desktop for First Time Worldwide." *StatCounter Global Stats.* http://gs.statcounter.com/press/mobile-and-tablet-internet-usage-exceeds-desktop-for-first-time-worldwide. [Google Scholar]
27. Taylor, James C. 2001. *Fifth Generation Distance Education.* Higher Education Division, Department of Education, Training and Youth Affairs. http://core.ac.uk/download/pdf/11034576.pdf. [Google Scholar]
28. Temple, Paul. 2008. "Learning Spaces in Higher Education: An Under-researched Topic." *London Review of Education* 6 (3): 229–241. doi: 10.1080/14748460802489363 [Crossref], [Google Scholar]
29. Temple, Paul. 2009. "From Space to Place: University Performance and Its Built Environment." *Higher Education Policy* 22 (2): 209–223. doi: 10.1057/hep.2008.30 [Crossref], [Google Scholar]
30. Thomas, Herbert. 2010. "Learning Spaces, Learning Environments and the Displacement of Learning." *British Journal of Educational Technology* 41 (3): 502–511. doi: 10.1111/j.1467-8535.2009.00974.x [Crossref], [Web of Science ®], [Google Scholar]

6

A Study of the Higher Education Sector in Telangana on the Impact of Teaching Resources in Online Teaching

Samala Anjaneyulu

Abstract

Almost every instructor has been forced to teach online and give the output due to the Covid pandemic that broke out in the early days of 2020. Most traditional academics in the higher education sector were unfamiliar with online pedagogy and needed training in digital technologies that require online teaching. This minimal level of training clearly concerns the efficacy of online teaching and forces us to consider the need for teaching resources or trained human resources in successful online teaching. That's why this article intends to look at Telangana current teaching resources and the attitudes of students and educators about digital teaching approaches.

The present paper has taken 100 samples with a mixed approach for assessing the impact of teaching resources in online teaching in the higher education sector in Telangana state. The paper concludes that teaching resources in Telangana receiving nominal training on transacting online education could not significantly impact the way digital platforms are used in education. Further, the paper suggests that online education must stay smooth and need good teaching resources. Higher education cannot be a dynamic entity alone; thus, more induction programmes must be initiated to offer instructors hands-on experience and assistance in setting up the necessary infrastructure.

Keywords : digital teaching, online courses, higher education sector, skilled faculty, online teaching.

1. Introduction

Higher education, like other sectors, has undergone several transformations, with the digitisation of learning materials and online teaching serving as significant milestones. The rapid emergence of the Covid pandemic compelled the state to shut down conventional classrooms and educate online in order to avert the deaths of children[1]. It was decided that two academic years of online teaching would be needed for the teaching resources to carry out their responsibilities. Digital education had previously meant merely using PowerPoint presentations for most academics at the university level[2]. Still, now that online teaching has been introduced, these traditional academics are learning about video courses, virtual classrooms, smart boards, and a host of new ways to educate that were previously unavailable to them. Since the effectiveness of online education relies on qualified resources, this function must be thoroughly investigated before making any long-term commitments[3].

Online ICT infrastructure, which is accessible to both teachers and students, is critical to the success of online teaching[4]. This infrastructure may be found in metropolitan areas, state-funded institutions, and centers of excellence. However, the availability of this infrastructure varies greatly across urban and rural regions, corporations, state institutions, and centers of excellence[5]. Telangana, the country's newest state and home to 40 percent of the country's urban higher education institutions, represents all of these qualities, as well as the educated and untrained resources they represent, in equal measure. Telangana is also known for having a mix of prestigious institutions and colleges with less-than-stellar facilities, including a number of central research institutes. As a result, we can draw generalisations about the future of online education by looking at the currently available resources. For the same reasons as Telangana, the state's public universities haven't held recruiting efforts for the previous seven years. Given the shortage, it's reasonable to wonder whether good teaching resources are available to support online education at all. Online teaching, even its sophisticated forms like MOOCs, has both advantages and disadvantages that may be better understood in the context of Telangana.

2. Review of literature

Young, S. (2006)[6]. He entitled his work **"Student views of effective online teaching in higher education."** For this study, the researcher surveyed students on their experiences with online learning in higher education courses. A web-based instrument was used to gather data from 199 online students. It included elements that were believed to be linked with successful online teaching. A successful teaching item was regressed onto a total of twenty-five items in order to discover a core set of factors that were most significantly linked to effective teaching. Seven main themes emerged: being responsive to the requirements of students, providing relevant examples, inspiring students to achieve their best, successfully running the class, giving a worthwhile course, effectively communicating, and demonstrating care for student development. These seven factors may define effective online teaching, accounting for 86.2 percent of the variance ineffectiveness. According to the students' open-ended remarks, good instructors are engaged in the learning process both visually and actively, work hard to build trusted connections with their pupils, and maintain a controlled yet flexible classroom atmosphere.

Daniel W. Surry, Robert M. Gray Jr. and James R. Stefurak (2011)[7]. Entitled his work **"Technology Integration in Higher Education: Social and Organisational Aspects."** Researchers attempted to examine how combining regular classroom instruction with online learning may affect the economy. The cost and benefit aspects explored by the authors by splitting the cost of adopting online education into four separate categories, such as the zero cost element that enables everyone to access online education like open-access learning sources, are included in these facets. Little fees, such as yearly memberships that Affordability may take advantage of, allow micro- and minor stakeholder organisations (MSOs) to participate in online education. Still, high costs limit participation in high-end institutions and state-sponsored organisations'. For this study, the authors used a three-tiered questionnaire to acquire basic information on each factor's influence on participants. They found that the incremental advantages of online education outweigh the initial costs because of the second and third-order questions, which were based on the first-order questions and focused on the macro-level characteristics of online education.

Geryk M. (2020)[8]. Entitled his work **"Sustainable Development in Higher Education in Kantola."** Researchers have carried out an empirical examination of the need to boost multi-national education systems to satisfy the skill requirements of global entities and prepared a paper on sustainable development objectives for higher education. Using the principles of the World Commission for Environment and Development principles, Gery examined the relationship between educational institutions and technological platforms to speed up the integration of teaching resources and online environments. He concluded that new partnerships between academic institutions and technology platforms are required.

Afzal Sayed Munna et.al (2021)[9]. They have entitled their work **"Online Learning: A View from Higher Education, Cross-Currents."** For successful crisis management, academics have explored the function of online education. Their conclusions are essential to note: if online education is well-designed, it will be beneficial only if the course content and its pedagogy are well-crafted. The authors concluded that technology used to promote online education should be included in instructional materials to maximise learning results. According to Syed & Mazumdar, their research findings of top British institutions led them to these conclusions.

Srinivasa Rao, K. (2021)[10]. He entitled his work as **"Online Education –fallacies and reality"** The researcher studied how online education is implemented in Andhra Pradesh. These southern Indian state houses twelve state universities and three private universities and concluded that the current use of the online platform has been reactive to the imposed lockdown by the state, creating a gap in teaching resources and students. This may not be the case for a lengthy period of time, during which online education adoption must be proactive. According to the author, online education has contributed to the enrichment of instruction that has to be translated into academic synergy by institutions' efforts.

3. Gaps in the literature

Research shows that Western education has done a great deal of work in developing and spreading online courses via MOOCs. In contrast, the university system in states like Telangana hasn't moved as quickly to move away from traditional teaching methods. There is also a lack of research to show a relationship between the quality of teaching materials and online teaching in states like Telangana. This study, therefore, aims to establish a relationship between the following things.

4. Objectives of the study

1. To examine the benefits and drawbacks of online education.
2. To detect Telangana higher education teaching resource shortages.
3. To evaluate the efficacy of online teaching with the use of qualified teaching resources.

5. The need for the study

These goals try to develop a relationship between online teaching efficiency and training and exposure levels of teaching materials to provide the primary features of boosting online teaching. Only a few edutech companies have been able to connect with students regardless of their educational background or level of expertise with the instructors, who are the primary resources of online education. This is an evident reality. Therefore, it is necessary to identify the features of teaching resources that may be included in online and traditional teaching to achieve a blended approach.

6. Scope of the study

The breadth of this paper's analysis of the relationship between teacher exposure to online teaching and the success of online education is limited. Still, a wide range of other variables affects the online educational environment. Only Telangana teaching resources are examined in this paper's geographical scope.

7. Methodology

Its first objective is to analyze the advantages and disadvantages of online education in the current context using secondary data from various sources. Its second objective is to identify the aggregate position of teaching resources in Telangana using data on Professors, Associate Professors, and Assistant Professors and the corresponding vacancies in each of these three ranks and their respective positions. Because gaps in teaching materials at every level must be tallied to evaluate whether the resources are appropriate for an online education environment, when it comes to the third aim, gathering primary data to verify the hypothesis, we use a Likert scale and the Chi-Square test.

8. Size of the sample

For the purpose of testing the hypothesis of this article, one hundred academics in the higher education sector of Telangana in both rural and urban regions are surveyed. Random cluster sampling is used to pick the participants.

9. Null Hypothesis

H0: The use of skilled teaching resources does not substantially influence online education's efficacy.

10. The Benefits and Drawbacks of Online Teaching

Throughout the academic spectrum, it is frequently discussed whether online education can replace or supplement traditional teaching methods. A better knowledge of the benefits and drawbacks of online learning is essential, particularly in recently established states like Telangana, where the distribution of educational institutions and students across urban and rural areas is more evenly divided. The pros and cons of online teaching are much like any other instructional method. However, it is well-established that a technique or model must be accepted if the incremental advantages outweigh the incremental costs, valid for online education.

Students who couldn't afford to attend a university or college for different reasons might benefit from online education since many institutions can interact with students via virtual classrooms and teach the courses to those who otherwise couldn't afford it. Additionally, online education should be commended for allowing students more freedom in choosing when and how they want to study and the ability to make changes to their course offerings[11]. Using the most up-to-date educational tools like 3D visuals and simulators, educators may better explain ideas in a virtual environment while teaching online. Millions of students may have signed up for a single course taught by one instructor in a digital platform like Course Era without encountering the issue of maintaining an optimal student-to-teacher ratio [12]. Some of the advantages of using online teaching to develop an interface between instructors and students are listed below.

With that said, there are certain drawbacks to online schooling as well. Students' receptive levels can't be assessed and tuned to the band digitally because of the absence of direct connectedness and nonverbal communication features like direct eye contact. It is also criticised because it lacks the opportunity to build a personal relationship between the instructor and student. Strong alumni associations and student devotion to such associations can only be fostered via personal relationships among students, as shown by the success stories of top-tier colleges. First, it is possible to establish an initial impression that online education cannot replace traditional teaching, but rather may complement it to better serve students, given that teachers are well-trained to recognise and address these advantages and disadvantages.

Table 1: Status of teaching resources

S. No.	Designation	India (2019-2020)	Telangana (2019-2020)
1	Number of Professors	139797	7190
2	Associate Professor	160137	7444
3	Assistant Professor	1023519	62123
4	Tutors	80172	3207

Source: Telangana State Council of Higher Education.

As can be observed from the Table 1, Telangana has a far lower percentage of professors (7190 out of 139797) than the national average, which is in stark contrast to the state's overall population. Associate professors and assistant professors showed similar trends, with 4.6 percent and six percent, respectively. Similarly, the last section of the above table represents tutors. Because of this, online learning is on the rise in Telangana in both a proactive and reactive manner. Data on the state's regular and on-demand supply of teachers, including vacancies and temporary substitutes, may be used to examine the situation further.

Table 2: The present Status of Teaching Resources in the Universities of Telangana

S. No.	University	Contract Teachers	Regular Teachers	SFC Teacher
1.	Kakatiya University	182	133	49
2.	Osmania University	370	249	121
3.	JNTUH	265	185	80
4.	MGU	49	13	36
5.	Telangana University	52	39	13
6.	Telugu University	22	-	22
7.	Satavahana University	39	33	06
8.	Palamuru University	100	43	57
9.	RGKTU -Basara	136	136	-
10.	JNTUA(Fine Arts)	99	24	75
11.	BRAOU	21	-	21
	Total	**1335**	**855**	**480**

Source: The Telugu News Daily: Enadu help desk, June 2021.

Table 2 shows that there is a wide disparity in the number of teaching resources available throughout the state's eleven institutions, and part of this disparity is alleviated by contracts and ad hoc recruitments made on behalf of the state. Additionally, the state's most prominent institutions like Osmania University and JNTU show a lack of regular and skilled teaching resources, which negatively influences efforts to digitalise the higher education system and promote online teaching.

Table-3: Status of faculties in universities of Telangana

S. No.	Designation	Sanctioned	Vacant	Working
1.	Number of Professors	395	238	157
2.	Associate Professor	910	781	129
3.	Assistant Professor	1,532	850	682
	Total	**2,837**	**1869**	**968**

Source: The Telugu News Daily: Sakshi e-paper, 05th September 2021. https://epaper.sakshi.com/c/62913091

Online education requires the presence of competent teaching resources to carry out the programme; however, the accompanying data shows that there are 238 vacancies among the sanctioned strength of 395 Professor Cadre resources, representing a 60 percent deficit. An unhealthy resource deficit must be filled on a war footing basis before any attempts at online education, or other digital academic activities can materialize. The associate and assistant professor cadres shortage is 85.5 percent and 55.5 percent, respectively.

11. Testing of Hypothesis

Table 4: Pivot table and observed frequency

The Pivot table and observed frequency						
	Agree	**Disagree**	**Neutral**	**Strongly Agree**	**Strongly Disagree**	**Grand Total**
All of the above	8	9	7	15	7	46
Fills the gap of teaching resources	8	3	8	4	2	25
It helps enrich the academic knowledge of teachers and students	6	8	5	6	3	28
Helps in effective HR management				1		1
Grand Total	**22**	**20**	**20**	**26**	**12**	**100**

Source: Primary Data.

Table 5: Expected frequency

MOOCs is beneficial in communicating the subject compared with the traditional teaching							Chi-Square
	Agree	**Disagree**	**Neutral**	**Strongly Agree**	**Strongly Disagree**	**Grand Total**	
All of the above	10.12	9.2	9.2	11.96	5.52	46	
Fills the gap of teaching resources	5.5	5	5	6.5	3	25	
It helps enrich the academic knowledge of teachers and students	6.16	5.6	5.6	7.28	3.36	28	0.5598
Helps in effective HR management	0.22	0.2	0.2	0.26	0.12	1	
Grand Total	**22**	**20**	**20**	**26**	**12**	**100**	

Source: Primary Data.

12. Interpretation

The null hypothesis could not be rejected because the estimated value of 0.5598 is less than the table value of 3.55 for the specified degrees of freedom. As a result, online education in Telangana is unlikely to be considerably impacted by the state's skilled teaching resources.

13. Conclusions

The residual values obtained from testing the hypothesis in this paper allow us to conclude that teaching resources in the state of Telangana receiving a nominal training on transacting online education could not significantly impact the way digital platforms are used in education. Online education must stay smooth and need good teaching resources. Higher education cannot be a dynamic entity alone; thus, more induction programmes must be initiated to offer instructors hands-on experience and assistance in setting up the necessary infrastructure.

References

1. Bartolic, S. K., Boud, D., Agapito, J., Verpoorten, D., Williams, S., Lutze-Mann, L., ... & Guppy, N. (2021). A multi-institutional assessment of changes in higher education teaching and learning in the face of Covid-19. Educational Review, 1-17.
2. Mishra, L., Gupta, T., & Shree, A. (2020). Online teaching-learning in higher education during lockdown period of Covid-19 pandemic. International Journal of Educational Research Open, 1, 100012.
3. Gourlay, L., Littlejohn, A., Oliver, M., & Potter, J. (2021). Lockdown literacies and semiotic assemblages: Academic boundary work in the Covid-19 crisis. Learning, Media and Technology, 46(4), 377-389.
4. Pham, Q. D., Dao, N. N., Nguyen-Thanh, T., Cho, S., & Pham, H. C. (2021). Detachable web-based learning framework to overcome immature ICT infrastructure toward smart education. IEEE Access, 9, 34951-34961.
5. Muthuprasad, T., Aiswarya, S., Aditya, K. S., & Jha, G. K. (2021). Students' perception and preference for online education in India during Covid-19 pandemic. Social Sciences & Humanities Open, 3(1), 100101.
6. Young, S. (2006). Student views of effective online teaching in higher education. The American Journal of Distance Education, 20(2), 65-77. Available at: https://www.tandfonline.com/doi/abs/10.1207/s15389286ajde2002_2
7. Daniel, W. Surry, Robert M. Gray Jr. and James R. Stefurak (2011). Technology Integration in Higher Education: Social and Organizational Aspects, Issue-1 Vol. 4, Page 428.
8. Geryk, M. (2020). Sustainable Development in Higher Education in: Kantola. AHFE 2020. Advances in Intelligent Systems and Computing, Vol. 1209. Springer, Cham.
9. Afzal Sayed Munna, Dr. Anupam Mazumdar (2021). Online Learning: A View From Higher Education, Cross-Currents: An International Peer-Reviewed Journal on Humanities & Social Sciences, Volume-7, Issue-2.
10. Srinivasa Rao, K. (2021). Online Education –fallacies and reality, journal of higher Education, Issue-2, Vol.1.
11. Glazier, R. A. (2021). Connecting in the online classroom: Building rapport between teachers and students. JHU Press.
12. Lau, K. W., & Lee, P. Y. (2015). The use of virtual reality for creating unusual environmental stimulation to motivate students to explore creative ideas. Interactive Learning Environments, 23(1), 3-18.

7

A study on Undergraduation Student's Perception towards Entrepreneurship Education in Telangana

Swetha Konatham

Generally, economics social and psychological factors are affecting to become successful entrepreneur but education is the good equipment to change the world and education can you play a role to understand outside the world.

Education is one of the mechanisms to provide knowledge and skills to understand day to day transactions so it may help to lead to empowerment and play important role in providing entrepreneurs.

Entrepreneurs need for economic growth due to this reason universities and teachers institutions, corporate and governments are focusing attention on entrepreneurship education iron government is taking as a challenge to faster economic development for this government is trying to facilitate many entrepreneur training programmes to the students hence education system has to be changed to encourage youth towards entrepreneurship for this universities and teachers and educational institutions need to provide entrepreneurship education in our education system.

This study aims to study the situation of entrepreneurship education and education offered by Degree colleges in Telangana and Degree educational institutions are recognised as a profession or not, how students are getting motivation to get new ideas and innovations to become entrepreneur with under graduation education in Telangana and this study trying to know entrepreneurship education training programmers are conducting by educational institutions.

Entrepreneurship education is human right so this study how under graduation students are getting entrepreneurship education in Indian education system at Telangana and entrepreneurs are not born they are made so this study would like to know educations institutions are taking this responsibility or not and this study focus on students are getting motivation from educational institutions, government training programmers, entrepreneur special courses, family, friends and self to become entrepreneur.

Keywords: education, entrepreneurship education, entrepreneur, aims, motivation, educational institutions, colleges, innovations etc.

Introduction

Entrepreneurship is nothing but starting a new business with new idea so we can say that it is practical world for upcoming new business people and entrepreneurs are need for economic growth to every country that for every developing country like India.

Entrepreneurship education need in economic development of a country Entrepreneurship education standup for decreasing unemployment in developing countries.

In every year a lakhs of graduates are passing out from various institutions in our country but they are looking to get the job not focusing on how to create employability.

Technical development alone cannot lead to economic growth, unless technology used by the entrepreneurs.

Entrepreneurs play role in capital creation, creation of employment, increasing standard of living etc. And social sustainability and regional imbalance we can bring by encouraging entrepreneurs in developing countries like in India.

Entrepreneurial opportunities are there like tourism, automobile, textiles, social ventures, software, engineering goods, franchising, education and training, e-commerce etc in India.

Entrepreneurship education give information about real time skills to implement new ideas for solve real time problems and entrepreneurs may not born as entrepreneurs but they can made as entrepreneurs by providing entrepreneurship education in educational institutions because educational institutions play key role student's forming knowledge and skills.

Literature Review

Fatima Sirelkhatim and Yagoub Gangi-Cogent Business and Management 2 (1), 1052034, 2015

This paper studied entrepreneurship education curriculum content and teaching methods in the tertiary level and find this study common practices of entrepreneurship education programmes content.

Nasra Ahmed Mohamed and Ali Yassin Sheikh Ali - Entrepreneurship education : systematic literature review and future research directions- World Association of Sustainable Development (WASD)-: 43 – From

Volume: 6 Issue: 1/2, to Volume: 17 Issue: 4: This paper deeply investigates the literature on entrepreneurship education to help entrepreneurship education decision-makers to develop better solutions.

Luke Pittaway, Jason Cope, Business Journal 25 (5), 479-510, 2007- A Systematic Review of the Evidence: This SLR has provided an effective method for mapping out thematically the field of entrepreneurship education and for allowing this field to be viewed holistically; linking forms of research together that have not been linked previously. The review highlights a number of areas of evidence that are making significant contributions to our understanding of entrepreneurship education, however, there are also areas for development, gaps in the knowledge base and research themes where one would have expected more cross-fertilisation of knowledge. The thematic framework presented in this paper confirms much of the conclusions made be the NCGE (2004b) study, which used a narrative method.

The next step in this research might be to conduct a deeper content analysis (using textual analysis software such as NVivo) of the articles in each thematic cluster to show a more in-depth discussion of each identified theme. In a content analysis there are no restrictions on the format of the archives, as is required for the bibliometric software treatment.

Finally, some study's limitations should be pointed out. However, it must be recognised that all the limitations are due to the compulsory decisions for applying a bibliometric technique like SciMAT. First, a methodological bias was introduced during the co-word analysis because it was necessary to group some of the keywords such as those representing the same concept as the authors' criteria. Second, the maps generated depended on the selected parameters. In this sense, different similarity measures and different clustering algorithms may have been implemented. Expertise in appropriately configuring the SciMat programme was very important in setting the best parameters to avoid the appearance of strategic diagrams that are too complex to analyze.

Research gap in literature

Research shows that government has taking as challenge to encourage new entrepreneurs for developing economic growth meanwhile educational institutions also focusing attention on entrepreneurship education to encourage youth towards entrepreneurship and there is lack of research shows educational institutions and teachers are reaching students towards entrepreneurship education at under graduation education to get new ideas, innovation and confidence to became entrepreneur like in Telangana.

Objectives of the study

1. To know educational institutions and teachers are reaching students towards entrepreneurship education at under graduation education to get new ideas, innovations and confidence to became entrepreneur.
2. To examine under graduation education is helping to became entrepreneur.

Need for the study

Education is the machine so we can change world with education weapon for economic development there is need to identify the entrepreneurship education is reaching to students that at under graduation education because youth have chance to braining storming at this level so education providing by educational institutions and teachers these people can motivate and create awareness and can build confidence to became entrepreneur by giving entrepreneurship education.

Scope of the study

This study examine the under graduate student perception towards entrepreneurship education in Telagana and how educational institutions and teachers are playing role to became entrepreneur.

Research methodology

Data collected from primary and second source so primary data collected through structure questionnaire method secondary data collected from various books, journals and websites etc.

Sample size

Randomly data collected from various districts in Telangana from B.Com, B.Sc., and BA and BBA students from 250 respondents but only 200 students are responded across Telangana state.

Data tool

Tables and percentages.

Drawbacks of the study

This study done towards student perception not focused on educational institutions and teacher's perception towards entrepreneurship education at undergraduation education in Telangana.

Benefits of this study

This study will give information to know and examine educational institutions and teachers perception towards entrepreneurship education in Telagana.

Data analysis

A. Demographic Profile

Data collected through structure questionnaire from undergraduate students i.e. from B.Com, B.Sc, BA and BBA courses in different districts in Telangana with sample size 250 but only 200 are students are responded and 40 percent respondents are female students, 60 percent respondents are male students. 50percent respondents are B.Com, 15% respondents are B.Sc, 10 percent respondents are BA, and 25 percent respondents are BBA.

1. What is your Gender

Finding : As per this study 75 percent respondents are interested to start business but only two percent respondents are started business, 80 percent respondents don't have entrepreneurship education as a syllabus in their undergraduation, 20 percent respondents have other than entrepreneurship educational workshops and getting information about entrepreneurship education in their educational institution, 2 percent respondents educational institutes are conducting entrepreneurship education workshops and sending to other places where entrepreneurship education workshops and 15 percent respondents are felt that teachers are providing awareness and motivating to get new ideas and innovation to

GENDER	RESPODENTS percent
FEMALE	40
MALE	60
UNDER GRADUATION	**RESPODENTS percent**
B.Com	50
B.Sc	15
BA	10
BBA	25

	B.PROFESSIONAL QUESTIONS	YES percent	NO percent
3.	are you interested to became entrepreneur	75	25
4.	are you started any business	2	88
5.	entreprenuer education subject do you have in your pursuing degree	10	80

6. your educational institution is conducting any workshops	20	80
7. your educational institution is giving information related to attend workshops at others place	20	80
8. your educational institution is conducting any entrepreneurship educational workshops	2	98
9. your educational institution is sending you to the entrepreneurship educational workshops	2	98
10. teachers are providing awareness about entrepreneurship education training programmes	15	85
11. teachers are motivating for new idea and innovation to became entrepreneur	15	85
12. your undergraduation is helping to became entrepreneur	2	98
13. do you have any idea about entrepreneurship training programmes' in Telangana	10	90
14. do you have any idea about entrepreneurship training programmes in India	10	90
15. your undergraduation subjects are helping to get any new ideas	5	95
16. your teacher teaching methods are helping to get new ideas	7	93
17. why you unable to entrepreneur		
a. no new ideas	20	80
b. not getting confidence to start	78	12
c. no money	72	28
d. no labour	50	50
e. unable to understand market	88	12
f. no family support	70	30

became entrepreneur and 98 percent responding that their undergraduation education is not helping to get new ideas and to became entrepreneur, 10 percent respondents have about entrepreneurship education training programmes in Telangana and in India, five percent respondents and seven percent respondents are observed that their under graduation education subjects are helping to get new ideas.

20 percent respondents unable became entrepreneur due to no ideas with them, 78 percent respondents are not getting confidence to start, 72 percent respondents don't have money, 50 percent respondents don't have suitable labour, 88 percent respondents unable to understand market and 70 percent respondents don't have family support to start business.

As per this study 75 percent respondents are interested to became entrepreneur but two percent respondents started business and 80 percent respondents have new ideas but unable to became entrepreneur due to no confidence to start business, no labour, no money, unable to understand market and no family support but education is equipment can change anything in the world but only 80 percent educational institutions and teachers are not conducting general workshops and entrepreneurship educational workshops and also educational institutions and teachers are not motivating, not creating awareness, not conducting training programmes and also teaching methods, learning subjects are not helping to get new ideas, to get confidence to start business and to became entrepreneur.

Conclusions and Suggestions

Educational institutions and teachers need to focus on entrepreneurship educational workshops and training programmes and other workshops, teachers should learn new teaching methods as per the global and technological and economical changes to motivate, create awareness and confidence towards entrepreneurship education.

Training is required in all subjects to the teachers from subject experts and industry experts in practical and real time practical's to resolve problems.

Entrepreneurship education should not be treated as specialised subject by the teachers and educational institutions and governments it should be part of every subject to create new ideas, innovation and it should not be treated as a separate profession.

Undergraduation education treating as required qualification to go post-graduation and to get job but not giving priority to create new ideas and innovation and confidence and need give priority on getting new ideas and innovations and confidence because to became entrepreneur need getting new ideas and innovations and confidence are the primary keys.

References

1. Bennett, R. (2006). Business lecturers' perceptions of the nature of entrepreneurship. International Journal of Entrepreneurial Behavior & Research, 12, 165–188.10.1108/13552550610667440 [Crossref], [Google Scholar]
2. Chang, J., & Rieple, A. (2013). Assessing students' entrepreneurial skills development in live projects. Journal of Small Business and Enterprise Development, 20, 225–241.10.1108/14626001311298501 [Crossref], [Google Scholar]
3. Cope, J. (2011). Entrepreneurial learning from failure: An interpretative phenomenological analysis. Journal of Business Venturing, 26, 604–623.10.1016/j.jbusvent.2010.06.002 [Crossref], [Web of Science ®], [Google Scholar]
4. Hannon, P. (2006). Teaching pigeons to dance: Sense and meaning in entrepreneurship education. Education and Training, 48, 296–308.
5. Covid Pandemic, B. (2004). Entrepreneurship education: Toward a model of contingency-based business planning. Academy of Management Learning and Education, 3, 258–273. http://dx.doi.org/10.5465/AMLE.2004.14242112

6. Jones, C. (2010). Entrepreneurship education: Revisiting our role and its purpose. Journal of Small Business and Enterprise Development, 17, 500–513. http://dx.doi.org/10.1108/14626001011088697
7. Cope, J. (2011). Entrepreneurial learning from failure: An interpretative phenomenological analysis. Journal of Business Venturing, 26, 604–623. http://dx.doi.org/10.1016/j.jbusvent.2010.06.002
8. Lee, S., Chang, D., & Lim, S. (2005). Impact of entrepreneurship education: A comparative study of the US and Korea. The International Entrepreneurship and Management Journal, 1, 27–43. http://dx.doi. org/10.1007/s11365-005-6674-2
9. Pardede, E., & Lyons, J. (2012). Redesigning the assessment of an entrepreneurship course in an information technology degree programme: Embedding assessment for learning practices. IEEE Transactions on Education, 55, 566–572. http://dx.doi.org/10.1109/TE.2012.2199757
10. Wang, Y., & Verzat, C. (2011). Generalist or specific studies for engineering entrepreneurs?. Journal of Small Business and Enterprise Development, 18, 366–383. http://dx.doi. org/10.1108/14626001111127124
11. P & quot; Sharma, Economic Entrepreneurship, Growth, Inclusive Entrepreneurship, Initiatives, Government, India
12. https://doi.org/10.1111/j.1460.8545.2004.00101.x
13. https://doi.org/23311975.2015.1052034
14. https://doi.org/10.1108/IJEBR-04-2018-0258
15. https://doi.org/10.1108/wjcmsd.07-2020-0084

8

National Educational Policy 2020 : Some Insights

Dr P. Venugopal

Abstract

After a 34-year wait, the country finally got a New Education Policy 2020. The drafting committee submitted its final draught to the union cabinet for approval on July 29, 2020, and it was accepted and approved. The new strategy aims to prepare the ground for significant changes in the country's school and higher education sectors. This was one of the primary initiatives taken to change the country's education system, which was badly needed. The goal of this research is to look at the areas where the policy has suggested action, although they appear to be in poor condition. It is impossible to have a policy that requires us to construct an entire infrastructure. During the implementation of this policy, a thorough reform and a drastic change should be considered. Education is a concurrent subject, and the plan under the New Education Policy 2020 will be implemented based on future laws from the centre and state. The paper focuses on the features, benefits, drawbacks and discusses possible outcomes of the NEP 2020.

Education is essential for realising one's full potential, creating a just and equitable community, and advancing national progress. The key to India's continuous rise and leadership on the global arena in terms of economic growth, social fairness and equality, scientific advancement, national integration, and cultural preservation is to provide universal access to high-quality education. Over the next decade, India will have the world's largest population of young people, and our ability to provide them with high-quality educational opportunities will define our country's future.

Key words: NEP, Higher Education, GDP, GER.

The knowledge landscape in the globe is rapidly changing. Many unskilled jobs may be taken over by machines as a result of various dramatic scientific and technological advances, such as the rise of big data, machine learning, and artificial intelligence, while the need for a skilled workforce, particularly involving mathematics, computer science, and data science, as well as multidisciplinary abilities across the sciences, social sciences, and humanities, will become increasingly in demand. With climate change, increased pollution, and decreasing natural resources, there will be a significant transition in how we fulfil the world's energy, water, food, and sanitation demands, requiring new skilled labour in biology, chemistry, physics, agriculture, climate science, and social science once again. The increasing occurrence of epidemics and pandemics will necessitate joint research in infectious disease management and vaccine development, as well as the socioeconomic issues that will arise as a result.

The Union Cabinet of India approved the National Education Policy 2020 (NEP 2020) on July 29, 2020, which defines the goal for India's new education system. The 1986 National Policy on Education has been replaced with the new policy. In both rural and urban India, the programme provides a comprehensive framework for basic through higher education, as well as vocational training. By 2021, the strategy intends to completely alter India's educational sector. The NEP's language policy is intended to be a broad guideline and advisory in nature, with states, institutions, and schools deciding how to implement it. Numerous reforms to India's education policy are enacted by the NEP 2020. It aspires to raise public education spending from roughly four percent to six percent of GDP as quickly as practicable.

A group led by former Cabinet Secretary T. S. R. Subramanian began the consultation process for the New Education Policy in January 2015. A panel chaired by former Indian Space Research Organisation (ISRO) chief Krishnaswamy Kasturirangan released a draught NEP in 2019 based on the committee report from June 2017. The Ministry of Human Resource Development later announced the Draft New Education Policy (DNEP) 2019, which was followed by a series of public discussions. The NEP Draft was 484 pages long. "Over two lakh proposals were received from 2.5 lakh grame panchayats, 6,600 blocks, 6,000 Urban Local Bodies (ULBs), and 676 districts," according to the Ministry. The vision of the National Education Policy is: *"National Education Policy 2020 envisions an India-centric education system that contributes directly to transforming our nation sustainably into an equitable and vibrant knowledge society by providing high-quality education to all."*

Individuals that are exceptional, thoughtful, well-rounded, and creative must be developed through quality higher education. It must allow a person to study one or more specialised areas of interest in depth and to develop character, ethical and constitutional values, intellectual curiosity, scientific temper, creativity, service spirit, and twenty-first century skills in a variety of fields, including sciences, social sciences, the arts, humanities, languages, personal, technological, and vocational subjects. The new education policy makes some significant changes to the current system, with multidisciplinary universities and colleges being established in or near every district, student curricula, pedagogy, evaluation, and support being revamped for a better student experience, and a National Research Foundation being established to support excellent peer-reviewed work and effectively need study at universities and colleges.

The main issues confronting the Indian higher education system include forced separation of qualifications, early specialisation and student streaming into restricted research areas, a lack of competitive peer-reviewed academic research funding and large affiliated universities leading to low levels of undergraduate education, and a lack of focus on research at most universities and schools. Institutional restructuring and consolidation aims to end higher education fragmentation by transforming higher education institutions into large multidisciplinary institutions, producing well-rounded and innovative individuals, and transforming other countries educationally and economically, with the gross enrolment ratio in higher education, including vocational training, increasing from 26.3 percent in 2018 to 50 percent by 2035.

All human capacities—mental, cultural, social, physical, emotional, and moral—should be improved through holistic and multidisciplinary education. In the long run, this type of comprehensive education will be the standard for all undergraduate programmes, including medical, technical, and vocational schools. A comprehensive approach to learning environments and student assistance includes a sufficient curriculum, engaged pedagogy, consistent formative assessment, and enough student support.

Objectives of NEP 2020

The Union Cabinet approved the New Education Policy (NEP) to introduce a series of big changes, including allowing top foreign universities to open campuses in India, increasing the proportion of students receiving vocational education, and moving towards multi-disciplinary institutes like IITs. The policy's goal is to turn India into a "global knowledge superpower." One of the policy's stated goals is to instil "deep-rooted pride" in being Indian, not just in thought but also in spirit, intellect, and deeds, as well as to develop knowledge, skills, values, and dispositions that support responsible commitment to human rights, sustainable development, and global well-being.

Increased access, equity, and inclusion are also goals of the programme, as well as "light but tight" regulation by a single regulator for higher education. According to the NEP, by 2040, all Higher Education Institutions (HEIs) must strive to become multifunctional institutions with 3,000 or more students. By 2030, every district will have at least one significant multidisciplinary institution in or near it.

By 2035, the goal will be to raise the Gross Enrolment Ratio in higher education, including vocational education, from 26.3 percent to 50 percent. Over time, single-stream higher education institutions will be phased away, and all will strive to become interdisciplinary. In 15 years, the system of "associated colleges" will be phased out. The country's current complicated nomenclature of HEIs, such as 'deemed to be university', 'affiliating university', 'affiliating technical university,' and 'unitary university,' will be replaced simply with the term 'university.'

A university shall be defined as a multidisciplinary institution that offers undergraduate and graduate programmes, as well as high-quality teaching, research, and community service.The term will allow for a range of institutions, from those that place equal emphasis on teaching and research (Research-Intensive Universities) to those that place a greater emphasis on teaching (Teaching-Intensive Universities). The terms "deemed to be university," "affiliating university," "affiliating technical university," and "unitary university" will be phased out. Even technical schools like IITs will shift to a more holistic, multidisciplinary education that includes more arts and humanities. Arts and humanities students will strive to learn more science.

Features of NEP-2020

Scope for Higher Education

In India, the many regulators of higher education (HE) will be merged into the Higher Education Commission of India (HECI) as a single regulator for HEIs. The certification bodies (NAAC and NBA) will be replaced, and a strong National Certification Council (NAC) will be established. The National Research Foundation would promote higher education research and innovation funding. For higher educational institutions, the NEP has required a multidisciplinary education paradigm. These institutions should have a minimum of 3000 students on campus. The deadline for becoming multidisciplinary is set for 2030, and by 2040, they are expected to have a student body of 3000. Furthermore, these multidisciplinary universities should either focus on research or teaching, and can specialise in one of these areas. The colleges have the option of becoming self-contained and awarding their own degrees, or they can join an existing university.NEP also discusses strategies to boost student enrollment in various types of educational institutions. GER has long been a source of worry in India, and the current education strategy places a special emphasis on it. NEP places a strong emphasis on a holistic, multidisciplinary education approach, and research is presently supported only at the undergraduate level. With cross-disciplinary and outcome-based education, current policy emphasises a student's overall development. At the national level, there is a proposal for an Academic Bank of Credit to enable flexibility in obtaining degrees and different entry-exit options at all levels of education. Several digital platforms will be launched, or existing ones will be updated, to promote online learning and library digitisation (NEP, 2020). Instead of the current teacher-centered teaching approach, a student-centered teaching and learning method will be implemented. The evaluation paradigm will be changed from a choice to a competency-based model.The evaluation and assessment mechanism will also shift from an end-of-semester exam to a continuous assessment system. Skill education will be a priority for all HEIs. They should also have counselling centres with counsellors to look after the emotional health of students. Traditional education is undergoing a significant upheaval as it transitions to a market-driven model. The Indian government wants to build world-class educational institutions and recruit a large number of overseas students. Furthermore, a student's courses taken at overseas universities will be given credit and considered equal in India. This will allow students to begin their studies overseas and finish them in India (NEP, 2020).

Scope for Private Institutions

All non-public universities would be given graded autonomy, according to the proposal. Accreditation, engagement in research innovation, and the delivery of high-quality education will all contribute to their autonomy.

They'd also have to keep their financial dealings clear. There should be no financial irregularities, and a system must be in place to monitor them. In every course, private HEIs would be required to grant free-ships and scholarships to deserving/ meritorious students. During the accreditation procedure, a mechanism has been established to keep an eye on this. There would be no distinction between government and private institutes when it came to research funding, which should be awarded entirely on the basis of the ideas' merits.Otherwise, private HEIs will be forced to close due to a lack of 3000 students (NEP, 2020).

Benefits of NEP-2020

The NEP-2020 is expected to close the gap in India's educational standards. It will aid in the internationalisation of education in the country as well as the instillation of innovation. The NEP 2020 draught paper is a forward-thinking document that was created after extensive consultation with all stakeholders. It is recommended that children begin formal schooling at the age of three. The policy's main focus is on developing manpower, encouraging entrepreneurship, and creating jobs. It is founded on the principles of equality, autonomy, and empowerment of society's weakest members.

The NEP created a foundation for higher education institutions to thrive. They will have more freedom in terms of admission, teacher appointment, reservation quota excmption, research support, and staff retrenchment and layoff. Private colleges are free to create their own admissions and cost structures. In this regard, government directives must be followed by public entities.The NEP calls for a multidisciplinary approach to education that focuses on developing skills and making students employable. It included provisions for autonomous institutions to offer self-degrees at both the undergraduate and graduate levels. Accreditation and ranking systems are required to maintain control over educational quality. The Proposal incorporates the knowledge and opinions of numerous advisors from various industries. NEP 2020 was created with the objective of achieving the United Nations' Sustainable Development Goals (SDG) by 2030. It also emphasised lifelong learning and included various entry-exit options to allow students to complete their degrees at any point in their lives. Under RTE, education must be provided to all elements of society, and it must be based on equality, with no discrimination based on caste or gender.There is a specific provision for students from economically disadvantaged backgrounds. Teachers' education and training have been suggested as improvements to improve the quality of teaching in higher education institutions.

Only a select group of institutions will be permitted to provide the B.Ed. programme. This would be made a requirement for all students in elementary school. Every library would be converted to a digital format. It is intended to encourage extensive research at both the undergraduate and graduate levels, with financing provided by the National Research Foundation. Lecturers will have the freedom to design their own class delivery, evaluation, and research-innovation strategy. Higher education degrees can now be earned through online distance learning, which is expected to be a useful tool in increasing GER.Universities/Institutions in India can now openly collaborate with international universities on all forms of educational and research projects. It is proposed to set up National Research Foundation with initial capital of INR 20000 crores. This body has been given mandate to provide funding support to all public and private institutions (NEP, 2020).

Drawback of NEP

It appears to be written to encourage the privatisation of education in India, as evidenced by the paper. It mentions, among other things, encouraging the top 100 foreign institutions to open stores in India. It's arguable if this is to further the cause of education or to facilitate profiteering. Although NEP 2020 mentions the need for increased openness, particularly in relation to price structures, it makes no mention of a strategy for dealing with the growing problem of capitation fees charged by private universities, which are largely run by influential politicians and religious groups. As a result, universal education will remain a pipe dream. The NEP 2020 does not specify how to operationalise and guarantee the right to education, particularly for excluded and disadvantaged groups (2020).

Discussion

The National Education Policy-2020 outlined a path for progressive education while preserving the essence of Indian tradition, culture, and values in order to establish a new country with a forward-thinking perspective.

India has a rich historical legacy, and education has long been a part of it. After extensive talks with stakeholders from all sectors, the NEP 2020 was developed. Its goal is to provide multidisciplinary skill-based education in order to create jobs; it also aims to increase student enrollment in all types of educational institutions by 2030. This will necessitate significant adjustments in the current educational system. As a result, at all levels, each stakeholder must be held accountable.

Conclusion

The new National Education Policy (NEP) 2020 is an excellent policy since it intends to make the educational system holistic, adaptable, and multidisciplinary, as well as related to the demands of the twenty-first century and the Sustainable Development Goals of 2030. In many ways, the policy's goal appears to be ideal, but the key to success resides in its implementation.

The National Education Policy 2020 aspires to move education toward a more scientific approach. It will assist in catering to the child's abilities at various phases of development. Cognitive, social, and physical development are all part of this process. When fully implemented, the policy will bring India up to speed with the world's leading nations.

Works Cited

1. Chopra, Ritika (2 August 2020). "Explained: Reading the new National Education Policy 2020". The Indian Express.
2. https://static.pib.gov.in/WriteReadData/userfiles/NEP_Final_English_0.pdf

9

NEP 2020: A Review in Post Covid Scenario

Dr C. Rama Mohan Reddy

Abstract

In the midst of all the negativity enveloping the world as a result of the issues created by the Covid- 19 pandemic, the Government of India's New Education Policy (NEP 2020) was a welcome shift and fresh news. Many people were taken aback by the announcement of NEP 2020. Many educators did not see the changes indicated by NEP 2020 coming. Though education policy has had an equal impact on school and college education, this article focuses mostly on NEP 2020 and its implications for higher education. This paper also discusses the key aspects of NEP and how they impact the current educational system.

Key Words : New Education Policy, Higher Education, Covid-19.

In the aftermath of the Covid-19 epidemic, the Indian government's New Education Policy (NEP 2020) is a welcome news and a positive development among the world's pessimism. The recently announced National Education Policy 2020 envisions an India-centered education system that contributes directly to transforming our nation into an egalitarian and vibrant knowledge society by providing high-quality education to everyone.

It is a well-known fact that change is the law of nature, and we must change with the times if we are to live. In the same way, every institution, policy, and law must be revised on a regular basis to satisfy the needs and goals of inhabitants. The cabinet approved a new education policy with the purpose of improving and expanding educational options for inhabitants. The new method emphasises holistic growth and prioritises practical knowledge above academic information.

Key Features: The key features of the new education policy are as follows:-

1. The school grounds will be used for various educational purposes for adults outside of the school's formal operating hours.
2. The new strategy emphasises vocational studies and encourages students to sample practical courses such as metal work and carpentry, as well as internship opportunities, in order to foster holistic development.
3. The policy also emphasises the importance of digital advancement, stating that a new body under the MHRD would be established to oversee E-education requirements for both high schools and higher education.
4. The NEP 2020 establishes a high requirement for teachers' educational qualifications. They want to create an integrated four-year B.Ed. degree programme that will be the minimum requirement for any person who wants to become a teacher.
5. A single governing body will be established to oversee all higher education in the country, including legal and medical education.
6. The education sector's GDP expenditure will be boosted to six percent of GDP.
7. The policy also encourages schools to participate in bag-free days and to teach the "three language formula" in all states.
8. The policy also weakens the stream separation policy and supports a more open realm of topic choice for students, with the goal of blurring the distinction between vocational and academic study.
9. The policy strives to provide students with a variety of exit choices if they decide to drop out of a course in the middle of it. Certificates, diplomas, and degrees will be granted according to a specified frame.
10. The new programme also focuses on developing multidisciplinary institutions across the country, which will provide students with a variety of new opportunities.

The new strategy not only fosters holistic growth, but it was also carefully planned to turn vision into action. "Action speaks louder than words," as the adage goes. As a result, the new policy not only promises a brighter future with a praiseworthy vision, but it also has various provisions that will help us realise that vision and make India a "knowledge centre" in the near future.

Vision of the policy

The National Education Policy 2020 examines an education system based on Indian values that directly contributes to the transformation of India, or Bharat. Its goal is to maintain and care for the present thriving knowledge society by delivering high-quality education to all, regardless of religion, gender, caste, or creed, giving everyone an equal opportunity to grow and develop. It is also an important step toward India becoming a global knowledge superpower. According to the Policy, our institutions' unified curriculum and pedagogy must instill in students a deep respect for the Fundamental Duties, as well as Constitutional values, patriotism, and a cognizant knowledge of one's tasks and obligations in a changing world.The Policy's vision is to instill in learners a deep sense of pride in being Indian and love for the country, not only in thought but also in spirit, intellect, and deeds, as well as to develop knowledge, skills, values, and dispositions that support responsible commitment to human rights, sustainable development, and global well-being, reflecting a truly global citizen.

Reforms in Higher Education

As we turn the pages of NEP-2020, we come across a proposal for the country's higher education to be remodelled. We discover that it discusses the construction of reputable universities with good standards, much as DS Kothari suggested in his Kothari Commission report in 1964-66. Kothari mentioned the need of establishing quality institutions, and that the foundations of the standard will start with the admissions process. According to the commission report, each institution would have a set of criteria for admission, and a kid will be admitted to that institution only if they meet those criteria. However, after the adoption of the Right to Education Act of 2010, maintaining the standard has become a concern, and institutions must now follow the RTE-2010 guidelines. Now, how will higher education in a huge country like India, which has more than 800 existing universities and 39,000 colleges, alter dramatically in each decade discussed in the NEP-2020? The policy also mentions self-financed courses, but no clear rules as to how they will be run in institutions with insufficient resources and money are provided. Each institution, as we all know, requires adequate facilities and infrastructure. Fees will always be a key worry in this area, and charge hikes will be the biggest roadblock. The requirements for preserving educational excellence are provided, but how will this be accomplished without enough resources?

Since independence, the constitution has stated that education should be free and obligatory until the age of fourteen. This means that every person is entitled to free and obligatory education. However, we as a country failed to attain the aim until 2009, despite the fact that the constitution had been in place for 59 years. As a result, the government enacted the Right to Education Act of 2010 (RTE-2010), which took effect on April 1, 2010. We've come a long way in the ten years since then, but can we say that we've progressed even half way? Creating laws and enforcing them in a vast country like ours does not work. In addition, the NEP-2020 anticipates allocating six percent of GDP to the education sector. Let us not forget that the government has been imposing a two percent tax since 2004. Let us not forget that the government has been imposing a two percent education cess since 2004 in the hopes of improving the Indian educational system. In the face of a financial crisis, how will the centre be able to raise funding is a huge question that must be answered. The subject to be taught is whether the educational cess would be a component of the primary budget or an additional tax, as originally envisioned.

Challenges of NEP 2020

1. Opening universities every week is a herculean task

In today's India, there are over 1,000 universities spread across the country. To achieve one of the policy's stated goals of doubling the Gross Enrolment Ratio in higher education by 2035, we will need to open one new institution every week for the following 15 years. It is undeniably difficult to open a university every week on a continuous basis.

2. The numbers are no less daunting in reforms to our school system

The National Education Policy 2020 intends to bring two crore children who are currently not in schools, back into the school system. Whichever way you look at it, accomplishing this over 15 years requires the setting up of around 50 schools every week.

3. Funding is a big challenge in the Covid era

This is not a challenge for the faint of heart in terms of funding. The National Education Policy 2020 calls for a rise in education spending from 4.6 percent of GDP to six percent of GDP, or INR 2.5 lakh crores per year. This money will be properly spent on expanding schools and colleges around the country, hiring instructors and professors, and covering operational costs like giving free breakfast to students. The fact that this policy is implemented at a time when the economy has been hammered by Covid-19-related lockdowns, government tax collections are abysmally low, and the fiscal deficit was large even before Covid complicates things.

4. Current focus on healthcare and economic recovery to lower the execution speed

Economists have been calling for large stimulus packages amounting to double-digit percentages of GDP, despite the strain on the exchequer.

5. Need to create a large pool of trained teachers

The policy envisions a major structural re-design of the curriculum, which is a very positive move. However, in order to properly offer this curriculum, we need teachers who have been trained in and understand the pedagogical requirements. Many of the curriculum modifications necessitate significant mental shifts on the part of both teachers and parents.

6. Inter-disciplinary higher education demands for a cultural shift

In higher education, the National Education Policy 2020's focus on inter-disciplinary learning is a very welcome step.

Targets and Timelines

Here are the policy's key targets as well as the deadlines set :

- The entire policy will be implemented by 2040.
- 100 percent Gross Enrolment Ratio from Pre-School to Secondary level by 2030.
- Teachers to be prepared for assessment reforms by 2030.
- Common standards of learning in public and private schools.
- Mission to focus on foundational numeracy and literacy of all students by Grade 3.
- Universalising early childhood care and education by 2030.
- Vocational training for at least 50 percent learners by 2025.

Opportunities of NEP 2020

The unfinished agenda of NEP 1986 is the starting point for New Education Policy. The NEP was founded in a completely different India in 1986. In terms of access and equity, significant progress has been done throughout the years. Enrollment in primary school has reached nearly universal levels, with a subsequent growth in enrolment in higher education (GER: 26.3 percent). However, there has been a decline in the quality of education in public schools, which has resulted in an exodus of the upper and middle classes. As a result, accountability systems have weakened. Despite low learning returns, remuneration structures in public systems have gradually improved.

Plausible Loopholes in the Application of NEP 2020

True, the policy was created with great care and attention to every need of kids and instructors, but there are still certain flaws in the policy that the government will discover once it is implemented. The following are some possible loopholes in the implementation of NEP, 2020 :

1. The policy establishes a clause that specifies that regional languages should be used to instruct kids until they reach the eighth grade. True, this measure will make it easier for pupils to learn in their native language, but every state has transfer students and migrant students. If there is no standard language of instruction in the country, it will be extremely difficult for such pupils to cope and catch up with their peers.
2. The new policy encourages on-site learning, which means children will visit a variety of enterprises, and Indian parents' possessiveness does not contradict this vision. Students in grades 6 through 12 are required to intern for various vocational programmes, which is a completely new notion for Indians to accept. This will be the government's most significant issue in implementing the NEP, 2020.
3. The education system is set to be overturned after 30 years of implementation; so, implementing the new policy and getting residents to accept it would be difficult. It is natural for people to form attachments to existing systems, and the previous policy had been in effect in India for over 30 years, making the implementation of the new policy considerably more challenging.
4. According to various reports, India is still in the developmental stage, with poverty being one of the most prevalent issues; digital learning will undermine the learning aspirations of the poor sections of society, as owning a laptop and other electronic devices is still considered a luxury in India for the marginalised. The new policy supports digital learning to a large level, which will have an impact on the learning capacity of the poor.

It is clear that the policy clearly promotes numerous new agendas that were not taken into account in the previous policy; yet, no policy can be perfect, and this policy, too, has potential gaps that will be highlighted during the policy's application process.

Criticism of NEP 2020

Below is the criticism which have been leveled, or which may be leveled, against the NEP 2020 :

- The NEP skirted around parliamentary supervision, debate, and examination. This is a rushed approach, one that appears to be targeted at scoring a political point, given that it was brought at a time when parliament was not operating because to Covid-19. This isn't the first time something like this has happened. Members of Parliament have been excluded from essential talks on numerous occasions during the last six years, preventing them from critically scrutinising policies or otherwise expressing their opinions and recommending revisions.
- The policy is a vision plan that fails to include the poorest members of society and provides little to no relief to women, caste and religious minorities, since it glosses over long-standing issues about access to education.
- There is no comprehensive roadmap or coherent implementation strategy in place to carry out this big goal, and many milestones and financial commitments required to carry out this plan are unclear. Take, for example, the following line: "The Centre and States will collaborate to expand public investment in the Education sector to at least six percent of GDP." There is no concrete commitment that the government can be held accountable for.
- Three-language formula: While the policy does not require this, it is written in such a way that students, instructors, and schools have limited option and freedom. It's also in blatant violation of a Supreme Court ruling. The layout of this is certain to conjure up memories of the anti-Hindi agitation of 1965, which protested the central government's decision to make Hindi an official language. Political parties in the South regard this as a ploy by the Modi government to force Hindi on states that do not speak the language. This is despite the fact that the federal government has stated that it will not impose any language on any state, leaving the final decision to the state.
- The RTE Act is not mentioned in the NEP 2020, therefore, education universalisation will be impossible without legislative backing: there is no mechanism to link primary and secondary education to the RTE. Legally, the center/state is not bound by this. "The final policy talks about universalisation of school education from 3-18 years, without making it a legal right," the RTE forum stated in a statement. As a result, there is no binding mechanism in place for the federal and state governments to make it a reality. Universalisation will be difficult without the RTE Act."

Conclusion

Every country's economy, social standing, technology adoption, and healthy human behaviour are all influenced by higher education. The education department of the country government is responsible for improving GER so that every citizen of the country has access to higher education opportunities. The National Education Policy of India 2020 is working toward this goal by enacting innovative policies to improve the quality, attractiveness, affordability, and supply of higher education by opening it up to the private sector while maintaining strict quality controls in every higher education institution. NEP-2020 is expected to achieve its goals by 2030 by encouraging merit-based admissions with free-ships and scholarships, merit and research-based continuous performers as faculty members, merit-based proven leaders in regulating bodies, and strict quality monitoring through biennial accreditation based on self-declaration of progress through technology-based monitoring.

All higher education institutions with the current affiliation of affiliated colleges will grow into multidisciplinary autonomous colleges with degree-granting authority or become constituent colleges of their affiliated universities. The National Research Foundation, an independent organisation, will provide funding for innovative projects in the basic sciences, applied sciences, and social sciences and humanities. The higher education system will become more student-centered, allowing students to choose core and allied studies within and across fields. Within the policy framework, faculty members also have the freedom to choose curriculum, methodology, pedagogy, and evaluation approaches. These transformations will begin in the academic year 2021-22 and will last until 2030, when the first phase of transformation will be noticeable.

Works Cited:

1. Nandini, ed. (29 July 2020). "New Education Policy 2020 Highlights: School and higher education to see major changes". Hindustan Times.
2. https://static.pib.gov.in/WriteReadData/userfiles/NEP_Final_English_0.pdf

10

Higher Education at Cross Roads: Post Covid-19 Scenario in India

Dr T. Sasikanth Reddy

Abstract

The impact of Covid-19 can be seen in every sphere of life. Especially when it comes to education; this is the biggest sector that has been adversely affected by this pandemic. It forced many great nations to enforce lockdown thereby bringing everything to an abrupt halt for a certain period of time. Right from the big businesses to educational institutions this Pandemic has literally altered and devastated the traditional ways of carrying out these things. The educational sector has been fighting to survive the crises. The teaching learning and evaluation methodologies have been completely altered by this pandemic. The digitalisation of education became a necessity in order to provide seamless education. Despite of all these challenges, the Higher Education Institutions (HEIs) have reacted positively and managed to ensure the continuity of teaching-learning, research and service to the society with some tools and techniques during the pandemic. This article highlights on major impacts of Covid-19 on HEIs in India and the world. Some measures taken by HEIs and educational authorities of India and the world to provide seamless educational services during the crisis are discussed. Due to Covid-19 pandemic, many new modes of learning, new perspectives, new trends are emerged and the same may continue as we go ahead to a new tomorrow. So, some of the post Covid-19 trends which may allow imagining new ways of teaching learning of higher education in India are outlined.

Keywords : Covid-19, Higher Education, Professional Development, Digital Lessons, Online Teaching, E-Conferences.

On March 11, 2020 World Health Organisation (WHO) declared Covid-19 as a pandemic. Covid-19 has affected more than 4.5 million people worldwide (WHO). In India, the first affected case of Covid-19 was detected on 30 January 2020 in the state of Kerala and the affected had a travel history from Wuhan, China. In India, the first death was reported on March 12, 2020 and the nation observed Janta Curfew for a day on March 22,

2020. India again observed 14 hours Janta Curfew on March 24 to combat the Coronavirus pandemic and assess the country's ability to fight the virus. Then, the 1st phase of lockdown was announced by the Prime Minister on March 25, 2020 for 21 days. The Indian government has been extending the lockdown duration in stages as the virus's impacts have been monitored, and lockdown 5.0 was issued on April 30 and was in force from June 1 to June 30, 2020. After the lift of lockdowns, a new variety known as OMICRON has begun to spread throughout India. Throughout all periods of the lockdown, educational institutions around the country have never been given permission to resume their educational activities. As a result, the pandemic Covid-19 had a tremendous influence on the school sector. According to a UNESCO estimate, Covid-19 has impacted over 68 percent of the global student population as of the first week of June 2020.

Impact of Covid-19 in India

The severe limitations and the nationwide lockdown for Covid-19 have impacted more than 32 crores of students in India. According to a study report on higher education conducted by the Ministry of Human Resource Development (MHRD), Government of India, there are 993 universities, 39931 colleges, and 10725 stand-alone institutions listed on their webpage that contribute to education. Even though the country has adapted to new-age learning, there is still a roadblock in the way of complete success because only 45 crore people out of the country's total population have access to the internet/e-learning. People in rural areas are still mostly without access to technology, which is hampered the cause of online education. By allowing educational institutions to adopt online learning and develop a virtual learning culture, the Covid-19 pandemic showed the entire society that need is the mother of invention. With technological innovation and developments, the pandemic has been propelling the education industry forward. The epidemic has had a tremendous impact on higher education. Over 320 million students in Indian schools and universities are currently affected, according to UNESCO. The pandemic has forced the globe to rethink how it will cope with the 'new normal.' It's vital to grasp the short- and long-term impacts, as well as future measures, after the initial phase of total overhaul. Can India emerge from this crisis with a refreshed perspective and boost to higher education? Going digital was a quick and successful reaction to the situation. To provide continuity in learning, it is now vital to develop effective online platforms. However, in a developing country like India, where students' socio-economic backgrounds and educational institutions are vastly different, the transition has not been easy. As the crisis worsens, the digital divide has grown even wider, requiring immediate intervention from both public and private sector participants.

Students will stay engaged and active in the learning process if they have good teachers, updated curricula, and effective tools.

Pandemic Covid-19 has had a significant impact on India's and the world's educational systems, but some of the most badly afflicted fields of higher education in India are included below:

1. **Destabilized all educational activities:** The Covid-19 outbreak has forced lockdown in all sectors, including education. With the cessation of educational activity, the institutions were closed, posing numerous issues to the stakeholders. As a result, many activities such as admissions, exams, entrance tests, and competitive examinations held by various boards/schools/colleges/universities have been postponed. Many entrance exams for higher education were cancelled, posing a significant problem in the life of a higher education student. To provide support services to students, HEIs have begun holding orientation programmes, induction meetings, and counselling sessions using various e-conferencing systems such as Google Meet, Skype, Youtube live, Facebook live, WebEx, and others. This effort aims to develop an effective virtual environment for teaching and learning, as well as to motivate students to participate in online activities. Teachers and students improved their usage of electronic media for information sharing by using WhatsApp, Google Drive, Telegram, and Twitter, among other platforms.
2. **Mixed impact on Academic research and Professional Development:** On studies, Covid-19 has both bad and beneficial effects. On the downside, it has made it impossible for scholars to travel and collaborate with others on a national and worldwide level. Some collaborative study or project work is made more difficult to finish. Some scientific laboratory tests and research projects were unable to be completed. On the plus side, academicians now have more time to strengthen their theoretical studies. Academics improved their research by becoming more familiar with technology methods. Webinars and e-conferences have become common ways for students and academics all around the world to share their expertise on similar themes.
3. **Severely affected the educational assessment system:** The majority of external exams have been rescheduled, while nearly all internal evaluations have been cancelled. Assessment cancellation has a negative impact on students' learning.

4. **Reduced employment opportunities:** Many job recruitment entrance tests were cancelled, posing a significant problem in the life of a student in higher education. Indians who had been working abroad were likewise dissatisfied with their job losses. Because of the pandemic condition, there is no recruitment in the government sector in India, and fresh graduates are under pressure to fear losing job offers from business sectors.

Emerging approaches in India

The Indian Government has taken a variety of steps to prevent the spread of the pandemic Covid-19. The MHRD and the University Grants Commission (UGC) have made several arrangements for students to continue their learning by launching a number of virtual platforms with online depositories, e-books and other online teaching/learning materials, educational channels through Direct to Home TV, and radios. ICT initiative of MHRD (eBroucher- https://mhrd.gov.in/ict- initiatives) is also a unique platform which combines all digital resources for online education (Pravat, 2020a). UGC has released Guidelines on Examinations and Academic calendar in view of COVID-l9 pandemic and subsequent lockdown on 29th April, 2020 (UGC notice). All terminal examinations have been postponed and shifted to July 2020 and suggested commencement of classes from August 2020. UGC has also prepared complete calendar for the academic session 2020-2021with new dates keeping in view of the lockdown. Some of the digital initiatives of UGC and MHRD for higher education during Covid-19 are pointed as below:

- **e-GyanKosh** is a National Digital Repository to store and share the digital learning resources which is developed by the Open and Distance Learning Institutions of India.
- **Gyandarshan** is a web- based TV channel devoted to educational and developmental needs for Open and Distance Learner. A web-based TV channel devoted to educational and developmental needs of the society.
- **Gyandhara** is an internet audio counseling service offered by IGNOU.
- **Swayam** provides Massive Open Online Courses (MOOCs) with 140 universities approved credit transfer feature. Swayam Prabha provides high quality educational programmes through 32 DTH channels transmitting educational contents.
- **National Digital Library of India (NDLI)** is a repository of e-content on multiple disciplines for all kinds of users like students (of all levels), teachers, researchers, librarians, library users,

professionals, differently abled users and all other lifelong learners. It is being developed at Indian Institute of Technology Kharagpur.

- **e-Yantra** provides hands on experience on embedded systems. It has about 380 Lab and made 2300+ colleges benefited.
- **FOSSEE** is short form for Free and Open-Source Software for Education, which is developed to promote open-source software for education as well as professional use.
- **Virtual Labs** has developed web-enabled curriculum-based experiments designed for remote operation.
- **National Educational Alliance for Technology (NEAT**) is an initiative for skilling of learners in latest technologies through a Public-Private partnership model between the Government (through its implementing agency AICTE) and the Education Technology companies of India. It brings the best technological products in education pedagogy on a single platform for the convenience of learners.

DISHTAVO- The E- Learning platform called Dishtavo was especially developed during the COVID crises. It is very complex and holistic as it extraordinarily addresses the different study packages that consists of; B.A, B.Com, B.Sc. and so forth under the Goa University at the UG and PG degree level.

Post Covid-19 Trends of Higher Education in India

Change is unavoidable, and it has been forced upon society as a result of Covid-19. The prospects afforded by the Covid-19 pandemic will lead to a brighter future. Tomorrow will be a new day, and we will have complete control over it. Traditional paradigms like as classroom lectures, modalities of learning, and forms of assessment will undoubtedly be challenged by new technology. The education sector will be able to envisage new ways of teaching and learning as a result of the new trends, which include the following:

1. **May encourage personalised learning:** Learning does not have to be limited to classrooms or defined bounds. In the new age, students may be virtual learners, with one teacher instructing dozens of students. To fulfil the learners' objectives and needs, the learning modules can be adjusted to fit different learning styles and the learning contents can come from a variety of sources. Students may choose to continue their education under the new paradigm.
2. **Learning with social distancing may continue:** For a long time, everyone will keep social distance and avoid warm handshakes, hugging, personal greetings, and intimacy. Invisible constraints

may limit the enjoyment and fun of university life. Sports, gyms, and competitions may remain in low gear for a longer period of time, resulting in fewer students participating in physical activities. Because of the necessity for social distance, there may be fewer students in each class. As a result, most educational institutions may work in multiple shifts throughout the day, putting additional pressure on the institution's teaching and administrative staff to manage.

3. **Teaching learning may run with technology:** For teaching, studying, entertaining, and communicating with the outside world, an increasing number of students will rely on technology and digital solutions. Students will use the internet to communicate electronically with their teachers and classmates via e-mail, WhatsApp, videoconferencing, instant messaging, webinars, and other means. Artificial Intelligence (AI) may make it easier for teachers to deal with assessment, evaluation, generating mark sheets, and monitoring each student's performance. All may make considerable use of the digital platform to relieve examiners of the load of managing examination and evaluation processes. Academicians would be able to focus more on course development, qualitative teaching-learning, and skill development if these activities were simplified.
4. **Demand for Open and Distance Learning (ODL) and online learning may grow:** To meet the challenges there is more demand for ODL and online modes of education and the same trend may continue in future also. Blended learning combines both face to face and online learning modes.

Conclusion

Because online classes were used as a substitute for traditional classes during the Covid-19 pandemic, internet and technology services should be regarded a necessity rather than a luxury. To encourage remote learning, online libraries, books, and periodicals should be made available. Sarkar (2020) maintains that adequate facilities must be developed for differently-abled students. There is a need to work collaboratively with other universities and Edutech companies to bring about innovative solutions in making digital learning hassle-free and effective. According to Judith Boettcher, an expert in online teaching, "we learn as social beings in a social context" (Miller, 2016). Students have the opportunity to interact with the facilitator and other students in a face-to-face setting. Meetings with instructors, classroom debates, and discussions improve social connectivity among teachers and students in such an environment. Because students are affected by the presence and absence of their peers and teachers, online learning programmes must account for social connectivity in their design. According to Miller (2016), encouraging of cooperation and faculty-student connections are two of the principles of Chickering and Gramson and these are connected to the idea of interpersonal connectedness. The only alternative left after the Covid-19 pandemic is moving to an online mode of teaching learning. Thus, educationists, academic leaders and others are constantly trying to find out whether the students are actually intellectually engaging with the course and its materials when they are at home or at any other place away from the university campus and when there is no scope for face-to-face learning (Miller, 2016). The Bloom's taxonomy acts as a tool to assess the intellectual complexity of the learning activities of the student and thus, gives an opportunity to focus on the cognitive processes that the students should engage in (Miller, 2016).

The goal of education is to empower individuals to improve the world in which they live. Technology has become a necessity in today's world. It's difficult to envision higher education without the usage of digital tools, which have supplied a wealth of educational and academic knowledge. It's also important to remember that it shouldn't promote power and inequality patterns. It should not create a digital divide between the wealthy and the less fortunate. Due to India's diverse socioeconomic situations, we cannot anticipate all essential resources to be available in a country like India. Online learning can be the ideal way of education if it is accessible to all members of society; nevertheless, it can be a threat if certain members of society are unable to use it, resulting in isolation. As a result, it is critical to recognise the importance of online education and to develop treatments that prioritise increased inclusion, connectedness, and equitability. It is critical that colleges and universities comprehend students' experiences and concerns, and prepare accordingly, as well as plan the study schedule in such a way that all students benefit.

Works Cited:

1. Pravat Ku Jena. Impact of Pandemic COVID-19 on Education in India. Purakala. 2020b;31(46):142-149.
2. MILLER, M. D. (2014). Online Learning: Does It Work? In *Minds Online: Teaching Effectively with Technology* (pp. 19-41). Harvard University Press. https://www.hup.harvard.edu/catalog.php?isbn=9780674660021&content=toc
3. Sarkar, A. (2020, June 18). *Online Classes during lockdown in Bengal.* Dalit Camera. Retrieved July 23, 2020, from https://www.dalitcamera.com/online-classes-duringlockdown-in-bengal/
4. Tripathi, S. K., & Amann, W. C. (2020, May 4). COVID-19 and Higher Education: Learning to Unlearn to Create Education for the Future. UNITED NATIONS. Retrieved July 23, 2020, from https://academicimpact.un.org/content/covid-19-and-highereducation-learning-unlearn-create-education-future

11

UGC and Higher Education in India

Dr K.S.C. Rangarao & Dr V. Govindu

Abstract

The Indian higher education system is one of the largest such systems in the World. It is estimated that during the Eleventh Five Year Plan period, there will be a tremendous pressure of numbers on this system and a large number of additional students will be knocking at the doors of higher education institutions in the country. There are also new challenges of management and regulation being faced by these institutions, which require serious attention, both at the institutions in the public sector and also those in the private sector now growing at a fast pace. Besides, the demands of the society for equity and accommodation cannot be neglected any more. The new regime under WTO where competence is the cardinal principle of success in international operations has made it abundantly clear that the country should exploit its excellent potential in higher education and training facilities and prepare itself to export the Indian brand of education to foreign countries. Policy planning and evolving strategies for this task are somewhat new for the country. In this context, an attempt is made in this paper to throw light on the role of University Grants Commission (UGC) which is playing the crucial role in governing higher education in India.

Keywords : Role of UGC, Higher Education system, youth empowerment, Institutional Framework, Educational Reforms.

Introduction

It is one of the most important bodies when it comes to higher education in India. It has made valuable contribution in improving the education in India and will continue to do so in the future. It is said that India has the best education in the world. This is exactly why UGC must be given the credit for this achievement. It is a statutory body that was started in 1956. It was set up by the Union Government of India to ensure that the standard of the University education in India is maintained. Professor Ved Prakash was heading this institute when it started and he was a great academician.

The UGC has its headquarters in New Delhi. As of today the offices can be located in all the major cities including Kolkata, New Delhi and Bangalore.

Post independence the government of India thought that education must be given the maximum importance from the elementary education to the highest levels of education such as the PhD degree. This is exactly why they wanted to come up with a body that will ensure that the education in India meets a certain standard. The UGC was originally looking into Aligarh University, Benaras University and Delhi University. In this article we will discuss about what is UGC and what is its role in the academic world of India. First of all UGC acronym stands for University Grants Commission, India.

OVERVIEW OF HIGHER EDUCATION

Higher Education sector has witnessed a tremendous increase in the number of Universities/University level Institutions and Colleges since Independence. The number of Universities has increased 34 times from 20 in 1950 to 677 in 2014. The sector boasts of 45 Central Universities of which 40 are under the purview of Ministry of Education, 318 State Universities, 185 State Private universities, 129 Deemed to be Universities, 51 Institutions of National Importance (established under Acts of Parliament) under MoE (IITs - 16, NITs – 30 and IISERs – 5) and four Institutions (established under various State legislations). The number of colleges has also registered manifold increase of 74 times with just 500 in 1950 growing to 37,204.

The quantum growth in the Higher Education sector is spear-headed by Universities, which are the highest seats of learning. In India, “University” means a University established or incorporated by or under a Central Act, a Provincial Act or a State Act and includes any such institution as may, in consultation with the University concerned, be recognised by the University Grants Commission (UGC) in accordance with the regulations made in this regard under the UGC Act, 1956. Every year, millions of students from within the country and abroad, enter these portals mainly for their graduate, postgraduate studies while millions leave these portals for the world outside.

Higher Education is the shared responsibility of both the Centre and the States. The coordination and determination of standards in Universities and Colleges is entrusted to the UGC and other statutory regulatory bodies. The Central Government provides grants to the UGC and establishes Central Universities/Institutions of National Importance in the country. The Central Government is also responsible for declaring an educational institution as “Deemed-to-be University” on the recommendations of the UGC.

At present, the main categories of University/University-level Institutions are:- Central Universities, State Universities, Deemed-to-be Universities and University-level institutions. These are described as follows:

Central University:- A university established or incorporated by a Central Act.

State University:- A university established or incorporated by a Provincial Act or by a State Act.

Private University:- A university established through a State/ Central Act by a sponsoring body viz. A Society registered under the Societies Registration Act 1860, or any other corresponding law for the time being in force in a State or a Public Trust or a Company registered under Section 25 of the Companies Act, 1956.

Deemed-to-be University:- An Institution Deemed to be University, commonly known as Deemed University, refers to a high-performing institution, which has been so declared by Central Government under Section 3 of the University Grants Commission (UGC) Act, 1956.

Institution of National Importance:- An Institution established by Act of Parliament and declared as Institution of National Importance.

Institution under State Legislature Act:- An Institution established or incorporated by a State Legislature Act.

OVERVIEW OF UGC

The depiction of UGC we have today is the result of numerous intense steps taken before and after the Indian Independence. Come, let's become a part of the establishment journey of the University Grants Commission.

The first attempt to have an education system was made in the year 1944 with the Sargent Report. It was the Report of the Central Advisory Board of Education on Post-War Educational Development in India. Through the recommendation, the University Grants Committee was formed in 1945, which took upon the responsibility of supervision of three Central Universities of Aligarh, Banaras, and Delhi. In the year 1947, the committee got the responsibility to control all the universities of that era. In 1948, the University Education Commission was set up, whose chairman was Dr. Sarvepalli Radhakrishnan. The commission suggested that the existing University Grants Committee should be transformed into University Grants Commission India like the UK.

On 28 December 1953, Maulana Abul Kalam Azad (former Minister of Education) inaugurated University Grants Commission. And in November 1956, UGC (University Grants Commission) was formally established as a statutory body of the Government of India via 'University Grants Commission Act, 1956' of the Parliament. The vision was to supervise the coordination, determination, and maintenance of standards of university education in our country. Thereafter in 1994 and 1995, UGC introduced six centers at Pune, Hyderabad, Kolkata, Bhopal, Guwahati, and Bangalore to control the region-wise education system in India. Currently, the head office is locating at Bahadur Shah Zafar Marg in New Delhi.

Power and Main Aims of UGC : The main aim and role of UGC in higher education is to provide funds to universities and coordinate, determine and maintain the ethics in institutions of higher education. The commission upholds the interpretation among the universities, government, and the community. UGC has also set some standards for the universities for being UGC Approved Universities. With the growth of higher education in India, many top, medium, and small universities are being established day by day. Among these universities, there are many universities that are fake and not fit as per the UGC standards.

Organisational Structure of UGC : The University Grants Commission follows a structural chain of command that starts from the UGC Chairman. Here, you can read the detailed analysis of UGC Members and the composition of UGC.

Chief Officials/Members of UGC : UGC Chairman - The present UGC Chairman's name is Prof. Dhirendra Pal Singh (D. P. Singh). He owns 34 years of experience in educational planning and administration, institution building, teaching and training, research and development, international cooperation, etc.

He has also served as the Director of the National Assessment and Accreditation Council (NAAC) and Vice-Chancellor of three universities - Banaras Hindu University (BHU), Varanasi, Dr. Hari Singh Gour University, Sagar and Devi Ahilya University, Indore.

Prior to becoming the UGC Chairman, Prof. D.P. Singh has also been a member of various committees to improve the depiction of the higher education system of India.

He also possesses awards like the Environment Leadership Award, Environmentalist of the Decade (Poorvanchal) Award, Bharat Jyoti Award, U.P. Ratan Award, Agra University Gaurav Shri Award, Raja Balwant Singh Shiksha Samman, Nation Builder Award, etc.

UGC Vice Chairman - Dr. Bhushan Patwardhan has been appointed as Vice Chairman of UGC.

UGC Secretary - Shri Amit Khare is currently serving as the Secretary Department of Higher Education, Ministry of Human Resource Development. He has many years of professional experience in teaching, research, administration, institution building, and corporate training.

UGC Scholarships and Awards - Complete List of UGC Fellowships: Various UGC scholarships and fellowships have been planned by the commission which provides enormous opportunities to the students who are continuously contributing to the growth of our educational system.

With the help of UGC scholarships, the students who are not financially strong but are capable to induce positive changes in the higher education system can continue their education without any financial hindrances.

UGC Research Awards & Honours:- The University Grants Commission (UGC) always put steps for encouraging teaching and research. For promoting excellence in research in higher education UGC has arranged UGC Research awards and honours. Every year many brilliant researchers and Lecturers are bestowed with UGC Awards and Honours by the commission.

The awards are –

UGC Hari Om Ashram Trust Awards

UGC Swami Pranavananda Saraswati National Awards

UGC National Veda Vyas Sanskrit Awards

At this point, we are concluding the hopefulness that you have streaked all the important aspects of UGC (University Grants Commission India). You might have liked this blog on what is UGC and what are the major roles played by these organisations. If it is so, please share the information with your mates. If you have any queries, then share them with us through the comment box below.

Activities and Programmes UGC:- In 1957 almost all the universities came under the control of the UGC. It is the only grant giving institute in the country. It provides funds and it also arranges for the coordination and maintenance of the universities in India. The UGC controls the following in India:

1. Maintaining the standard of research, teaching and examination in the universities.
2. Promoting university education.

3. Making regulations to maintain the minimum standard of education in the country.
4. It is a link between the union government and the institutes of higher education.
5. It also advises the government about the steps to be taken in order to improve the education system.
6. Allocates grants to the universities and colleges out of its own funds for their development or other general purpose.
7. Advises the central and state government on disbursing grants to the universities out of the Consolidated Fund of India.
8. Advises any authority on the establishment of new university or on the proposal seeking expansion of any university.
9. Collects information on university education in India and in other countries.
10. Seeks information from the universities from time to time. The information may range from the financial position of the university, their various branches of learning to the rules and regulations followed in a particular university.
11. Imparts education to the students in various streams through its Country wide classroom teachings and a four-year old 24 hours educational channel 'Vyas'.
12. Conducts National Eligibility Test (NET) through its National Educational Testing Bureau in a bid to determine eligibility for lectureship. It also awards Junior Research Fellowship (JRF), which has been set as the minimum standards for Indian nationals to enter teaching profession and research. Humanities (including languages), Forensic Science, Computer Science, Social Sciences, Environmental Sciences, and Applications and Electronic Science are the subjects in which a student can appear for a JRF.
13. The University Grants Commission has recently launched an 'e-scripting' course in television for all those students who want to make a career in broadcast media. The course is being run by its Consortium of Educational Communication, an Inter University Centre of the UGC on electronic media.

You can make out from the list above that UGC plays a vital role in the education of the country. It has ensured that a system it followed in higher education. UGC also ensures that the education in all these top universities is of the same standard so that the students passing out of these colleges can be considered equal. India is a vast country as a result there are thousands of colleges offering different courses. It is impossible to ensure that a common standard is maintained. However, UGC indeed makes this impossible task possible.

Funding Works of UGC:- Recurrent and capital grants are used to fund universities funded by the UGC. The former is intended to assist universities with their academic work as well as administrative tasks. The latter is used to fund significant construction projects as well as modest campus improvements.

1. Recurrent Grants:- The majority of recurring payments are distributed to universities on a triennial basis to coincide with the academic planning cycle and in the form of a block, grant to give universities the most freedom in internal deployment. After allocations are authorised, institutions have a lot of leeway in selecting how to best employ the resources they have. The amount of money given to universities is mostly determined by a formula. The funding formula is the most important factor in determining the needs of colleges. However, while making funding recommendations, the UGC considers the unique needs of particular universities as well as other factors not reflected by the formula and will make extra formulaic changes as needed. Funding suggestions will be made to the Government and approved by the Legislative Council in accordance with the mechanisms set by the government.

2. Capital Grants:- University capital projects are funded by capital grants, which are requested from the Administration on an annual basis through two pathways: the Capital Works Programme and the Alterations, Additions, and Improvements (AA&I) block allocation. The two paths are distinguished by a two-approval procedure in which all proposals must first be assessed by the UGC before being presented to the legislature for funding consideration. There is an additional step for UGC-approved projects to be exposed to a competitive selection process by the Administration in the Capital Works Programme.

Suggestions and Recommendations

For Higher Education Institution : The following are the few important suggestions and recommendations for the overall enhancement of Higher Education Institution in India in the near future :

1. The Governmental control in the Universities must be reduced, so that the University autonomy and accountability are strengthened and academic decisions are taken on merit.
2. New methods and procedures of financial regulations should be devised and direct interference of the finance department in the

financial management of Universities, which is counter productive should be stopped.

3. As the Colleges are the feeding sources of the Universities, a better coordination in their working and activities is very much required. The participation of the teaching faculty in through a democratic process should be ensured.
4. Complete transparency should be maintained in the working of Executive/Academic Bodies and other Governing Councils of the Universities. There is an urgency to review the University Acts in different States and revise the same in the light of the new requirements and the challenges being faced by the Universities. New technologies of information and communication should be utilised for obtaining administrative efficiency.
5. Higher Education should be developed as an infrastructure for social and economic growth of the Country.
6. Students involvement in the area of University/College governance should be encouraged.
7. Political interference in the appointment of University teachers and administrators should be totally stopped.
8. To initiate UGC scale salary to all the NAAC accredited colleges and universities in India.
9. Encouraged NAAC accreditation to all the colleges and universities of India.
10. To initiate awareness programme to all parents or guardian of the students.
11. Regular supportive supervision to NAAC accredited colleges and universities by a NAAC nominated team etc.

For UGC: The following are the few important suggestions and recommendations for UGC development.

1. It has been successfully doing its role for almost half a century and will continue to do so even in the future. One of the best ways to ensure that the education in all these universities is at par is to ensure that the teachers are equally good. This is exactly why the final approval of the UGC is required before a lecturer is appointed in any of these colleges.
2. We hope that by now you have got a fair idea of what the UGC is and the role that it plays in the education system. The UGC also conducts the NET, which is the name of a qualification that is

essential for a person to teach in the graduation and post-graduation colleges.

3. There are totally sixteen institutes that are controlled by the UGC. To name some of them are AICTE, RCI, DCI, etc. It also funds these colleges. The verdict of UGC is final when it comes to education in these institutes. In the 2009 it was proposed that UGC should be closed and AICTE (All India Council for Technical Education) should take up the role of UGC. However, the UGC still continues to operate.
4. UGC is important for a student. Well it is very important. When you apply for any higher education in India you must check if the college is approved by UGC and specifically it is not there in the list of fake universities. Only when the college is approved by the UGC you should take up the course. If a college is not approved by UGC it may not be a good place to get your degree from. If the degree is not approved by the UGC it will not have much value in the future.
5. UGC with the help of BSNL had launched the UGC-Infonet. The idea was to connect all the colleges that are approved by UGC. This would ensure that the students and the students from these different colleges can interact and exchange their point of views. This would be a state of the art technology for these colleges. The concept is good but it still needs some more time before it can be actually implemented. There is a team that is working hard on making this a possibility.

Conclusion

It is one of the most important bodies when it comes to higher education in India. It has made valuable contribution in improving the education in India and will continue to do so in the future. It is said that India has the best education in the world. This is exactly why UGC must be given the credit for this achievement.

Accreditation plays a critical role in the institutional overall improvement, enhancing its societal image and status. It helps the institution to know its strengths, weaknesses, opportunities, challenges and identifies internal areas of planning and resource allocation. It also enhances interpersonal relationships and collegiality on the campus. Many Institutions have updated the curriculum and initiated innovative and modern methods of pedagogy for the benefit of students. Accreditation gives the institution a new sense of direction and identity with greater sense of accountability and enhanced credibility.

References

1. Sawant, D.G. ¯Role of IQAC in maintaining quality standard in teaching, learning and evaluation. Pacific Science Review B: Humanities and Social Sciences 2 (2016) 66-69.
2. Arimoto Akira Structure and Functions of Financing Higher Education in Higher Education in the World 2006, GUNI (2006) series on the social commitment of universities. Palgrave, New York. (2006)
3. Adams, D. Defining educational quality. Improving Educational Quality. (1993.
4. www.ugc.ac.in and NAAC's Newsletter, Vol.XVI (2),July 2019.
5. Dr. B. Ilango, 2013. Accreditation of educational institutions and programmes in India, IEEE India Info Vol. 8, No. 4, April 2013.
5. http://www.NAAC.gov.in/docs/RevisedAccreditation Framework for Website 27 July2017. Pdf
6. http://www.onlinecollege.org/2011/05/03/accreditation and-higher-education-what-do-you-need-to-know/
7. Chauhan, C.P.S. Modern Indian Education Policies, Progress and Problems, Kanishka Publishers, Distributors, New Delhi (2007).
8. Adams, D. (1993). Defining educational quality. Improving Educational Quality Project.
9. **Publication #1: Biennial Report. Arlington, VA: Institute for International Research.**
10. **Anderson, L. (1991). Increasing teacher effectiveness. Paris: UNESCO.**
11. Anderson, S. E. (2000). A coordinated district consultant/teacher centre approach.
12. *A Decade of Dedication to Quality Assurance* (2004), NAAC publication.2004, Pub-141.
13. Daniel Stufflebeam Meta-Evaluation, December, 1974.
14. http://www.naac.gov.in/publications.asp (New Manual for Assessment and Accreditation - For Affiliated Colleges, New Methodology, Effective from 1st April 2007) (accessed on 04 February 2011).
15. http://www.naac.gov.in/Publications/IQAC_2005.pdf (Guidelines for the Creation of the Internal Quality Assurance Cell ((IQAC) in Accredited Institutions – A Post Accreditation Quality Sustenance Activity, (accessed on 04 February 2011)
16. http://www.ugc.ac.in/financialsupport/xiplan/guideline.html. (accessed on 04 February 2011)
17. *http://sjec.edu.in/pdf/Paper%20Presentation%20-Mithun%20Kumar.pdf*
18. *http://www.ugc.ac.in/pdfnews/0722837_guidelines-autonomous-colleges.pdf (Accessed on 14-03-2016)*
19. *Institutions Accredited by NAAC*, (2007), NAAC Publication No. 199.
20. *Judgement on Institutional Accreditation* (1997), NAAC Publication No. 28.

12

Emerging Trends in Higher Education Union Industry Government Partnership

Aditya Sharma

Abstract

Education is the right and necessity of every child, for a bright and secure future, to shatter the cloak of darkness and ignorance and fly to the light of enlightenment. It is crucial for all nations to invest on education as it is an investment to turn human resource to human capital and not an expenditure that can be ignored. As for the indulgence of change to the greatest of degree, the equitable efforts of both the union government and private stakeholders are necessary. For we can take into consideration the theory of multiplier as suggested by, John Maynard Keynes the father of macro economics. This theory states that for every unit of money spent by the government, multiplied benefits can be derived. This concept yet remains relevant in lieu with education industry.

The primary objective of this paper would be so as to propose a model for union and government partnership through which the distribution of education in the society can be increased, intern to increase the revenues earned by the nation and develop its human capital. For these references of countries like Finland which has free education. Norway with the highest education expenditure in terms of percentage of gross domestic product (6.6% of 2020), USA, etc can be taken.

The literacy rate of India is at a sulking low of 66.54 percent. There are a number of reasons for this like:

1. Dense population structure (138 crore as per 2020 estimates)
2. High average cost of education (Rs 64763 in urban areas, and Rs. 32127 in rural areas per annum for secondary education)
3. Low union expenditure of Rs. 993 billion for 2020

Sentient ways so as to extend quality education services to even the most downtrodden portion of the society would act as a driving factor for reducing the inequalities in the society and increase the literacy rate of the nation, through a hybrid model of private and public sector partnership.

The paper aims at finding out the problems and shortcomings in the education sector and proposing possible solutions to them while examining and predicting the scope of the industry currently and in the future as well. An in-depth scrutiny of the new education policy 2021, field trends of secondary education across the world pre and post Covid, shall be done.

Introduction

The following research paper aims to entail a detailed analysis of the changes occurring, or bound to occur in the future both structurally and economically in lieu with the field of education and training. As education is one of the basic necessities of every individual in this robust and ever changing world, it would cease to miss the education sector from the bigger picture of the economy as a whole. To gain control of the education sector is a task with penultimate importance as, education would be a remedy for unemployment, poverty and exploitation. Enlightenment would mean to as to solve these social evils from the grass root level. The following paper looks forward to how the education system has evolved and molded itself during the Covid-19 pandemic. The following articles of research aim at proposing a state and private partnership to increase the reach of education to even the most secluded parts of the society. So as to make the utopia of an educated and civilised society possible.

Current trends in the education industry

The economic output of the education industry have been confusing, yet promising. As education has now become possible through the method of online learning and e-tutors. Despite the inequalities and inconsistencies in the society today, most people have kept up as they have smart phones. The results have been so far so good, even promising to the future, keeping in mind the two years of pandemic also took a toll on students and learners alike:

1. The number of private unaided schools in India is 22.38 percent, with a staffing of about 37.18 percent. This indicates insufficient staff for government schools which needs to be considered so as to take necessary steps to keep up the balance.
2. Private schools account to almost 25 percent of the total k-12 schools in India as per estimates. Total of 253 million students study in these, with 60 percent students in public schools.
3. The literacy rate of the country is 74.04 percent, with 82.14 percent in males and 65.46 percent in females which indicates to inequality in the educated demography.
4. Kerala had the highest literacy rate of 93.91 percent, and lowest at 63.82 percent in Bihar.

5. 1.8 trillion hours and counting of in learning loss due to Covid-19 lockdown globally.
6. These learning losses can cause this generation of students a loss of $17 trillion of their lifetime earnings.
7. Online governmental courses have excelled, with almost 37+ lakhs students who successfully completed 2300+ unique courses under the skill India scheme.

New education policy 2020

The new education policy bill was passed in the Lok Sabha on 29 July 2020. The bill is ambitious in the sense that it aims at achieving a number of milestones which would revolutionise and diversify the education sector of India using infrastructure development by the government and credibly backed support of the private sector as well. It is based on the double engine model of the Modi government. The following are the set of goals that are to be achieved in the future:

1. Ensuring Universal Access at All Levels of schooling from pre-primary school to Grade 12;
2. Ensuring quality early childhood care and education for all children between 3-6 years;
3. New Curricular and Pedagogical Structure (5+3+3+4);
4. No hard separations between arts and sciences, between curricular and extra-curricular activities, between vocational and academic streams;
5. Establishing National Mission on Foundational Literacy and Numeracy;
6. Emphasis on promoting multilingualism and Indian languages; The medium of instruction until at least Grade 5, but preferably till Grade 8 and beyond, will be the home language/mother tongue/ local language/regional language.
7. Assessment reforms - Board Exams on up to two occasions during any given school year, one main examination and one for improvement, if desired;
8. Setting up of a new National Assessment Centre, PARAKH (Performance Assessment, Review, and Analysis of Knowledge for Holistic Development);
9. Equitable and inclusive education - Special emphasis given on Socially and Economically Disadvantaged Groups (SEDGs);
10. A separate Gender Inclusion fund and Special Education Zones for disadvantaged regions and groups;

11. Robust and transparent processes for recruitment of teachers and merit based performance;
12. Ensuring availability of all resources through school complexes and clusters;
13. Setting up of State School Standards Authority (SSSA);
14. Exposure of vocational education in school and higher education system;
15. Increasing GER in higher education to 50 percent;
16. Holistic Multidisciplinary Education with multiple entry/exit options;
17. NTA to offer Common Entrance Exam for Admission to HEIs;
18. Establishment of Academic Bank of Credit;
19. Setting up of Multidisciplinary Education and Research Universities (MERUs);
20. Setting up of National Research Foundation (NRF);
21. 'Light but Tight' regulation;
22. Single overarching umbrella body for promotion of higher education sector including teacher education and excluding medical and legal education- the Higher Education Commission of India (HECI)-with independent bodies for standard setting- the General Education Council; funding-Higher Education Grants Council (HEGC); accreditation- National Accreditation Council (NAC); and regulation- National Higher Education Regulatory Council (NHERC);
23. Expansion of open and distance learning to increase GER;
24. Internationalisation of Education;
25. Professional Education will be an integral part of the higher education system. Stand-alone technical universities, health science universities, legal and agricultural universities, or institutions in these or other fields, will aim to become multi-disciplinary institutions;
26. Teacher Education - 4-year integrated stage-specific, subject-specific Bachelor of Education;
27. Establishing a National Mission for Mentoring;
28. Creation of an autonomous body, the National Educational Technology Forum (NETF) to provide a platform for the free exchange of ideas on the use of technology to enhance learning, assessment, planning, administration. Appropriate integration of technology into all levels of education;

29. Achieving 100 percent youth and adult literacy;
30. Multiple mechanisms with checks and balances will combat and stop the commercialization of higher education;
31. All education institutions will be held to similar standards of audit and disclosure as a 'not for profit' entity;
32. The Centre and the States will work together to increase the public investment in Education sector to reach six percent of GDP at the earliest.
33. Strengthening of the Central Advisory Board of Education to ensure coordination to bring overall focus on quality education.
34. Ministry of Education: In order to bring the focus back on education and learning, it may be desirable to re-designate MHRD as the Ministry of Education (MoE).

Estimates

The estimates for a union industry and government partnership based education system have been by far positive. This is only due to the heavy governmental expenditure and the fast connectivity of the modern technology. Many industry experts give the following estimates for the future:

1. India is a nation of youth with 580 million of its citizens within the age bracket of 5-24 years. This points at the potential for a robust demand in the future.
2. India has more than 250 million schools, which is far more than any other country, found to increase due to the dense population structure and liberalisation schemes and policies.
3. Applications from foreign students for study in India programme increased by 146 percent in 2021.
4. Large portion of the population is proficient in English with a rank of 50 out of 100 in English proficiency index 2020.
5. 100 percent fdi is allowed by the government in the field of education.
6. Education market to amount $225 billion in fy2025.
7. India might become hotbed for edtech entrepreneurs.

Hybrid learning model of public private partnership and technology

As from the experience we gained from the erstwhile Covid-19 pandemic, a certain hybrid model of education is to be proposed where there would be a blend of both online and offline the details are yet to be confirmed as it is still an experiment for as to incorporate technology and making learning more interactive and easier for the child. But it proposes a new set of problems that are yet to be come across.

This is yet a dream which can be seen from successful entrepreneurial ideas like byjus, white hat junior, etc. but many experts are yet certain that this is the future for education aided by technology is not very far away but just requires a push of governmental initiative and market demand.

1. The state and private stake holders can undertake equally financed schools, or
2. State can provide grants and tax deductions for schools,
3. industry tie up schools can also be encouraged,
4. TV programmes can be started, special YouTube channels for education.

These are some of the suggested ways that can be used to as to support and grow educational institutions.

Conclusion

We can conclude to the fact that education sector would grow if and only if the private sector initiates innovations using the latest technology and new and advanced ideas, backed up by the support of governmental schemes and infrastructure. We can be ambitious that the education today would change for good, where the sky is the limit and it's only through everyone's efforts that we can cause revolutions unimaginable. Industry experts believe that we are not limited by knowledge or technology, but our creativity to use what we have.

We can positively say that economic growth would accelerate due to the multiplier effect of growth in the education sector.

References

1. The future of learning: 12 views on emerging trend in higher education, WJ Flynn and Jeff Vredegvood.
2. FICCI, education report March 2014.
3. Census, 2011, government of India report.
4. UNICEF report 17 September 2021.
5. World bank, Economic article 6 December 2021.
6. National education policy bill 29 July 2020, ministry of human resource development, India.
7. Union budget 2021, ministry of finance, India.
8. IBEF, article on education industry analysis 3 December 2021.

13

Impact of Covid-19 on the Higher Education System of Rural Areas in Telangana

Tula Ravikumar

Introduction

A total of 1.3 billion learners around the world were not able to attend schools or universities, and approximately 320 million learners were affected in India alone. It has changed the traditional education system to the educational technologies model in which teaching and assessments are conducted online. The Covid-19 pandemic has created challenges and disrupted the Higher Education system under these circumstances government-imposed nation-wise lockdown on March 25, 2020, to combat Covid-19, which has created an impact on the education system. India has the world's second-largest school system, after China. According to UNESCO, 63 million teachers were affected in 165 countries. This paper aims to analyze the impact of Covid-19 on thc Indian Education System, focusing on education during online teaching and assessment of students getting online classes at home during the pandemic, especially in rural areas of Telangana state. The positive and negative impacts of Covid-19 on the Telangana Education system are observed. Telangana is the 29th state of India, formed on the 2nd of June 2014. The state has an area of 112,077 sq. km. and has a population of 3,50,03,674. The Telangana region was part of the Hyderabad state from Sept 17th, 1948 to Nov 1st, 1956, until it was merged with Andhra Pradesh state to form the Andhra Pradesh state.

Telangana state profile information Districts 33, Revenue Divisions 74, Towns 141, Municipal Corporations 13, Municipalities 129, Zilla Praja Parishads 32, Mandal Praja Parishads 540, Gram Panchayats 12769,

Revenue Mandals 594, Revenue Villages (as per Census, 2011) 10,434 Inhabited Villages (as per Census, 2011) 9,834 Un-inhabited Villages (as per Census, 2011) 600.

Covid-19 and Academic Achievement as students have suffered throughout the pandemic, to get their learning. In the fall of 2020, according to some assessments, many students appeared to have made gains from the previous year, though in most cases, significantly smaller ones than in the prior year which includes a five to ten percentile point drop in math achievement on NWEA's MAP Growth assessments. Data at the state and district level last fall also painted a mixed picture, with some reports finding that students had made academic gains by fall 2020 but in amounts that were less than in previous years and uneven across subjects.

Pre-Pandemic Disparities- As this sections documents, pre-pandemic disparities in resources, opportunities, and outcomes experienced by many students of colour set the foundation for additional race-based disparities in educational opportunities as a result of Covid-19. Resources Disparities in schools and at home before Covid-19 State budgets for public education have been tight for more than a decade, affecting many schools and students.

The shutdown and lockdown of educational institutions have been proposed by the Indian Government as a logical option to enforce social separation within communities. The country's education sector, particularly for pupils from remote, has been severely impacted by the statewide lockdown. The current situation has made the functioning of educational institutions particularly challenging because the Indian education system is dominated by classroom learning.

Exams, school admissions, university entrance tests, competitive examinations, and other educational activities take place during this time. The closure of schools and institutions across the country is having a significant impact on learning as the days pass without an immediate way to stop the spread. The Indian education system's framework, including learning methodologies, teaching strategies, and evaluation methodologies, has been significantly impacted, leading to a transition to online education with the help of technology.

To achieve the defined goals and objectives, most people turn to virtual education. However, only a few schools and colleges can implement such procedures, and low-income private and public institutions are inefficient in doing so, resulting in a closure.

Objectives

- The impact of Covid-19 on the Indian education system, with a focus on the role of teachers and students through online education.
- In the context of online education, how is the positive impact beneficial to students, parents, and teachers?
- How might Covid-19 have a less detrimental impact on students, allowing them to continue with their studies.

Methodology

The study's data and information come from a variety of publications and articles on the impact of the Covid-19 epidemic released by national and international organisations. Information is also gathered from a variety of reliable websites. Some journals that refer to the impact of Covid-19 on the educational system are also referred to.

Purpose of Study

Every system has its own set of strengths and flaws. The goal should be to maximize strengths while reducing shortcomings to avoid missing out on opportunities to progress. The study's major goal is to assess Covid-19's impact on the Telangana educational system. Covid-19's impact on rural and urban students, as well as higher education institutions, is discussed.

The positive and negative impacts of Covid-19 on the Telangana Education system are observed. Telangana is the 29th state of India, formed on the 2nd of June 2014. The state has an area of 112,077 sq. km. and has a population of 3,50,03,674. The Telangana region was part of the Hyderabad state from Sept 17t,h 1948 to Nov 1s,t 1956, until it was merged with Andhra Pradesh state to form the Andhra Pradesh state.

Telangana state profile information Districts 33, Revenue Divisions 74, Towns 141, Municipal Corporations 13, Municipalities 129, Zilla Praja Parishads 32, Mandal Praja Parishads 540, Gram Panchayats 12769, Revenue Mandals 594, Revenue Villages (as per Census, 2011) 10,434 Inhabited Villages (as per Census, 2011) 9,834 Un-inhabited Villages (as per Census, 2011) 600.

Impact on Teacher and Student

During online education, both professors and students face numerous obstacles. At home, there were substantial concerns such as a lack of basic amenities, external distraction, and family disruption during teaching.

Assistance hurdles in educational institutions included a lack of funding for advanced technology purchases, a lack of training, a lack of technical support, and a lack of clarity and direction. Teachers had their own set of problems with technology. The issues were categorised as a lack of technical support, which included a lack of technical infrastructure, a lack of knowledge of online teaching platforms, and security concerns. Teachers' issues, such as a lack of technical understanding and course integration with technology, are limiting their willingness to teach online.

POSITIVE IMPACT ON THE EDUCATION SYSTEM

Even though the outbreak of Covid-19 has had numerous detrimental effects on education, Indian educational institutions have acknowledged the challenges and are doing their utmost to give students with smooth support services during the pandemic. The Indian education system now can evolve from a traditional system into a modern one. The following are some of the positive effects that can be evaluated.

- Develop the usage of soft copy learning resources- Because students were unable to acquire hard copies of study materials during the lockdown, the majority of students relied on soft copy material for reference.
- Improvements in collaborative work- There is a new opportunity for collaborative teaching and learning to take on new forms, thanks to the pandemic.
- Increase in the online meeting- The pandemic has resulted in a massive increase in teleconferencing, virtual meetings, webinars, and e-conferencing opportunities.
- Digital literacy increased as a result of the pandemic scenario, which encouraged individuals to learn and use electronic media for information sharing. Learning materials are easily shared among students, and related questions are answered via e-mail, SMS, phone calls, and various social media platforms such as WhatsApp or Facebook.

Educators and students were exposed to peers from all around the world. Learners were able to adjust to a global setting. Enhanced time management-during pandemics, students in online education can manage their time more effectively. Demand for open and distance learning- During the epidemic, most students favored Distance Learning since it encourages self-learning and allows them to learn from a variety of resources while also tailoring their education to their specific needs.

No.	District	GDCs	WDCs	Teachers Education	Medical & Nursing	Others	Total
1	2	3	4	5	6	7	8
1.	Adilabad	3	3	1	2	1	9
2.	Bhadradri Kothagudem	5	4	1			10
3.	Hyderabad	11	1	1	9	2	24
4.	Jagtial	4	1			1	6
5.	Jangaon	1	1			1	3
6.	Jayashankar Bhupalpally	2	2			1	3
7.	Jogulamba Gadwal	3	-				3
8.	Kamareddy	4	1				6
9.	Karimnagar	5	2			1	7
10.	Khammam	5	2				8
11.	Kumaram Bheem Asifabad	1	1				2
12.	Mahabubabad	4	2				7
13.	Mahabubnagar	3	2	1	1		9
14.	Mancherial	4	-				5
15.	Medak	3	2				6
16.	Medchal	2	-		1		10
17.	Mulugu	2	-			1	4
18.	Nagarkurnool	7	3				9
19.	Nalgonda	6	2	1	2		11
20.	Narayanpet	1	-				1
21.	Nirmal	2	1			1	4
22.	Nizamabad	7	4		1		11
23.	Peddapally	3	-				4
24.	Rajanna Sircilla	2	2		1		5
25.	Rangareddy	5	6		3		9
26.	Sangareddy	7	2		1		8
27.	Siddipet	7	2		1		10
28.	Suryapet	2	1		1		4
29.	Vikarabad	2	1				3
30.	Wanaparthy	4	1				5
31.	Warangal Rural	3	1		2	2	3
32.	Warangal Urban	3	2	1	1		8
33.	Yadadhri Bhongir	2	1				3
	Total	**125**	**54**	**6**	**26**	**13**	**221**

1.	Government Degree Colleges	123	*Collegiate Education*
2.	Social/Tribal/MinorityWelfare Residential Degree Colleges	53	*Welfare Dept. & Societies*
3.	Government Colleges of Teachers Education	6	*SchoolEducation*
4.	GovernmentMedicalandNursingColleges including Pharmacy	26	*MedicalEducation*
5.	Other Government Colleges	13	*OtherDept.*
A	***Total Public HEIs***	***221***	

Telangana's state government manages a total of 221 higher education institutions. There are 123 Degree colleges managed by Social/ Tribal/ Minority Welfare departments through Residential Education Societies, six colleges of Teachers Education Department, and 26 Colleges related to Medical Profession (medical, Ayurveda / Homeopathy, nursing, and pharmacy) managed by the Directorate of Medical Education.

Negative Impact on the Education System

Covid-19 has had a significant impact on India's educational system. It has had several detrimental effects on education, including the following:

School closure and class cancellations have impacted educational activity. Annual examinations and entrance tests have already been postponed across India by various boards.

Teachers and students are unprepared for online education; they were not prepared for this abrupt move from face-to-face to online learning. Parents' role- Some Educated parents in urban areas can guide their children, but others may lack the necessary education to instruct children at home. Digital gadgets: Many students, particularly in rural areas, have little or no internet connectivity, and many students may not be able to afford a computer, laptop, or supporting cell phone in their house, resulting in a digital divide among pupils. According to numerous sources, the lockdown has disproportionately affected impoverished students in India, with the majority of them unable to study online teaching-learning methods producing a significant divide between rich and poor students, as well as urban and rural students.

Observation and Recommendation

The pandemic has exposed some of India's education system's main flaws. The shutdown of schools has had a particularly negative impact on pupils from low-income families.

One of the most important trends to watch is the necessity for a combined approach to online learning, as well as increased investment in educational institutions' technological infrastructure. The importance of teacher education should be emphasised. All higher education institutions are now aware of the value of technology and should take steps to implement technology-driven education using the learning management system. Technology should be used in all parts of educational institutions, according to experts. This pandemic demonstrates that the technological and educationalrelationship is here to stay.

Another idea is that educational institutes divide courses into traditional and online instructions, which will aid in the integration of technology into classrooms. Teachers and students will get more digital literacy as a result of online teaching, which will boost their exposure and learning while also making them more employable in the digital world, contributing to societal sustainability.

Conclusion

India's education industry has been greatly impacted by Covid-19. Despite the numerous obstacles it has produced, it has also resulted in a variety of opportunities. To deal with the current Covid-19 dilemma, the Indian Government and several educational stakeholders have looked into the idea of open and distance learning through the use of various digital technologies. India is not yet ready to use digital platforms to bring education to every corner of the country. Due to the current selection of digital platforms, pupils who are not as fortunate as others may suffer. The objective should be to use digital technology to help millions of young Indian students gain a competitive advantage. It is imperative that educational institutions improve their knowledge and information technology infrastructure in order to be prepared for scenarios like to Covid-19.

Even if the Covid-19 situation lasts longer, attempts to maximize the use of online platforms are urgently needed. During the Covid-19 pandemic, India should devise innovative measures to ensure that all children have access to learning. Because kids gain greatly from online practice, it should be continued after the lockdown. To investigate the impact of Covid-19 on India's education system, a more extensive statistical analysis may be conducted.

References

1. https://en.unesco.org/covid19/educationresponse
2. https://www-indiatodayin.cdn.ampproject.org/v /s/www.indiatoday.in/amp/education- today/featurephilia/story/covid-19-impact-digital-education-conventional-education

3. http://www.educationinsider.net/detail_news.php?id=1326
4. http://www.education.ie/en/Schools-Colleges/Information/Information-CommunicationsTechnology-ICT-in-Schools/Digital-Strategy- for-Schools/ Building-Towards-a-Learning-Society-ANational-Digital-Strategy-for-Schools- Consultative-Paper.pdf
5. Times of india
6. Eenadu
7. The Hindu

14

Covid-19: Implications for Equity and Inclusion in Higher Education

Ananya Behera and Abbas Mohammad

The National Educational Policy 2020 (NEP 2020) is the third educational policy developed in India after a gap of 34 years from the second policy.The first education policy was announced in 1968 based on the reports and recommendations of the Kothari Commission, and the second education policy was announced in 1986 (Rao, 2021).

The National Education Policy was announced on July 29, 2020. According to the Government of India's own claim, the NEP 2020 was formulated after having considered over two lakh suggestions from different levels of local self-governing bodies, 2.5 lakh gram panchayats, 6,600 blocks, 6,000 ULBs and 676 districts with the aim of holistic productivity and contributing citizens for building an equitable, inclusive, and plural society with an increased Gross Enrolment Ratio (GER) of 50 percent by 2035 (Anuja, 2020). Aspects of equity and inclusion are central to the NEP 2020. This is in sync with UNESCO's Education 2030 Agenda, which is part of a global movement to eradicate poverty through 17 Sustainable Development Goals (SDGs) by 2030. Education, essential to achieve all these goals, has its own dedicated Goal 4, which aims to "ensure inclusive equitable quality education and promote lifelong learning opportunities for all". The UNESCO in its *Guidelines for Inclusion* viewed inclusion 'as a process which is concerned with the identification and removal of barriers' of education and ensures the presence, participation, and achievement of all students and their diversities. One of the most crucial aspects of NEP is the recognition of growing inequality and inequity plaguing the country's education system (Rao, 2021).

While the NEP 2020 seeks to "ensure inclusive and equitable quality education and promote lifelong learning opoortunities for all" by 2030, it has moved away from the traditional sites of exclusion and has broadened the categories of Socio-Economically Disadvantaged Groups (SEDGs) by including individuals and crucial intersectionalities such as migrant communities, transgender individuals, students of villages, and aspirational districts. The clubbing of categories had potential risks of preferential treatment not being put forward during the implementation, more so for refugee children, students of LGBQTI communities and internally displaced communities who did not find recognition in any of the National Educational policies including NEP 2020 (*ibid*). In this respect the NEP 2020 can be said to be unique.

The NEP puts emphasis on mother tongue-based education in the early years of schooling. This will be a significant factor in improving access to education for a large number of students for whom medium of instruction stood as a formidable barrier. Of course, this may take a few years for fruition. Translating knowledge texts into more easily understood familiar languages will be a great step forward. The effort is on to translate textbooks of varied subjects, including engineering into local languages. In the next sections, we will be discussing the concepts of equity and social exclusion.

Evolution of the concept of Equity

Various scholars have interpreted the concept of equity in different ways and tried to show how these are closely linked to the fundamental issues such as rights and social justice. Benadusi (2006) proposes an analysis of the issues that have been the focus of debates in the scholastic system over the years; in other words, how the concept of equity has evolved. These are:

- the concept of efficacy and efficiency, adopted in the 60s and 70s
- the issue of quality, which emerged in the 80s and 90s
- and finally, the equity approach, which began to emerge in the late 90s and in the first few years of the new millennium

It is pertinent to discuss some fundamental issues relating to the concept of equity and see the difference between the ideas of 'equity' and 'equality'.

Equity and equality

The debate on the comparison between equity and equality had been highlighted by Sen (1982), who, in reference to the concept of equality, asked the question: "equality yes, but of what?" The problem was posed thus: where does the concept of equality end and where "fair" inequality begins. In other words, it was asked if quality must be "of outcomes" or "of treatment", or if equity corresponds to a concept of "fair equality in the distribution of the final asset, which is combined with a fair inequality in the distribution of capital goods" (Benadusi, 2006, p. 23).

What emerges from the most recent studies is that the concept of "equity" must include, and at the same time transcend, that of equality, taking up position at a level that is more abstract and of broader conceptualisation. Understood in this way, the concept of equity also includes that of social justice, and frees itself from being limited to the practices of "equality", which, theoretically, are not necessarily "fair". While the principle of "equality", promoting the same treatment for all, "would guarantee the continuation of initial inequalities associated with different starting points" (Maitzegui-Onate and Santibanez-Gruber, 2008, p.375). In so far as education is concerned, the term "equity" acknowledges the need for unequal treatment in education processes, in order to make groups from disadvantaged backgrounds equal.

The fundamental idea is that since education is a basic right, fair distribution of "educational assets" must be safeguarded. If equity is not present in the educational system, some people could be deprived of choices, therefore failing to achieve their full potential (*ibid*).

Reflecting on how the issue of equity in education has been addressed in the policies and programmes of OECD countries, Marginson (2011) notes the coexistence of different and sometimes contradictory strategies and objectives underlying national and international policies.

From a conceptual standpoint, there are two possible strategies: try to increase the participation of those from socio-economic groups that until now have been under-represented in the scholastic system, or focus on the proportional distribution among students from different social groups. In this context two theories of justice have been put forward by Sen in "The Idea of Justice" (2009). The first theory is about the concept of *hypothetical social contract,* the reference authors of which are Thomas Hobbes, John Locke, Jean-Jacques Rousseau, Immanuel Kant, and John Rawls. This theory proposes an approach to justice that Sen defines as "transcendent institutionalism" (Marginson, 2011, p.5). The second tradition of justice, according to Sen, is that proposed by Adam Smith, Marquis de Condorcet, Mary Wollstonecraft, Jeremy Bentham, John Stuart Mill and Karl Marx, which Sen defines as realisation-focused comparison (*ibid,* pp. 6-7). Margison says that "whichever approach to equity is preferred, the ultimate rationale of any strategy for the enhancement of social equity, in higher education and other sectors, is its potential to advance human freedom".

The documents published by the international organisations that are mainly involved in social welfare and educational issues (OECD and UNESCO) discuss the issue of equity in the following terms: (1) equity in learning opportunities and in results (PISA 2009 results: overcoming social background",2010; "Equity and quality in education: supporting disadvantaged students and schools", 2012); (2) equity in compensatory measures for resources; study support (Education at a glance", 2011); (3) equity in the access to education: participation in primary, secondary and tertiary education ("education at a glance", 2011); (4) equity as inclusion ("Equity and inclusion in education", 2010).

Based on a reinterpretation of the most recent institutional policies for equity of the scholastic system, Maitzegui-Onate and Santibanez-gruber (2008), note the existence of three principles, namely:

(a) horizontal equity: equality of treatment for those who start from the same point;

(b) vertical equity: the series of compensatory measures directed towards minority groups or toward groups at risk of disadvantage (such as women, ethnic minorities or less affluent classes);

(c) equal education opportunity: the series of initiatives designed to ensure that everyone has the same opportunities for success (starting from different conditions and resources).

Concept of Social Exclusion

We can have a better understanding of the idea of inclusion by examining the concept of social exclusion. The idea of social exclusion was first introduced by sociological writers to refer to new sources of inequality. Social exclusion refers to ways in which individuals may become cut off from full involvement in the wider society. David Gordon distinguishes four dimensions to social exclusion: poverty or exclusion from adequate income or resources; labour market exclusion, service exclusion, and exclusion from social relations (Gordon et.al, 2000).

The NEP 2020 was announced right in the midst of the pandemic. While there was a pause in normal activities in various aspects of the national life it would not be fair to expect any significant advancc in the implementation of the NEP during this period. Needless to say, implementing those aspects of the policy which are related to equity and inclusion would be still more challenging. From March 2000 when a nation-wide lock down was announced by the Prime Minister, till February 2022, for full two years, almost all educational institutions of the country including those of higher education remained closed. Thus, class room teaching remained suspended. However, there was an attempt at a major shift to online teaching during this period. Jim Frindert, a member of the OECD Youthwise youth advisory board, underlines the challenges many faced as learning shifted online. He opines how "a mix of financial troubles, social isolation and pressure to perform have resulted in mental health issues distracting from education—changing the university period from best years of life to the worst". He underlines how the pandemic had put the spotlight on those without the hardware and know-how for online learning, while cramped living spaces and lack of parental support for some made the challenges even more acute (Gooch, 2022).

Delivering online training through existing digital infrastructure, micro-credentials were coming to be seen as a panacea. From a policy perspective, they may offer a way to democratise access to skills, aligning with government objectives to promote social mobility. However, this may not always be true. According to James Robson, Deputy Diector at the Center for Skills, Knowledge and Organisational performance at the University of Oxford, often technical in nature, the skills gained can be specific to particular jobs and employers and may lack long-term utility. Micro-credentials, put individuals who already have knowledge and cultural capital at an advantage over those who do not. Thus there is a risk of existing social inequalities getting widened. This goes well with the narrative of what has been variously called the "meritrocracy trap" or the "tyranny of merit", concepts coined by Daniel Markovits and Michael Sandel respectively. According to Sandel, the age of globalisation brought the greatest benefits to the well credentialed, but little to ordinary workers, placing greater economic and social value on those with better qualifications and ignoring those without such qualifications (*ibid*).

But there is a counterpoint to this. As per this view, despite its flaws, meritocracy is better than any alternative at reconciling the two great tensions at the heart of modernity- "between efficiency and fairness on the one hand, and between moral equality and social differentiation on the other". For Adrian Wooldridge, author of *The Aristocracy of Talent* (2021), treating people as moral agents is the only moral way to encourage people to discover and develop their talents (*ibid*).

In a seminar on 'Diversity, Inclusion and Internalisation: Comparative Perspectives' and Launch of Report on 'Diversity and Inclusion: Towards Building a Diverse, Equitable and Global University',Virandar S. Chauhan, Chairman, National Assessment and Accreditation Council (NAAC), cited the example of John Neumann from Oxford and Humboldt who says "people should come to you from all walks of life, you should learn inside and outside the class and you should be able to interact in the evening in the common rooms in a university which allows different ideas, opinions, allows you to accept somebody else's ideas and so on......" (Press Trust of India, 2019)

In the subsequent sections, we will be looking at the gender gap; digital divide in general; rural–urban digital divide; public-private divide in the field of technical education like engineering and medicine; divide in digital readiness of public and private institutions in the context of the pandemic. Since the strength of the pillars of higher education is dependent upon the quality of primary and secondary education, some data with regard to schools have also been given.

Gender Gap Post-Pandemic

As the household income of families dropped, female students had to bear the maximum brunt of school closures. Since schools were closed, more number of boys had access to digital infrastructures such as mobile phones, internet services, radio and other forms of media. Thus, boys had greater opportunity to attend online classes. It is important to note that there exists 50 percent gender gap in mobile internet users in India where 21 percent of women and 42 percent of men use mobile internet. This became even more evident due to the sudden shift from classroom learning to virtual learning during the pandemic. There was a 'gender-based digital divide' that made the situation worse for female students. Due to the lack of access to technology, digital schooling further disengaged girls from education and widened the educational inequalities among male and female students.

Digital Divide in General

It is often assumed that unequal access to online education impacts school education more severely. In reality, the digital inequity is bound to impact both school and higher education. Digital education can never be a substitute for on-campus tertiary education. A study by the Azim Premji Foundation showed that almost 60 percent of school children in India cannot access online learning opportunities. Over one-and-a-half years since the Covid pandemic broke out in India, the digital divide continues to pose challenges in remote teaching and learning, according to experts. Only 20 percent of school-age children in India had access to remote education during the pandemic, of which only half participated in live online lessons, according to a new national sample survey by ICRIER and LIRNEAsia, a think tank working on digital policy.

Rural-Urban Digital Divide After Covid-19

The Indian education system is characterised by a huge rural-urban gap when it comes to literacy, expenses incurred at household level, and accessibility to technology. The current pandemic further amplified the digital divide — four percent of rural households had access to computers compared with 23 percent of urban households between July 2017 and June 2018. A recent NSO survey on education— Household Social

Consumption: Education —throws more light on these existing differences. It highlights that up until higher secondary education, the average cost of education in a rural household is Rs 28,157, and that for an urban household is Rs 84,712. This could be attributed to urban households using private schools for education. With regards to accessibility, 92.7 percent households in rural areas and 87.2 percent of households in urban areas have had access to primary schools within one km of their houses. However, the gulf is wider when it comes to secondary schools within a kilometre — only 38 percent of rural household as opposed to 70 percent urban households. When it comes to technology, only 15 percent rural households had access to the internet as compared to 42 percent of urban households. While calculating the availability of a computer, smartphones were not taken into consideration. In terms of operating a system — amongst people aged 15-29 years —around 24 percent in rural areas and 56 percent in urban areas were able to operate a computer. 25 percent of people aged between 15-29 years were able to use the internet 30-days prior to the survey in rural areas against 58 percent in urban areas. A study by Oxfam India found that even among students of urban private schools, half of the parents reported issues with internet signal and speed. One-third of students struggled with the cost of mobile data.

In a recent newspaper debate the Chairman UGC, while admitting that access to quality higher education remains a challenge despite the existence of 1050 universities and 45000 colleges, expressed the hope that "the proposed Digital University can entirely solve issues related to seats in our universities". Quality education can be imparted through digital technologies, he asserted (Kumar, 2022, TOI, dated 17.03.2022). This is exactly what is stated in the NEP. It says; "Open Distance Learning (ODL) and online education provides a natural path to increase access to quality education". There are many scholars who differ from this line of thinking. For example, according to Prof Anita Rampal, students' feedback on the School of Open Learning (SOL) and related sites says it is for the poor, for those with low marks in Board examinations or for those who are preparing for entrance tests. Due to this a shadow industry of coaching flourishes, she claims. She argues that uncontrolled expansion of online courses may result in an irreversible and regressive compromise with quality and equity (Rampal, 2022, TOI 17.03.2022).

Sometimes, people may think that the issue of inclusion can be promoted through the mechanism of distance education, in general and online education in particular. This may be partially true, but not true in the entirety because without face-to-face interaction, some of the pre-existing disadvantages and disabilities of students may not be adequately addressed.

Public-Private Divide in Medical and Engineering Education

It is a well known fact that there is serious shortage of medical personnel in India. There is shortage of paramedic professionals as well. This shortage was dramatically highlighted during the pandemic. It is obvious that the country needs more doctors and paramedical staff. There are 596 medical colleges in India with a total number about 90,000 seats only. Every year 7-8 lakh aspiring students appear in the NEET exam. A little more than 50 percent get admission in government medical colleges. Since private medical education is expensive and unaffordable, thousands of students go abroad for medical education. Going by the current trend, rural areas are likely to suffer from shortages of doctors even if the demand-supply gap is bridged as most medical graduates who spend fortunes to earn their degrees are expected to prefer urban areas for placement. The increasing dependence on high-cost private colleges for medical education is not going to make access easier for the socially and economically disadvantaged.

The situation with regard to engineering education is different. The insane race for private engineering education came to a halt around 2014. Though many private institutions provided poor quality education new colleges continued to receive government approval. There were around 32 lakh seats in engineering colleges in 2014-15. Since then 400 institutions have closed and enrolment has fallen to 12 lakhs. (Rampal, 2022). Clearly there has been a serious mismatch between the demand for and suppy of engineering education.

Gap in digital readiness of private and government institutions

Many private higher educational institutions were quick in making the transition from physical to online learning mode. On the other hand, majority of government educational institutions struggled to make this transition with the exception of premier institutes like IITs, NITs, IIMs and some of the central universities. Some of the challenges faced by those institutions lagging behind in the online mode of teaching are lack of digitised content, lack of training to their teachers/faculty in the use of virtual teaching and assessing tools and poor or no investment in technology. That part of skill education which is supposed to be a part of tertiary education is expected to suffer due to absence of on-campus teaching. The experimental parts dependent on lab facilities is going to be adversely affected, in so far as vocational education is concerned.

Notwithstanding the fact that online education has many disadvantages, it may be said that it has its own advantages also. Let us now focus on some of the advantages associated with the shift to internet-based learning.

Advantages of internet-based learning

The flexibility and convenience associated with internet-based learning cannot be denied altogether. Globalisation and technological advance have enabled the creation of a global market in higher education. Because of these, higher education has assumed an international dimension. Opportunities like involvement in cross-national research projects, participation in international conferences have become possible. Through web-based learning and the formation of 'e-universities', education and qualifications have become more accessible to students of higher education across the globe, including India. Certificates and degrees can now be acquired outside the world of classrooms and traditional educational spheres. A large number of institutions in India are entering the education market due to the process of globalisation. This spearheads competition and striving for quality education to meet the needs of the competitive market (Giddens, 2006).

While technology can open door for a large number of opportunities, it has to be acknowledged that there is no such thing as an easy 'techno-fix'. Developing countries like India, which are struggling with mass illiteracy and lacking telephone lines and electricity need an improved educational infrastructure before they can truly benefit from new technologies (*ibid*). We have seen earlier, how technology widens the gap along lines of gender and class and broadens the urban-rural divide. New information and communication technologies may widen these gaps post-pandemic. However, if new technologies are crafted keeping in mind the components of equity and inclusion, there is a possibility the gaps may be bridged and the country will move towards effective implementation of the NEP 2020.

Equity and inclusion are key issues in higher education, and the state is obliged to address these issues. Questions of equity and inclusion are particularly important in India because diversity is deeply embedded in the fabric of the nation. And all higher educational institutions need to be as inclusive as possible because they can add significantly to the achievement of national development efforts and nation-building.

References

1. *60 % students do not have internet access in India*. India Today Web Desk, New Delhi, November 15, 2021 (https://www.indiatoday.in/education-today/news/story/60-students-do-not-have-internet-access-1876720-2021-11-15).
2. *Access,equity: key challenges to improving quality of higher education*, says scholars. Press Trust of India, 20 March 2019 (https://www.business-standard.com/article/pti-stories/access-equity-key-challenges-to-improving-quality-of-higher-education-say-scholars-119032000794_1.html).

3. Anuja. 2020. "NEP 2020: Making Education More Inclusive". *The Times of India*, August 18 (https://timesofindia.indiatimes.com/blogs/voices/nep-2020-making-education-more-inclusive/).

4. *COVID-19 pandemic affected implementation of NEP: UGC Chairman*.Press Trust of India. Indore. November 09,2021, (https://www.business-standard.com/article/current-affairs/covid-19-pandemic-affected-implementation-of-nep-says-ugc-chairman-121110901725_1.html).

5. Giddens, Anthony. 2006. *Sociology*, Cambridge: Polity Press.

6. Glaring digital divide in education in India: COVID-19 gives opportunity for digital inclusion.

7. Goastellec, Gaeleand and Jussi Valimaa. 2019. "Access to Higher Education". *Social Inclusion* 7(1) 7. doi: 10.17645/si.v7i1.1841.

8. Gooch, Anthony.2022 "Equity in Education after COVID-19: Tackling the challenges ahead", January 17. (https://www.oecd-forum.org/posts/equity-in-education-after-covid-19-tackling-the-challenges-ahead).

9. Harper, Shaun R. 2020. "COVID-19 and the Racial equity:Implications of Reopening College and University Campuses". *American Journal of Education*, 127(1). https://doi.org/10.1086/711095.

10. *Inclusivity vis-à-vis NEP 2020*. Delhi: National Law University January,2021(https://nludelhi.ac.in/download/publication/Inclusivity%20vis% 20a%20vis%20NEP%202020.pdf).

    India Today Web Desk, New Delhi, September 11, 2020 (https://www.indiatoday.in/education-today/featurephilia/story/glaring-digital-divide-in-education-in-india-covid-19-digital-inclusion-1720817-2020-09-11).

11. Kumar, C.Raj."The Way Forward for Implementing NEP".2021 The Tribune, July 28 (https://www.tribuneindia.com/news/comment/the-way-forward-for-implementing-nep-289073).

12. Kumari, Ranjana.2022. "Girls education among the post-pandemic scenario", Times of India,Voices, January 31 (https://timesofindia.indiatimes.com/blogs/voices/girls-education-among-the-post-pandemic-scenario/).

13. Mukherjee, Arjun.2020. "Education in time of COVID: pandemic amplifies rural-urban digital divide", Financial Express, July 24 (https://www.financialexpress.com/education-2/education-in-time-of-covid-pandemic-amplifies-rural-urban-digital-divide/2033459/).

14. *New UNESCO Global Survey Reveals Impact of COVID-19 on Higher Education*, UNESCO, 15 July,2021 (https://en.unesco.org/news/new-unesco-global-survey-reveals-impact-covid-19-higher-education).

15. Satyam, Nishtha. 2020. "Indian Education's new digital wave after Covid left behind women." *The Print*, January 28 (https://theprint.in/opinion/indian-educations-new-digital-wave-after-covid-left-behind-women/593491/).

16. Srinivas, A. 2021. "Pandemic-hit children need better education". *The Hindu Business Line* Agust 14 (https://www.thehindubusinessline.com/news/national/i-day-special-pandemic-hit-children-need-better-education/article35913876.ece).

15

Higher Education in India: Contemporary Issues and Remedies

Dr M. Sriramulu

Introduction

Generally, we consider that the education imparted after the junior college education is termed as higher education; which is conferred on the students through the institutions of higher education. Almost all countries provide some form of education beyond secondary schooling. The institutions vary considerably in requirements for admissions in the purposes they serve. As a general rule, however, they undertake to train students for vocations, to prepare them for professions or for the study in advanced professional schools, or to give them a broad cultural background is intended to help the student become a concerned and well-informed citizen as well as to enrich his or her personal life. In the US and Canada, the word college has at least two meanings; one an independent school that offers four year courses in liberal arts leading to the bachelor's degree; and two; division or unit offering courses within a particular field or study.

A true university is a group of colleges under the same administration. Innumerable students are taking their degree and post-degree education through different universities across all over the world. When, in India, colleges for more advanced were first started, there was no difficulty in staffing them. Actually, they were first staffed locally. Obviously there was no specially literate class of Englishmen in India previous to 1854. However, the peculiarly delicate and responsible nature of educational work was not socially recognized, and the only standard of value of accepted is salary and prospectus, the less advantage terms on which 'education' men work, result in real lowering in public esteem, and this disparagement has undoubtedly exercised a somewhat depressing effect on the atmosphere of educational work. Therefore, at least, let the Indian public acknowledge what it owes to those by whose labour and devotion the educational system has been built up, and by renewed efforts, brought nearer to thoroughness and efficiency. This is said for the men of then higher educational service first, because in them, is vested a certain primacy in virtue of the qualifications demanded of them and of their relation to Government. But it is said also for all classes of educational workers; for the Provincial Service, for the Subordinate and Lower Subordinate Services, all in their places and degrees, and for the numerous workers of all grades outside Government Services in doing faithful educational service of any kind.

This paper aims to highlight the present challenges to the higher education. It also attempts to highlight theoretical and practical experiences; skill of learning in present situation. It also throws light on what the major issues in curriculum design and set up of syllabi, management of higher education, health consciousness and professional ethics and value education are.

Challenges to the Higher Education

Lack of predominance of the universities in the project of the higher education area in India, erosion of their autonomy, undermining of undergraduate education, the increasing distance between knowledge areas and the separation of universities from the real world outside and crass commercialisation are some of the problems, which characterise the development of the Indian higher education system. It is significant that we develop an understanding of these issues before suggesting strategies to renovate and rejuvenate higher education in India.

Distances and Disconnects

As for invisible walls, it is often indicated that our undergraduate and graduate programmes are so 'theoretical', the implication being that they are destitute of 'practical' experiences. Without looking into familiar epistemological issues, we can say that a theory is as good as the power it has to explain the visible world. A theory is put to practice when a student attempts to use it to make sense of what he or she notices in the world. Conversely, by noticing something in the world and seeking an explanation for it, a student feels the need to have a theory. The chasm that exists between theory and practice combined with the fragmentation of the idea of knowledge leads to the confusion that our system of higher education is suffering from. To outwit this, it would be necessary that the universities adopt a auricular approach which treats knowledge in a holistic manner and creates exciting opportunities for different kinds of interfaces between the disciplines, which is inconsiderable today in most of the universities and institutions of higher learning. It is important that universities relate to the world outside and the walls of disciplines are porous enough to let other voices be heard. It would also be necessary that the university education is treated in its perfection and subject areas have not to be designed in isolation.

Art of Learning

At present, many students coming out from their institutions of higher education have do so without achieving the kind of skills they really need to work in a real world situation. Among the drawbacks many students face are lack of ability to analyze or solve problems, relate problems to different contexts, communicate clearly and have an integrated understanding of different branches of knowledge. These problems can be addressed if the processes by which curriculum is designed and then syllabi are determined undergo improvement.

Curriculum Issues and Restructuring of Syllabus

It is necessary as to what is the objective of a university, especially at the undergraduate level, and then use the answers to develop a curriculum. Presently, the design of curriculum and syllabi is reflective of the entrenched examination system under which the student is asked to face a question paper at the end of the year, or in some universities, at the end of the semester. This archaic examination system, ostensibly used as a means of certifying the ability of students, unfortunately does not really test the kind of skills they need to be successful in either the pursuit of pure theoretical knowledge or in practical real world situations. The examination system, even in the case of the comparatively better equipped in less rigid institutions, has left quite manifestly traditional and incapable of distinguishing between different talents of students in a tangible manner. Similar to what happens at the school level; university-level evaluation practices also simply widen the scope of memory-based questioning, with the occasional rote-based 'application' question masquerading as real-world problem solving. In doing so, they entrench the student's lack of ability to examine and understand the real world, as a result of which their engagement with people or issues remains scarce once they enter the world of work, with implications for their abilities as workers and citizens.

Management of Higher Education

The Indian higher education system is one of the largest such systems in the World. It is estimated that during the Tenth Five Year Plan period (2002-07), there will be a tremendous pressure of numbers on this system and a large number of additional students will be knocking at the doors of higher education institutions in the country. There are also new challenges of management and regulation being faced by these institutions, which require serious attention, both at the institutions in the public sector and also those in the private sector now developing at a fast step. As a result of which the old structures of management established in pre-independent India and working during most of the twentieth century are now needed to undergo faster changes.

In spite of this, the demands of the society for equity and accommodation cannot be neglected any more. The new chapter under WTO where competence is the cardinal principle of achievement in global operations has made it quite clear that the country should exploit its excellent potential in higher education and training facilities and prepare itself to export the Indian brand of education to foreign countries. Policy planning and evolving strategies for this task are somewhat new for the country. But, this is an opportunity which India should not neglect, as it offers interesting possibilities to strengthen the nation's talent and resourcefulness.

Health Consciousness and Physical Fitness

Physical fitness and sports are two sides of the same coin and are mutually dependent on each other. As the famous dictum goes, mind is the key to man and eyes cannot see what mind cannot perceive. The relationship between mind and body has been acknowledged scientifically. It is generally believed that a healthy body has a healthy mind; but it could be the other way around also, i.e., a healthy mind has a healthy body. However, this requires appropriate training.

Today's education is largely academic. In real sense, this orientation is required to changer a balanced development through inculcating health conscious amongst students. This will cover the development at physical, mental and social levels. With the increasing stress on academics in the world of employment and elsewhere and the rapid progress in science and technology all over the world, parental force has been exercising academic training at the cost of health and physical fitness of the youth. It is in this context that there is now an urgent need to lay a strong foundation and strengthen physical education and sports programmes in the higher education field. This invites the integration of physical education, sports, yoga and recreation activities in the higher education system for the superficial good of the younger generation.

Ethics in Profession and Value Education

The faster developments in science and technology and the challenges of globalisation are bringing some more challenges to the education system in the country. This is also the time when parental care to the children is on the wane. The adverse effects of the media on the mental development and moral values of the younger generation are indispensably being felt increasingly in all spheres of life. Gross consumerism has distorted the view of persons into one of equating possessions with richness. Exploitation of natural resources is going on without reference to sustainability. The discrepancy between the rich and the poor is growing wider. While the education system needs to keep step in step with the scientific and technological developments in terms of building the skills and knowledge, it also needs to focus attention on the more fundamental issues of the social and moral consequences of such unregulated activities. In this context, there is now a growing demand to lay greater emphasis on education to inculcate, nurture and develop values, particularly among the youth of the country.

Conclusion

Exaggerative emphasis on one at the cost of the other would be counter productive. Hence accessibility and quality upgradation are not separable and indispensable dimensions of higher education. As India is a wide and sub-continental in size a population above one billion, the quantitative expansion of education (i.e., dimension accessibility) is of paramount importance to mitigate disparities across regions, gender and social strata in the field of cducation. This should be given due consideration.

A well-planned and structured interaction to be developed between Centres of Academic Excellence and other Universities/ Institutions; (1) While restructuring the syllabi and courses, efforts should be made to develop an optimal combination of acquisition of theoretical and practical skills. The courses should be so designed that critical reading and interpretation of classics, practical field work wherever relevant, and application of readings and other skills are given importance; (2) Quality of higher education can improve considerably through an extensive and optimal use of audio-visual technologies and Internet. The courses should be so designed to make good use of these modern developments; (3) In restructuring of syllabi, all stakeholders such as students, teachers and users of services should be involved. However, teachers should be given flexibility within the norms and benchmarks decided by the stakeholders and (4) Quality of higher education can also be improved by inducting quality oriented objectivity in merit promotions of teaching faculty. UGC, ICSSR and other research funding bodies should encourage interdisciplinary/multi-disciplinary Seminars/ Conferences/ Research projects. These bodies could allocate at least 50 percent of their research funds for inter-disciplinary activities. UGC could also take initiatives to open Centres/Schools for promoting multi-disciplinary teaching and research.

Works Cited

1. Mayhew, Arther, H.R. James. *Development of Education System,* (ed.) Shastri Book Distributors, 2003.
2. Muzumder, N.N., *History of Education in Ancient India,* McMillan, 1917.
3. Trevelyon, C.E. *On the Education of the People of India,* Longman, Orme, Bross, Green & Longmans, 1838.
4. Report of the Universities Commission of 1902. Howell (Arthur), Education in British India, Calcutta.

16

Adoption of Foreign Policies and Practices in Promoting Equality and Inclusiveness in the Education

Nooreen Gowher

ABSTRACT

The national education policy 2020 is the first education policy of the twenty first century that aims to address many growing developmental imperatives of our country. This policy proposes the revision and revamping of all aspects of the education structure, including regulation and governance to create a new system that is aligned with aspirational goals of the twenty first century education including SDG4, while building India's traditions and value systems. The new education policy emphasises on the provision of quality education to all the students irrespective of their place of residence with particular focus on historically marginalised, disadvantaged and underrepresented groups as education serves as best tool for achieving economic and social inclusion equality.

In this paper I would like to address and discuss about the adoption of various foreign policies in order to achieve equality and inclusiveness in education thereby developing an egalitarian society creating alma metersto attend learning outcomes related to all curricular areas.

Keywords: Inclusive education , Equity in education, marginalised groups, SDG4, policy, national policy, NPE, egalitarian society.

Introduction

Impact of Covid-19 on Higher Education

Covid-19 outbreak has caused a downward spiral in the world economy and caused a huge impact on the higher education system. The sudden closure of campuses as a social distancing measure to prevent community transmission has shifted face-to-face classes to online learning systems.

This has thrown the focus on utilising eLearning tools and platforms for effective student engagement which may have limitations of accessibility and affordability for many students. The pandemic has exposed the shortcomings of the current higher education system and the need for more training of educators in digital technology to adapt to the rapidly changing education climate of the world. In the post-pandemic situation, the use of eLearning and virtual education may become an integral part of the higher education system .There are a variety of subjects with varying needs. Different subjects and age groups require different approaches to online learning. Online learning also allows physically challenged students with more freedom to participate in learning in the virtual environment, requiring limited movement. Also Internet bandwidth is relatively low with lesser access points, and data packages are costly in comparison to the income of the people in many developing countries, thus making accessibility and affordability inadequate. Policy-level intervention is required to improve this situation. Further exploration and investigation on effective pedagogy for online teaching and learning is an area for research. Need for developing tools for authentic assessments and timely feedback is found to be another area of study. The affordability and accessibility for all the learners of varied economic background is identified as a challenge, for which the educational tools developer could focus on customisation. The policy level intervention is also vital. Education system across the world needs to invest on the professional development of teachers, especially on ICT and effective pedagogy, considering the present scenario. Making online teaching creative, innovative and interactive through user-friendly tools is the other area of research and development. This would assist and prepare the education system for such uncertainties in the future.

However, the higher education institutions and universities need to plan the post-pandemic education and research strategies to ensure student learning outcomes and standards of educational quality.

National Education Policy 2020

The life cycle of the national education policies can we track back from 1968, 1986 and finally the most recent policy of 2020.

1. According to NPE 1968 the government of India resolves to promote Free and compulsory education for the development of education.
2. The focus of NEP 1986 was primarily on ensuring universal access to and providing quality education to wide base of learner's from different categories of marginalisation like the children from

economically poor urban slum communities, migrant children, children of migrant workers and agricultural labourers, children dwelling from forest dwelling communities in remote areas.

3. The NEP 2020 — the final educational policy was developed after 34 years. It has drawn much attention towards the theme of inclusive and equitable education.

A major critique of this policy was that the implementation strategies did not fully account to a corresponding legal framework, policy or implementation programme to drive it further.

Statement of the Problem

"Adoption of Foreign Policies and Practices in Promoting Equality and Inclusiveness in the Education"

Objectives of the Study

Keeping in view of the problem for the present study the following objectives have been framed:

1. To study about NEP 2020 and it's perspective on higher education
2. To study about the principles of NEP in setting up inclusive and equitable education
3. To study the practices in foreign countries to promote equity and inclusiveness in education for future use

Research Questions

1. What are the issues in Inclusive and Equitable set up in education post Covid-19?
2. How adoption of foreign policies or practices would promote inclusiveness and equity in education at all levels of education ?

Operational Definitions

Inclusive Education

For the present investigation, inclusive education means the provision of services to the students with special needs in their neighbourhood schools with necessary support services-and supplementary aids for both students and teachers. It means meeting the requirements of children with special needs for free and quality public education in the least restrictive and most effective environment.

Equitable Education

In education, the term equity refers to the principle of fairness. Equity in education is when every student receives the resources needed to acquire the basic work skills of reading, writing, and simple arithmetic. It measures educational success in society by its outcome, not the resources poured into it.

Students with Special Needs

Students with special needs are those who deviate from the norm in mental or physical characteristics to such an extent that they require a modification in school practices or special education services in order to develop to their maximum capacities.

Methodology

A qualitative study - comparison between education with inclusive and equity in India and foreign countries with emphasis on the report established by UNESCO (United Nations Educational, Scientific and Cultural Organisation).

Equitable and Inclusive Education by NEP 2020

NEP 2020 aims to ensure that no child loses any opportunity to learn and excel because of the circumstances of birth or background. Special emphasis will be given on Socially and Economically Disadvantaged Groups (SEDGs) which include: gender identities (particularly female and transgender individuals), socio-cultural identities (such as Scheduled Castes, Scheduled Tribes, OBCs, and minorities), geographical identities (such as students from villages, small towns, and districts), disabilities (including learning disabilities), and socio-economic conditions (such as migrant communities, low income households, children in vulnerable situations, victims of or children of victims of trafficking, orphans including child beggars in urban areas, and the urban poor).

Inclusive and Equitable Education Set Up in India by NEP 2020 at Higher Levels of Education

- Aim to increase GER (Gross Enrolment Ratio) in higher education including vocational education from 26.3 percent to 50 percent by 2035
- Rationalised institutional architecture
- Establishment of Single regulatory body for higher education

- National research foundation to catalyze and expand research and innovation across the country
- Financial support to the students
- Open and distance learning
- Motivated, Energised and capable faculty
- Effective governance and leadership
- Use of technology in education
- Online and digital education
- Tech based option for adult learning through apps,TV channels
- Availability of E-courses in regional languages
- Common entrance exam for all colleges

What are the issues / challenges in Inclusive and Equitable set up in education ?

- Fragmentation of higher education system
- Less Students Enrolment due to poverty trauma post Covid-19
- Escalation in cost of higher education
- Lack of appropriate funding to provide an equitable opportunity to learn during covid 19.
- Lack of Competencies among teachers to adapt new methods of teaching
- Large class sizes
- Inadequate pre-service training and professional development
- Negative Attitude of Parents / Unawareness of parents
- Inadequate Infrastructure and facilities
- Lack of access to high quality early childhood education
- Less collaboration of higher educational institutes with industries
- Gap between supply and demand
- Higher dropout rates
- Failure to distribute resources for learning to all students in fair, balanced and equitable manner, etc
- Lack of access specially in socio-economically backward areas.

Inclusive and Equitable Education Set Up by Foreign Countries with Emphasis on a Report- The International Commission on the Futures of Education Established by UNESCO

The global health pandemic has shined a harsh light on the vulnerabilities and challenges humanity faces. It has provided a clear picture of existing inequalities—and a clearer picture of what steps forward we need to take, chief among them addressing the education of more than 1.5 billion students whose learning has been hampered due to closure of educational institutions.

How adoption of foreign policies or practices would promote inclusiveness and equity in education at all levels of education ?

In this report, the International Commission on the Futures of Education—established by UNESCO in 2019 and composed of thought leaders from the worlds of academia, science, government, business and education—presents nine ideas for concrete actions today that will advance education tomorrow.

1. Commit to **strengthen education as a common good**. Education is a bulwark against inequalities. In education as in health, we are safe when everybody is safe; we flourish when everybody flourishes.
2. Expand the definition of **the right to education** so that it addresses the importance of connectivity and access to knowledge and information. The Commission calls for a global public discussion—that includes, among others, learners of all ages—on ways the right to education needs to be expanded.
3. **Value the teaching profession and teacher collaboration**. There has been remarkable innovation in the responses of educators to the Covid-19 crisis, with those systems most engaged with families and communities showing the most resilience.We must encourage conditions that give frontline educators autonomy and flexibility to act collaboratively.
4. **Promote student, youth and children's participation and rights**. Intergenerational justice and democratic principles should compel us to prioritise the participation of students and young people broadly in the co-construction of desirable change.
5. **Protect the social spaces provided by schools** as we transform education. The school as a physical space is indispensable. Traditional classroom organisation must give way to a variety of ways of 'doing school' but the school as a separate space-time of collective living, specific and different from other spaces of learning must be preserved.
6. **Make free and open source technologies available to teachers and students.** Open educational resources and open access digital tools must be supported. Education cannot thrive with ready-made

content built outside of the pedagogical space and outside of human relationships between teachers and students. Nor can education be dependent on digital platforms controlled by private companies.

7. **Ensure scientific literacy within the curriculum.** This is the right time for deep reflection on curriculum, particularly as we struggle against the denial of scientific knowledge and actively fight misinformation.
8. **Protect domestic and international financing of public education**. The pandemic has the power to undermine several decades of advances. National governments, international organizations, and all education and development partners must recognize the need to strengthen public health and social services but simultaneously mobilise around the protection of public education and its financing.
9. **Advance global solidarity to end current levels of inequality**. Covid-19 has shown us the extent to which our societies exploit power imbalances and our global system exploits inequalities. The Commission calls for renewed commitments to international cooperation and multilateralism, together with a revitalised global solidarity that has empathy and an appreciation of our common humanity at its core.

Conclusion

Though there are several obstacles and challenges related to educational system which hinders to promote inclusive education. It is not impossible to attain success in inclusive education in nation through effective strategies and other means but at the same time there are some issues as well as some challenges which we have handle by soft hands. To make inclusion appropriate teacher preparation, awareness and attitude towards disabilities, retention of special children, underrepresented children, children from different backgrounds in the community etc. must be made compulsory in all programmes irrespective of elementary, secondary level and higher education. Further quality resources, faculties and facilities must be supplied to each institution to make inclusive and equitable education programme successful.

Recommendations

- Planning the transition towards inclusive quality education at all levels, including tertiary education, training teachers, and having the necessary supports and resources.

- Designing and implementing a plan with goals and deadlines providing reasonable adjustments in the education system even when a high level of support is needed.
- Allocating enough budgetary resources.
- Carrying out awareness and diverse culture promotion related campaigns.
- Guaranteeing accessibility, reasonable adjustments and supports to children with different disabilities and also to the children from diverse underrepresented groups.
- Practices to decrease higher levels of grade repetition, drop out rates and greater age.

References

https://www.education.gov.in/sites/upload_files/mhrd/files/document-reports/NPE-1968.pdf

https://legalreadings.com/critical-analysis-on-new-education-policy-2020/

https://nludelhi.ac.in/download/publication/Inclusivity%20vis% 20a%20vis%20NEP%202020.pdfNational Law University, Delhi Press Sector 14, Dwarka New Delhi 110078

Draft National Education Policy 2019.

https://www.researchgate.net/publication/348564487_International_ Perspectives_on_Inclusive_Education_Vol_15__Resourcing_Inclusive_Education

https://www.unicef.org/india/media/1191/file/Making-Schools-Accessible.pdf

Ainscow, M and Halle-Giorgis M, (1998). "The Education of Children with Special Needs: Barriers and Opportunities in Central and Eastern Europe"', UNICEF, Innocenti Occasional Papers, Economic and Social Policy Series. no. 67, Florence – Italy.

https://en.unesco.org/sites/default/files/education_in_a_post-covid_world-nine_ideas_for_public_action.pdf

17

Impact of Technology on Education after Covid-19

Dr Ratna G. Chandak

Abstract

Twenty first Century is witnessing a rapid growth in technology in every field of life. Education is no exception. The use of information and communication technologies in education can play a crucial role in providing new and innovative forms of support to teachers, students, and the learning process more broadly. Advances in technology drive and digital transformation have made it necessary to equip students with necessary skills to succeed in their careers. Their knowledge should match the technological advances. The curriculum has to be updated as per requirement of the high-demand jobs. Technology has brought revolutionary changes in all areas of life, from interpersonal communication, economy, entertainment industry, even education. It seems that today, more than ever, students are faced with changes that not only fundamentally alter the way they learn, but their everyday life as well. It is simply impossible to ignore the tremendous impact that modern technologies have on new generation of students.

The present generation of children grow up with laptops, tablets, various gadgets and modern digital systems, so they have long been ready for the modernisation of education. With that in mind, the importance of technology in education only becomes more obvious. Learning styles have changed over the years, gradually introducing new technologies with a potential to improve teaching. Students' readiness for technology in the classroom is excellent news, because the digital age brings new challenges, not only in education, but in all other areas of life as well. Therefore, it is important that students learn to harness all the potential of modern society while still at school. Given that they use social media and the Internet and play video games on a daily basis, children expect information to be presented in a similar way at school. Lesson content should be pictorial and entertaining, it should captivate their attention and contain as little redundant information as possible, which is one of the major shortcomings of the traditional approach to education.

The Covid-19 pandemic has been a great teacher in demonstrating the importance of online education by integrating technology in education. Online teaching-learning has emerged as a powerful educational tool. Use of technology can make teaching livelier by creating favourable learning environment.

Benefits of Education Technology

It should not be forgotten that technology is only a means and not an end in itself. Its success depends on how it is used by the educators. The benefits of the use of technology are-

- Digital learning tools in classrooms can increase student engagement and accessibility. In the past, students spent a large part of their time searching for information. Nowadays, the search for information is digitized and practically everything can be found on the Internet. Instead of going to the library, students can find the desired content on Google or any other search engine. This way, the learning environment becomes an online environment that provides information in all possible formats (text, audio, video, photographs, infographics, etc.). Thus, students get a better understanding of the teaching material that enables better learning in line with the standards of the twenty first century skills. This advanced approach is based on tools – fast Internet, stable WiFi and a laptop (tablet or mobile phone) and therefore many educational institutions make great efforts to give each of their students access to a computer.
- It can hclp teachers improve their lesson plans. Teachers can leverage technology to achieve new levels of productivity, implement useful digital tools to expand learning opportunities for students, and increase student support and engagement. It also enables teachers to improve their instruction methods and personalise learning.
- Schools can benefit from technology by reducing the costs of physical instructional materials, enhancing educational programme efficiency, and making the best use of teacher time.
- Technology allows 24/7 access to educational resources. Classes can take place entirely online via the use of a laptop or mobile

device. Hybrid versions of learning combine the use of technology from anywhere with regular in-person classroom sessions. In both scenarios, the use of technology to tailor learning plans for each student is possible. Teachers can create lessons based on students' interests and strengths. An added benefit is that students can learn at their own pace. When they need to review class material to get a better understanding of essential concepts, students can review videos in the lesson plan. The data generated through these online activities enable teachers to pin point students who had to struggle with certain subjects and offer additional assistance and support. Thus, technology helps in personalised learning.

- It vastly increases collaboration and communication. Educational technology can foster collaboration. Not only can teachers engage with students during lessons, but students can also communicate with each other. Through online lessons, students get to work together to solve problems. In collaborative activities, students can share their thoughts and ideas and support each other. At the same time, technology enables one-on-one interaction with teachers. Students can ask classroom-related questions and seek additional help on difficult-to-understand subject matter. At home, students can upload their homework, and teachers can access and view completed assignments using their laptops.
- It helps in sparking inquisitiveness and imagination for search for knowledge among students. Through engagement with students, teachers can spark inquisitiveness in children and boost their curiosity, which leads to academic success. Curiosity helps students to get a better understanding of basic concepts. Students can interact with other students from across the globe.
- The importance of technology in education is particularly evident when it comes to the development of critical thinking. Different educational approaches allow students to express themselves in original ways, thus arriving at different solutions. In that process, they approach information critically, thinking about each available piece of information to reach the desired result.
- The place that used to belong to textbooks and notebooks is now occupied by tablets, videos, animations, Internet, audio recordings, colleges, etc. This way, students can communicate in a way that is most familiar and relatable to them, so even shy students or those who struggle with teamwork now have the opportunity to shine and achieve better results.

- With technology and access to resources beyond classroom walls, students are inspired to become problem-solvers, critical thinkers, collaborators, and creators. Where technology has been successfully integrated into classrooms, students develop a lifelong love of learning.
- Perhaps the most obvious change has occurred in the classroom of modern schools. The only 'gadgets' that were available in the traditional classroom were the blackboard, chalk and the classroom globe, whereas nowadays, they have access to state-of-the-art technological advances, even artificial intelligence. Thanks to virtual reality, students can visit any part of the planet in geography classes, or watch a 3D movie about the ancient world in history classes. Education has come a long way from using a projector in class. The technology is being used extensively in higher education where resources allow a wider and more comprehensive application of the latest technologies for research purposes.
- There is an overall improvement in the quality of education. It enables students to explore new subjects and deepen their understanding of difficult concepts.
- Records of students and their progress are digitised.
- Evaluation and testing can be done using different apps for students.
- Through the use of technology inside and outside the classroom, students can gain twenty first century technical skills necessary for future occupations.

Challenges to Educational Technology

The challenges to educational technology are many:

- The use of technology has yet to gather momentum. Only less than 10 percent of institutions have been reported of having these tools in their classrooms.
- Additional concerns include excessive screen time, the effectiveness of teachers using the technology, and worries about technology equity.
- Stress on students is also reported.
- Access is an added concern — for example, not every school has resources to provide students with a laptop. Internet connectivity can be unreliable in homes and remote areas. Some students thrive

in online education settings whereas others lag for various factors like support resources.

- Online education may also pose challenges for teachers, especially in places where it has not been the norm. Educators unfamiliar with some of the technology used in education may not have been exposed to the tools as they prepared for their careers or as part of their professional development. They may be required to be specially trained in using the technology. Teachers looking to make the transition and acquire the skills to incorporate technology in education can take advantage of learning opportunities to advance their competencies. For individuals looking to help transform the education system through technology, universities should introduce special courses in teaching to equip them with essential tools to become leaders.
- School systems have the hard decision of choosing devices and technology models that will help achieve their visions of transforming learning. Device decisions should be made by working with multiple stakeholders and evaluating how educators and students use the devices for day-to-day learning. Stakeholders should take into account appropriate grade-level curriculum, content needs, and how the devices will be used inside and outside the classroom. It's no easy task, but considerations such as compatible digital curriculum and content, assessment requirements, manageability options, security features, device functionality, and the overall cost of ownership are key to choosing the right device. A secure and robust IT infrastructure is the foundation of a 360p learning experience, and supports digital content, protects key student data, boosts operational efficiency, and provides the security and privacy protection.

Tools of Technology in Education

Gamified Learning

In 2022, people's attitude to learning is changing. Learning is not boring anymore. Learning is fun, engaging, and interactive. Gamified learning is the main proof of such a tendency. There is a common misconception that gamified learning is the most suitable for kids. Of course, kids play games more often than adults. But it does not mean that old learners will not enjoy playing games that bring both joy and benefit. Moreover, gamification has a positive effect on socialisation. Students learn how to behave in a competitive environment. They form positive social and behavioural patterns under competitive conditions. They learn to self-educate and adjust to different learning formats. Games are all about positive impressions from the lesson. Make your students forget about mundane tasks and boring homework. Introduce gamification into the learning process.

3D Printing

3D printers are being incorporated into a wide variety of disciplines, from computer science and math, to more traditional vocational subjects. Students interested in engineering principles, for example, are combining 3D printing with CAD software to create mini-models. Science teachers may print out 3D models of subject matter such as atoms and anatomy for students to touch and study.

SMART Boards

With more allocation of funds, SMART boards are making their way into more and more classrooms. These computer-connected white boards use a projector and special pens to allow teachers to write the day's lesson, as well as record it. Teachers can use the board to explain a concept, then save the lesson for students to re-watch later. Some institutions are incorporating LCD screens on students' desks that allow lesson interaction, the use of educational apps, and even the ability to connect with other students around the world.

Cloud Computing

Laptops and tablets are common in the classroom these days. Now, institutions are moving to cloud computing programmes that allow teachers and students to upload assignments, interact with one another, and even access their textbooks.

Nano Learning

The information age has brought with it an increase in screen fatigue. As a result, students are physically unable to concentrate and process large amount of information. The answer to this problem is Nano learning. It involves providing students with information in smaller amounts, over a shorter period of time. Learning in short bursts is proven to increase the ability to take in and retain information.

Virtual Reality (VR) and Augmented Reality (AR)

While the concept of VR is not particularly new, technological advances in recent years are now making it possible to produce VR equipment that is both cheap and high enough quality to provide a comfortable immersive user experience. While there is plenty of room to improve, VR is close to a mainstream breakthrough. (Emerging Technologies, A conversation with Michael Bodekaer Jensen, Founder, Labster)

Virtual reality has undergone a lot of changes over the last few years as the technology has matured and companies have gotten a better handle on what applications are most appropriate for VR. When VR first came to the forefront of consumer awareness, most of the expected uses were around gaming and entertainment. Now, however, we're seeing a shift to more pragmatic use cases in education and enterprise applications like architecture.

We'll see hardware prices for VR devices drop sharply within the next several years, which will create more opportunities for schools to integrate them into their technology portfolio. Even as prices drop, the devices will get more powerful, with higher resolution screens and faster processors. This will happen alongside the rollout of high-speed 5G networks, all of which will contribute to richer, more immersive VR environments that really increase the sensation that users are actually somewhere else.

In education, we'll see VR experiences being used to provide experiences that are hard or even impossible to bring to students today. Google Expeditions, for example, enables students to take field trips to faraway places without the logistical complexity, while companies like Labster let students run full labs without any lab equipment or supplies. More and more of these applications will be created, letting students have a wide range of experiences with a lower investment in highly specific classroom equipment. (Emerging Technologies, A conversation with Dan Lindquist, Expeditions Product Manager, Google)

On the one hand, teachers can stick to the traditional educational approaches and methods. But in this case, they should accept the fact that they can do little to affect students' performance. On the other hand, they can go hand in hand with the emerging trends in educational technology and introduce VR or AR into learning. By doing so, teachers will show their students that a classroom isn't a place of boredom. It's a place where big technological changes go live. VR (Virtual Reality) and AR (Augmented Reality) also are the current trends in educational technology.

Immersive VR experiences require a VR headset. This has a digital interface which projects images, creating a real or virtual world that users can see and interact with. It also includes gesture controls and easy-to-use teacher controls. While some VR headsets are undoubtedly expensive,

Google Cardboard and similar alternatives offer a more affordable VR experience – the user only needs to insert a smartphone into the viewer. AR, on the other hand, can be accessed simply through a smartphone or tablet. Students engage with digital technologies like VR because it inspires them to think beyond the four walls of the classroom.

AR and VR can be incorporated into the classroom in the following ways:

(i) **Field trips** – Field trips are helpful for art, geography and history lessons, among others. VR can take students on a tour around the best galleries, museums and cities in the world, without leaving the classroom.

(ii) **Virtual careers** – VR offers the opportunity for students to find out about a range of careers. It literally puts the student in another's shoes, meaning they can gain first-hand experience of what it's like to do different jobs.

(iii) **High-tech training** – It is highly influential for students who are thinking about pursuing a career in areas like the military or medicine, VR and AR can project real life training. For example, it can show students the anatomy of the body from inside out.

(iv) **Language immersion** – The best way to learn a language is total immersion. VR can immerse students in a foreign language, by virtually placing them in the middle of a virtual world, hearing only their target language.

Project-based Learning

Project-based learning is a teaching method that actively engages the students in real-life projects. The idea is that students 'learn by doing', with teachers acting as the hands-on facilitator.The objective is to have students investigate and respond to an authentic, engaging and complex question or issue. They will develop critical-thinking, creativity, collaboration and communication skills; all of which are highly sought after twenty first century skills, valued by employers.

Some suggested topics for projects include:

- Finding solutions to a local environmental problem.
- Coming up with alternative energy sources.
- Analysing photography or photojournalism.
- Voicing opinions on a popular debate.

Project-based learning may be implemented in the classroom in the following manner:

(i) Put students in groups of four or five.
(ii) Ask them to brainstorm some ideas for their project.
(iii) Have class feedback and choose the one they will focus on.
(iv) Then ask students to research their particular subject area together.
(v) Next ask them to put together a presentation digitally so they can practise using design and technology.
(vi) Finally, ask students to present their project to the rest of the class and encourage feedback and discussion.

Experimental Learning

Student disengagement is on the increase. Often, teachers find them on their mobile phones, zoning out or talking to friends. However, a new way to tackle this is gaining momentum which is experiential learning. This learning approach is becoming common worldwide. This learning approach involves immersing students in real-world situations. It offers first-hand experiences in which they need to practice planning, decision-making, teamwork and more.

Experiential learning activities may involve:

1. **Collaborative exercises** by providing students with a problem or debate in teams and ask them to come up with ideas and solutions. This could be a philosophical debate or a mock business problem to get them thinking about a range of scenarios.
2. **Role-playing** by getting students to act out different scenarios. An imaginary situation can teach students how different actions and behaviours can affect outcomes.
3. **Field work** by asking students to go out and collect data. This could be done online through questionnaires and surveys, which can then be presented to the class.

Conclusion

The importance of technology in education is tremendous, and its impact is growing. However, it is crucial to implement technology in education in the right way, because many traditional teaching methods should continue to exist. In addition, the computer is not applicable in every situation, nor is learning with it necessarily more efficient. Therefore, it is up to teachers to strike a balance between future-ready education and the good old offline teaching. The physical proximity between a teacher and a student cannot be replaced with the use of modern gadgets. Teacher should have a rapport and personal touch with students. He should even have a knowledge about student's family background and of the social environment to which he belongs. **Education at its heart is about human connections and relationships.** While we can never replace the magic that happens between great teachers and students in an in-person environment, we should focus on the social aspects of technology to enhance connections from a distance. Much more attention must be directed on how technology will enhance teaching and learning in a blended learning environment reaching students, both in school and at home.

References

1. World Strides.com
2. Pearson International Schools blog
3. Drexel University School of Education
4. The top five educational trends to look out for in 2021 by Charlotte Stace
5. AnzhelikaDanielkievich, Content Manager, Blog
6. https://edu.google.com/
7. Internet websites and blogs

18

Liberalising India's Private Vision of the National Education Policy 2020

Ch. Bikshapathi

Abstract

National Education Policy (NEP) 2020 has laid out a vision of education that's necessary for the twenty first century. It recognizes that children today need to learn skills both 'foundational skills' of literacy and numeracy as well as 'higher-order' cognitive skills such as critical thinking and problem solving, and social and emotional skills such as cultural awareness and empathy, perseverance and grit, teamwork, leadership, communication. To address the issue of overburdening of students, NEP recommends rationalising content in the curriculum focusing on essential concepts, flexible streams and vocational courses allowing students to make wider choices suited to their career aspirations, a change in board examination structure with examinations focused on core capacity rather than memorisation of content reducing the need for coaching as well as a single entrance exam for college admissions. These academic reforms are both necessary and progressive, and if implemented properly, can propel Indian education into the twenty first century.

According to United Nations Development Programme (UNDP) estimates, the total financial requirement for India to reach Sustainable Development Goal 4 to "Ensure inclusive and equitable quality education and promote lifelong learning opportunities for all" by 2030 is $2,258 billion, which for the years 2017-30 averages $173 billion per year, far exceeding the current government budget of $76.4 billion a year for education. It would be unrealistic to expect such large investments coming solely from the government and purely philanthropic initiatives. All efforts must be made to improve the quality of public education but there's no reason why for-profit private schools can't coexist. In fact, private schools should be co-opted as partners in the delivering of the educational vision laid out by the NEP. The lessons learnt from 30 years of liberalisation should be now implemented in the education sector, thereby ensuring that India achieves the demographic dividend.

Keywords: NEP, UNDP, Skill, higher education, private.

The National Education Policy (NEP) 2020 aims to transform education, keeping the learner at the centre. The NEP builds on recommendations from the Education Commission (1964–66) and Justice J.S. Verma Commission (2012) as well as the previous version of the policy – National Policy on Education 1986, modified in 1992 (NPE 1986/92), Right of Children to Free and Compulsory Education Act, 2009 and Rights of Persons with Disabilities (RPWD) Act, 2016. The NEP 2020 is a huge stride in the right direction — it focusses on the holistic development of students by ensuring access, relevance, equity, quality and strong foundational learning. The new policy has numerous take aways for education sector stakeholders. This report, which is KPMG in India's point of view, analyses the impact of the NEP and puts forth various opportunity areas emerging from the new policy. Significantly, the policy lays emphasis on four key areas of reforms viz. curricular changes to build strong foundational skills, improving quality of learning across all levels of education, shift in the ways of assessment and, finally, need for systemic transformation. The NEP envisages creating synergies in the curriculum across Early Childhood Care and Education (ECCE) to school and the higher education segments. The NEP stresses on creating a national curricular and pedagogical framework, which is competency-based, inclusive, innovative and focuses on comprehensive development of children. School curriculum is expected to imbibe the human value system and provide greater flexibility and expose students to acquire future skills in the areas of computation, coding, design thinking, digital literacy, ethical and moral reasoning etc. The NEP promotes building of strong foundational skills right from early childhood. Also, there is a new way of envisioning vocational education in the policy by integrating it across secondary and higher education and developing a credit framework to offer vertical and horizontal mobility between vocational and higher education. One of the stronger themes across the entire policy document is around quality improvement in the learning outcomes. A series of initiatives has been highlighted in the NEP around quality learning environments, use of ICT tools for training, experiential learning, improving the quality of faculty among others. Recommendations on moving ECCE and school pedagogy to the 5+3+3+4 structure and a three-tiered institutional architecture in the higher education segment (research focus, teaching focus and autonomous degree-granting colleges with strong employability focus) are welcome steps from the sector standpoint. Educational institutions must plan to leverage suggestions in the policy. It has rightly translated the learners' needs by offering them increased flexibility in choosing subjects mapped to their aspirations. Furthermore, multiple entry and exit points along with the concept of academic credit bank will ensure their continued learning.

The next focus area is around assessment reforms, a much-awaited change. The NEP emphasises upon the need for formative assessments, making the examinations less strenuous and thereby inducing a practice of self or peer review among the learners. Steps such as creation of a National Assessmen.

Having seen the components of liberalisation, let's understand the advantages that the private sector can bring to improve the quality of education: a Efficiency in terms of costs: The study in Andhra Pradesh also showed that the APS deliver a slightly better learning 16 achievement levels to public schools at one-third the cost . Of course these achievement levels represent only the bare minimum learning levels. But a fairer comparison of efficiency of cost would be that of what the state spends on public education as compared to what similarly priced private schools would achieve. In 2016-17, Telangana spent nearly Rs 42,000 per student across all their public schools. A quick search shows nearly 100 private schools in the 30-50K / annum fee range, all of which would deliver much higher quality of learning 18 as compared to the average or even the best performing public school. A simple thought experiment would do it: if a parent was given a voucher of 42K to spend on a school of choice, how many parents across the country would choose a public school over a private school?

Educational Innovations

Public school systems due to their systems and built-in inertia don't have the capacity to innovate pedagogy or delivery mechanisms to improve learning outcomes. Private schools especially when they achieve a scale will invest their discretionary surplus into research and development in usage of technology, hiring and training of teachers and other areas to improve educational outcomes while also minimising costs. While much of the discourse in education is focused on ensuring delivery of the basic literacy and numeracy skills, it must be recognized that this alone doesn't suffice in meeting the needs of the twenty first century workplaces which require higher order skills. Public schools that are struggling to meet the basic literacy and numeracy requirements don't even have the twenty first century skills in their sights. Middle and especially high income private schools are far better placed to deliver these twenty first century skills and for that to extend to the APS, innovation, paradigm shifts and technology needs to be used for which private players are best placed.

Virtuous selection

In India, teaching in schools is not a preferred career for talented people. Similarly, education as a sector doesn't really attract high quality people as entrepreneurs, researchers or administrators other than in unregulated educational sectors such as educational technology, private tutoring or coaching centres for competitive exams. The right regulations and incentives can bring high quality people as entrepreneurs, researchers, teachers and administrators into private schooling. Further, by allowing large investments and attracting quality people to the schooling sector will either force current operators (at all income levels - BPS or otherwise) to either improve their quality or will force them to shut shop. Entrepreneurs will also innovate to bring efficiency at a large scale. Parents will switch over from schools that don't offer value for money once liberalisation allows many new schools to start which will compete on both quality and costs. Allowing market forces to Private players can solve difficult educational problems through economies of scale and innovation. For example competition and the opening of the telecom sector improved access many fold at much lower costs. Today, 1GB data costs Rs 18.5 in India as compared to the 24 global average of around Rs 600. And this is the case despite many issues with regulations of the Telecom sector. Similarly, at this point of time, there's no educational system as yet in the world that delivers high quality at low costs. Liberalisation is the only way through which private players may find the right solution to the education problem at competitive prices. A senior level employee at a large venture capital firm told us on the request of anonymity, "Vouchers can be given to parents and this should help the market find its way in terms of quality". The private sector can bring about the broad benefits of agency, intense competition and innovation (in delivery and in curriculum).

LIBERALISATION

While indeed education is a public good, however the stark reality is that Indian education is in a mess. Movement from public to private school continues in large numbers, while learning outcomes continue to remain poor. Therefore, liberalisation is a necessity for educational standards to rise - it's a desperate need for India. This should not become an ideological battle. India's experiences with liberalisation with the right regulation has been 25 good in sectors such as telecom, airlines, banking and automotive sector. Recently, healthcare too has been liberalised. In fact, the government's initiative of ensuring universal medical insurance for low-income families under Ayushman Bharat, has partnered with a 26 number of private hospitals. A recent report shows that under Ayushman Bharat, 75 percent of all the total claim amount of Rs 3,767 Crore were made in private hospitals with only 25 percent going to government hospitals, clearly showing the preference towards private hospitals for even low-income families when they can afford better private hospitals due to the insurance 27 scheme. This shows that the government can find innovative ways to use the private sector to provide a public good rather than making it an unnecessary ideological battle. Given Indian's political, economic and social background and dispensation, it's important to recognize that a proposal to liberalise the school sectors will bring about a lot of objections. It's therefore essential to address these objections, whether they are purely ideological or based on real issues that might happen if the private sector is liberalised. Why only schooling? Educational technology has become big in the last decade. The coaching class industry which consists of coaching for competitive exams as well as tutoring for school and board 29 exams is huge in India (estimated at $40 billion). Both these are for profit. There's no logic in allowing coaching classes, and EdTech companies to make profits, while private schools can't make profit. In fact, this makes the adverse selection issue a much bigger issue as the best people in the education industry gravitate towards coaching classes or EdTech where they can make profits, or get well paying jobs.

The equity issue: There's widespread fear that if private schools are liberalised, private schools will deliver far better quality as compared to public schools, but only to the middle class and beyond thereby exacerbating the current inequity in the system. There are two arguments against this: (a) Furthermore, we already have a huge equity issue whereby good quality education is out of the reach of most low income families. (b) If the government funds parents rather than schools, it will allow all parents access to better quality private schools rather than only those who can afford to pay for themselves. Therefore, by getting a strong supply side response from the private sectors for low cost schools will actually improve access to quality education rather than reducing it.

Conclusion

Fierce critics of liberalisation of private schools point out that the best education systems in the world consist of public run and/or non-profit private schools. However, given the state of education in India, if we don't make drastic changes to our education policy, we will lose any chance of using the demographic dividend to our advantage. Liberalising schools in India is a necessary and desperate step to ensure access to quality education for all as public education has failed to deliver. The last question to address is whether the private school market is attractive enough for private sectors to invest in a big way, either as a whole or specific segments, the focus.

References

Bhattacharya, Saumya. "How entrepreneurship for private schools is being stifled by the government", Economic Times, 2016, https://economictimes.indiatimes.com/small-biz/entrepreneurship/how-entrepreneurship-for-private-schools-is-being-stifledby-the-government/articleshow/51300086.cms?utm_source= contentofinterest&utm_medium =text&utm_campaign=cppst

Bhargavi, Anjuli. "Declare education 'for profit': Educationists, private schools urge govt", Business Standard, 2020, https://www.business-standard.com/article/education/declare-education-for-profit-educationists-private-schools-urge-govt120012801670_1.html

See Appendix 2 & 3 for case studies on the liberalization of the Indian Aviation and Telecom sectors

Nayyar, Dhiraj, "Who is afraid of profit in education?", ETV Bharat, 2020, https://www.etvbharat.com/english/national/business/business-news/who-is-afraid-of-profit-ineducation/na20200803165011772

Centre for Civil Society, "FACES OF BUDGET PRIVATE SCHOOLS IN INDIA Report 2018", (pg. 9) https://ccs.in/bpsreport/2018

Das, Gurcharan. Launch of the State of the Sector Report on Private Schools in India, Central Square Foundation, Jul 2020, https://www.youtube.com/watch?v=0wmdehjv1Jc

Sahlgren, Gabriel Heller. "REGULATION AND FUNDING OF INDEPENDENT SCHOOLS - Lessons from Sweden", Fraser Institute, 2016, https://www.fraserinstitute.org/sites/default/files/regulation-and-funding-of-independent-schools-lessons-fromsweden.pdf

Sahlgren, Gabriel Heller. "Regulation and Funding of Independent Schools: Lessons from Sweden", Fraser Institute, 2016.

https://www.fraserinstitute.org/studies/regulation-and-funding-of-independent-schools-lessons-from-sweden Moorhead, Joanna, "Profit-making schools: good or bad idea? "The Guardian, 2013.

https://www.theguardian.com/education/2013/mar/04/profit-making-schools-debate Brooks, Katie. "What The Latest Data Say About Chile's School Voucher System", Echoic, org, 2018,

https://www.edchoice.org/engage/what-the-latest-data-say-about-chiles-school-voucher-system/ "What is DBT (Direct Benefit Transfer)?". National Payments Corporation of India (NCPI), 2019, https://www.npci.org.in/what-dbtdirect-benefit-transfer

Mantri Rajeev & Gupta Harsh. "The conclusive case for school choice", LiveMint, 2013, https://www.livemint.com/Opinion/LI8HU3WD2LsgNO8lPVyhgK/The-conclusive-case-for-school-choice.html

Bhasin, Karan. "Facts, no fiction: Moving towards education vouchers for India's public schooling system". OpIndia, 2019 https://www.opindia.com/2019/01/facts-no-fiction-moving-towards-education-vouchers-for-indias-public-schooling-system/

Hussain, Sadaf and Vijaylakshmi Yadav. "How the voucher system can improve the nation's quality of education". DNA, 2016, https://www.dnaindia.com/analysis/column-how-the-voucher-system-can-improve-the-nation-s-quality-of-education-2216116

Kingdon Geeta and Panagariya Arvind. "Heart of the problem: NEP 2020 charts new road map, but fails to make public school teachers accountable."
Times of India, 2020, https://timesofindia.indiatimes.com/blogs/toi-edit-page/heart-of-the-problemnep-2020-charts-new-road-map-but-fails-to-make-public-schoolteachers-accountable/

Mantri, Rajeev & Gupta Harsh. "The conclusive case for school choice", Live Mint, 2013, https://www.livemint.com/Opinion/LI8HU3WD2LsgNO8lPVyhgK/The-conclusive-case-for-school-choice.html "Govt. spends[1] 41k per student: Srihari", The Hindu, 2017,

https://www.thehindu.com/news/cities/Hyderabad/govt-spends-41kper-student-srihari/article19999743.ece

19

Holistic, Multidisciplinary and Futuristic Aspects of Education in the Light of NEP-2020

Dr Asit Mantry

Education has the power to transform the world as it is indispensable for the development of any nation. Education plays a pivotal role in developing a country in all aspects whether it be a cultural, social, moral or economical. As it develops a country's economy, therefore it is a milestone of nation's development. Right after independence initiatives were made by the govt. of India to educate the natives. One of the millennium development goals is to provide universal primary quality education to all. So, the country started focusing on quality education which is considered as the most powerful tool for the development of individuals and society as a whole. Several initiatives have been taken to develop sound education system and forming policies are one among them. The first education policy in India rolled out in 1968 and after that National policy on education 1986 came into existence.NPE-1986 concentrates on overall development of the child and focuses on improving education in the country. But with the advancement in Science and Technology and to compete globally our education system deemed to be unsuccessful. In order to meet the global needs of the society, after a long gap, National Education Policy was launched in 2020. The main motto of NEP-2020 is to concentrate on interdisciplinary and multidisciplinary form of education. It emphasised on holistic education in which the child would be exposed to educational, co-curricular, and extra-curricular subjects and activities on an equal footing. We are living in the twenty first century which is highly advanced as compared to previous era. To survive in this century, we need broad-based multidisciplinary education. Multidisciplinary education brings holistic development of an individual. The concept of holistic and multidisciplinary education is not new in India, it was followed in the ancient India also. In ancient times, it is considered that education means attainment of 64 kalas (skills or arts) by the individual. These 64 kalas enabled an individual to live a prosperous life. Multidisciplinary education is need of the hour in the present times also. In future, this type of education will produce more productive individual which leads the nation to the height of success.

Keywords: Education, Holistic, futuristic, development, multidisciplinary.

Introduction

Education has the power to transform the world as it is indispensable for the development of any nation. The system of organised education in India has a long history, started with gurukul to current system of education. Education plays a pivotal role in developing a country in all aspects whether it be a cultural, social, moral or economical. Education is the backbone of any country; it plays a crucial role in technological developments and imparts various skills, values, and awareness. Since independence, India has focused on improving the literacy rate. Right after independence initiatives were made by the govt. of India to educate the natives. One of the millennium development goals is to provide universal primary quality education to all. So, the country started focusing on quality education which is considered as the most powerful tool for the development of individuals and society as a whole. Several initiatives have been taken to develop sound education system and forming policies are one among them. The first education policy in India rolled out in 1968 and after that National Policy on education 1986 came into existence. NPE-1986 concentrates on overall development of the child and focuses on improving education in the country. Revised programme of action (1992) envisioned that up to 14 years of children, free and compulsory education should be provided. By 2000, Government of India have decided to spent six percent of gross domestic product (GDP) will be spent on education. Government of India unquestionably put high priority not only on universalization of education but also on quality education. In between various initiatives such as Mid-Day meal (1995) and Sarv Shiksha Abhiyan (2001) brought revolution especially in rural areas in the form of enrollment and retention of students and of course in the field of education. But with the advancement in Science and Technology and to compete globally our education system deemed to be unsuccessful. In order to meet the global needs of the society, after a long gap, National Education Policy was launched in 2020. The main motto of NEP-2020 is to concentrate on interdisciplinary and multidisciplinary form of education. It emphasised on holistic education in which the children would be exposed to curricular, co-curricular, and extra-curricular topics and activities in an equitable manner.

Holistic Aspect of Education

Our primary educational goal has been the holistic development of individuals since independence, but the government has now legally adopted holistic education under the NEP-2020. Education with the perspective of holistic is concerned with the development of physical, intellectual, emotional, social, artistic, creative and spiritual potential of every individual. It attempts to engage students in the teaching-learning process and encourages personal and collective responsibilities. Holistic education instills eagerness and cultivates social and communication skills; makes learning natural and meaningful. It helps the children to make connection with subjects by using their creative skills and it's the only way with the help of which realisation of self and development of nation is possible. NEP-2020 covers the total span of holistic education by talking of education right from the first year to lifelong learning. Now the pattern of education is 5+3+3+4 years of education integrating curricular and pedagogical framework leading to holistic development of the child. In order to achieve the holistic development of child, Ministry of Education launched **NIPUN** Bharat mission in July 2021. The mission keeps in mind the main themes of NEP-2020 and emphasized three developmental goals which encircled the gamut of different domains of development. The several domains of development prepare a youngster to deal with difficult life events. All of these domains were organised around three key objectives:

First: Good health and well-being of the children.

Second: Development of effective communication.

Third: Physical involvement of the learner and interconnectedness with their environment.

It takes into account what is required to make the nation prosperous and self-reliant. So, NEP has a holistic vision on transforming learning and learners.

Multidisciplinary and Futuristic Aspect of Education

We are living in the twenty first century which is highly advanced as compared to previous era. To survive in this century, we need broad-based multidisciplinary education, so that our citizens will be prepared to face the challenges of this modern society. An approach in which students are allow to learn and explore different subjects or curriculum from diverse disciplines in one course is known as multidisciplinary approach. In this approach, one course does not remain isolated from other courses. For example, a student from science stream can adopt a subject from humanities stream and a student of engineering can adopt any Indian language as subject in his course. Multidisciplinary approach is based on the principle of "Integrated curriculum" that emphasizes on the blending of different disciplines under a particular course. Students' interpersonal skills, empathy, and marketability as future professionals and engaged citizens improve when they are prepared to work in and on multidisciplinary teams. (Herremans, & Murch 2003; Lam, Kolomitro, & Alamparambil, 2011). Through multidisciplinary approach, students will be able to appreciate others' personal and professional perspectives. It also develops critical and reflective thinking among students. The base of multidisciplinary is 'liberal education'. Liberal education is a blender of academic and pedagogical approach. It develops various competencies among the students by assimilating formal and informal learning opportunities. These learning opportunities includes teaching, research, interdisciplinary subject and engagement with community. A multidisciplinary institution provides the students with choice of various subjects. Through exposure to various subjects a well-rounded personality develops among the students.

Role of Multidisciplinary Universities and Colleges

The primary aim of NEP-2020 for the higher education is to create multidisciplinary universities and colleges. Through the creation of these multidisciplinary institutions will put an end to the fragmented higher education system of India. It will put all the fragmented higher education institutes under the umbrella of multidisciplinary university. Multi-disciplinary higher education institutions will reduce many challenges that are faced by the higher education in the present times. It will help in breaking the silos between the departments by providing interdisciplinary curriculum. Within higher education, breaking down divisions between departments and modelling the value and impact of interdisciplinary approaches should be woven into the curriculum. (Herremans, & Murch, 2003). It will promote cross-disciplinary research which is the requirement of this twenty first century. It will form an association of diverse scholars and peers so that they can gain knowledge from each other. It will bring holistic development in the students. It will promote the pooling of the human as well as materialistic resources across the higher education that will tackle the problem of the lack of resources in the higher education institutions. This mission of transforming standalone university into multidisciplinary university will be proceed in a thoughtful and systematic manner by restructuring the exist institutions.

Multidisciplinary Education in the Context of Ancient India

In India, holistic and multidisciplinary education is not a new notion, it was followed in the ancient India also. In the ancient India, education (Vidhya) is imparted to the students by the 'gurus' or 'acharya' (teachers) in the 'gurukuls' (schools). Those gurukuls were purely operated on the bases of multidisciplinary approach. In that time, the curriculum includes life skills, martial arts and knowledge of Vedas. In ancient times, it is considered that education means attainment of 64 kalas (skills or arts) by the individual. Those 64 kalas enabled an individual to live a prosperous life. Multidisciplinary education is not only peculiar in the ancient times but it has its relevancy in the present times also. The prominent universities like Takshashila and Nalanda were also runed on multidisciplinary approach in which millions of students were studied from across the world. The current educational system was emerged during the British rule in India. The main focus of the British education was just to prepare English-speaking clerks so that the tasks of British govt. administration were easily executed. But that type of education did not fulfill the need of the Indian society. That's why in this twenty first century, India again brings back its traditional system of education because it is the need of the hour in the present times also.

Futuristic Aspect of NEP-2020

The main motive of the NEP-2020 is to produce skillful citizens in the future. It is mentioned in the policy that. The goal of education will not only be cognitive development, but also character development and the creation of holistic and well-rounded persons with critical twenty first century skills. For this purpose, NEP 2020 offered vocational education at from initial stage i.e. from upper primary level to university level. In a nutshell, the focus of this policy is to make the Indian education system productive so that it will be transformed into a educationally and economically sound country in the world.

Conclusion

The NEP-2020 was centred on a child's overall development. The holistic development is possible when the multidisciplinary curriculum is provided to the child in an integrated manner. This curriculum makes the citizens of the India productive and skillfull which leads our country to the path educationally and economically developed country.

References

Singh, A.K. (2022).NEP 2020: Vision and Pathways. *Yojana, 66* (02), 9-12.

Yadav, S. (2022). Skilling youth for future. *Yojana, 66* (02), 21-24.

https://www.education.gov.in/sites/upload_files/mhrd/files/NEP_Final_English_0.pdf

Raghav Bansal (2020). *Times of India*-Is Education the most important step in the development of the country?

Pajankar & Pajankar (2010). Development of school education in India. Journal of social science, 22(1): 15-23 (2010).

https://aryaurukul.in/blog/the -impotance-of-holistic-education-in-our-school-curriculum.

20

Promoting Critical Thinking Skills in Students

Dr B. Prathima

Abstract

Critical thinking is a scope of various complex skills related to a higher level of thinking. It is a self-directed thinking that produces new and innovative ideas and solves problems. It assumes reflecting critically on learning experiences and processes, and making effective decisions by avoiding common pitfalls.

Through technology, the amount of information available today is massive. This information explosion is likely to continue in the future. Students need a guide to weed through the information and not just passively accept it. Students need to "develop and effectively apply critical thinking skills to their academic studies, to the complex problems that they will face, and to the critical choices they will be forced to make as a result of the information. Because critical thinking is a mental habit that requires students to think about their thinking and about improving the process, it requires students to use higher-order thinking skills – not memorise data or accept what they read or are told without critically thinking about it (Scriven & Paul, 2008; Schafersman, 1991; Templeaar, 2006). Therefore, critical thinking is a product of education, training, and practice.

This paper throws light on what critical thinking is, essential aspects of critical thinking, barriers to critical thinking and strategies to promote critical thinking skills in students.

Key words: Critical Thinking, Acquired Skills, Logical Reasoning, Egocentric, Classroom Assessment Techniques, Cooperative Learning Strategies.

As the world economy shifts away from manufacturing jobs and towards service industry and creative jobs, there's a consensus among parents, educators, politicians and business leaders that it is crucial students graduate into university or the workforce with the ability to identify and solve complex problems, think critically about information, work effectively in teams and communicate clearly about their thinking. Oliver & Utermohlen (1995) see students as too often being passive receptors of information. Through technology, the amount of information available today is massive. This information explosion is likely to continue in the future. Students need a guide to weed through the information and not just passively accept it. Students need to "develop and effectively apply critical thinking skills to their academic studies, to the complex problems that they will face, and to the critical choices they will be forced to make as a result of the information explosion and other rapid technological changes" (Oliver & Utermohlen).

What Critical Thinking is?

Critical thinking is defined as the ability to make decisions and solve problems based on logical reasoning and evidence while leaving out emotions to enable evaluation and improvement of one's own thought process. While this seems like a simple thing to do, most people do not possess the ability to apply critical thinking to their decision-making process. The problem starts from school, where students are tested for remembering the lessons more than developing their ability to apply them in real life situations.

A recent report by Foundation for Young Australians points that the number of employers seeking new employees with innate critical thinking skills has grown by more than 158 percent over the past three years. This huge surge in demand also shows that there's a shortage of availability. The good news is that critical thinking is an acquirable skill and anyone can develop it with enough practice. When examining the vast literature on critical thinking, various definitions of critical thinking emerge. Here are some samples:

- "Critical thinking is the intellectually disciplined process of actively and skillfully conceptualising, applying, analysing, synthesizing, and/or evaluating information gathered from, or generated by, observation, experience, reflection, reasoning, or communication, as a guide to belief and action" (Scriven, 1996).
- "Most formal definitions characterise critical thinking as the intentional application of rational, higher order thinking skills, such as analysis, synthesis, problem recognition and problem solving, inference, and evaluation" (Angelo, 1995).
- "Critical thinking is thinking that assesses itself" (Center for Critical Thinking, 1996b).

- "Critical thinking is the ability to think about one's thinking in such a way as : 1. To recognize its strengths and weaknesses and, as a result, 2. To recast the thinking in improved form" (Center for Critical Thinking, 1996c).
- Perhaps the simplest definition is offered by Beyer (1995) : "Critical thinking... means making reasoned judgments". Basically, Beyer sees critical thinking as using criteria to judge the quality of something, from cooking to a conclusion of a research paper. In essence, critical thinking is a disciplined manner of thought that a person uses to assess the validity of something (statements, news stories, arguments, research, etc.).

Essential Aspects of Critical Thinking

In the book, Critical Thinking, Beyer elaborately explains what he sees as essential aspects of critical thinking. These are:

- **Dispositions:**
  Critical thinkers are skeptical, open-minded, value fair-mindedness, respect evidence and reasoning, respect clarity and precision, look at different points of view, and will change positions when reason leads them to do so.
- **Criteria:**
  To think critically, must apply criteria. Need to have conditions that must be met for something to be judged as believable. Although the argument can be made that each subject area has different criteria, some standards apply to all subjects. "... an assertion must... be based on relevant, accurate facts; based on credible sources; precise; unbiased; free from logical fallacies; logically consistent; and strongly reasoned" (p. 12).
- **Argument:**
  Is a statement or proposition with supporting evidence. Critical thinking involves identifying, evaluating, and constructing arguments.
- **Reasoning:**
  The ability to infer a conclusion from one or multiple premises. To do so requires examining logical relationships among statements or data.
- **Point of View:**
  The way one views the world, which shapes one's construction of meaning. In a search for understanding, critical thinkers view phenomena from many different points of view.

- **Procedures for Applying Criteria:**
  Other types of thinking use a general procedure. Critical thinking makes use of many procedures. These procedures include asking questions, making judgments, and identifying assumptions.

Barriers to Critical Thinking

There are various types of Barriers to Critical Thinking that hinders with one's personality and overall individuality. To combat and overcome the Barriers to Critical Thinking in one's life, the person has to realise and figure out the same. Some important barriers to critical thinking are discussed below:

1. Egocentric Nature and Thinking Patterns

Egocentric nature or behaviour is a natural tendency and is many a time difficult to overcome. Such a barrier is making the person think about himself and leads to the inability to not to sympathise with others to understand their issues and problems. And one's ego can be one of the most significant Barriers to Critical Thinking. It is more of a character flaw, and despite several attempts of change; it is quite difficult for one to change. Such people lack to evaluate the perspective and feelings of others and make it disturbing for other people to work with them in a team.

2. Group Thinking

Group thinking is yet amongst the harmful Barriers to Critical Thinking, plus it is also quite unhealthy. In such a case, the person doesn't have his own opinion or decision in any given case or situation. To overcome the same, it requires the individuals of the group to stand apart and question and formulate their thoughts, opinions, and ideas.

3. Drone Mentality

Drone mentality barrier can be explained as when a person doesn't pay attention during the important work meetings and discussions. And it hails upon any time and on anyone affecting the process of critical thinking. Very often, daily and mundane routines make a person fall prey to drone mentality. The managers and the HR department of the firm must keep the employees intrigued with challenging tasks and motivational factors.

4. Social Conditioning

Many of us have a habit of thinking within our comfort zones, and we refrain to even think outside our spectrum as we are taught to think in a certain way and manner owing to the various social conditions.

Barriers to Critical Thinking owing to social conditioning involves stereotyping things and people around us and having unwanted assumptions that make it quite difficult for people around us in the organisation to work. It requires cultural and social awareness to overcome this behaviour and barrier.

5. Biased Nature and Experiences

Having a personal bias is one of the biggest Barriers to Critical Thinking as its curbs and prohibits a person from making decisions that are fair, open-minded, and transparent. It also prevents the person to use logical reasoning, experience, and the basic common sense to make decisions that are informed and valid.

6. Work pressure

Quite many numbers of times at our workplace, we are overloaded with stringent deadlines, and it does affect our skill of critical thinking. But the silver lining is that a person can also sharpen his critical thinking skills and abilities amidst the tough and tight deadlines. When the time is short, and a deadline needs to be met, we often go for an option of completing the work without any strategic thinking and long term vision. **And here is when the barrier arises to thinking critically.**

7. Arrogance

Arrogance is a bad attitude and often hinders with critical thinking abilities. It makes a person with a closed mindset and with an opinion that he knows everything and there is no further need for learning new things. Arrogance makes the person fail on a long term basis as he has closed his channels of learning and is unable to assess the rewards and benefits of critical thinking.

8. Stubborn Nature

One of the Barriers to Critical Thinking to stubborn nature as a person with such a nature has his own set of beliefs and ideologies. And such a barrier is not very welcomed in the world of business, especially the corporate world as it is ever-evolving and dynamic in nature and its approach. The person has to be open to changes and come out from his present beliefs understanding that the world of business is quite fluid and fast-paced and demands flexibility and adaptability.

9. Fear

Fear often acts as a barrier not only to critical thinking but also for the overall growth and development of a person. Fear makes him unconfident, demotivated, and not very agile to think out of the box and come up with the ideas and strategies. Fear can arouse out of the various reasons such as anxiety, depression, self-esteem issues, and other such personal reasons affecting a person's professional life as well.

10. Laziness

Critical thinking requires a person to do a lot of research, study literature that is work-related, and be open to learning new things for growth and development. But when a person is lazy, it acts as one of the Barriers to Critical Thinking.

Strategies to Promote Critical Thinking

The 1995, Volume 22, issue 1, of the journal, Teaching of Psychology, is devoted to the teaching critical thinking. Most of the strategies included in this section come from the various articles that compose this issue.

CATS (Classroom Assessment Techniques)

Angelo stresses the use of ongoing classroom assessment as a way to monitor and facilitate students' critical thinking. An example of a CAT is to ask students to write a "Minute Paper" responding to questions such as "What was the most important thing you learned in today's class? What question related to this session remains uppermost in your mind?" The teacher selects some of the papers and prepares responses for the next class meeting.

Cooperative Learning Strategies

Cooper (1995) argues that putting students in group learning situations is the best way to foster critical thinking. "In properly structured cooperative learning environments, students perform more of the active, critical thinking with continuous support and feedback from other students and the teacher".

Case Study /Discussion Method

McDade (1995) describes this method as the teacher presenting a case (or story) to the class without a conclusion. Using prepared questions, the teacher then leads students through a discussion, allowing students to construct a conclusion for the case.

Using Questions:

King (1995) identifies ways of using questions in the classroom:

1. **Reciprocal Peer Questioning**

   Following lecture, the teacher displays a list of question stems (such as, "What are the strengths and weaknesses of...). Students must write questions about the lecture material. In small groups, the students ask each other the questions. Then, the whole class discusses some of the questions from each small group.

2. **Reader's Questions**

   Require students to write questions on assigned reading and turn them in at the beginning of class. Select a few of the questions as the impetus for class discussion.

Conference Style Learning

The teacher does not "teach" the class in the sense of lecturing. The teacher is a facilitator of a conference. Students must thoroughly read all required material before class. Assigned readings should be in the zone of proximal development. That is, readings should be able to be understood by students, but also challenging. The class consists of the students asking questions of each other and discussing these questions. The teacher does not remain passive, but rather, helps "direct and mild discussions by posing strategic questions and helping students build on each other's ideas" (Underwood & Wald, 1995, p. 18).

Use Writing Assignments

Wade sees the use of writing as fundamental to developing critical thinking skills. "With written assignments, an instructor can encourage the development of dialectic reasoning by requiring students to argue both [or more] sides of an issue".

Dialogues

Robertson and Rane-Szostak (1996) identified two methods of stimulating useful discussions in the classroom:

1. **Written dialogues:**

   Give students written dialogues to analyze. In small groups, students must identify the different viewpoints of each participant in the dialogue. Must look for biases, presence or exclusion of important evidence, alternative interpretations, misstatement of facts, and errors in reasoning. Each group must decide which view is the most reasonable. After coming to a conclusion, each group acts out their dialogue and explains their analysis of it.

2. **Spontaneous Group Dialogue**

   One group of students are assigned roles to play in a discussion (such as leader, information giver, opinion seeker, and disagreer). Four observer groups are formed with the functions of determining what roles are being played by whom, identifying biases and errors in thinking, evaluating reasoning skills, and examining ethical implications of the content.

Ambiguity

Strohm & Baukus advocate producing much ambiguity in the classroom. Don't give students clear cut material. Give them conflicting information that they must think their way through.

Conclusion

The goal for educators who want to instil critical thinking skills in their classrooms is to think of their students not as receivers of information, but as users of information. Learning environments that actively engage students in the investigation of information and the application of knowledge will promote students' critical thinking skills. However, as with any skill, critical thinking requires training, practice, and patience. Students may initially resist instructional questioning techniques if they previously have been required only to remember information and not think about what they know. They may struggle with assessment questions that are not taken from the book. However, by encouraging students throughout the process and modelling thinking behaviours, students' critical thinking skills can improve. The effort is worth the reward: students who can critically think for themselves and solve real-world problems.

References

Astleitner, H. (2002). Teaching critical thinking online. *Journal of Instructional Psychology*.

Bartlett, J. E. (2002). Analysis of motivational orientation and learning strategies of high school business students. *Business Education Forum*.

Catanach, A. H., Croll, D. B., & Grinaker, R. L. (2000). Teaching intermediate financial accounting using a business activity model. *Issues in Accounting Education*.

Davis, L., Riley, M., & Fisher, D. J. (2003). Business students' perceptions of necessary skills. *Business Education Forum*.

Ennis, R. H. (1993). Critical thinking assessment. *Theory Into Practice*.

Flavell, J. H. (1979). Metacognition and cognitive monitoring: A new area of cognitive-development inquiry. *American Psychologist*.

Gurses, A., Acikyildiz, M., Dogar, C., & Sozbilir, M. (2007). An investigation into the effectiveness of problem-based learning in a physical chemistry laboratory course. *Research in Science & Technological Education*.

Hannon, S., McBride, H., & Burns, B. (2004). Developing creative and critical thinking abilities in business graduates: The value of experiential learning techniques. *Industry and Higher Education*.

Kang, N., & Howren, C. (2004). Teaching for conceptual understanding. *Science and Children.*

Kumar, M., & Natarajan, U. (2007). A problem-based learning model: Showcasing an educational paradigm shift. *Curriculum Journal, 18*(1), 89–102.

MacKnight, C. B. (2000). Teaching critical thinking through online discussions. *Educause Quarterly.*

Rippen, A., Booth, C., Bowie, S., & Jordan, J. (2002). A complex case: Using the case study method to explore uncertainty and ambiguity in undergraduate business education. *Teaching in Higher Education*.

Sandholtz, J. H., Ogawa, R. T., & Scribner, S. P. (2004). Standards gaps: Unintended consequences of local standards-based reform. *Teachers College Record, 106*(6).

Scriven, M., & Paul, R. (2007). *Defining critical thinking.* The Critical Thinking Community: Foundation for Critical Thinking. Retrieved January 2, 2008, from http://www.criticalthinking.org/aboutCT/define_critical_thinking.cfm

21

Teaching Learning Strategies in Higher Education

Dr Ch. Prasad

Abstract

Contemporary teaching is concerned not only with imparting knowledge but with developing skills and strategies for further learning. Teaching and learning is a process that includes many variables. These variables interact as learners work toward their goals and incorporate new knowledge, behaviours, and skills that add to their range of learning experiences. Individual students may be better suited to learning in a particular way, using distinctive modes for thinking, relating and creating. The notion of students having particular learning styles has implications for teaching strategies. Because preferred modes of input and output vary from one individual to other, it is critical that teachers use a range of teaching strategies to effectively meet the needs of individual learners. Sound health instruction should incorporate a variety of teaching methods intended to complement the learning styles of children. This research article described issues related to Teaching, Learning Strategies for quality education.

Kcy words: *Quality Education, Teaching Strategies, Visual Presentation, Academic Strategies, Creativity Learning.*

Statement of the Problem

Institutions of higher learning across are responding to political, economic, social and technological pressures to be more responsive to students' needs and more concerned about how well students are prepared to assume future social roles. Faculty are already feeling the pressure to lecture less, to make learning environments more interactive, to integrate technology into the learning experience, and to use collaborative learning strategies when appropriate. Some of the more prominent strategies are outlined below. For more information about the use of these and other pedagogical approaches, contact the programme in support of Teaching and Learning. Teaching and learning is a process that includes many variables. These variables interact as learners work toward their goals and incorporate new knowledge, behaviours, and skills that add to their range of learning experiences. Individual students may be better suited to learning in a particular way, using distinctive modes for thinking, relating and creating. The notion of students having particular learning styles has implications for teaching strategies. Because preferred modes of input and output vary from one individual to other, it is critical that teachers use a range of teaching strategies to effectively meet the needs of individual learners. Sound health instruction should incorporate a variety of teaching methods intended to complement the learning styles of children. This should lead to young learners who are both intrinsically and extrinsically motivated to inquire, infer, and interpret; to think reflectively, critically and creatively; and in the finally analysis to make use of the knowledge and skills they have gained by becoming effective decision makers.

The success of any education system depends on the quality of teachers, which, in turn, depends on the effective teaching-learning process. Teacher's role is of vital significance for the development of society and appropriate changes in the society. Thus, the quality of higher education depends upon quality of those who impart it. The role of the teacher assumes greater significance in this deteriorating scenario of higher education. It is a daunting task for the teachers to improve the quantity, quality in higher education. It is said that a good teacher can bring the entire world to the class room. The teacher being a sculptor has to play multidimensional role to inspire the students.

Challenges before Educational Policies

Ideally and materially education for sustainable development revolves around the quality of basic and professional education that is essentially determined by curriculum relevance, liberation oriented pedagogy, teacher's development dynamism and the practice of wide participatory democratic school governance. Let us discuss these variables. Curriculum is one of the main input for quality education whereby emphasis is supposed to be given on local cultural environment. Education is linked to production in the sense that the activities of learning leads to preparation of products which have intrinsic values. As was the case in traditional informal education systems, one learnt as (he) grew up and again one learnt as one produced.

Teachers' quality both in terms of professional excellence and social behaviour greatly influence the education outcome. This makes the professional development of teachers. It is expected to give them induction courses on critical issues, so as to enable them adopt to changing students' characteristics, changing nature of teaching and social expectations of teaching in the light of fast pace of the growth of knowledge. The efforts have been taken to establish and develop teachers. The policy-makers are hard to engage development partners in assisting in meeting such needs in schools.

In order to evaluate performance of an institution in the light of sustainable development and being about a measure of accountability a mechanism of accreditation has been developed by UGC. This is an autonomous council under UGC called National Accreditation and Assessment Council with a purpose to carry out periodic assessment of universities and colleges. NAAC has evolved a methodology of assessment which involves self-appraisal by each university and college and an assessment of the performance by an expert committee. Similarly, for technical education AICTE has been established its own accreditation mechanism for its institutions through the National Board of Accreditation. NBA has also undertaken a detailed exercise for benchmarking the performance of reference for evaluation. Both NAAC and NBA are in the right direction and need to be encouraged and strengthened.

Educational institutions have been trying their best for providing education for sustainable development. Yet, there are Obstacles and problems that have to be tackled in this area. These include: Inadequate capacity to support and provide learning about sustainable development. This goes together with lack of competent teachers (quality of teachers); lack and shortage of teaching tools; low quality of instructional materials and inadequacy of infrastructures. The agenda of sustainable development needs skilled practitioners and professionals from all walks of life. These roles place demands on human resources, and require, action by teaching institutions to improve the understanding and skills of educators. Sustainable development is all too classified sector-wise both by separating responsibility for its components, or by making it the sole concern of a specialised unit or person. There is a contention that establishing units as centers of expertise/excellence will help in capacity building and ensure efficiency and efficacy but unless used properly, they may lead others to feeling that they have no responsibilities for sustainable development in their organisations or communities.

Quality Education and Learning Process

Quality education is the solution to all the problems and teachers are the main ingredients in giving quality education. It is said that quality is not destination, it is a continuous journey. Quality means doing the right things right. Doing this right is efficiency and doing right things is effectiveness. Quality education is the education that best fits the present and future needs of the learners. It is the education that provides students with the tools to deal with and find solutions to challenges confronting mankind. In a changing world of rapid technological advances, this means that what was considered quality education yesterday might not meet the standard of what will be understood as quality tomorrow.

The term teaching strategy, in its simple meaning, stands for the type of strategy used by the teacher in carrying out his teaching. Strategy, as a term is quite in vogue in military science and warfare. Here, it stands well for the effective plans, means and ways derived and employed for winning a war. A chess player may also be said to employ effective strategies for winning his game. In the same thing, a teacher may also need the use of strategies for carrying out his task of teaching as effectively as possible. E. Stones and S. Moris (1972) in their book, Teaching Practice: Problems and Perspectives they write, "Teaching is a generalised plan for a lesson which includes structure, desired learner behavior in terms of goals of instruction and an outline of planned tactics necessary to implement the strategy". Special features of teaching strategy:

(1) It stands for a generalised plan, ways and means for carrying out the task of teaching
(2) The plan is directed towards teaching-learning objectives
(3) Teaching strategy is devised and employed to help the learners

Teachers may be different types of teaching in different teaching-learning situations for the effective realisation of their objectives. These strategies may be broadly classified as autocratic teaching strategies (content centred and teacher dominated) and democratic teaching strategies (student centred and democratically organised)

Autocratic Strategies	**Democratic Strategies**
Lecture strategy	* Group discussion strategy
Demonstration strategy	* Question-answer strategy
Tutorial strategy	* Problem solving strategy
Supervised study strategy	* Dramatic strategy
Narrated strategy	* Project strategy
Description strategy	* Dramatic strategy
Explanation strategy	* Role-play strategy
Illustration strategy	* Assignment strategy
Review strategy	* Excursion strategy
Recapitulation strategy	* Brainstorming strategy

Let us try to know in detail about some of the autocratic and democratic teaching strategies. Every strategy has merits, demerits and limitations.

While making use of the lecture as a teaching strategy, a teacher tries to present a segment or unit of the desired content material of a subject to a group of learners through lecturing (verbal communication of ideas). It aims to attain the specific teaching-learning objectives related particularly to the cognitive and effective domains of the learner's behaviour. The lecture strategy, as an oldest traditional mode of teaching, may prove quite advantageous in so many ways for the present-day classroom teaching-learning. The main criticism labeled against the use of it lies in its focusing to organise the teaching-learning act merely on the memory level rather than the understanding and reflective levels. The group discussion strategy involves some sort of discussion, i.e. exchange of ideas between students and teacher or among a group of students resulting in some learning for the realisation of the predetermined teaching-learning objectives. It may prove quite helpful in a number of teaching-learning situations if handled properly in an able leadership. The demonstration strategy refers to the visual presentation of the action and activities, practical work, or the experiments related to the facts and principles of a delivered lesson by the teacher in the classroom to facilitate the teaching-learning task. The discovery strategy aims for the development of an attitude of problem solving or discovery among the learners. In adopting this strategy, the teacher's task is to persuade the students to solve any confronted problem independently by providing the essential facilities, guidance, instructions, etc. The Project Strategy requires on the part of the students to select an appropriate project and then make it a centre of their teaching-learning activities under the proper supervision and guidance of their teacher, who should provide them the needed information and knowledge irrespective of the subject area it belongs as and when needed.

The Problem solving strategy refers to a teaching strategy that provides opportunity to the students for analyzing and solving a problem on the basis of their previous stock of the knowledge enriched with the present means. The narration strategy calls for the capacity and ability of a teacher to produce before the students a well-ordered and sequenced verbal account of the objects and events related to the teaching-learning of a particular topic or subject in a most interesting way. The illustration strategy involves the use of verbal examples and concrete illustrations for making the abstract ideas of the presented learning material quite clear, interesting and comprehensible on the part of the students.

What need to be done?

The question-answering strategy refers to the art and skill of managing the task of teaching and learning by putting questions and responding to them by both the teacher and the students in a quite appropriate and interactive way. The exposition strategy pays a lot of considerations to the manner of putting the subject matter before the students in a simple, interesting and clear style to make them understand it easily and properly. The description strategy refers to an act of representing an object, event or person through words (oral or written) on the part of a teacher as thoroughly as possible for providing its total mental picture to the students. It differs from narration in the sense that it calls for a relatively large details of a thing or event and is not limited to the oral communication. In making use of the explanation strategy, a teacher goes a step further to the exposition strategy for making the things more plain and explicit. In exposition he places facts clearly and vividly before the students, whereas in explanation he aims at showing facts in their proper relation to others in a system. In making use of the dramatisation and role-playing strategies, a teacher tries to make his students understand the concept and vents related to his subject by converting them into an act of play. In role-playing, it is essential on the part of students to enact the roles of the persons involved in the learning episode, but in dramatisation a teacher may himself take this responsibility for the purpose of making an audio and a video presentation of the things and events. By the utilisation of the independent study or self-study strategy a teacher aims for the development of a habit of independent knowledge regarding a topic in hand. In the adoption of the supervised study strategy, he goes a little ahead in its overall management by allowing the students to get engaged in their self-study or group study under his properly planned and organised vigilance and supervision. In addition to using a number of teaching strategies helpful in the presentation of the subject matter, a teacher has to make room for the adoption of some suitable strategies for heir fixation in the minds of the students. The review strategy, drill work, and assignment strategies may prove quite beneficial in this direction. The tutorial strategy, on the other hand, may help in supplementing or enriching the traditional classroom instruction by calling up on a tutor to provide his personalised and individualised services to a student or a small group of students (tutees for their required betterment). The brainstorming strategy, is utilised by a teacher with a group of students to explore a number of ideas related to a situation or solution of a problem without passing any judgement or censure.

It is, therefore, especially useful in the development of higher cognitive abilities like reflective thinking, creative imagination, and problem solving among the students. A teacher should also make use of the sensitivity-training strategy for providing adequate training to the youngsters for the proper development and nourishment of their sensitivity (ability to make proper use of their sense organs and remain sensitive to their environment).

Summing up

From the above discussion it may be concluded that a teacher in the classroom needs to adopt a particular strategy or a number of strategies in combination depending upon the available teaching-learning situations and the realization of the set teaching-learning objectives. The success of a particular teaching-strategy, however, rests on the selection and use of proper teaching tactics that play a central part in its implementation. By definition, teaching tactics may be said those behaviours or activities of a teacher, verbal or non-verbal, which he works out and makes use for the development and application of a particular teaching strategy. A teaching strategy can always be implemented by employing suitable teaching tactics, i.e. the components or basic units of teaching behaviour through which the teacher, the students and the subject matter interact.

References

1. Sampth, K. *Introduction to Educational Technology,* Sterling Pub, Fourth Ed, 2001. Delhi.
2. Aggarwal, J.C, *Landmarks in the History of Modern Indian Education*, Vikas Pub. Delhi, 1999.
3. Mangal, S.K. *Essentials of Educational Technology* PHI Learning Pub, 2012, New Delhi.
4. Cyril Arun Kumar, L. ***Recent Trends in students anti social Behaviour implications for the future Education***, Roshan Pub, 2018, Tenali.
5. Ram, N.The Hindu speaks on Education, Kasturi Sons Ltd, 1997, Chennai.
6. Ausubel, D. P. 1988. *Educational Psychology: A Cognitive View*. New York: Holt, Rinehart & Winston.
7. Bruner, J. S. 2017. *Toward a Theory of Instruction.* New York: W. W. Norton.
8. Bruer, T. John. 2013. *In Search of Brain-Based Education*. *Phi Delta Kappan* (May 1999), 649-57. http:// www.pdkintl.org/kappan/kbru9905.htm
9. Deutsch, M. 2005. A Theory of Cooperation and Competition. Human Relations, 2: 129-52.
10. Freire, Paulo. 1997. *Pedagogy of the Oppressed*. New York: Seabury.
11. Gardner, LHoward. 1993. *Frames of Mind: The Theory of Multiple Intelligences*. New York: Basic Books.

Related Websites

www.eduprestine.com

www.zapmate.co.in

22

Higher Education Access and Equity in Dalit in India

Dr Enapa Upender Rao

Abstract

The Dalits, also known as the scheduled caste or untouchables, have experienced consistent denial to access to education since the 1850s. This decade coincided with Britain's established control over India, which meant many of the improvements to Dalit education were coming from outside influences, rather than from the national government. Because of unchanging social norms and behaviour, incentives to pursue education were minimal for the Dalits who were still physically and emotionally harassed. Increasing efforts to eliminate caste discrimination combined with additional attempts to increase the accessibility and appeal for education have contributed to the slow progression of Dalit education. The responsibility for social equalisation fell fully upon the Indian government when it gained its independence from Britain in 1948. While some benefits of social programmes and government policies designed to increase primary education rates can be noticed, the Dalit literate population still remains much lower than that of the rest of India. There remains still, hostility, oppression and flaws in social programmes in Indian society that prevent an increase in education growth. Despite efforts to decrease caste discrimination and increase national social programmes, the Dalits of India continue to experience low enrolment rates and a lack of access to primary education in comparison to the rest of India.

Introduction

The organisation of the caste system and its entrenchment within Indian history has resulted in centuries of hostile interaction between classes. In rural areas, Dalits were excluded from temples, village wells and tea shops. In some areas of the country, the Dalits were not permitted to walk in daylight for their shadows were considered pollution (Nambissan 1011). In addition to the cruel and humiliating circumstances the Dalits have been put in, their efforts to improve their situation have often been squashed by assault, rape and murder by upper castes threatened by the Dalits' search for equality (Bob, 173). The cruel and unjust treatment imposed upon the Dalits has decreased in frequency as history has progressed, although it still continues in today's society.

Social Exclusion: The denial of equal opportunities imposed by certain sections of society on others which leads to inability of individuals and groups to participate wholly in the political, economic, cultural and social functioning of the society they live in.

- Discrimination: As per the United Nations definition, discrimination includes any conduct based on a distinction made on grounds of natural or social categories, which have no relation either to individual capacities or merits, or to the concrete behaviour of the individual person. It implies immoral and undemocratic behaviour which undermines the principles of equality.
- Equity in Education: Equity requires securing every child's right to education, in education and through education. It not only means providing equal opportunity, but also conditions that allow the socially excluded children to avail the opportunity. It means making institutional changes to allow all children achieve their aspirations and potential in and through education.
- Inclusion in Education: Requires responding to diverse needs of children by increasing their participation in learning, culture and community. It involves changes in classroom practices, curriculum and teaching methodology that will allow children's experience to participate.

After the introduction of the Scheduled Caste and Scheduled Tribe Prevention of Atrocities Act of 1989, the practice of the caste system became illegal in India. Despite increased government intervention, the discrimination and mistreatments of individuals of lower castes still occur. Today, the Dalit population represents 16 percent of the country's population and still struggles to achieve social equality. There remains geographic division within Indian cities and villages which exemplify the role that the caste system plays in today's society (Desai *et al*). Many Dalits have attempted to avoid the caste system by converting from Hinduism to other religions, although this rarely allows these individuals to escape their social and economic hardships.

The Dalits have experienced a bit of progress in establishing an equal position in Indian society. Under the Poona Pact, a reserved number of seats in the national legislature were reserved for Dalit candidates only who would be elected based solely on the votes of their Dalit constituents

(Bob). Their movement has also been encouraged by slow societal shifts towards a greater acceptance of Dalit equality and a greater role played by local and international nongovernmental organisations (Bob, 173). The Dalit population continues to struggle for equality, though the progress of the past few decades shows hope for an improved level of equality within Indian society.

The Importance of Education

Before beginning to examine methods of improving enrolment in primary education and literacy rates, it is important to know why education is such an important topic in development studies. The past century has been characterised by a global expansion of education. Alongside this growth in education has also been an increase in the gap between different social strata (Desai & Kulkarni). Education can be a way to increase the incomes of impoverished people. Education helps to ensure that benefits of growth are experienced by all. Economic perspectives see education as a means to make individuals more productive in the workplace and at home. It can also be seen as a means of empowering socially and economically deprived groups into seeking political reform. By using any of these reasons as motivation to pursue educational development, governments are attempting to generate some form of social or economic equality for the population.

Some of those who study development see education as a means of improving social welfare through economic means. When compared to secondary and university level education, rates of return are highest for primary education, which means that the costs associated with providing basic education are much lower than the benefits received from learning to read and write. About 17.2 percent of economic growth in Africa and 11.1 percent in Asia between the 1950s and 1960s have been credited to increases in education (Psacharopoulos, 102). In addition to an increase in economic growth, primary education is also said to lead to greater income distribution. Providing primary education to 10 percent more people would equate to a decrease in the inequality index of 5 percent (Psacharopoulos, 103). The economic advantages of increasing enrolment rates for primary education emphasise the importance of increasing education accessibility for the dalits of India.

An alternative reason to study education is for its ability to empower the individual to strive for an improved quality of life. A big factor impacted by education is that human beings often base their life goals and everyday actions on what they perceive to be feasible (Simon Wigley & Akkoyunlu-Wigley, 290). Education expands the knowledge of possibility to poor individuals, and is often a necessary factor in providing incentive to escape poverty and social oppression.

Development projects focused on increasing access to basic education, rather than ones that increase capital to improve current levels of education, ensure governments are able to know that the benefits of these programmes are experienced by all, rather than a select few. As mentioned previously, the rates of return for primary education exceed those of secondary and university levelled education. It is therefore of greater value for governments to focus first on increasing access to primary education before moving onto to increase levels of education. By focusing development on a human-capabilities approach, governments and aid organisations are able to increase the number of people with the fundamental skills of reading writing and arithmetic (Simon Wigley & Akkoyunlu-Wigley, 288). These skills allow individuals to communicate, argue, count, and problem solve so that they are able to become more aware and in control of their own lives. This allows them to better deal with problems in their everyday lives including taking a loan out from the bank, defending them in a court of law, escaping unhealthy personal relationships or avoiding jobs which would expose them to unsafe working conditions (Simon Wigley & Akkoyunlu-Wigley, 293). Even the value of holding a basic education is in itself a frequently overlooked asset. Education has had an independent effect on life expectancy, increasing the age for educated individuals (Simon Wigley & Akkoyunlu-Wigley, 290).

One of the most important Dalit political activists who saw the value of social equity within India was Bhimrao Ramji Ambedkar, who became the chief architect of India's constitution after years of social activism. Throughout the first half of the twentieth century, Ambedkar dedicated a significant portion of his life to improving the quality of life and social status of Dalit Indians. He established the People's Education Society in 1945 which believed that increasing access to education to the Dalits would increase their empowerment. He thought that a higher level of education would cause the Dalits to realise their position so that they would aspire to the highest of Hindu positions, and that they would consequently use political power and influence as the means to an end to their oppression (Nambissan, 1014). Ambedkar believed that the value of education was in the empowerment of Dalits to pursue political action for social reform through informed lobbying.

A History of Education

The 1991 census of India reported that Dalit communities were one of the least literate social groups in the country, with only 30 percent of Dalit children recognised to have basic reading and writing skills (Nambissan 1011). These high levels of illiteracy are a result of insufficient access to primary education. Reasons proposed for this low primary education rate amongst the Dalits have ranged from blaming family values to universal acceptance of social behaviour. In reality, it is a history of constant oppression and missing incentives that have been the reason why India's lowest caste has struggled to take advantage of public education programmes.

For centuries, the Dalit population of India were forbidden from gaining access to education. Originally reserved for upper castes only, the denial of conventional education to Dalits was designed to prevent them from increasing their quality of life and to highlight caste divisions. Caught in a colonial struggle between European nations, Indian society had no motivation to determine who should manage social programmes until the British established control over India. Then, during the 1850s, the British began the long process of increasing the accessibility of education to all citizens on India.

Signed in April of 1850, the Caste Disabilities Removal Act theoretically abolished all Indian laws which challenge the rights of those who are members of any caste or religion. To most, this was the first step towards social equalisation within India. It was also the beginning of a series of attempts to increase accessibility to education for members of the dalit caste. To coincide with the signing of the act, the Indian education system became accessible to every member of society. However, one hundred and sixty years after the Dalits were granted permission to attend schools, the primary education rates of the Dalit population compared to those of upper castes remain as low ever.

There have been a number of suggestions proposed as to why the Dalits have yet to take advantage of open access to education. Some have suggested that Dalits possess an apathetic attitude towards education, and so the thought of attending school seems unappealing and inefficient compared to entering the workforce or doing nothing at all. Another suggestion of the cause for lower access to education to Dalits is that most families are caught in a vicious cycle of illiteracy and poverty. Therefore, not only do parents have no incentive to have their children attend school, but they also frequently lack the financial means to send them to the fee-based schooling system of India (Nambissan, 1011). The final and often most realistic reasons for why the Dalits have failed to take advantage of their access to education is a combination of a history of oppression and a lack of access to local, quality education systems.

A historical back-drop of mistreatment and class hierarchies has provided little incentive for the Dalits to pursue education.

Throughout the 1800s and into the mid 1940s, conditions for Dalit children within the Indian education system were very poor. Due to discrimination from higher castes, the Dalits did not feel comfortable attending schools. Dalit children were required to sit outside the school, listening on the veranda while those in higher castes would be taught inside. Teachers, who refused to touch the Dalit children even with sticks, would throw bamboo canes as undeserved punishment while children of other castes were permitted to throw mud. The Dalit children, who knew retaliation would result only in increased abuse, would be essentially scared into not attending school (Freeman, 67). Of the limited number of Dalit children who were attending school, the majority were male; a trait which continues even today (Nambissan, 1012).

The 1948 independence of India prompted an increase in responsibility for the government to promote the economic and educational interests of the lower castes and to protect the Dalits from social injustices and exploitations. Over the next few decades, the Dalits would see very little action to support the claims and progress made during the fifties to help improve their access to primary education. The 1950s saw subtle improvements in the number of schools being built in India, as well as the amount of money being allocated towards primary education programmes. The efforts being put forward by the government lost momentum over the next few decades however, as the rate of primary schools being constructed slipped from 5.8 percent in the 1960s, to 2.1 percent during the 1970s, and eventually down to only 1.3 percent through the 1980s (Nambissan 1015). This was complemented by a shift in funding from primary school education to middle school education. This transition exemplified the government's shifted focus from increasing primary enrolment rates to increasing the quality of the education provided to those already provided with sufficient access to education.

Between 1983 and 2000, improvements in access to education for all of India have been made, although the difference between education rates for Dalits, especially females, and those in higher castes remained constant. In the seventeen year period, enrolment rates for Dalit boys grew from only 47.7 percent to a meagre 63.25 percent. When compared to those males in upper castes, enrolments jumped from an already relatively impressive 73.22 percent to 82.92 percent. Even poorer results were observed when looking at the female Dalit enrolment rate, which inched from 15.72 percent to 32.61 percent, when compared to their upper-caste counterparts whose enrolment climbed from 43.56 percent to 59.15 percent (Desai & Kulkarni). The education gap can also be understood to translate through the entire schooling system, with the proportion of Dalit to non-

Dalit success remaining at a constant low rate through primary, secondary, and post-secondary schooling. Although large improvements have been made to increase enrolment rates in India, statistics show that there has been little progress in decreasing the education gap between castes.

The lack of success in increasing primary enrolment rates for Dalits over the past one hundred and fifty years is evidence that very few projects have had any success in increasing social equality within the Indian Caste system. In the next section, the paper will look at some of the programmes which have attempted to provide incentive for India's poorest to seek primary education.

Education-Based Development Programmes: Can they Work?

When discussing methods which seek to improve enrolment rates, it is important to analyze which circumstances prevent Dalit children from attending school. A family's financial situation plays a role in whether or not they are able to afford to send a child to school. This is a major contributor to low Dalit enrolment rates since Dalits have considerably lower incomes than those in upper castes, and therefore have a hard time paying for education. Distance also plays a key role in determining a child's ability to attend school. Because Dalit homes are often located outside of a village, it is more dangerous for Dalit children to travel to and from school by themselves without risking assault, sexual abuse or abduction (Desai & Kulkarni). In addition, teachers at the schools are often members of upper castes who set low expectations for the Dalit children and rarely seek to provide them with a positive learning environment. There are many factors that act as obstacles for Dalits attempting to gain a primary education, and which many development methods have attempted to overcome.

India has attempted many different strategies to help increase the incentive to receive education for Dalit children. Earlier strategies focused on finding ways to give Dalit children an education without exposing them to the harshness of upper castes. As time progressed and the caste system began to weaken in India, there was a greater shift towards equalising society so as to provide safer and more positive learning environments. Since gaining its independence, the Indian government has continued to make progress on improving the quality of life for India's lowest caste. Modern exposure to international thought has increased access to ideas and methods on how to increase education rates for the Dalits, providing for some of the best results in recent years (Nambissan 1011). The remainder of this section will examine some of the strategies used over the past one hundred and fifty years, attempting to look at how effective they really were.

Following the creation of the Caste Disabilities Removal Act, the British government attempted to increase Dalit school attendance through methods which took into consideration the sensitivity of the caste society. Because the Dalit children were often harassed when they attended schools, the British chose to propose alternative teaching methods, rather than directly addressing the caste issue. One proposed alternative was the use of night schooling for Dalit children. In this manner, children would not need to worry about attending school with members of upper castes, but would still face dangers of travelling without daylight to and from school. Another proposed solution was the use of all-Dalit schools. This solution eliminated the dangers associated with night-time schooling, but also did not help to decrease hostility between the classes. These two methods combined resulted in a four percent primary enrolment rate for Dalit children by 1931, 81 years after education was first opened to all citizens on India. Of these Dalit children, 93 percent were attending all-Dalit schools. A problem occurred when there were insufficient all-Dalit schools at which children could pursue secondary education. Only one percent of all students at the time ever made it past primary education (Nambissan, 1012). It was because of this, that when the British handed over control of the country to India in 1948, the Indian government began thinking of new ways to increase access to education.

Often, governments try to bring in international assistance in dealing with a national crisis like severely low primary enrolment rates. Prescribed to the Indian government by the World Bank, the District Primary Education Programme was designed to increase primary enrolment rates within India. The goal of the programme is to reduce differences in enrolment between gender and social standing to five percent, and to decrease the dropout rate to 10 percent. The DPEP receives the majority of its funding from the World Bank. It calls for the formation of local committees that oversee the hiring and management of Para-teachers. These Para-teachers are trained teachers hired by the DPEP programme to fill growing vacancies in primary schools. They are hired on a short term basis but are offered extended terms as an incentive to perform well (Kumar, Priyam, & Saxena, 565). They are a low-cost alternative to permanent teaching staff and their performance is often higher due to increased incentives. Since the introduction of the DPEP, India has actually managed to see decreasing primary enrolment rates (Kumar, Priyam, & Saxena, 567). It is possible that national campaigns to increase enrolment in primary education fail to have a direct intended impact. Instead, the management of such programmes are so focused on a top down approach to education development that they are not able to discover and acknowledge specific issues.

A smaller scale, and more capital based approach to development and increasing primary enrolment rates is the allocation of additional textbooks to a community. In developing countries, textbooks are often the only basis for a curriculum in a subject. If a school is not able to purchase its own textbooks, then knowledge resources will be limited. By increasing the amount of textbooks, development projects are attempting to increase the ability of schools to take in more students and they hope that additional resources so that performance in school will increase (Crossley & Murby, 111). The biggest concern which arises out of providing textbooks is that it will not increase enrolment rates. New textbooks provide little incentive for Dalit children to attend classes as they do not alleviate any of the barriers currently blocking them from access education. Increasing access to text books has assisted in increasing the quality of education despite having little or no impact on enrolment rates.

Lastly, this paper will look to an outside approach to increasing school enrolment and attendance by observing how school-based drug treatments to common diseases attempt to provide incentive for enrolment. Many preventable diseases, including hookworm, roundworm and whipworm affect millions of children worldwide every year, preventing them for attending any sort of school or doing any physical labour (Miguel & Kremer, 159). In this sense, the free drugs associated with this programme not only provide incentive for children to come to school and learn, but they also serve a second purpose in that they keep students healthy, ensuring they are physically capable of returning to school. Children who attended schools which offered this programme not only remained healthy, but felt more comfortable attending school on a regular basis. It has been proven that programmes which offer medical incentives decreases absence rates by 25 percent. This method has also proven to equally increase the amount of girls and boys who are being enticed to attend regular primary schooling (Miguel & Kremer, 190-191).

In a case examined by Miguel and Kremer, female attendance increased by 10 percent in subject areas, nearly two times that of males (Desai & Kulkarni). The medication has also proved more cost effective for the organisations administering the medication. This method been proven as a more effective way of increasing education levels compared to food incentives. On average the annual $5 cost of administering deworming medication to a child is six times cheaper than providing the same child with food incentives. School uniforms, which are often so expensive as to prevent young girls from attending school, have had relatively equivalent success in increasing enrolments rates in young females. Deworming, however, remains more effective because costs associated with deworming medication are twenty times less expensive than providing school uniforms (Bossuroy & Delavallade). Using medication and deworming medicines as incentives, international organisations including the World Health Organisation and The Forum of Young Leaders' campaign, Deworm the World, have developed a successful outside-the-box approach to increasing enrolment and attendance rates.

Conclusion

There have been many attempts over the past one hundred and fifty years to help increase the quality of life for the Dalits of India through development focused on enrolment in primary education. Education provides individuals with the means to increase their income and to engage in economic activities. In addition, it can help empower individuals to lobby for social change through political activism. The lack of incentives to pursue education for the Dalits of India can be traced back to a long history of mistreatment and oppression. Still occurring today, caste harassment makes teaching environments unstable for caste children, it places caste homes on the outskirts of towns so that children have greater distances to walk to school, and it economically suppresses the Dalits so that they are unable to pay for their children's education. Many suggestions, both traditional and modern, have arisen on how to go about resolving issues surrounding Dalit primary enrolment. Night classes and all-Dalit schools provided a safer learning environment for the Dalits, but did not address any issues of caste conflict. Twentieth century policies helped officially decrease some of the animosity and inequality between groups so that the Indian government could have a greater focus on national primary enrolment rates. Larger operations, including the DPEP cooperative project with The World Bank failed to resolve some of the grass-root issues which deterred Dalits from attending school. Funding increasing supplies of textbooks to Indian schools do not address any of the core reasons as to why dalits are not attending school. Instead of increasing enrolment, additional textbooks only had an effect on increased performance levels. Providing free deworming medication at school has proven successful both in increasing the health of children which prevents absenteeism, and in increasing enrolment levels. Minor increases in incentives for Dalits to pursue primary education have been beneficial, but not sufficient in equalising the enrolment gap between the Dalits and members of upper castes. In order to significant progress to be made in increasing the primary enrolment rates of Dalit children, development organisations must continue to explore varying levels of incentives and pursue national social equality in India.

Reference

Bossuroy, Thomas and Clara Delavallade. "Giving schoolchildren a chance." Web. Nov. 17 2008. http://www.livemint.com/2008/11/17211850/Giving-schoolchildren-a-chance.html. Accessed Jun. 11 2010.

Construction of a New Human Rights Issue." *Human Rights Quarterly* 29.1 (2007): 167-193. Print.

Crossley, Michael, and Myra Murby. "Textbook Provision and the Quality of the School Curriculum in Developing Countries: Issues and Policy Options." *Comparative Education* 30.2 (1994): 99-114. Print.

Desai, Sonalde, and Veena Kulkarni. "Changing Educational Inequalities in India in the Context of Affirmative Action." 45.2 (2008): 245-270. Print.

Desai, Sonalde, and Veena Kulkarni. "Changing Educational Inequalities in India in the Context of Affirmative Action." *Demography* 45.2 (2008): 245-270. Print.

Desai, S., C.D. Adams, and A. Dubey. 2006. "In the Margins: Social Inequalities in Children's Educational Outcomes in India." Paper presented at the annual meeting of the Population. *Association of America*, March 30–April 1, Los Angeles.

Freeman, James M. *Untouchable: An Indian Life History*. illustrated edition. Stanford University Press, 1982. Print.

Kumar, Krishna, Manisha Priyam, and Sadhna Saxena. "Looking beyond the Smokescreen: DPEP and Primary Education in India." *Economic and Political Weekly* 36.7 (2001): 560-568. Print.

"Looking beyond the Smokescreen: DPEP and Primary Education in India." *Economic and Political Weekly,* 36.7 (2001): 560-568. Print.

Miguel, Edward, and Michael Kremer. "Worms: Identifying Impacts on Education and Health in the Presence of Treatment Externalities." *Econometrica* 72.1 (2004): 159-217. Print.

Nambissan, Geetha B. "Equity in Education? Schooling of Dalit Children in India." *Economic and Political Weekly,* 31.16/17 (1996): 1011-1024. Print.

Psacharopoulos, George. "Education and Development: A Review." *The World Bank Research Observer* 3.1 (1988): 99-116. Print.

Simon Wigley, and Arzu Akkoyunlu-Wigley. "Human Capabilities versus Human Capital: Guaging the Value of Education in Developing Countries." *Social Indicators Research* 78.2 (2006): 287-304. Print.

"The Caste System in Hinduism." Web. 2005. http://www.friesian.com/caste.htm. Accessed 30 Mar 2010.

23

Teaching, Learning and Evaluation (TLE) in Higher Education Institutions during Covid-19 Havoc: Some empirical findings and amicable suggestions

Dr Gopala Sudarshanam

Abstract

Higher education is the most indispensable mechanism in shaping and molding the landscape of any nation. Irrefutably, it is always the key socio-economic device and has positively proportionate relation with any state's GDP, Health indicators, industrial growth and multifaceted development. If it is not strived in the designed, expected and needed dimension, the devastation it causes can be copious and unpredictable too. Our Indian higher education, which is the largest in the world with 70 million enrolments, 1000 plus different universities and 45000 HEIs is not an exception to this widely proved doctrine. As UN- General Secretary commented, 'The Present notable Covid-19 disaster has triggered history's biggest disruption of education, affecting 1.6 billion students worldwide (70% of the world student population) and some 23.8 million students may not be able to return to schools to next year because of economic fallout'. 'It is critical that education is at the heart of international solidarity'. (The Hindu, 09-08-2020). The Research and other forms of scholastic endeavours, which indeed are more consultative and collaborative in nature, have completely paused desperately at greater extent and caused on insurmountable obstacle. Unfortunately, as in most other developing and underdeveloped countries, in India too, there were no predetermined pathways to combat and compete with the precarious pandemic type cataclysmic circumstances. Still we should enshrine with huge hope to face and fight the unprecedented challenges thrown by the pandemic.

Thus, the entire education system was shut abruptly as many other nations across the globe. Further, it is facing the discontent of the most concerned parents, students and educationists for not being ready with remedies to bring the 'mother' of all systems in to the mainstream and a blur is prevailed in addressing issues of digital divide. In these circumstances, the researcher has made an attempt to look into the matter based on the primary and secondary data coupled with meager amount of personal interaction with his peers and disciples he teaches. He has also tried to observe the paradigm shift on different faces and facets and identified suitable ways and means to bounce back teaching, learning and evaluation process through this study.

Therefore, present study reveals that majority of the respondents jointly from both groups were in the productive age bracket of 21-31 years, which is on far with close to the nation's mean productive age of 30 years. It was further found from this study that close to 80 percent of the students and 72 percent of faculty are the habitants of rural and urban areas respectively. This finding also reflecting the statistics of majority of students is hailing from rural and semi-urban places in the country for seeking their higher education. When socio-economic status of the respondents was analyzed, 96 percentage of students and 54 percent of faculty were belonging to SC, ST and BC together and their monthly economies fall under the range of ten to twenty thousand and twenty to forty thousand respectively. Finally it was also found that they were not much satisfied with virtual or online teaching, learning and evaluation mechanism. But forced to adopt, as there was no other suitable and amicable either substitute or alternative.

Key Words : Empirical, Paradigm, Covid-19, HEIs, Online TLE and Technology.

Introduction

Undoubtedly, Higher Education is the most key socio-economic device in shaping the superpowers of any nation on the globe. It always has a close nexus with any nation's GDP, Health indicators and multifaceted and multifold development. In an era of knowledge based economy, higher education will continue to play very significant role and its contributions certainly supports for brighter future of all its stakeholders. The paramount objective of education in any country has been the development of the individual in many faces and facets. The minimum level of education that was necessary to achieve this goal in the agrarian society was primary and in the industrial age, secondary. In the present boundary less informative society, education needs to be able to respond to copious demands of a rapidly progressing world by raising awareness of environment, peace, cultural and social diversity, increased competitiveness, and the emerging concept of a global village. Education prepares the individual to connect - and live in harmony - with the multiple environments around him. Higher education is a very important sector for the growth and development of human resources which can take responsibility for social, economic, and scientific development of the country. But this sector is now very badly affected as many others due to novel COVID-19 fiasco.

Our Indian higher education, which is the largest in the world with 70 million enrolments, 1000 plus different universities, 45000 HEI,s and 10,011 stand alone institutions is not an exception to this widely proved doctrine. As UN- General Secretary commented, 'The Present notable Covid-19 disaster has triggered history's biggest disruption of education, affecting 1.6 billion students worldwide (70 percent of the world student population) and some 23.8 million students may not be able to return to schools to next year because of economic fallout'. 'It is critical that education is at the heart of international solidarity'. (The Hindu, 09-08-2020). The Research and other forms of scholastic endeavours, which indeed are more consultative and collaborative in nature, have completely paused desperately at greater extent and caused on insurmountable obstacle. Unfortunately, as in most other developing and underdeveloped countries, in India too, there were no predetermined pathways to combat and compete with the precarious pandemic type cataclysmic circumstances. Still we should enshrine with huge hope to face and fight the unprecedented challenges thrown by the pandemic.

In this connection the researcher has tried to make a lucid study on new strategies adopted in teaching, learning and evaluation of higher education during this carona pandemic. Further, he has also made an attempt to examine the impact of such online pedagogical methods on satisfaction levels of students, parents and teachers. Eventually, the initiatives of governments to cope up the situation and to bring new normal were also included in his study.

Statement of the problem

Appreciable amount of research work has done on the broad area of higher education and its allied areas like transformation of higher education in India, role of various agencies in the development of higher education and challenges and opportunities of higher education in knowledge based economy. Perhaps, there are a very few attempts on how to face the challenges and prompt strategies to extract the opportunities from Covid like disasters. Hence the present study is aimed at examination the need and impact of online teaching, learning and evaluation in higher education in India. Further the researcher has also made an attempt to present the lucid picture on satisfaction levels of students, teachers and teachers on this new pathway. Observation of emerging trends, areas of concerns and expectations from contemporary higher education pedagogy and sector were also covered.

Objectives of the Study

Following are the main objectives of the present study entitled, "Teaching, Learning and Evaluation (TLE) in Higher Education Institutions during Covid-19 Havoc: Some empirical findings and amicable suggestions".

1. To study the components of new pedagogy, adopted in higher education teaching, learning and evaluation (TLE) during Covid-19 fiasco.
2. To examine the satisfaction levels of Students, Parents and Teachers with online TLE methods.
3. To present a lucid picture on the initiatives of governments to bring new normal.
4. To state some empirical observations and concerns for better tomorrow.

Scope of the Study

The present study is very crisp about the half a year saga of Indian Higher Education during novel Covid-19 pandemic. Lucid effort has been made to make some observations and concerns over the journey of Indian Higher education during Covid-19 fiasco. Further this paper also throws light on the other subtle issues like students, parents and teachers satisfaction levels on shifting the focus from offline to online and manual to machine centered. An attempt to find the expectations of the interested parties of higher education in one hand and higher educational institutions on the other hand also made. But for the present study, the technical education was excluded from the pool of higher education, with an assumption that the study may become too lengthy and high time consuming process. Further the chosen sample of respondents 300 comprises of students 200 and teachers 100.

Though interacted over phone with very limited number of parents, their number is not included in sample size but their opinions have presented in the description. Select sample has taken from undergraduate and post-graduate institutes of government and private sectors, belongs to three districts such as Siddipet, Karimnagar and Jangaon of the Telangana state. Finally this study has conducted for the period of 45 days only during August- September, 2020. Therefore the results may not be generalised for entire country as sample size, jurisdiction of the study and sample frame have their own technical limitations.

Research Methodology

It is irrefutable that the research methodology is the scientific approach and road map adopted for the preparation of any report, dissertation, thesis or a piece of research paper. Present work is not an exception to that. Hence for the present paper and for the purpose of the study major portion of the data have been collected from secondary sources exclusively. Necessary secondary data on conceptual frame work and a few previous works are collected from online, offline and open access Journals, Newspapers, Periodicals, Reference Books, and various other publications. To produce authenticate and reliable recent statistics on composition of higher educational institutions and their contribution to the core, the MHRD prepared 8th AISHE-2018 report is used. Further to present and cover the qualitative conceptual perceptions on higher education and its performance indicators like GER and PTR an empirical approach was also lay down. Interviewing senior faculty members working in degree colleges, universities and other technical institutions is part of it, besides, conduct of debates, group discussions in Management Teachers Consortium (MTC, Chennai Based) and brainstorming sessions among them. The websites like Google, MHRD, UGC and other official sites of the government of India have also used for data collection for the information on different legal and statutory aspects of the study. To analyze, summarise and present the quantitative data for easy comprehend, statistical tools such as normal tables, percentages and simple averages were used.

Previous Studies

Crawford, J, Butler – Henderson, K and et.al (2020): in their research paper 'Covid-19: 20 Countries higher education intra period digital pedagogy responses' have opined that the responses of higher education providers have been diverse from no response to social isolation strategies on campus and curriculum development for fully online offerings. They have also stressed on agility of higher education in preparing for the pandemic.

Schwartz, Andrew, M and et.al (2020): in their empirical research output titled 'Managing resident workforce and education during the Covid-19 pandemic: Evolving strategies and lessons learned' have observed that the residencies are faced with new challenges to provide care and education in the face of safety, resource redistribution and erosion of classic learning opportunities.

Pravat Jena (2020): through his research article on 'Impact of Covid-19 on Higher Education in India' has found many new models of learning, perspectives and trends, also opined as the same may continue, as we go ahead to a new tomorrow.

Richard E. Ferdig et.al. (2020): in their study on 'Teaching, technology and teacher education during the Covid-19 pandemic: stories from the field' have identified remote co-teaching, creating learning management, creating a support network to sustain student centered, active pedagogy in emergency online education, virtual professional learning by retired teachers and experiential learning through video observation as the significant components of TLE during pandemic type disasters.

N. Kapasai, P. Paul and et.al (2020): have conveyed that about 70 percent of learners have involved in e-learning during lockdown inspite of several challenges. Through their paper ' Impact of lockdown on learning status of undergraduate and postgraduate students during Covid-19 pandemic in West Bangal, India' have also suggested strategies needed to build a resilient education system, that ensure to develop the skills of the young minds.

T. Karalis (2020): in his paper entitled ' Planning and evaluation during educational disruption: lessons learned from Covid-19 pandemic for treatment of emergencies in education' has supported the responding of governance to emergencies in education at various levels, such as National, State and Regional have pacified the panic over education among students, parents and even teachers.

Sandeep Grover, Swaprajeet Sahoo and et.al (2020): in their field survey paper titled 'Psychological impact of Covid-19 lockdown: An online survey from India' have found that more than 2/5 of the people are experiencing anxiety and depression due to lockdown and prevailing Covid-19 pandemic. Their praiseworthy study also suggests that there is a need of expanding the mental health service to everyone in the society during this pandemic situation.

Ms Veena Shenoy, Ms. Sheetal Mahendra and Ms. Navita Vijay (2020): have stated that during lockdown period majority of the faculty have undergone the process of technology adoption and students are involved with various online modes of learning. They have also observed lot of fear, anxiety and consciousness among students and faculty regarding Covid-19. Significant finding of their paper is that the students' attendance and involvement for online learning is on par with the regular face-to-face class engagement.

Aziz Naciri, Mohamed Amine Baba and et.al (2020): in their paper 'Mobile learning in Higher Education: Unavoidable alternative during Covid-19' have reflected the role of mobile learning as remote teaching strategies sustaining students centered learning. Further they stressed upon mobile learning is unavoidable alternative during Covid-19.

Dr. Amit Kumar Maity and Sanglap Maity (2016): in their research article entitled 'Evolution of Higher Education in India', emphasized education as the most important weapon of social progress and development. They were also opined that the higher education must be meant for making skilled leader in the different fields of society.

Dr. Gopala Sudarshanam and Y. Sharadha (2016): in their research paper, 'Transformation of Indian Higher Education' has observed the higher education as an important element of social change. They have also opined, the higher education must also reach to the masses at affordable cost and assure them at least minimum living of life in the society but it is not up to the mark even after 69 years of independence.

Analysis of Data and Interpretation

Under this head, the researcher has made an attempt to analyze the data collected through a structured questionnaire link using 'Google form'. For this he used statistical tools such as averages, percentages and ratios. Further, the collected data is also compiled in the form of tables.

Respondents Profile

Initially researcher has tried to analyze the profile of the chosen respondents, in terms of their age, sex, habitation, socio-economic background and the core discipline they were engaged with. For this the data collected from primary source was compiled in the following Table 1, which reveals that 63 percentage of Students and Faculty were in the age bracket of 21 years and 31 years and above respectively. Regarding to sex more than 60 percent of the students and faculty are male. Interestingly from the students pool almost 80 percent are the habitants of the rural area in contrast to this about 72 percent of faculty are hailing from urban area. The researcher has also made an attempt to find socio-economic background of the both respondents and found that almost 96 percent of the students are from SC, ST and BC together, whereas only 54 percent of the faculty were belonging to this satra. Out of the 200 and 100 samples of students and faculty 74 and 40 respectively were with Commerce as their core discipline for either to study or to teach. Finally from the table it was also revealed that the majority families' monthly income of the students was ranging between 10,000 to 20,000 and against to this 88 percent of the faculties have been earning their monthly emoluments between twenty thousands to forty thousands.

Therefore, based on the description of the respondents profile, in it may be inferred that majority of the students and faculty were in the mean age of demographic dividend of the nation i.e. 20 and 30 respectively. As many scholars have emphasized, much of the students and faculty were the habitants of rural and urban respectively. From this data, it was also seen and found that significant number of students and teachers have been selecting Commerce discipline as their core subject after engineering courses. Bothersome observation at the end was, faculty was not paid either on far with their counterparts working in the government sector or even respectable emoluments to meet their family requirements. Further faculties were also not paid their salaries for almost four months, as class room and physical work missing. But a few institutions have mitigated them with half of their pay roles. Hence it may be concluded that neither students not teachers were happy with the changed paradigm during the novel Covid-19 period. They were strongly felt the more concerned intervention of government regarding salaries payment to teachers and supply of devices or tools to students to attend their new teaching, learning and evaluation methods, initiated by their respective teachers and Colleges. Above numbers can be found in the below given Table 1 lucidly.

Table 1: Respondents Profile

Students (200)			Faculty (100)		
Characteristics	**No.**	**%**	**Characteristics**	**No.**	**%**
Age:			**Age:**		
20 years and Below	74	37	30 years and Below	37	37
21 years and Above	126	63	31 years and Above	63	63
Sex:			**Sex:**		
Male	126	63	Male	69	69
Female	74	37	Female	31	31
Residential Area:			**Residential Area:**		
Rural	158	79	Rural	28	28
Urban	42	21	Urban	72	72
Community Status:			**Community Status:**		
SC	31	16	SC	08	08
ST	19	09	ST	04	04
BC	142	71	BC	42	42
General	08	04	General	46	46
Core Program of Study:			**Program of Teaching:**		
Arts	28	14	Arts including languages	17	17
Commerce	74	37	Commerce	40	40
Science	46	23	Science	27	27
Computers	52	26	Computers	16	16
Family monthly income:			**Monthly emoluments:**		
10,000 to 20,000	128	64	20,000 to 30,000	31	31
20,000 to 30,000	52	26	30,000 to 40,000	57	57
30,000 and Above	20	10	40,000 and Above	12	12

Source: Primary data collected through a structured questionnaire link using 'Google form'.

Technology Adopted in new paradigm

As all we believe, change is dynamic, constant, pervasive and inevitable. In almost all walks of our day to day conversations and professional association, we witness it as the most invaluable. But people have the tendencies of resisting change without contemplating in to its need, significance and purpose, here as they have no suitable alternative to cope up the change have adopted the technology with mixed perceptions. Selected institutions of the study have used variety of pedagogy in their new teaching, learning and evaluation process. Amicable orientations to students and required need based training to the faculty members on application of virtual class rooms have regulated the resistance of usage of technology for new normal and to tune their mindsets for the same. Therefore the researcher has tried to know the devices and tools used by the both respondents. So from the given below Table 2 it is found that to attend the virtual classes through online significant number of students (90%) have depended on their Cell Phones, whereas 48 percent of Cell Phones and 34 percent of Laptops were used by the faculty. In both cases usage of desktops was very meager.

Hence from the study it may be read between the lines that despite of much trauma nexuses with qualitative internet connection, bandwidth, uninterrupted power supply and gigantic challenge of students engagement, higher education institutions and their respective stakeholders have either willingly or unwillingly have accepted journey with available technology to embrace the present but temporary pandemic crisis. Surprisingly, it was also found that, after short trainings and periodical instructions of the Commissioner of Collegiate Education (CCE) Telangana state, huge sunk of faculty and students were using virtual modes for their informal meetings,

Table 2: Devices used for attending/engagement of online Pedagogy or online TLE

	Students (200)		Faculty (100)		
Component or tool used	**No.**	**%**	**Component or tool used**	**No.**	**%**
Laptop	12	06	Laptop	34	34
Cell Phone	179	90	Cell Phone	48	48
Desk top	07	03	Desk top	12	12
Others	02	01	Others	06	06
Total	**200**	**100**	**Total**	**100**	**100**

Source: Primary data collected through a structured questionnaire link using 'Google form'.

orientations, faculty development programmes, seminars, conferences, workshops, staff meetings, students mentoring and counseling, alumni meetings, club activities, conduct of various competitions to students and even to organise condolence meetings to sad demise of any faculty member (Veeresham, retired faculty, GDC-Siddipet) during this catastrophic Covid-19.

Platform used for attending/engagement of online TLE

To find the results pertaining to the third objective of this empirical study, research was also included a few questions pertaining to online platforms, with which students and faculty were associated during this disaster. The tools used by the faculty for engagement of their assignments and students to attend their classes includes Zoom App, Google Class Room/ Google Meet, Skype, YouTube Live and other sources such as Google hangouts, LMS and ICT etc. From this study, Table 3 reveals that 88 percent of Faculty and almost equal size (87%) of the Students have been using Zoom App for their virtual teaching, learning, and evaluation activities. When it was attempted to find the reason for the same majority of the respondents have opined, Zoom App is user friendly, less associated with technical jargons and less dependency were contributing factors for choosing the App.

Therefore, regarding to online platform it may be concluded that majority of the students and staff were well versed with Zoom app for their virtual engagement. Apart to this faculty were also sharing own made E-content, PPTs and Recorded and downloaded Videos to students in general and among themselves in particular. For this they were using students Watsap groups, College websites and Mail ids.

Table 3: Platform used for attending/engagement of online Pedagogy or online TLE

Variable	Students (200)		Faculty (100)	
Platform used	**No.**	**%**	**No.**	**%**
Zoom App	174	87	88	88
Google Classroom/Google Meet	14	07	08	08
YouTube Live	02	01	02	02
Skype	00	00	00	00
Others	10	05	02	02
Total	**200**	**100**	**100**	**100**

Source: Primary data collected through a structured questionnaire link using 'Google form'.

Satisfaction levels of Students and Teachers with online TLE

The researcher has also made a lucid attempt to find the satisfaction level of structured respondents in particular and student's parents in a cursory way. To find the degree of satisfaction over online teaching, conduct of examination, evaluation of students' performance application of technology, teacher-student relationship and other secondary aspects like timing of classes, usage of devices after class activities of their wards etc. Further an attempt was also made to know the faculty perception and level of content on new paradigm and its innovative attributes. From Table 4, it is found that there is vague and mixed response from the students regarding their satisfaction with online pedagogy and its components. It seems they were forced to adopt virtual platforms for coverage of uncompleted syllabus, competition of leftover assignments, test and examinations. Out 200 respondents major portion, i.e. 124 (62%) were in the range of very poor to average and only 38 percent were between good to excellent bracket. But it is reverse with faculty members. About 71 percent were feeling very happy and expressed they were doing quite excellent with changed TLE methodology and only 29 percentage of respondents were at 3rd, 4th and 5th point in 5 Point scale of satisfaction analysis.

Therefore, based on this available data it may be strongly inferred that students have no alternative to learn their academics except cope up with the present scenario. Similarly faculty too is adoptive with technological advancement for their sustenance and progress in their career.

Table 4: Satisfaction levels of Students and Teachers with online Pedagogy or online TLE

Sl.No.	Attribution	Students (200)		Faculty (100)	
		No.	%	No.	%
1.	Excellent	40	20	31	31
2.	Good	36	18	40	40
3.	Average	80	40	19	19
4.	Poor	34	17	06	06
5.	Very Poor	10	05	04	04
	Total	**200**	**100**	**100**	**100**

Source: Primary data collected through a structured questionnaire link using 'Google form'.

Evaluation System during Covid Period

Assessment and evaluation system of higher education was vehemently affected. College level assessments like internal examinations, various kinds of tests, project works and class room presentations were completely cancelled. Most of the external and semester-end examinations and project viva voce have been postponed. Perhaps, this phenomenon may have absolute and direct impact on the students' academic and occupational career. Further this disruption may also create huge anxiety, panic and psychological imbalance for the future of students, not only among students but also in faculty and parents. Pravat (2020), has warned prevalence of reduced employment opportunities and people's struggle for food rather education. However, after certain initiatives being drawn by the state and central governments at different levels, many colleges have been managing said internal examinations, tests, assignments and even viva-voce for final projects, dissertations and thesis evaluation through online modes.

Governments Initiatives to strike the balance

Central and state governments of India through their apex level educational agencies, bodies and commissions, such as MHRD and UGC and Telangana State Council of Higher Education (TSCHE) and their affiliated organisations and universities, have designed some digital platforms to ease the students and teachers from unforeseen distress and devastation. The brief description on a few such initiatives can be seen as under (UGC Website).

- To store and share the digital learning resources, **'e- Gyankosh'**, a national digital repository has developed. It is indeed created and protected with registered copyright by IGNOU.
- **'Swayam'**, the massive open online courses (MOOCs) with 140 universities approved credit transfer facility is facilitated by the UGC. This programme also includes 32 DTH channels enabled, swayam prabha and e- PG pathashala.
- Through **'e-Adhyayan'**, provided more than 700 e-books and play-list of video content to the PG courses across the nation.
- **'Gyandhara'** is another initiative, being designed by the IGNOU, which provides internet audio counseling service. As it is a web based radio, students can listen to the live discussions by the concerned subject experts and teachers.
- **'FOSSEE',** it is short form for free/Libre and Open source Software for education, which is developed to promote open source software for education as well as professional use.
- **'e-ShodhSindhu'** is one more important resource. It is a collection of e-journals, e-journal archives and e-books. This source is much praised and equipped with more than 10,000 e-journals and around 3.5 Million e-books.
- For the benefit of research students with repository of Ph.D thesis, a novel platform is created, called **'Shodhganga'**. It has ability to capture, index, store, dissemination and preserve, electronic thesis and dissertations submitted by the research scholars.
- **VIDWAN, e-pathya, Gyandhara, SAKSHAT, NEAT and virtual labs** are other facilities provided by the MHRD and UGC

together for procurement of needy information on education, research and developmental aspects of the students and teachers.

- Commissioner of Collegiate Education, Telangana (CCE-TS) has come forward with wonderful vision of creating big pool of e-content to almost all undergraduate students of varied disciplines. It has trained its 2000 plus teaching staff to gear up to create video lessons in their respective disciplines for their 1.5 lakh students. All of them have produced at least one video lesson on every day with 40 minutes span. This process has continued for about 30 days, by which more than 60,000 video lessons have been produced and uploaded in YouTube channel. It has made great help to students and equally to the faculty members for future reference.

Consolidated Observations and Concerns

Therefore, now after panic and pathetic situation prevailed and penetrated in to the minds of all the people, institutions, agencies and governing authorities at utmost level, the debate, discourse and contemplation has been shifting from frustration to alternative solutions, to restore the imperative previous days with added features and breakthrough. As blessings in disguise, online and blended teaching-learning apparatus, various LED/TED/PEP/MED/QED talks, usage of virtual platforms and applications (Apps), Live TV and recorded Video lessons have arrived to redeem. For more conducive and to resilience, new pathways have been paved, such as optimum utilisation of IT, design of effective integrative and collaborative teaching-learning, MOUs with pioneering institutions of higher education and devices for play mode learning. Further, LIW (living, innovating and Working), LIC (Learning Is Continuous), SMART, Team and Digital learning and delivering variety of Talks by experts have perpetuated as new success mantras to reinstate the higher education and its fascinated stakeholders. The significant role and contribution of College websites, Social networking sites, Columnist writings, Psychologists counseling, advisory essays of professional doctors in their respective specialisation and benefaction of qualitative E-content developers is paramount and highly applauded. Eventually it is worth to note and follow that "The only thing we know about the future is that it will be different" (Peter F Drucker), hence we should *make* future ready for Covid like situation with optimum utilisation of our most exponential demographic dividend (68%) in one hand and espouse with ever innovative and creative think tank coupled with human touch on the other hand.

Findings of the present study

After through study of the available literature, meticulous computation of the collected data and keen analysis of the opinions and perceptions it is found that majority of the respondents jointly from both groups were in the productive age bracket of 21-31 years, which is on far with close to the nation's mean productive age of 30 years. It was further found from this study that close to 80 percent of the students and 72 percent of faculty are the habitants of rural and urban areas respectively. This finding also reflecting the statistics of majority of students is hailing from rural and semi-urban places in the country for seeking their higher education. When socio-economic status of the respondents was analyzed, 96 percent of students and 54 percent of faculty were belonging to SC, ST and BC together and their monthly economies fall under the range of ten to twenty thousand and twenty to forty thousand respectively. Faculty members of the private colleges have openly expressed their agony for not being paid salaries during lockdown period, similarly government employees have expressed their dissatisfaction over deferment of their three months salaries. Regarding usage of tools and platform for attending virtual classes whooping size of students (90% and 87%) were using cell phones and Zoom App respectively. But faculty are using both cell phone and laptop together as tool and Zoom App as platform. Subsequently for evaluation process predominantly faculty were depending on Google forms. Finally it was found that they were not much satisfied with virtual or online teaching, learning and evaluation. But forced adopt as there was no other suitable and amicable either substitute or alternative.

Conclusion

For this jostle journey of paradigm shift, the researcher has also expressed his concern that the teachers of varied capacities must see to resilient their delivery mode than in previous. Further, they should incorporate successive strategies for the betterment of students in their rescue plans and policies. As technology evolving rapidly, we have explored to endless opportunities to connect through artificial intelligence and virtual communication, so we as the prominent pillar and harbingers of the education apparatus, must be equipped with required advancements. Always we should thought students success holistically and find the vulnerabilities of them, so as to build the amicable sterilised environment and design solutions for their stability in success. Hence, the workforce associated or enthusiastically engaged with the broad spectrum of education must gear up to accept, adopt and get leveraged with such kaleidoscopic phenomenon of change. Subsequently, all stakeholders of education must be of the opinion that sensitisation and sanitisation of needy skills, abilities, knowledge and competencies in once core area of specialisation will be BEACON forever. Ultimately a genuine teacher will be perpetuated as the predominant source of information, instruction and inspiration to the students in general and scholastic society in particular. Eventually no other source or resource either substitute or replace him.

References

1. Aziz Naciri & Mohamod Amine Baba and et.al (2020): 'Mobile Learning in higher Education: unavoidable alternative during Covid-19', published in Aquademia, 2020, Vol-4, Issue-1.
2. Crawford, J and Butler-Handerson, K and et.al (2020): 'Covid-19: 20 Countries higher education intra-period digital pedagogy responses', Journal of Applied Learning & Teachining, Vol.3, No.1, pp. 1-20.
3. DNS Kumar (2020): Impact of COVID-19 on Higher Education. Retrieved on May 25, 2020 from https://www.highereducationdigest.com, April-29, 2020.
4. Dr. Gopala Sudarshanam(2016): 'The Transformation of Indian Higher Education from Pre-Independence to Post- Independence: Some observations and Concerns'. Manjeera Journal for Research in Social Sciences, Vol.III, No.1. January- June, 2016, ISSN-2394-5605.
5. Enadu telugu daily news paper research articles for last couple of months.
6. 'Globalization of higher education and cross-border student mobility'- NV Varghese-2008.
7. "Impact of Globalization on Education in India"- Paper presented at the National Seminar on 8th & 9th February 2008, by Prof. Rahul. P. More at Abeda Inamdar Senior College Pune-1.
8. India Today (2020). Effect of Covid-19 on Campus: Major steps being taken by Colleges to keep education going. 1668156-2020-04-17.
9. Indian Higher Education Reform: From Half backed socialization to half backed capitalism-Deesh Kapur & Pratap Bhanu Mehta –Presented at Bookings NCAER india policy Forum-2007 New Delhi, dated July 2, 2007.
10. Internationalization of Higher Education: Towards a conceptual framework- Policy future in education 2003.
11. Ms. Veena Shenoy, Ms. Sheetal Mahendra, Ms. Navita Vijay (2020): 'COVID 19-Lockdown: Technology adaption, Teaching, Learning, Students Engagement and faculty experience', Mukt Shabd Journal, Volume IX, Issue IV, pp. 698-702, April, 2020.
12. N. Kapasia, P. Paul and et.al (2020): 'Impact of lockdown on learning status of undergraduate and postgraduate students during Covid-19 pandemic in West Bengal, India'. Children and Youth services Review- ELSEVIER, Volume 116, September, 2020.
13. Pravat Jeva (2020): 'Impact of Covid-19 on Higher education in India' International Journal of Advanced Education and Research, Vol-5, Issue. 3, pp. 77-81.
14. Richard, E. Ferdig and et.al (2020): 'Teaching, Technology and teacher Education during the Covid-19 pandemic: Stories from the field'. Association for the advancement of computing in education-ISBN: 978-1-939797-49-0.

15. Sandeep Grover, Swaprajeet Sahoo and et.al (2020): "Psychological impact of Civid-19 lockdown: An online survey from India", Indian Journal of Psychiatry, Vol. 62, Issue-4, pp. 354-362.
16. Schwartz, Andrew.M and et.al (2020): 'Managing Resident workforce and Education during the Covid-19 pandemic: Evolving strategies and lessons learned', JBJS Open Access: April-June, 2020, Vol. 5, Issue-2, p. 45.
17. T. Karalis (2020): Planning and Evaluation during Educational disruption: Lessons learned from Covid-19 pandemic for treatment of emergencies in education'. European Journal of Education Studies, Vol-7, Issue-4.
18. The Hindu English Daily Newspaper an article 'The Present notable COVID-19 disaster has triggered history's biggest disruption of education' published on 09-08-2020.
19. UGC Annual Report, 2018-2019.
20. WHO, WHO Corona virus Disease (COVID-19) Dashboard, Retrieved on June-3, 2020.

24

India Joining the Mainstream of Global Standard Higher Education: A Review

Dr K. Krishna Murthy

Abstract

The primary goal of education is to support a nation's enormous expansion and development, the dynamic character of education brought about by global developments necessitates this specific occurrence in due course. As a result of these possibilities, each country's education system became more and more diverse, resulting in the birth of globalisation. Then it became apparent that curriculum needed to be revised to reflect the diverse socio-cultural aspects of the countries being studied. In order to promote relevant education, it aims to establish the importance of globalisation in the selection of relevant curriculum and creative teaching methods in higher education. Several ideas and theories were examined in order to support this study's stated goal. It was found that globalization influences teachers' and curriculums' creative natures, resulting in the dynamic nature of the educational process as a whole. It was therefore proposed that Teachers search out creative ways to boost their knowledge in their professional endeavours. Seminars should be conducted for the teachers in order to emphasize the necessity of increased inventive possibilities both locally and globally. As a result, it was advised that curriculum designers should keep in mind the demands of the society while designing educational curriculums. As a consequence of this, a wide range of people will be able to obtain knowledge since the wall of rigidity in education will be broken down. Due to the new delivery method and curriculum's flexibility, the learners will also be internationally relevant, therefore fulfilling the worldwide benchmark.

Key words: Globalisation, Higher Education, Teachers, Curriculums, Educational process, Professional endeavours, Seminars, Curriculum designers, Society, Educational commodities.

Introduction

Globalisation is the processes that lead to a single global society. The breakdown of borders between the several diversities. Globalisation is the reduction of barriers between countries, allowing for free access to social relations. Globalisation may be described as heightened global social relations that connects distant regions in such a manner that local events are influenced and vice versa. The process through which societies across the globe become more linked, so that what happens in one area of the world affects people and societies in other parts of the world.

These political, economic, cultural, and social events are more intertwined and have a greater influence in a world that is increasingly linked. In this way, the events of other cultures have an ever-increasing and ever-deeper impact on societies throughout the world.

People are becoming more conscious of the decreasing planet in each of these examples. Because of the World Wide Web, you may communicate with Websites all around the world. There are many additional examples, such as email (E-mail) and social media (Facebook, Twitter etc.

We now live in a global village, it is critical that countries' educational institutions and programmes keep pace with the rapidly changing demands of a globalising world by being more flexible, responsive to current technical, economic, and social issues. Adapting education to meet the needs of a rapidly changing world is essential for a peaceful and secure future. As a result, the "Millennial Development Goals" and "Sustainable Development Goals" are now often used interchangeably. This asks for national education programmes to be aligned with global concerns to ensure that the world is a healthier and more secure place.

To provide consistency across different national education systems while also acknowledging the distinct characteristics and problems that each educational system faces is a difficult balance to strike. Global difficulties also need international cooperation and programme to address the challenges. The world's governments and international organisations must make a concerted.

II. Objectives of Global Educational Standards

There are consequences for education, as the context and socio-cultural background of learners are seldom taken into account when conceiving and executing curriculum. In order to deal with this issue, teachers must incorporate lessons on peaceful coexistence in their curriculum in addition to those that emphasize national identity or citizenship.

III. Motivating Ideals for Global Standard Education

It was suggested that:

1. Teachers should look for unique ways to increase their dynamisms in their professional endeavours.

2. Teachers should attend seminars on the necessity of expanding their creative horizons on a national and worldwide scale.
3. The requirements of society should constantly be taken into consideration when curriculum designers design higher level educational curricula for greater efficiency and relevance in education. Government should also contribute their quota in providing the essential provisions that will facilitate the integration of globalisation towards the construction of applicable educational programmes for successful innovation and growth.
4. Education financing should be responsive to worldwide standards.

IV. A Step Towards Global Standard Education

There are strong reasons now for universities to take an integrated strategy to internationalisation rather than a one-dimensional one. Competing for top talent has never been more difficult, and the increased influence of institutional rankings, together with changes in global student flows. In the meanwhile, more and more people are realising the need of intercultural competency in today's increasingly varied and multicultural society, which serves as an additional source of motivation. Student interest in international and intercultural experience is developing as research shows an increasing need for university graduates with better global views and intercultural competency. Both global and more local multicultural concerns are at the centre of internationalisation.

Teaching, research, and service missions may all benefit from internationalisation. It's most effective when seen as a means to the fulfillment of more general business objectives, rather than a goal in and of itself. If internationalisation is considered as a goal in and of itself, it is less likely to be achieved than when it is integrated into university practice.

In order to be a responsible global citizen, we must acknowledge that the challenges we face are from economic, religious, and political issues. If individuals don't perceive themselves as global citizens and aren't ready to work together in new ways and take good action instead of just avoiding bad action, we have no chance of solving these challenges. Being a responsible global citizen involves more than just having a broad set of skills and knowledge. A collection of civic ethics or principles that have been internalised as part of our individual and societal obligation to address.

V. Ethical Part

The long-term advantages of a university education for students' social consciousness, it is necessary to carefully plan and design the curriculum.

The meaning of the word global citizenship may be construed in many ways, and they are not all positive. Every student has access to a wide range of perspectives. For our students to become global citizens who care, we need to do more than just teach them about global issues. It may be a valuable catalyst for curricular globalisation.

VI. Conclusion

Internationalisation in the disciplines is made possible by our contributions individually and together. Some of the ideas presented in this may be utilised to construct learning goals, learning activities, and assessment tasks as part of the process of internationalising the curriculum.

References

1. Anikpo, M.(in Okodudu, S. and Peterside, S.J., 2015). The Academic Legacies of Anikpo: With Reminiscences of Associates and Friends. Port Harcourt. Souldek Consulting.
2. Anthony, G. (1990). The Consequences of Modernity. Stanford: Stanford University Press.
3. Apple, M.F. (1996). Cultural Politics and Education. New York: Teachers College Press.
4. Essiet,U.(2019). Nigerian Curriculum not in tune with 21st Century Challenges Nigerian Vanguard Nov 14 2019 story by Olawole page.
5. Haralambos, H. &Holborn, M. (2008). Sociology: Theories and Perspectives (6th Ed). Collins London.
6. Jacques, H. & Muriel, P. (2000). Globalization and living together: The challenges for educational content in Asia. CBSE – IBE, 2000 (p.136).
7. Childress, L. 2009. "Internationalization plans for higher education institutions," Journal of Studies in International Education, Vol. 13, no. 3, pp. 289–309.
8. Childress, L. 2010. The Twenty-first Century University: Developing Faculty Engagement in Internationalization, Peter Lang, New York.
9. Clifford, V. 2009. "Engaging the disciplines in internationalizing the curriculum," International Journal for Academic Development, Vol. 14, no. 2, pp. 133–143.
10. Coates, H. 2005. "The value of student engagement for higher education quality assurance," Quality in Higher Education, Vol. 11, no. 1, pp. 25–36.
11. Cobbin, P. & Lee, R. 2002, "A micro-journal approach to internationalising the accounting curriculum," Journal of Studies in International Education, Vol. 6, no. 1, pp. 59–77.
12. Escrigas, C., Sanchez, J., Hall, B. &Tandon, R. 2014, "Editors' introduction: Knowledge, engagement and higher education: Contributing to social change," in Higher Education in the World 5: Knowledge, Engagement and Higher Education: Contributing to Social Change, Palgrave Macmillan, Basingstoke, pp. xxxi–xxxix.

25

Impact of Covid-19 on Higher Education in India : A Critical Review

Dr Mahesh Kumar Ganwar

Abstract

The impact of Covid-19 can be seen in every sphere of life. Especially when it comes to education; this is the biggest sector that has been adversely affected by this pandemic. It forced many great nations to enforce lockdown thereby bringing everything to an abrupt halt for a certain period of time. Right from the big businesses to educational institutions this Pandemic has literally altered and devastated the traditional ways of carrying out these things. The educational sector has been fighting to survive the crises. The teaching learning and evaluation methodologies have been completely altered by this pandemic. The digitalisation of education became a necessity in order to provide seamless education. This paper would be discussing the problems faced by the students in India who are pursuing higher education during this pandemic. This paper also tries to find out the positive and negative impact it had on the teaching, learning and evaluation methodologies at undergraduate level and what steps our policymakers have taken in order to provide seamless education to the students who are pursuing higher education in India. Some suggestions have also been pointed out in this paper with regard to how we can further revolutionise the teaching and learning process to improve the experience of both; teachers and learners during the pandemic.

Introduction

On March 11, 2020 World Health Organisation (WHO) declared Covid-19 as a pandemic. Covid-19 has affected more than 4.5 million peoples worldwide (WHO). In India, the first affected case of Covid-19 was detected on January 2020 in the state of Kerala and the affected had travel history from Wuhan, China (Wikipedia). In India, the first death was reported on 12 March, 2020 and the nation observed Janta Curfew for a day on

22 March, 2020. India again observed 14 hours Janta Curfew on May 24 for 21 days. Monitoring the effects of the virus, Indian Government has been extending the lockdown period in different phases and the lockdown 5.0 was declared on April 30 which is effective from 1st June to 30th June 2020. In all the phases of lockdown starting from lockdown 1.0 to lockdown 5.0, the educational institutions throughout the nation have never got any relaxation to start their educational activities. Thus, pandemic Covid-19 impacted significantly on the education sector. According to the UNESCO report, Covid-19 has affected nearly 68 percent of total world. The outbreak of Covid-19 has forced many countries to enforce lockdowns that brought everything to a standstill including the teaching and learning process. The educational sector suffered the most due to this pandemic. This pandemic has made the world to observe social distancing in the public space. Covid-19 was first identified in Wuhan, China and then it gradually started spreading in other parts of the world. It was only in 2020 the WHO declared it as pandemic. It has claimed millions of lives across the world. According to the UNESCO report more than 90 percent of total student population in the world was affected due to the pandemic during the initial phase of its outbreak. It has caused a serious and very deep rooted impact on the social, economic and also psychological life of people in different parts of the world. The guidelines that were issued by the WHO which were ratified by the most of the countries across the world compelled the governments to shut down the institutions of mass gatherings. So along with the educational institutions the academic year end exams and also competitive exams were postponed indefinitely. This step was taken in order to slow down and contain the spread of Corona virus in India by segregating the people who were infected with Covid-19. This process came to be known as Lockdown wherein the Govt. had imposed severe restrictions on the movement and the gatherings of the people in order to control the spread of this airborne disease. So ultimately in this process all the educational institutions closed.

It has raised multiple issues right from the health to the wealth also affecting the day to day functioning of the life due to its rampant spread across the world and India is definitely not an exception to it. The economy has suffered severe setback which can be reflected in different sectors. One of the major and devastating impact this pandemic brought in the global education is, it led to sudden shift of education from classroom teaching to the online mode of teaching and learning that has affected the teaching and learning process in Universities, colleges and schools and thus it has significantly disrupted the higher education sector in India. This shift in education has brought a great change in the pattern of learning with certain positive and negative impacts.

In the case of the country like India this online teaching has registered devastating impact on the lives of those students who are underprivileged and coming from very poor section of the society. In India it has also brought certain severe effects on the conventional learning process of face-to-face interaction even when some technical aids were introduced in the classrooms. However, also it is important to note that there are still certain educational institutions in India which are not very well equipped to the modern technological facilities in the classroom. Thus, we can say that with the introduction of new method of learning through digital mode of learning, learning became very easy to the students as they can sit at home and get access but at the same time some students also had to face problem due to the poor internet connectivity which brings to the notice that even after India is adapting to online learning methods, still there lies an obstacles as entire population donot have access to internet and E-learning facility. Rural people are still deprived of technology. Therefore, it is important to understand that there are positive as well as negative effect on the Indian society. This paper intends to understand the issues that are associated with the higher education in India due to Covid-19 and also to focus on certain drawbacks in the context of online education and its psychological impact on the lives of the students.

Objectives of the Study

To study the Highlight the impact of Covid-19 on higher education sector.

To study the Enlighten various emerging approaches of India for higher education.

To understand the put few suggestions for continuing educational activities of HEIs facing the challenges created by Covid-19.

Methodology

Various reports of national and international agencies on Covid-19 pandemic are searched to collect data for current study. As it is not possible to go outside for data collection due to lockdown, information are collected from different authentic websites, journals and e-contents relating to impact of Covid-19 on higher educational system of India.

Results and Discussion

Around the second week of March 2020, state government across the country began to shut down the schools, colleges due to Covid-19. As we all know that this was the crucial time for students as different University, college examination are usually held during this period and also different entrance test of various universities and competitive examination were to be held during this period. And since there found to be no immediate solution to prevent the outbreak of COVID 19, college, school and university closure had to be made compulsory to prevent the spread of virus. It has affected more than 285 million young learners in India. Students had to face severe problem as they were not aware of the future examination especially students who were in the final year and also those who were to answer entrance test. This closure of educational institutions disrupted the structure of learning.

1. Destabilised all educational activities: Outbreak of Covid-19 has compelled lockdown in every sector including education. The institutions got closed with cease of educational activities and created many challenges for the stake holders (Pravat, 2020a). So, the various activities like admission, examinations, entrance tests, competitive examinations conducted by various boards/schools/colleges/ universities are postponed. Many entrance tests for higher study got cancelled which created a great challenge in the life of a student of higher education. The primary challenge was to continue teaching learning process when students, faculties and staff could no longer be physically present on the campuses. The obvious solution for the institutions was to depend online teaching learning. However, within a relatively short time, HEIs have been able to provide support to the students through online modes. Covid-19 has accelerated adoption of digital technologies to deliver education. It encouraged all teachers and students to become more technology savvy. The HEIs have started conducting orientation programmes, induction meetings and counselling classes with the help of different e-conferencing tools like Google Meet, Skype, Youtube live, Facebook live, WebEx etc. to provide support services to the students. This initiative has taken to create an effective virtual environment of teaching learning and to create motivation among students for online activities. The teachers and students improved the use of electronic media for sharing information by making use of WhatsApp, Google drive, Telegram, Twitter etc. They have been sharing important documents with the group members and creating online local repository also. Students are advised to submit the scanned copies of the assignments to the institution through email. Institutions have also started receiving internship reports and projects through email during the lockdown for Covid-19.

2. Mixed impact on Academic research and Professional Development: Covid-19 has both negative and positive impacts on research. If we take the negative side, it has made impossible for researchers to travel and work together with others nationally and internationally. Some joint research work or project work are made complicated to complete. Some scientific laboratory testing/research work could not be conducted. If we look at the positive side, academicians got much time to improve their theoretical research work. Academicians got acquainted with technological methods and improved their research. Webinars and e-conferences became normal methods for sharing expertise among students and academicians around the globe with similar issues. They could get much time to concentrate on professional development by doing research and to improve knowledge by sharing ideas through webinars and e-conferences. They enhanced their technical skill and could get the scope for publishing articles in journals, publishing books in this free time.

3. Severely affected the educational assessment system: Most of the external examinations have been postponed and almost all the internal assessments have been cancelled. The cancellation of assessments has negative impact on students' learning. Many institutions have been managing the internal assessments through online mode using different digital tools but the postponement of the external assessments, has a direct impact on the educational and occupational future of students' life. This uncertainty has created anxiety among students as they are stuck in the same grade/ class without promotion. Similarly, many students who had appeared final/ board examinations would suffer a lot as by the time they get their certificates, it might be too late for them to apply for the forthcoming academic year in other countries due to lockdown.

4. Reduced employment opportunities: Many entrance tests job recruitments got cancelled which created negative impact with a great challenge in the life of a student of higher education. The Indians who have been doing their jobs abroad became upset of their job withdrawal also. In India, there is no recruitment in Govt. sector and fresh graduates are in pressure of fearing withdrawal of job offers from corporate sectors because of the pandemic situation. Many students may lose their jobs from India and overseas. The pass out students may not get their job outside India due to various restrictions caused by Covid-19. All these facts imply towards increase of unemployment rate due to this pandemic. With increase of unemployment situation, the interest for education may gradually decrease as people struggle for food rather than education.

- **Swayam** provides Massive Open Online Courses (MOOCs) with 140 universities approved credit transfer feature. Swayam Prabha provides high quality educational programmes through 32 DTH channels transmitting educational contents. e-PG Pathshala (https:/ /epgp.inflibnet.ac.in/) is for postgraduate students. Postgraduate students can access this platform for e-books, online courses and study materials. The details of these three digital platforms are described by the author in the previous paper.

- **National Digital Library of India (NDLI)** is a repository of e-content on multiple disciplines for all kinds of users like students (of all levels), teachers, researchers, librarians, library users, professionals, differently-abled users and all other lifelong learners. It is being developed at Indian Institute of Technology Kharagpur. It is designed to help students to prepare for entrance and competitive examinations, to enable people to learn and prepare from best practices from all over the world and to facilitate researchers to perform inter-linked exploration from multiple sources. It is a virtual repository of learning resources with a single-window search facility. It is also available to access through mobile apps.
- **e-Yantra** provides hands on experience on embedded systems. It has about 380 Lab and made 2300+ colleges benefited.
- which is developed to promote open-source software for education as well as professional use.
- **Virtual Labs** has developed web-enabled curriculum-based experiments designed for remote operation. It has over 100 Virtual Labs consisting of approximately 700+ web-enabled experiments which are designed for remote-operation. It provides remote- access to Labs in various disciplines of Science and Engineering. These Virtual Labs caters to students at the undergraduate level, postgraduate level as well as to research scholars.
- **National Educational Alliance for Technology (NEAT)** is an initiative for skilling of learners in latest technologies through a Public-Private partnership model between the Government (through its implementing agency AICTE) and the Education Technology companies of India. It brings the best technological products in education pedagogy on a single platform for the convenience of learners.

Post Covid-19 Trends of Higher Education in India

1. May encourage personalised learning: Learning may not be confined to classes or to any specific boundaries. Students may be the virtual learners with one teacher leading dozens of students in the new age. The learning modules may be modified to suit different learning styles and the learning contents may come from different sources to meet the learners' aspirations and needs. Students may pursue their learning in the new paradigm as per their choice. Many parents may be reluctant to send back their children to schools/colleges suddenly after the end of lockdown. Some poor family parents who have lost their livelihood during the pandemic may not be able to afford the expenditure to send their children to institutions. This may lead to home education for another few months. Student safety and well-being issues are important deciding factors for students and their parents for movement to international institutions for higher study. New modes of social distancing will continue for quite some time and may affect on-campus face-to-face teaching learning. Most of the parents will prefer to find workable alternatives closer to their home and may restrict for less movement within the country due to the pandemic. The international education has also been affected by the crisis. Many international universities have been closed and are delivering all educational activities online. Many international conferences in higher education have been cancelled or turned into a series of webinars. So, the national and international student movement may be diminished.

2. Demand for Open and Distance Learning (ODL) and online learning may grow. Covid-19 has forced the human society to maintain social distancing. It has created more challenges to continue teaching learning by maintaining social distancing. To meet these challenges there is more demand for ODL and online modes of education and the same trend may continue in future also. Blended learning combines both face-to-face and online learning modes. Covid-19 has accelerated adoption of digital technologies to deliver education and encouraged the educational institutions to move towards blended mode of learning. All teachers and students became more technology savvy. The traditional face-to-face mode with post Covid-19 technology mode will lead the education towards blended mode of teaching learning and it may transform the structure of the education system. In India, lots of students or their parents take education loans for higher education. If the employment market does not pick up, student debt crises may rise and create serious issue. Students may face increased stress, anxiety and depression due to their student loans. There is no recruitment in Govt. sector and fresh graduates fear withdrawal of their job offers from private sectors because of the pandemic Covid-19. Many Indians might have returned home after losing their jobs overseas due to Covid-19. Hence, the fresh students who are likely to enter the job market shortly may face difficulty in getting suitable employment.

Conclusion

The purpose of education is to enable oneself to better the world in which they live. Technology today has become need of an hour. It is difficult to imagine colleges and university education without the use of digital resources which has provided different educational and academic information. However it is also necessary to understand that it shouldn't reinforce structures of power and inequality. It should not create digital divide between rich and poor. As we cannot expect in country like India to have availability of all required resources due to different socio-economic conditions in India. Online mode of learning can be the best mode of teaching if it can be accessed by all the sections of the society however it can pose threat if certain section of society cannot avail this facility and thus exclusion. It is therefore important to take cognizance of online education and plan for interventions that will prioritize greater inclusivity, connectivity and equitability. It is important that colleges and University understands the experience and issues of the students and prepare according to the further and design the study pattern in such a way that all students benefits.

References

1. Pravat Ku Jena. Online learning during lockdown period for Covid-19 in India. International Journal of Multidisciplinary Educational Research. 2020c; 9, 5(8): 82-92.
2. Sandhya Ramesh. What it means for Covid to never go away and become endemic-like HIV, malaria, measles, 2020. Retrieved on June 2, 2020 from https://theprint.in/health/what-it-means-for-covid-to- never-go-away-and-become-endemic- like-hiv-malaria- measles/423217/
3. Freedman, J. L. (1984). The effect of television violence on aggressiveness. Psychological Bulletin, 96, 227-246.
4. Friedrich, L. K., & Stein, A. H. (1973). Aggressive and pro-social television programmes and the natural behavior of preschool children. Monographs of the Society for Research in Child Development, 38(4, Serial No. 151).
5. Friedrich-Cofer, L., & Huston, A. C. (1986). Television violence and aggression: the debate continues. Psychological Bulletin, 100(3), 364-371.
6. Gopinath, M. (2020, june 10). Covid-19 crisis brings opportunity to expand the autonomy of public universities. *The Indian Express*.
7. Gopinathan, K. R. (2015 , April 19). Is online the way forward? *The Hindu*.

26

Modernisation of Higher Education towards Achieving Equity

Dr Mohanraj N. Pattar & Dr Premchand Chavan

Abstract

In India, higher education is being imparted since ancient years as there are citations and remains of ancient universities. UGC has been established after independence to organise and manage higher education in India after independence. Due to globalisation and privatisation, there is increase in numbers of universities and higher educational institutions. Still, few classes of society are deprived from higher education and it is against equitable access to higher education. Further, many of the universities are with conventional streams of subjects which are not worth to suit modern employment requirements. Hence, it is suggested to introduce new courses based on skills required for the present employment requirements. For this purpose, scientific design of curriculum and courses based on skills that are required for jobs is essential.

Introduction

Education is a process by which a person's body, mind and character are formed and strengthened. It is bringing of head, heart and mind together and thus enabling a person to develop an all round personality identifying the best in him or her. Higher education in India has expanded very rapidly in the last six decades after independence yet it is not equally accessible to all. India is today one of the fastest developing countries of the world with the annual growth rate going above 9 percent. Still a large section of the population remains illiterate and a large number of children's do not get even primary education. This is not only excluded a large section of the population from contributing to the development of the country fully but it has also prevented them from utilising the benefits of whatever development have taken place for the benefit of the people (Sheikh, 2017).

Higher education has been given an important position in the Indian society since ancient days. Fa-Hien and Huen Tsang, Chinese travellers who visited India and they were found important education centres at Takshashila, Kanchipura, Nalanda, Vikramashila and such other places, which were established between Fifth to Sixth Century BC. There were also ancient education centres such as Nagavi Vishwavidyalaya in Kalaburagi district of Karnataka.

The new approach to higher education has been given by the British during 1818 when College of English Education was started in Serampore, Calcutta. Later, McCauley's minute (1835) promoted English education in India. Charles Woods' Dispatch (1854) helped to establish the Universities at Calcutta, Bombay and Madras in 1857 and the Government has provided Grants to these universities. Hunter Commission is the major milestone in higher education which provided major impetus to higher educational development in India.

There were 20 Universities and 500 affiliated colleges with 0.2 million students studying in these colleges and Universities in 1947. After independence, Radhakrishnan Commission (1948-49) recommended for establishment of the University Grants Commission (UGC). Later, Secondary Education Commission (1952), the National Policy on Education (1986) and such other commissions were set up for the developmental plans in higher education. As a result, 47 Central Universities, 28 Institutions of National Importance, 347 State Universities, 130 Deemed Universities, 237 Private Universities, and more than 34000 colleges were imparting higher education and research in India in 2016.

Problems in Higher Education

Higher education has been facing many of the problems and challenges in modern period especially after globalisation. Higher educational disparity is one of the most significant problem faced in India. Due to lower status of women, their enrolment to higher education and research courses is lower and discriminatory. It is due to conventional ideas and beliefs that women are having secondary status, they are for household work and don't need education and even many would think that women's education is just additional economic burden. Hence, there is gender inequality in higher education. Globalisation has encouraged privatization so as to attain quality. Of course, privatisation has led competition and modernisation of higher education, on the other hand, it has led to commercialisation of higher education and as a result, higher education has become dream for poor people. The main drawback is the high tuition fees associated with it. Most parents belonging to the lower middle class with more than one child to educate usually find it impossible to afford such a luxury. Privatised institutions are being symbolised by the rich and elite sections of our society (Kaur and Kaur, 2018).

There is also challenge of enrolment as less than 20 percent of the entire Indian population is getting higher education and there is disparity on access to higher education based on caste, gender, religion, class, etc. Few of the States have also neglected the recruitment of teachers to universities, which has become decrease in quality of higher education. Limited numbers of universities and higher education institutions, that is only 722 are imparting higher education and when compared to population, the total institutions are needed at least 1500 universities.

On the nature of higher education, it is found that more concentration is made by majority of the universities on conventional and theory based subjects rather than skills and technology oriented or even employment oriented higher education. Hence, the quality of education in terms of needs of present employment is not matched. The present day education is neither imparting true knowledge of life and nor improving the talent of a student by which one can achieve laurels in the field one is interested (Sharanabasappa and Kadamudimatha, 2017).

Modernisation of Higher Education: Towards Equity and Balanced Development

As there are limited numbers of universities and institutes of higher education, it is suggested to establish more universities to impart higher education. Of course, participation of private sector is important to increase quality and competition in higher education, but restriction on the fees charged by these private educational institutions should be put, so that poor can get qualitative education. Reservations for the marginalised groups such as scheduled castes, scheduled tribes, women, other backward classes, etc should be given for the admission in private universities and higher educational institutions. More and scholarships and fellowships are essentially needed by the Government to encourage higher education of all groups in India.

With a few exceptions, India's colleges and universities have grown into enormous, under-funded, and unmanageable institutions. Politics has intruded into campus life at several of them, influencing academic appointments and decisions at many levels. Underfunding of libraries, information technology, laboratories, and classrooms makes providing high-quality training and engaging in cutting-edge research extremely difficult. The rises in the number of part-time teachers and the freeze on new full-time appointments in many places have affected morale in the academic profession. The lack of accountability means that teaching and research performance is seldom measured. There are minimal incentives to perform under this system. Bureaucratic inertia hampers change. Student unrest and occasional faculty agitation disrupt operations. Nevertheless, with a semblance of normality, faculty administrators are able to provide teaching, coordinate examinations, and award degrees (Arunachalam, 2010).

It is essential to revise curriculum of all the courses including the change of subjects as per the interests of the students and nature of employment opportunities is essential. For this purpose, there is need to analyse the skills required for different jobs that are available and generated in India. Then, skills required for different jobs and works should be ascertained and based on such needs, the curriculum to different courses should be designed. New courses by freedom of choice of subjects to students should be introduced. Student-centred education and employment of dynamic methods of education will require from teachers new attitudes and new skills.

The combination of arts subjects and computer science and science and humanities or literature should be introduced so that such courses could be useful for the students to do jobs after recruitment in some companies which would reduce unnecessary rush to higher education. The programme must be focused on graduate studies and research and developing strategies and mechanisms for the rapid and efficient transfer of knowledge and for its application to specific national and local conditions and needs.

There is need to identify the Corporate Social Responsibility, where the corporate sector helps the educational institutions and universities in building up of higher education infrastructure and also increase the employment at corporate organisations based on the skills imparted by the universities and higher educational institutions. In this respect, the corporate organisations have to come forward and collaborate with universities. Imparting knowledge should be one of the important aspects needed in higher education rather than just completing syllabus and awarding degrees. For this purpose, there is need for reform examination system, modernisation of library and learning facilities.

It is strongly suggested to the Government to allot and release funds liberally to the universities and higher educational institutions so as to build modernised infrastructure. There is need for constant and continuous inspection of the universities and higher educational institutions by autonomous committees and commissions so as to measure quality in terms of curriculum, examinations, skills imparted through various courses, industry-university collaborations, modernisation, library, etc.

Concluding Remarks

There is need to revise the higher education by adopting scientific and equitable means. For this purpose, it is essential to provide adequate financial resources to universities and higher educational institutions by the Government. Further, reservation is essential for all the classes of society in admissions so as to encourage equity in higher education. Scholarships and fellowships are needed to encourage education of the poor. The industries should analyse the skills required for jobs and employment and collaborate with universities so that these institutions can impart essential skills needed for jobs. For this purpose, more job and profession-oriented courses are essentially to be introduced at universities. There is need to revise curriculum of existing courses and introduce new courses based on job-oriented skills on the part of the universities. Continuous modernization of teaching practices and library infrastructure is needed to impart modern knowledge to students and researchers. The Government has to set up autonomous committees and commissions regularly, so as to ensure quality and equitable higher education of the universities and institutions of higher education.

References

1. Arunachalam, P (2010): Higher Education Sector in India: Issues and Imperatives. ***Journal of Global Economy***, 6(4), July-August 2010, pp. 267-291.
2. Kaur, Navpreet and Kaur, Navneet (2018): Privatization and Commercialization of Higher Education. ***International Journal of Academic Research and Development***, 3(1), January 2018, pp. 456-458.
3. Sharanabasappa, CB and Kadamudimatha, Basavaraj Nagesh (2017): A Study on Higher Education in India: Issues, Challenges and Directions. ***International Journal of Multidisciplinary Research and Development***, 4(2), February 2017, pp. 188-191.
4. Sheikh, Younis Ahmad (2017): Higher Education in India: Challenges and Opportunities. ***Journal of Education and Practice***, 8(1), 2017, pp. 39-42.

27

Collaborative Learning Assessment

Dr Mrunali N. Deshpande (Lilhare)

Abstract

Many students cringe and groan when told that they will need to work in a group. However, group work has been found to be good for students and good for teachers. Employers want college graduates to have developed teamwork skills. Additionally, students who participate in collaborative learning get better grades, are more satisfied with their education, and are more likely to remain in college. This paper will discuss the use of group work in higher education.

Teaching and learning in higher education are changing. Active learning has become an important focus in this time of pedagogical change. While the term encompasses a broad array of practices, collaborative learning, or small group work, remains an important element of active learning theory and practice. Research suggests that students learn best when they are actively involved in the process (Davis, 1993). According to Wasley (2006), "Students who participate in collaborative learning and educational activities outside the classroom and who interact more with faculty members get better grades, are more satisfied with their education, and are more likely to remain in college" (p. A39). A collaborative learning environment, as opposed to a passive learning environment, helps students learn more actively and effectively (Murphy, Mahoney, Chen, Mendoza-Diaz & Yang, 2005). Additionally, research also shows that employers want college graduates to possess the ability to work in groups and have developed suitable teamwork skills (Blowers, 2000). This paper is designed to offer suggestions on how to use small groups in order to facilitate learning and instructional diversity in face-to-face classes. It will begin with an overview of the advantages and disadvantages of working in a group and then discuss some of the methods available to enhance group learning and communication. It will also provide some suggestions for evaluating and assessing group work. While many people detest the mere suggestion of group work, it can be an effective tool if used appropriately.

Keywords : Group work, collaborative learning, higher education pedagogy

Advantages

There are six advantages to working in a group: 1. Groups have more information than a single individual. Groups have a greater well of resources to tap and more information available because of the variety of backgrounds and experiences. 2. Groups stimulate creativity. In regard to problem solving, the old adage can be applied that "two heads are better than one." 3. People remember group discussions better. Group learning fosters learning and comprehension. Students working in small groups have a tendency to learn more of what is taught and retain it longer than when the same material is presented in other instructional formats (Barkley, Cross & Major, 2005; Davis, 1993). 4. Decisions that students help make yield greater satisfaction. Research suggests that students who are engaged in group problem solving are more committed to the solution and are better satisfied with their participation in the group than those who were not involved. 5. Students gain a better understanding of themselves. Group work allows people to gain a more accurate picture of how others see them. The feedback that they receive may help them better evaluate their interpersonal behaviour. 6. Team work is highly valued by employers. Well developed interpersonal skills were listed by employers among the top 10 skills sought after in university graduates (Graduate Outlook Survey, 2010).

Overall, effective student participation in group work is an important learning outcome for higher education courses (Elgort, Smith & Toland, 2008). Although many students feel as though they can accomplish assignments better by themselves rather than in a group, instructors find that group work helps the students apply knowledge (Elgort, Smith & Toland, 2008). However, merely assigning a group does not itself create critical thinking outcomes. Therefore, the instructor must be cognizant of how best to facilitate effective collaborative learning environments. There are four stages of group work. First, the instructor must decide that he/she wants to incorporate group work into the class. The group work should be designed into the syllabus. The second stage involves teaching the students to work in a group. Instructors cannot assume that students know how to work together, structure time, and delegate tasks. The instructor must be able to teach the students how to work proactively in groups. This leads to the third stage, which involves monitoring the groups. The last stage, and the most important to the students, is the assessment of the group. The instructor must develop a concrete rubric for grading the students.

Getting Started: The best place to start group work (much like anything else) is at the beginning. When developing a course syllabus, the instructor can determine what topics and theme lend themselves to group work. This is the time that instructors can think about how they will form their groups, help negotiate the group process, and decide how to evaluate the final product. Johnson, Johnson and Smith (1991) suggest that group tasks should be integral to the course objectives. This means that the group work should complement the learning objectives outlined in the syllabus. If one of the learning objectives is to promote critical thinking skills or writing enhancement, then the group work should support these areas.

Group size: The dynamics of group size is an important component of group work. A small group is often considered to consist of three or more people (Beebe & Masterson, 2003). Groups of two are called dyads and are not encouraged for group work because there are not a sufficient number of individuals to generate creativity and a diversity of ideas (Csernica *et al.*, 2002). In general, it is suggested that groups of four or five members tend to work best (Davis, 1993). However, Csernica *et al.* (2002) suggests that three or four members are more appropriate. Larger groups decrease each members opportunity to participate and often results in some members not actively contributing to the group. In situations where there is a shorter amount of time available to complete a group task, such as an inclass collaborative learning exercise, it is suggested that smaller groups are more appro-Assigning a Group Assigning the members of the group is integral to the success of the group. Some faculty members prefer to randomly assign students to groups. This has the advantage of maximizing heterogeneity of the group (Davis, 1993) and is an effective way of assigning group member in large classrooms. If the class size is small and the instructor is familiar with most of the students, the instructor can select the group members based on known attributes of the class. For example, the instructor can form the groups while taking to account performance levels, academic strengths and weaknesses, ethnicity, and gender (Connery, 1988). Additionally, some instructors allow the class the self-select their group; however, this has some disadvantages. Self selected groups often gravitate toward friends and roommates (Csernica *et al.*, 2002). This can result in the students self segregating and spending more time socialising than working on the group project (Cooper, 1990). Research suggests that groups which are assigned by the instructor tend to perform better than self-selected groups (Felder & Brent, 2001).

Teaching Students: It is difficult for teachers to design and implement group work effectively, and it is difficult for students to foster the group process, especially if they do not have the skills to make effective use of group work. Many students have never worked in a group before or lack the skills to work with others. Instructors cannot assume that students know how to work together, structure time, or delegate tasks. There are several ways that instructors can help. First, the instructor should make certain that each student understands the assignment. Students should know the purpose of the project, the learning objective, and the skills that need to be developed through group work. Successful group work is easier if the students know how the assignment relates to the course content and what the final product is supposed to be (Davis, 1993). Second, the instructor needs to reinforce listening skills and the proper methods to give and receive constructive criticism. These skills can be discussed in class and modeled during class activities. Some faculty use various exercises that are geared toward helping students gain skills to work in groups (Fiechtner & Davis, 1992). Small in-class group activities help reinforce cohesion and group unity Third, the instructor needs to help the students manage conflict and disagreements. The instructor should avoid breaking up the groups (this will be discussed in more detail later in this paper). When a group is not working well together, the students need to learn how to communicate effectively and establish goals for a successful group (Davis, 1993).

Monitoring the Group Process: One method to help groups succeed is to ask each group to devise a plan of action (Davis, 1993). The plan of action involved assigning roles and responsibilities among the group members. Each member should have a role, such as the note take or the group spokesman. The instructor can review each group's written plan of action or meet with each group individually and discuss their plan. Another method to help monitor a group's progress is to ask them to submit weekly progress reports. These reports (or weekly meeting notes) should outline what the group discussed, who attended the meeting, and the objectives set for the next week. In this manner, the instructor can monitor the group's activities and progress throughout the semester and assess the level of involvement from each member. Group Dissonance Groups will not always work well together. Some groups lack motivation, strong leadership, or simply have personality conflicts. Even when it appears that a group is falling apart, it is important to avoid breaking up the group. Not only will the group dynamics of the original group be affected if the members are reassigned, but the addition of members to other groups will disrupt their dynamics as well (Davis, 1993). One way to help prevent conflict and group members who shirk duties is to keep the group small. It is difficult to be a "loafer" or a "slacker" in a small group (Davis, 1993). Additionally, matching work assignment to skill sets will help separate the "loafers" from the students who are generally struggling (Freeman & Greenacre, 2011). Freeman and Greenacre (2011) suggest that instructors should help the students understand the benefits of working together as a group for the group as a whole, which will help students who are struggling (Freeman & Greenacre, 2011). Furthermore, the group should be encouraged to have assigned roles and responsibilities. It is more difficult to be a slacker if the goals are clearly outlined for each member. It is necessary to help a group work through disagreements and find resolution. Simply breaking up the group does not encourage the students to work though differences. Freeman and Greenacre (2011) suggest that group interventions should be aimed at the destructive group member, focus on the behaviour and not the person, and address the benefits of the group process for the group as a whole. Barkley et al. (2005) recommend designing the coursework in such a way that the success of the individual relies on the success of the group.

Evaluation: Evaluating a group is a difficult task and the instructor should have a clear idea of how he/she wants to evaluate the group work. First, the instructor should decide what is being evaluated: the final product, the process, or both. Next, it is necessary to deicide who assigns the grade: the students, the instructor, or both. Some faculty members assign each member of a group the same grade, which may promote unhappiness if some members devote more time and effort to the group and get the same grade. Some instructors assign each group member an individual grade, which may or may not foster competition within the group and may undermine the group solidarity (Davis, 1993). If the group is graded as a whole, it is suggested that the project or presentation should not count for more than a small percentage of the student's final grade (Cooper, 1990; Johnson, Johnson & Smith, 1991). If the aspect of process is going to be evaluated, it is important to give the students an opportunity to assess the effectiveness of their group. At the end of the process, they should be able to list their contributions, their group member's contributions, and the process as a whole. They should be able to identify the aspects that worked and the aspects that did not work. The student's group assessment allows the instructor to evaluate the group process and apply the most effective methods to future group projects. In the aspect of assessment, it is vital that the students know and understand how they will be evaluated. One method used to convey this information is with a structured grading rubric. A rubric is a scoring tool which lists the criteria by which a paper or presentation will be graded. The rubric lists, not only the criteria by which the work is judged, but also the student's mastery of the material (Finson & Ormsbee, 1998). Stevens and Levi (2005) advocate the use of rubrics because they: convey expectations to the students, help students focus their efforts, improve student achievement, reduce grading time for the instructor and improve the effectiveness of feedback. If the instructor is interested in assessing the group process and final product, two separate rubrics need to be created. For the process, the evaluation criteria should represent the learning objectives for class and for the group. Process evaluation might include: attendance and participation in meetings, time management skills, active listening, evidence of cooperative behaviour, and professionalism and engagement with the task. For evaluating the effectiveness of the product, a more concrete grading rubric might be necessary. The criteria can be outlined based on content, structure, organisation, accuracy, thoroughness, and general mechanics. Rubrics can be helpful for both students and instructors; they outline expectations and allow instructors to assign grades on a more objective basis. Rubrics provide detailed breakdowns of points that are awarded for each criterion and how those points are awarded. Additionally, rubrics are useful beyond grading; they also help students conceptualise the assignment (Mckeown, 2011). The instructor knows what the end product should look like, and it is his or her responsibility to effectively convey that expectation to the students (Finson & Ormsbee, 1998).

Conclusion

There is a well of information about group work and the benefits of collaborative learning. When students spend time meeting in groups, they are able to achieve a deeper learning themes covered in class as well as develop skills, such as writing and communication (Light, 2001). Wright and Lawson (2005) found that the bridging of in-and outside-class work encourages students to spend more time preparing for class, and having conversations with team members outside of regular class time. One of the most recent trends in collaborative learning appears to be the use of technology to advance group work. Elgort, Smith and Toland (2008) utilised the use of wikis in a class and found that most wikis encouraged student participation and group involvement, but did not counteract student preference to work alone rather than in a group. Additionally, many instructors use online discussion forums in their face-to-face classes to foster participation and engagement (Wright & Lawson, 2005). This has the advantage of engaging commuter students and students who have jobs in addition to taking classes. Utilising online or web based might help resistant students engage in and benefit from group work. Overall, it seems clear that when it comes to group work, the whole is greater than the sum of its parts. While creating, monitoring, and evaluating groups is a recursive process, active learning techniques are beneficial for students. Supplementing lectures with group work helps students feel engaged and subsequently learn more (Payne, MonlTurner, Smith & Sumter, 2004). Group work helps students develop teamwork skills and social interactions as well as learning about various backgrounds, culture, beliefs, and attitudes (Payne et al., 2004). Group work does not have to yield "group hate" and as long as the instructor is properly prepared to introduce and facilitate group involvement and participation, group work can produce very positive and lasting results. References Barkley, E. F., Cross, K. P., & Major, C. H. (2005). Collaborative learning techniques: A handbook for college faculty. San Francisco; Jossey-Bass Publishers. Beebe, S. A., & Masterson, J. T. (2003). Communicating in small groups. Pearson Education Inc. Boston: Massachusetts.

References

1. Connery, B. A. (1988). Group Work and Collaborative Writing. Teaching at Davis, 14(1), pp. 2-4. (Publication of the Teaching Resources Center, University of California at Davis)
2. Cooper, J. (1990). Cooperative learning and college teaching: tips from the trenches. Teaching Professor, 4(5), 1-2.
3. Davis, B. G. (1993). Tools for Teaching. Jossey-Bass Inc., San Francisco: California.
4. Elgort, I., Smith, A. G., & Toland, J. (2008). Is wiki an effective platform for group course work? Australasian Journal of Educational Technology, 24(2), 195-210.
5. Felder, R.M. and Brent, R. (2001). Effective strategies for cooperative learning. Journal of Cooperation & Collaboration in College Teaching, 10(2), 69–75.
6. Fiechtner, S. B., & Davis, E. A. (1992). Why some groups fail: A survey of students' experiences with learning groups. In A. Goodsell, M. Maher, V. Tinto, and Associates (eds.), Collaborative Learning: A Sourcebook for Higher Education. University Park: National Center on Postsecondary Teaching, Learning, and Assessment, Pennsylvania State University.

28

Role of Technology in Education Role in Media and Society

Dr N. Manikyarao

Abstract

Social network tools afford students and institutions with multiple opportunities to improve learning methods. Through these networks, you can incorporate social media plugins that enable sharing and interaction. Students can benefit from online tutorials through YouTube, online courses delivered by universities abroad through Skype and a wide array of resources that are shared through social networks. There is valuable knowledge to be gained through social media such as analytics and insights on various topics or issues for study purposes. The great thing about using social media in education is that you soon learn who the experts are in different fields and subjects. When you start following these experts you learn more and gain useful content from them, this empowers you to produce great results. Teachers also use social media as a medium to get new resources to support their lessons, activities to teach particular concepts, bulletin board ideas, information on new apps to do a follow up of certain topics as well as to network and know what is happening in schools all over the world. Media plays an effective and essential role for running the show of any formal or informal teaching-learning process. Communicating is sharing information or providing entertainment by speaking, writing, or other methods. Mass media is important type of communication to send message to large audience. Books are the one of the oldest methods of mass communication. The development of modern technologies there were many media that have been developed and used for educational development. Present day functioning of schools has been very much influenced by the media, especially by electronic media after globalisation of economy and culture. Penetration of television channels and increase in the awareness of general public due to open knowledge.

Keyword : education, social media, class room teaching,

Introduction

Education is the process of learning and knowing, which is not restricted to our school text-books. It is a holistic process and continues through our life. Even the regular happenings and events around us educate us, in one or the other way. It would not be an exaggeration to say that the existence of human beings is fruitless without education. An educated person has the ability to change the world, as he/she is brimming with confidence and assured of making the right moves. It Makes Better Citizens, Ensures a Productive Future, Opens New Vistas, Spreads Awareness, Helps in Decision-Making, Bolsters Confidence. The term media is derived from Medium, which means carrier or mode. Media denotes an item specifically designed to reach a large audience or viewers.

The term was first used with the advent of newspapers and magazines. However, with the passage of time, the term broadened by the inventions of radio, TV, cinemas and Internet. In the world of today, media has become almost as necessary as food and clothing. It is true that media is playing an outstanding role in strengthening the society. Its duty is to inform, educate and entertain the people. It helps us to know current situation around the world. The media has a strong social and cultural impact upon society. Because of its inherent ability to reach large number of public, it is widely used to convey message to build public opinion and awareness.

The role of media in education is evident today by the number of computer labs, television sets and libraries that have become part of curriculum in most schools today. Media comes in different forms and each form affects the way students learn and interpret information. Media has brought the world closer (globalisation) so that now students from different universities in different parts of the world are connected through a mere internet connection. Amidst the information revolution mass media has become such a massive part of our lives.

Objectives

Using media requires that the instructor step outside of the traditional lecture method and facilitate learning by encouraging students to learn through the media. This approach works best when students are primed. If students are not adequately informed about what they are expected them to learn, they will struggle to make the connection between the learning objectives and the media that they are exposed to.

Social Media in Education

Today, we can see education institutions adapting these developments into their systems and relying on group resources and mechanisms to improve student life. The use of social media in education helps students, teachers and parents to get more useful information, to connect with learning groups and other educational systems that make education convenient.

Social media has the ability to broaden your perspective on various subjects and gives illuminating, instant content that is new. Learning colleges have the ability to connect with students through social media networks such as Facebook, Google Plus groups, and YouTube. These channels can be used to communicate campus news, make announcements and provide students with useful information. This builds engagement between the college and students which help tackle many student issues through the group interactions.

Institutions can share supportive and positive posts that reach all students that are connected to the networks and pages. You can initiate hash tags on social media to engage students and online discussions that are helpful. A video is a prominent tool in social media trends that is effective and you can use it to share useful videos that inspire students and help them in their course subjects.

Through social mediums such as YouTube, Facebook or Instagram live video the engagements between students and the institution can be sustained. The benefits of social media in the education process don't have to stop at the teacher-student relationship. There are a lot of other benefits that can be extracted from the use of social networking at higher levels as well. For example, principals or administrators can find a new way to integrate social media. Like sharing school news via social networks, holding an online meeting with the parents or even starting fundraising for different projects.

Social media offers the audience and subject monitoring tools that are useful and it is one of the best platforms to extract data. You can find out how the majority people feel about a particular topic by creating Instagram/ Facebook Polls, or conduct a survey using Google Forms or Survey monkey, or how experts perceive and advice on specific issues by using forums like Quora.

Learning management systems (LMS) is networking software that delivers educational programmes and gives institutions other administrative activities. Social media learning in LMS can include instant chat functions, video, forums to share info and other lesson resources to help students.

Role of media in education: Television programmes, internet websites, feature-length films, newspapers, music tapes and CDs, magazines, billboards, radio programmes: essentially, a tool/technology which is used by someone to transmit a message to a large external audience is called mass media. John Dewey stated that education could not be limited within teacher and taught without social environment. So mass media is one such potent force in the social environment of education. Through modern electronic techniques and technologies, mass media prove that education is, really comprehensive not confined within four walls of the classroom. Really, mass media are the educational medium for the mass and mass education. Irrespective of caste, colour, geographical, sociological, economical diversities mass media prove as an important means for the education to all. Mankind gets a great deal of information from the widespread mass media i.e. newspaper, TV, radio, magazines, journals, films, etc. It is estimated that mass media may substitute the real classroom teaching in future.

The Use of Media in Teaching – Learning Process

Learning is a process to acquire knowledge. It needs hard work and sometimes will make students frustrated and get bored, so that they lose their attention to a lesson. In this case, the use of media in teaching- learning process is needed to attract students' attention and to make teaching learning activities more interesting and also effective. The use of media in teaching-learning process is not a new thing. Many teachers know that media will be helpful. Usually use of media is very useful to teach social studies by this we can use pictures from encyclopaedia or else, a globe, a map, and internet to teach social studies. The students had to find all-important information including the map, flag, landmark, famous buildings, mountains, traditions, etc. By using media in teaching, students' improvement can be seen clearly.

The use of media in teaching- learning process has also several advantages. Media could raise the students' interest of the lesson and media is important to lead students' attention. Media increase students' responsibility to control their own learning. In brief, we can say that the use of media in teaching- learning activity is good.

The Advantages of Using Media

- Many media sources (feature films, music videos, visualisations, news stories) have very high production quality capable of showcasing complex ideas in a short period of time. This helps develop quantitative reasoning.
- Media offers both cognitive and affective experiences. It can provoke discussion, an assessment of one's values, and an

assessment of self if the scenes have strong emotional content.

- The uses of media sources help connect learners with events that are culturally relevant. As a result, a positive consequence of utilising media is that instructors must keep their materials and examples up-to-date.
- News stories can be used to connect theories taught in the classroom with real world events and policies.

The Advantages of Media for Students

- Popular media (films, music, YouTube) are a familiar medium to students that helps gain attention and maintain student interest in the theories and concepts under discussion. Students can see the theories and concepts in action. In more than a figurative sense, theories and concepts leap from the screen.
- Students can hone their analytical skills by analyzing media using the theories and concepts they are studying.
- The use of media in the classroom enables students to see concepts and new examples when they are watching television, listening to music, or are at the movies with friends.
- Students can experience worlds beyond their own, especially if the media is sharply different from their local environment.

The Advantages of Using Social Media in the Classroom

- Interaction using social media provides students with a sense of belonging and creates bonds between students and their peers, and between students and the instructor.
- Students likely have some prior familiarity with sites such as Facebook or MySpace, lowering the "learning-curve" associated with using a new technology.
- Wikis and blogs provide avenues to increase collaboration between students. For additional reading consider: Whither the Wikis? and five Strategies for Using Wikis in the Classroom.

Using Social Media in the Classroom

- Students involved in projects can blog about their experiences.
- Social media content creators must protect the copyrights of others (see the page on cautions for more info).
- In the case of a wiki or a blog, clear authorship must be determined and maintained.

- Clear grading criteria must be provided to students to encourage their participation in the use of social media.
- An extensive list of best practices may be found on the Edutastic blog.

The Importance of Media in the Classroom

Media in the classroom engage students in learning and provide a richer experience. Media are useful tools for illustrating a lesson, allowing students to see examples of what they are learning. Interactive media such as Smart Boards allow students to move items on a screen for illustrative purposes. Students view media as exciting learning aids, making learning entertaining and less monotonous, according to the report "Benefits and Risks of Media and Technology in the Classroom" from the UCLA Office of Instructional Development.

Conclusion

The media has the power of educating people, the good and the bad. Since it affect the eyes, the ears and the mind simultaneously nothing can overcome the influence of the media. The media in the advanced society should perform a noble mission of enlightening people and discourage sectarian, communal and divisive trends. Media integration is consistently referred to as a relatively new phenomenon in education. Although complete media integration is not yet commonplace in classrooms throughout the country, media's use in the classroom, much like that of technology, is seemingly old hat Although "movie day in the classroom" has shifted from slides and projectors to DVDs and YouTube as a result of rapidly changing technologies in the twenty first century, media use in the classroom remains prevalent none the less. Hardly a country in the world is spared controversy in education, but when one looks behind the sometimes anarchic scenes, there is a lot about which to be optimistic and hopeful. Traditionally, the mass media and education have enjoyed a love-hate relationship. On one hand television and newspapers particularly, have provided extensive and extremely useful education content. On the other, however, their newsrooms never seem to hesitate when controversy rears its ugly head. The power of media is so extensive and huge; it can be used to educate people with very little cost. Media today is to inform the people about the latest happening around them and the world. They cover all aspects of our interest like weather, politics, war, health, finance, science, fashion, music, etc. The need for more and more news has evolved into creation of dedicated TV & radio channels and magazines. People can listen, watch and read latest news whenever and wherever they want.

References

1. Owell and Rhoten, (2009). Promotes individual learning, social interaction and immersion; and is highly customizable and collaborative.
2. Bloom, B., Englehart, M. Furst, E., Hill, W., & Krathwohl, D. (1956). *Taxonomy of educational objectives: The classification of educational goals. Handbook I: Cognitive domain*. New York, Toronto: Longmans, Green.
3. [1] Cates, W. M. (1995). The technology of educational restructuring: planning for change in teacher education. Computers in the Schools, 11(4), 1-22.
4. Change, J., & Moores, T., & Smith, D. K. (2005). Prepare your mind for learning. [3] Communications of the ACM, 48(9), 115-118.
5. Clark, R. E. (1994). Media will never influence learning. Educational Technology Research and Development, 42(2), 21-29.
6. Clark, R. E. (1992). Media use in education. In M.C. Alkin (Ed.), Encyclopedia of Educational Research (pp.805-814). New York: Macmillan.
7. Clark, R. E. (1983). Reconsidering research on learning with media. Review of Educational Research, 53(4), 445- 459.
8. Crick, R. D., & Wilson, K. (2005). Being a learner: a virtue for the 21st century. British Journal of Educational Studies, 53(3), 359-374.
9. Jonassen, D. H., & Carr, C., & Yueh, H. P. (1998). Computers as mind tools for engaging learners in critical thinking. Tech Trends, 43(2), 24-32.

29

Evaluation Assessment of Choice Based Credit System - A Critical Review

Dr Padala Thirupathi

Abstract

How does the CBCS change the understanding of a teacher's work or workload is missing from the prescriptive discourse on reform. Despite offering the least clarity in terms of its rationale and process, CBCS as a scheme has been implemented by diktat, framed in the discourse of preserving quality and maintaining standards by the UGC. The possibilities of it surviving in the higher education system far exceed its intrinsic merit on account of the political imperative for its implementation. Credit system demanded in terms of a shift in approach to teaching. Their quantum of teaching or "workload" as defined by the funding body, the UGC, had remained 16 hours a week of teaching within colleges, even before the adoption of the credit system. Higher Education Bill tabled in the Parliament in 2010, even though withdrawn, had been preceded by the centralised articulation of the Action Plan for Academic Reforms linked with conditions of continuation of state funding for institutions. This research to be discussed on "Evaluation and Assessment of Choice Based Credit System – A Critical Review".

Keywords : *Curriculum framework, Active Plan, Credit System, Internal Articulation, Academic achievement, Academic councils, curriculum design, standardization, curriculum implications.*

Introduction to the study

The study illustrates how the contestations over reforms and the accompanying institutional changes, although characteristic of and essential to the academic space, may result from an incongruence between the policy approach, the reform proposals, and assumptions about the decision-making processes within the university. The case of DU highlights how complex institutional dynamics play out and determine the experience and outcomes of the reform process. It also signposts the contextual embeddedness of the change process. The nature of contestations and resistance to reform proposals within the institution make visible the negotiations over the traditional organisational ideals of collegiality, autonomy, and participatory structures of self-governance.

The research questions that guided this exploration were :

- How was the process of institutionalisation of reforms managed in the Higher Education? What factors, internal and external, facilitated or inhibited the introduction of these reforms?
- What were the collective perceptions of the graduation and post-graduation academic community about the relevance, need, and politics of the reform initiatives? How did various actors resist or promote these changes? Where did resistance to reforms nest in the university and how was it negotiated during the implementation of reforms?
- How and in what terms, can we understand the resistance to, and the outcome of the reform process?

Methodology

This researcher study approach was adopted to study of reforms in Higher Education a review of choice based credit system an institutional context. An approach enabled the researcher to explore the ongoing processes and outcomes, while simultaneously engaging with the realm of institutional memory and history. It offered the flexibility for in-depth exploratory research. The need for a detailed institutional case study emerged from the context that academic reforms in universities and degree are subject to intense public debate, but also fall within the domain of a significantly under-researched domain. The researcher contested and negotiated space of academic governance and curricular planning in universities. The case studies document three qualitatively distinct approaches to initiating academic reforms. Even though the set of reforms seemed integral to each other in terms of their reference point and scope, yet, in terms of their life cycle in the University, they unfolded and played out in unique ways. The study attempted to capture the dynamics—academic, political and ideological, circumscribing the trajectories of these three reform initiatives in Higher Education.

Academic Reforms in Higher Education

The three reforms studied as part of the case study of the Higher Education had unique trajectories and outcomes. The Semester system and the choice-based credit system were introduced into the system, explicitly positioned as an institutional response in compliance with the national policy mandate and guidelines introduced by the UGC. The Four Year Undergraduate Programme, on the other hand, was conceptualised and projected as an institutional innovation in response to the national mandate. The experience of implementation of the three reforms was distinct from each other.

The proposal for introduction of the semester system at the undergraduate level had been in gestation in the University since the late 60s. Organisation and structural challenges in introducing examination reforms and enabling conditions for centrally managing the curriculum and evaluation processes in the relatively large college system of Higher Education had prevented its uniform implementation within the system. However, when it was finally introduced for implementation, it was positioned by the University leadership as a response to the UGC directive for change, amidst consequences of financial sanctions for non-compliance against colleges and university by the UGC.

Within this context, teachers opposed the introduction of change without due consultation on its feasibility and desirability, given that none of the earlier structural and organisational constraints in the system had been redressed. After a long-drawn conflict between college teachers and the university administration, the institutionalisation of change was completed through legal intervention. Even as the desirability and need for change to semester mode remained contested among the academic community, the Delhi High Court's judgment (Nandini Dutta and others v. Higher Education, 2013) in favour of the University's decision and process of implementation of the semester system enabled the assimilation of reform into the system.

Efforts to produce curricula that are more "relevant" and "responsive" have, over the past two decades, witnessed a global policy shift towards the credit and choice framework. The credit-choice discourse of university undergraduate curricula. For the majority of students, the undergraduate programme marks a terminal stage in higher education. A significant issue arises about the relevance of a discipline anchored framework, designed to sequentially link to postgraduate studies, for students who do not aspire or cannot progress in the academic stream for postgraduate studies and research. In the context of massification and the changing nature of the market economy, the undergraduate programmes, organised primarily on a disciplinary basis have been found lacking. The underlying assumption appears to be that curricular changes can overcome the existing gaps and facilitate a new culture of thinking and pedagogy that is more responsive to student diversity on campuses. The alternative proposed to the traditional disciplinary frame of organising undergraduate education has been provided by the credit framework (with inbuilt modularity) with the explicit aim of creating a student-centric learning environment with a commitment to strengthening interdisciplinarity.

The experience of other countries indicates that the outcome of the reform (policy) exercises and the restructuring of curricula within the credit exchange discourse has done little more than pressurising liberal arts and science institutions to provide a professional or vocational face to their existing academic provision. While the reform direction has promoted the move towards modularisation and the adoption of a learning outcomes framework, the shift has not been in absolute terms, with accommodations made in the new frame for older practices. Ensor notes in the context of South Africa that the approach of "apprenticeship" into a discipline (that highlights the continued dominance of the disciplinary discourse) has continued to guide the curricular organisation, and has been accommodated neatly into the credit framework. The promises of the credit framework for increased student choices and the possibility of multiple coherent pathways through modularisation are thus found challenging to realise within the given institutional constraints.

Student Choice Credit System

The disciplinary discourse...has persisted through the restriction on student choice, the tying of modules through pre- and co-requisites and the emphasis on induction into vertical knowledge sequences. So, while the imperatives for academic reforms are closely tied to the academic mission and objectives of the higher education system, its conceptualisation often steers far from the dynamics circumscribing the working of the system. The design of the reform process thus seems to neglect the implementation phase and its embeddedness in the nature and culture of the institution itself. The mission of the modern university has been tied closely to the developmental agenda of the nation-state and hence the goals or academic imperatives of the university, in turn, become aligned to the national policy mandate. Globalisation and the accompanying political and economic restructuring of the nation-states have also impacted education as one of the public institutions in varied ways. In many countries, the higher education system is currently undergoing fundamental changes in its governance, structure, funding and organisation. The direction of change, as Marginson and contend, is unlike what has been experienced before and demands alternative analytical frameworks to make sense of the effect of globalisation on higher education policy and practices. Higher education in every corner of the globe is being influenced by global economic, cultural, and educational forces, and the institutions themselves (as well as units and constituencies within them) are increasingly global actors, extending their influence across the world. Moreover, the political, economic, and educational contours of countries (and of regions and continents) are being reshaped by regional trading blocs that lead higher education to become more similar across national boundaries and more active in the regional market. With the adoption of neoliberal policy frameworks across nation-states within the context of globalised political economies, there is a simultaneous departure from the traditional conceptualisation of the role of higher education in a state-society and mechanisms of its organisation. The neoliberal framework, for instance, is characterised by a reduction of the state subsidisation of higher education, shifting of costs to consumers, the demand of accountability for performance and an enhanced emphasis on the role that higher education plays in the economy. Thus, the higher education institutions are not just embedded within a national system but have to reckon with the presence of the market in higher education. The study of the impact of these forces on higher education institutions has been attempted, in terms of the impact of state policies on universities' independence or universities' involvement and responsiveness to national markets.

UGC Guidelines on Credit System

The adoption of the credit-system by the University involved a shift towards a modular and choice-based approach to curriculum planning. While the credit- system had been seen to promote interdisciplinary studies and had its proponents within the UGC as early as the late 50s and 60s, it gathered more significant currency in the early 70s in the context of the reform of university examination system. The new wave of expansion in higher education and renewed state support for it since the Eleventh Plan proposal was accompanied by the UGC Action Plan (UGC, 2009) for implementation of the credit system, semester scheme and internal assessment. This was also accompanied by a change in policy stance concerning the institutional adherence to UGC guidelines, creating financial implications for institutions not implementing the academic reforms.

The "credit" discourse was present within the University's internal articulation of academic reform, in the form of proposals for restructuring made by the Academic Renewal Committee (1992), the BA Programme Restructuring (2002), and within the conceptualisation of the FYUP proposal. The policy of credit transfer was deliberated upon in the Academic Council Meeting. The proposal for credit transfer was critiqued as arguments were made for the institution of a credit system in the University as a first step. The submission to the Academic Council made by six elected members of the AC noted:

The provision of **credit transfer** requires the existence of a credit system. Save a few courses which make perfunctory mention of the credit system, the Higher Education does not have a credit system in place. Introduction of the credit system would require discussion at the level of every department, as per our best practices by the General Bodies of teachers of each subject and statutorily by the Committees of Courses and then the faculties before the AC can / should decide on the matter. Even if a credit system were to be accepted, courses have to be restructured to make it meaningful. Credit transfer would require a prior course structure which specifies how many papers and which kind of papers can a student pursue outside to qualify for a specific degree…

Credit system -Curriculum Design and Implications

While both, the semester reform as well as the structure and duration of an undergraduate degree are examples of organisational reforms, CBCS is a substantive curriculum reform and offers a different framework for curriculum development. Higher education curricular and pedagogical practices have remained stable over centuries but transformed significantly in the context of massification in the twentieth century. Modular and credit based courses, Betts and Smith (1998) note, had their origins in the USA in the late nineteenth century for a similar reason that developed a century later in the UK and other parts of the world. Higher education institutions experienced the pressure to change, as their student base diversified, creating an imperative for replacement of the uniform classical curricula with something more suited to contemporary needs. The academic principles and philosophical underpinnings for such a shift emanated from a growing acceptance of student-centred learning and of John Dewey's advocacy of "self-realisation" achieved through study fitting the individual's interest (Theodossin, 1986, p. 5, as cited in Betts and Smith, p.4). While the idea of the credit-based curriculum may have been first explored and adopted in the American context, it is no more an experiment (Sindhi and Shah 2015). All the major higher education systems across the world have over the year implemented a system of credits: European Credit Transfer System (ECTS) in Europe's universities, the "National Qualifications Framework" in Australia, there is a Pan-Canadian Protocol on the Transferability of University Credits; and UK has the Credit Accumulation and Transfer System (CATS). South Korea has developed an alternative to full time university-bound academic degree through a system of Academic Credit Banking System (ACBS).

What is the essential shift in a curricular approach that has garnered traction for the credit system? What is the problem which the credit-based curriculum reform seeks to address? How does the curriculum need to change to address this problem? Betts and Smith (1998) argue that the credit-based modular curriculum system has at its heart a revolutionary approach to HE, which challenged the centuries-old model of HE curriculum and pedagogy. University education was largely tutor-centred; this favoured the HE model of an elite club where only a few could be allowed to join, and a normative pace determined the rationale for success and failure of those who succeeded in taking admission. Heffernan (1973) notes that in the classical and ecclesiastical tradition, which characterised higher education up to the 1850s and 1860s, students were trained in basically the same subjects and sequences. Progress toward a degree was embodied in a relatively rigid, prescribed curriculum.

Students were expected to gain their degrees within a "normal" period of time. Any longer demonstrated that the student had failed to achieve the desired standards. On the other hand the rarer part-time degrees were lengthy affairs, often six years, doubling the time needed for the full-time degree, demonstrating there was no easy or backdoor route into the graduate club.

The credit system and its underpinning philosophy, therefore, form an attempt to place upon the rigid, traditional HE culture an educational philosophy which stresses flexibility and a revaluation of the "standards". It shifts the evaluation discourse to a "learning" and "learner-centric" discourse; questions the sanctity of "time" as a standard for evaluation, and creates the possibility of altering the system to allow for differential pace in learning and navigating the system. It entails a shift in curriculum thinking: a departure from teacher-driven curriculum towards the principle of what the student want is what the student gets notes that the traditional pedagogical systems (anchored on non-credit based principles) are usually organised around high-stakes tests, whereas, systems based on the credit hour articulate the purpose and hence modality of student assessment differently. Assessment in this frame need not merely be "assessment of learning", *but* could be seen as "assessment for learning" and "assessment as learning".

A Study on Credit Culture

The evaluation of student progress is more frequent and broken down into smaller units, such as three or four courses per semester, rather than the work of an entire semester or year. Indeed, the reality in a credit-hour system is that each course for which credit is awarded often has several assessments that are cumulated into a final course grade that determines whether credit should be awarded. Students receive more timely feedback on their progress, enabling them to make corrections and improvements as they move forward. In addition, these multiple and sometimes continuous assessments frequently employ a variety of measures of academic achievement, such as attendance, oral recitation, timed examinations, essays, research papers, and laboratory experiments.

Principles of a Credit Culture

From	To
Exclusion	Inclusion
Teacher	Learner
Process	Outcome
Direction	Guidance
Failure	Achievement
Margins	Mainstream
Professional Control	Individual Choice
Structures	Cultures

Source: Robertson (1994, p. 315) (cited in Trowler 1998, p. 8).

The shift in principles guiding curriculum design is accommodated well within a well-defined structure of degrees, examinations, and course-time units expressed in semester credit hour terms. The credit system, therefore, as Heffernan (1973) argues, becomes a logical choice. Once the units of educational accomplishment or outcomes are established, they can be linked to the management and cost of administrative operations, both being expressed in credit hour terms: tuition by credit hours elected, salaries by credit hours taught, facilities by credit hours produced, and programmes of study by credit hours required. The conceptualisation of the need for reform, therefore, has been broadly similar across different contexts. In the UK context, Betts and Smith (1998) note, the initiative for credit framework emanated not from mainstream universities and colleges, but polytechnics, and provide an insight into how the adoption of a modular-credit system indicated a systemic need:

In the European context, education has appeared in the process of European integration through the Bologna Process and establishment of a European Credit Transfer System (ECTS). The critical elements of ECTS are:

1. Institutions (departments/programmes) using ECTS are required to provide information on course contents, level, and workload;

2. Provide a transcript of record containing all of the information on credits and grades assigned to the student;
3. Create an ECTS learning agreement arranged between the sending and receiving institutions;
4. Provide ECTS coordinators at the institution and/or department who are responsible for the administration of ECTS and any transfer negotiations.

The adoption of a credit system as part of the Bologna Process essentially indicates institution of a process of creating easily readable and comparable degree; academic mobility for students and teachers; and uniformity in the degree type and system (such as undergraduate and graduate) across the EU area. The student-determined curricular choice and flexibility (*incoherence*). The tradeoff between "rigidity" and "incoherence", particularly at the undergraduate level remain a programmematic and curricular design challenge. At the threshold of the twenty first century, as HE systems across the world aim towards mass participation in HE, Betts and Smith argue, we should perhaps re-appraise the situation. Credit accumulation and transfer systems, and the parallel curriculum framework based on modular systems are part of that re-appraisal. If in many ways they liberate the student and teacher, in other ways they may also constrain them. Points out that the credit framework attempts to undermine one central assumption underlying the organisation of academic practices of teaching and learning in higher education system, namely that learning best takes place within one institution, over a fixed and limited period of time, according to rules best determined by academic staff. As evident from the Korean ACBS, and case of polytechnic and vocational education, academic learning is brought to the same level as learning acquired at work or elsewhere rather than being seen as superior. This blurs the distinctions between academic, experiential and other forms of learning. Thus, control over the curriculum within the credit-framework is conditioned by consumer choice rather than "producer control", also seen as a key aspect of neo-liberal thinking (Trowler, 1998).

The Credit-system:- Challenges in the Indian Context

The National Knowledge Commission (NKC) had called for the reform of existing universities to ensure frequent curricula revisions, the introduction of the credit system, emphasising internal assessment as critical to learning, encouraging research, and reforming the governance of institutions. The credit system and the emphasis on modularity in curriculum planning have been found useful in the process of revisiting the curriculum and linking each component of the programme with that of the overall programme objective. The modularity in curriculum design, obtained by specifying each curriculum unit in terms of credit weight/ as a quantum of work required to be completed to meet the requirements for the degree successfully, is relatively more facilitative in breaking the entrenchment of disciplinary domains. It is facilitative in re-configuring programmes (completely/partially) and revisiting them, apart from enabling student mobility and agency (through choice) in assembling a degree relevant for them.

The UGC proposal for academic reforms to establish a uniform credit system across universities in the country articulated its rationale in terms of an attempt to mitigate the diversity in evaluation practices across the country and variability in the credentials of degrees and programmes of the different universities. The CBCS framework aims at ensuring seamless mobility of students across higher education institutions in the country and abroad, with the possibility of credit transfer across universities in the country as well as internationally. The variability in the practices of defining the credit and programme requirements across universities that had already implemented the credit system was seen by the regulators as a challenge for streamlining degree credentials and ascertaining standards. UGC circulated the guidelines for CBCS structure in 2014 and drafted the model curriculum for 109 different academic programmes, drawing upon a select number of external experts. Universities were asked to introduce the CBCS from the academic year 2015-16. The Higher Education was amongst the first ones to adopt it. Within the history of academic reforms at DU, this moment seemed like an aberration as CBCS adoption process was significantly uncontested within the University bodies.

Standardized Credit System

The University Grants Commission Act specifies the main function of the Commission as coordination and maintenance of standards: laying down norms and qualifications to maintain a common standard. This articulation does not imply framing the syllabi as the task of the UGC, which is the prerogative of the academic bodies of the universities. Given the diversity in institutional profile across the country, the UGC has brought out model syllabi earlier as well, which are considered more as exemplars. Norms and regulations are expected to be of a broad generic nature to facilitate academic pluralism and allow for diversity in the institutional landscape. Curriculum framing remains and is a core task of the University's academic community: the structures of Departments/ Schools, Boards of Studies, Standing Committees of the Academic Council, an Academic Council and an Executive Council/ Syndicate exist to oversee the preparation of curriculum. This academic governance system and mechanism for maintaining standards exist within the framework of all University Acts as much as they are a part of the UGC Act.

What the CBCS guidelines provided for was a standardised template for credit parity and programme structure of the degrees offered by different universities. A significant difference exists in the approach and implications of providing guidelines for minimum standards and expectations from a degree, as opposed to specifying what to teach to the universities. The UGC Act does not supersede the academic autonomy of the universities, which are corporate entities in themselves, incorporated through Acts of State and Central Legislature. Adoption of CBCS in DU appeared to create a narrative around the imposition of the external body's will on to the University even as its internal governance bodies ratified the CBCS. The CBCS guidelines provided for a deviation of 30 percent from the stipulated UGC structure and for similar deviation in the course content also for those universities that decided to adopt the curriculum prepared by the UGC. The internal critique to CBCS as articulated by the different segments of the teacher association argued that University's conformity to CBCS guidelines mitigated the pluralism in methodologies that are informing knowledge growth and development in the social sciences, humanities and even the sciences.

What need to be done?

Curriculum planning and review is a complex process, which needs to be informed by the ground reality of the nature of teaching, preparedness, and aspirations of students as well as faculty orientation and strengths. Framing of a syllabus informed primarily by developments and configurations within a select disciplinary domain is in principle against a real-time engaged understanding of university classrooms and cultures. For curriculum review to be an organic process, both the content and processes have to be owned by the academic community. Many within the academic community feel the CBCS implementation as self-contradictory and destructive of academic and pedagogic innovation. While there is no dearth of literature which describes and analyses lack of academic and pedagogic innovation in the Indian HE system before the credit discourse; what is relevant to this perception is the fact that the structural rigidity of the affiliation system remains incompatible with the new philosophy and is inherently detrimental to any academic innovation.

Summing up and Concluding Remarks

The implementation of CBCS has, to say the least, brought to the forefront a range of issues around curriculum—both substantive and those related to design, in the context of general undergraduate education in the country. The broad narrative on the ground, against a distinct kind of regimentation feared through a new curriculum framework, emanates from two sets of challenges: infrastructural as well as cultural. In the Indian HE context, the need for infrastructural or organisational restructuring is well recognised and articulated but remains far from realisation. The schemes of autonomous colleges, for instance, barely redresses the perils of the affiliating system in the country. As long as colleges remain affiliated to universities, we continue to stifle academic resources in thousands of colleges in the country. The stifling of the curriculum project jeopardies innovation and rigour in teaching in the Humanities and Liberal Arts and Sciences, particularly in the undergraduate space. Given the maximum student diversity in the undergraduate space, most considerable flexibility and alternate learning trajectories are required within this domain. The CBCS framework contains the potential to facilitate this. Without the organisational reform, however, the effectiveness of merely the curriculum reform remains circumspect. Another question that remains unanswered is the processes by which reform in the architecture of the curriculum can translate to an altered and more engaged pedagogic culture in the universities and colleges. Without an academic culture that values self- and peer-review, organisational learning, reform achievements appear more as rhetorical claims, often untested and unverified.

The adoption of the Choice Based Credit System (CBCS) has, in the Indian context, has been focused primarily on the curriculum domain without a rethinking of the structures of affiliation or deliberation on the meaning and implications of the credit framework for curriculum thinking and the culture of teaching and learning. It appears as an imposition of the vocabulary of credits on the existing templates of both the curriculum as well as academic structures for curriculum planning. The credit exchange discourse aims to disaggregate curricula into modules that students can then fit together according to their interests and needs, and in doing that it makes a critical assumption that students at the first-degree level have the competence to do so independently. A lack of comprehensive understanding or realisation of the structural changes at the institutional level and the absence of a scaffolding approach and mechanisms needed to translate choices into coherent cognitive strategies or epistemic maps will continue to form a significant challenge to the process of changing epistemic contours of undergraduate curriculum and teaching.

References

Adelman, C., Kemmis, S. and Jenkins, D. (1980). Rethinking case study: notes from the second Cambridge conference. In H. Simon (ed.). *Towards a Science of the Singular,*. Norwich: Centre for Applied Research in Education, University of East Anglia.

Agarwal, P. (2021). *Indian higher education: Envisioning the future*. New Delhi: Sage.

Altbach, P.G. (2017). Book Notes: Great Expectations and Mixed Performance: The Implication of Higher Education Reforms in Europe, Ladislav Cerych and Paul Sabatier . *Comparative Education Review.*

Amaral, A. and Magalhães, A. (2004). Epidemiology and the Bologna Saga. *Higher Education, 48*(1).

Amin, S., Apoorvanand, Bhattacharjea, A. Datta, P.K., Deshpande, D., Kumar, K., Kumar, U. and Mahajan, S. (2013, April 14). DU S 4-year degree course..

Anand, C.L. & Buch, P. (1991). Research in Higher Education: A Trend report . In M.B. Buch (ed.) *Fourth Survey of Research in Education (1983-88),* Vol. II, 1339-1391. New Delhi: NCERT.

Anandkrishnan, M. (2007). Higher Education II: Critique of Knowledge Commission. *Economic and Political Weekly. 42* (7).

Baker, D. (2018). St. Stephens College, Delhi, 1881-1997: An Alexandria on the banks of Jamuna?. In M. Hasan (ed.). *Knowledge, Power and Politics: Educational Institutions in India,* pp. 66-113. New Delhi: Roli Books.

Baldridge,V. (1971). *Power and Conflict in the University: Research in the sociology of complex organizations*. New York: John Wiley & Sons, Inc.

Bali, A.P. (1986). *College Teachers: Challenges and Responses (A case study of Delhi University).* New Delhi: Northern Book Centre.

Bhattacharaya, S. (2015, 30 August). A Critical Note on Ambiguities and Anomalies in CBCS guidelines (14/08/15) issued by DU on Grading System. *Revolutionary Diaries: A new World Order.*

Bhushan, S. (2008). Financial Requirements in Higher Education during XI Plan Period in Sukhadeo Thorat (ed.) *Higher Education in India: Issues Related to Expansion, Inclusiveness, Quality and Finance,* 215-76. New Delhi: UGC.

Blackler, F., Crump, N., and Macdonald, S. (2000). Organizing processes in complex activity networks. *Organization, 7*(2), pp. 277-300.

Chandra, P. (2017). Governance in Higher Education-A contested space (making the university work). In Devesh Kapur and Pratap Bhanu Mehta (eds.), *Navigating the Labyrinth- Perspectives on India's Higher Education,* pp.235-264. Hyderabad: Orient Blackswan.

Chitnis, S. (1993). Gearing a colonial system of education and take independent India towards development. *Higher Education, 26* (1), 22-41.

Davies, J.L. & Morgan, A.W. (1982). The politics of institutional change. In L. Wagner (ed.) *Agenda for institutional change in higher education,* pp. 153-188. Guildford: Society for Research into Higher Education.

Delanty, G. (2002). The governance of universities: what is the role of the university in the knowledge society? *Canadian Journal of Sociology, 27* (2). pp. 185-198. UoD (1943). *Delhi University Magazine*. Vol.1, Issue 1.

Dungan, R. (1970). Higher Education: The effort to adjust. In Stephen R. Graubard and Geno Ballotti (eds.). *The Embattled Universities*. New York: George Braziller.

ECISS (2009, November 4). *A proposal for implementation of semester system at the undergraduate level in the Higher Education.* New Delhi: Higher Education. Retrieved from Democratic Teachers Front web archive: https://dtfnet. wordpress.com/2009/11/04/723/

Harman, K.M. (1989). Culture and conflict in academic organization: Symbolic aspects of university worlds. *Journal of Educational Administration, 27*(3), 30-54.

Harvey, C. (1988). *Retrenchment strategies in two Canadian universities: A political analysis*. Research Paper 88-08. Montreal: McGill University.

Heffernan, J. (1973). The Credibility of the Credit Hour: The History, Use, and Shortcomings of the Credit System. *The Journal of Higher Education. 44* (1), pp. 61-72. Stable URL.

Kapur, D. and Khosla, M. (2017) The Supreme Court and private higher education. In Devesh Kapur and Pratap Bhanu Mehta (eds.) *Navigating the Labyrinths: Perspectives on Indian Higher Education*, pp. 207-234. Delhi: Orient Blackswan..

Kaul, J.N. (1974). *Higher Education in India: 1951-1971.* Simla: Indian Institute of Advanced Studies.

Kogan, M., Bauer, M., Bleiklie, I. and Henkel, M. (eds.) (2006*). Transforming Higher Education: A Comparative Study, 2nd edn*, Dordrecht: Springer.

Nandini Dutta v. Higher Education (2013). WP (C) No. 2764/2011, Judgment of the High Court of Delhi, New Delhi (11 July 2013).

Narain, N. (2006). Restructuring of undergraduate education: Paper prepared for the Academic Renewal Committee of the Higher Education . *UGC Journal of Higher Education. 19* (2), pp. 274-280.

Pillai, J. K. and Mohan, S. (1986). *Working of the semester system: A review.* Madurai: Department of Education, Madurai Kamraj University.

Panda, A. (2012, August 17). DU students protest Meta College concept: Fewer takers for innovative B.Tech. Humanities. *The Tribune*. Retrieved from: http://www.tribuneindia.com/2012/20120818/delhi.htm#1

Powell, W.W. & DiMaggio, W.W. (eds.) (2011). *The new institutionalism in organizational analysis.* Chicago and London: The University of Chicago Press.

Rao, K.S. (2001). *Management of autonomy in institutions of higher learning: Case studies of autonomous and non-autonomous colleges. Independent study.* New Delhi: National Institute of Educational Planning and Administration.

Sharma, G.D. (2008). *Institutionality of change (NIEPA: Case Study in Educational Reforms).* Indian Institute of Education, Pune. New Delhi: National Institute of Educational Planning and Administration.

Simon, H. (ed.) (2009). *Towards a science of the singular*. Norwich: Centre for Applied Research in Education, University of East Anglia.

Sindhi, S. and Shah, A. (2015, September 12). India's controversial Choice Based Credit System-OpEd. *Eurasia Review.*

Singh, Amrik. (2003). *Fifty years of higher education in India: The role of University Grants Commission*. New Delhi: Sage.

Thompson, T.R. (2011). *From Bologna to Berlin 1999-2003: the initial steps of the Bologna Process and creation of the European Higher Education Area*. Unpublished PhD Dissertation, University of Pittsburgh.

Trowler, P. (2001). Captured by the discourse? The socially constitutive power of New Higher Education discourse in the UK. *Organization.*

Varghese, N.V. (2018). Education research and emergence of higher education as a field of study in India. In J. Jung, H. Horta, A. Yonezawa (eds.) *Researching higher education in Asia: History, development and future*, pp. 299-313. Singapore: Springer.

Related blogs, Websites and Internet Sources:

http://timesofindia.indiatimes.com/

http://www.jstor.org/stable/1980626

https://www.researchgate.net/publication/308647442

http://higheredstrategy.com/wp-content/uploads/2014/08/Intelligence-

http://old.tehelka.com/the- semester-system-is-a-free-market-utopia/

http://www.tribuneindia.com/2012/20120818/delhi.htm#1

https://cyber kam.blogspot.com/2015/08/a-critical-note-on-ambiguities-and.html

http://old.tehelka.com/the- semester-system-is-a-free-market-utopia/

https://www.eurasia review.com/12092015-indias-controversial-choice-based-credit-system-cbcs-oped/

https://www.youthkiawaaz.com/2015/03/du- choice-based-credit-system/

https://indiankanoon.org/doc/148675148/

30

Mobile-phone based Activities Programme for Teacher Educators

Dr Pagare Prashant

Today's Technology are generally expected to utilise some form of Information Communication Technology in regular teaching practice. The use of Information communication technology in the teaching-learning it can create innovative stress. UNESCO (1998) Information communication technology defined as Scientific technology and engineering discipline and management techniques used in information handling and their interactions with men and machines and associated, social, economic and cultural matters.

Information Technology implies telecommunication involving a combination of computers, networks, satellites, telephones, radio, television and the like Creating Multimedia projects in campus it's both challenging and exciting. Fortunately, they are many multimedia applications. This resources involve not only hardware Multimedia is an innovative teaching and learning method.

Related studies

1. Mujibul, H.S. (*Technology in Teacher Education*- 2004). Computer assisted instruction:- (CAI) CAI is defined as the use of computer and other associated technology with the intension of improving the academic performance (Everett, 1995). It is also known as computer assisted learning (CAL). Computer based education (CBE) computer based training. It is an integrated system comprising of computer hardware, software and courseware aimed at providing interactive, individualised or group learning the system provides an effective and directional student computer communication for presenting textual and graphic information and giving the student responses and assessing the needs of the students in an adaptive

manner. CAI is there a continuing online student computer dialogue in which the machine is asking the student questions and subsequently checking is responses and or is the machine directing the logical development of a new concept.

2. Krishnamurthy, R.(2004) Network based Teaching & Learning: Tarun Offset, Delhi Learning Strategies: These are following: P.I.P. Instruction: — (Personalized, individualised, and process instruction) It is first applied in the late 1950s in the form of programmed instruction(P.I) .The nation was over reacting to Sputnik at the time, and P.I. was among the panaceas devised to save elementary pupils from ignorance. Once again, however, higher education borrowed procedures designed for the very young, and college students found themselves going through very simple but very detailed programmes and recording very simple written responses. One of the results was consuming dullness.

3. Gopal, P. & Mishr A R. (2007) *Computer Assisted Instruction*. New Delhi:Mahamaya Publishing House. The world's most successful economies are longer powerhouses of industry, but rather powerhouses of information. For developing countries to complete new knowledge-based economy, they must provide access to the latest information, regardless of the subject. Educators, hence, have a challenging job in their hands. The teaching learning process now cannot be confined within the rigid dimensions of a classroom with the traditional teaching tools. It is becoming imperative to make use of any resource available within the reach of an educator, so as to enhance the teaching learning process. One such resource is that of information and Communication Technologies.

Good learning activities are one of the keys to success in distance learning. Today's Technology are generally expected to utilise some form of Information Communication Technology in regular teaching practice. The use of ICT in the classroom can create innovative teaching opportunities for learner–centre learning without giving them stress. Use of Cell-phone based activities programme to teacher educator for aware about E-learning tools for effective teaching, research activities, demonstrating lessons and practices adopted in the programme implementation. It helps to teacher educator to professional development. This paper mainly intended effectiveness of Cell-phone based activities programme for teacher educators.

Objectives of the Study

To study the Awareness about Mobile-phone among teacher educators (ODL)

To develop Mobile-phone based activities programme for teacher educators (ODL).

To evaluate the effectiveness of Mobile-phone based activities programme.

Hypotheses

There is no significance difference in achievement of teacher educator in various course related work by Mobile -phone based activity programme and regular activity programme.

Methodology of Research

To achieve the objectives of the study the experimental method was used. The sample was taken through the Purposive sampling technique. True experimental method use the 100 teacher educators (ODL) of experimental group was give Cell-phone based activities programme in the selected activities for the control group the same activities are taught through the regular distance mode method to the another 100 teacher educators (ODL).

Tool Used for data collection: Questionnaire, pre-test and post-test more specialised training will be given Procedure:-Step of programme - Firstly, prepare plan how to access content and activity during the programme where Counsellor (teachers) will be shown how to access content and activities from their cell phones and will clearly understand the different types of communication that can facilitate personal messages, session and group discussions etc. In Group discussion work focused on some question for the use of the mobile phones as learning tools some questions were suggested as per following :

- Where did you use the mobile phones?
- Was it better to read the text on the mobile phone screen or to listen to the voice interpretation?
- Did you use any alternatives to SMS for text based communication?

Secondly, counsellor (teachers) was assisted in downloading content mobile learner onto their cell phones. m-learning creates on-line communities of practice. The Internet can bring learners, teachers, specialist communities, experts, practitioners and interest groups together to share ideas and good practice.

How should learners get the learning material (in electronic form)?

- The learners get all the learning material in electronic form. This can be done by downloading from the Internet, or through e-mail, storing on computer laptops or on mobile phones.
- Laptops are good because one can write notes, and the screen is bigger compared to phones. Thirdly, what should be the role of the learner counsellor (teacher)?
- To spread information and knowledge and to coordinate his fellow learners to the source of information and knowledge.
- To help others in difficult areas in their studies.
- To assist learners in the use of e-learning.
- Scheduled interactive sessions will either be between smaller groups or will have a specific topic.
- How should study groups be organised?
- Learners taking similar activities should form groups.
- The counsellors (teacher) could help the learners to organise themselves into study groups.
- Workshops and e-mail, SMS and phones.
- Meetings at least two times a month.

Data Analysis and Interpretation: The researcher used mean, standard deviation, t-value as statistical measures to analyze & interpret the data.

Table : Showing 't' value for Equality of Post-Test of Experimental Group and Controlled Group in Main Experiment

Group	Teacher educators	Mean	S D	t- value	0.05 Level
Experimental	100	83.72	9.21	6.49	significant
Controlled	100	67..4	12.7		

Here, the observed value of t was 6.49, which was greater than the table value of t at 0.05 level of confident.

Conclusion

This experimental study reveals that there is significance difference in the achievement in research work and various syllabus related activities of the experimental group over the control group of Teacher educator in subject due to Mobile-phone based activities programme to the experimental group.

Therefore there should be Mobile-phone based activities programmes used in teacher educator training in distance mode.

100 percent teacher educator said that institute should provide internet services and free access, Mobile-phone communication services which can help the teacher and learner to develop learning skills and alert regarding self-studies.

97 percent respondents agreed that it is useful for the preparation of assignment, searching references of review of related literature; know the research presentation topics and project work.

98 percent respondents said that it is useful for interaction with peer learner and immediate solve the difficult about concept or content to interact with counsellors and also help how to complete exercise and project works with in particular period.

Implication of the study: The result of the will help to understand the need of teacher and In-service Teachers in computer will help to organize need based Mobile-phone based activities programme for them which in turn will benefit teacher-educators in teaching-learning process. It's help for successfully completing courses and builds self-knowledge and self-confidence and encourages learners to take responsibility for their learning. Its Reduces travel time and travel costs of learners.

We need competent teachers for effective utilisation of emerging technologies in present educational scenario, making teachers competent for emerging technologies that requires efforts at different use of new-Multimedia technology to communicate and collaborate with peers and the larger community. It is also used to various courses for learner motivation and completes the course with in time. Hence Mobile-phone based activities programme need to be in the academic as well as administrative level of educational institutes.

References

Joshy, S.K. & Seghal, C. (2014). *Educational Technology*. New Delhi: Pacific Book International.

Gupta, S.L. & Gupta, H. (2013). *Research Methodology*. New Delhi: International Book House.

Insung, J.,Tat M., Wong & Tian, B. (2013). *Quality Assurance in Distance Education ducation E-learning*. New Delhi: SAGE Publication.

Prashant P. & Sonkamble C.P. (2012). *Glocal Education & research*. Mumbai: ISST.

B.Chitrasen (2007). *Information technology in Modern Education*, New Delhi :Alfa Publications pp. 108-134.

Gopal, P. & Mishra, R. (2007). *Computer Assisted Instruction*. New Delhi:Mahamaya Publishing House. (Ref.no340478)

Agrwal, J. C. (2007). "*Essential of Education Technology :Teaching Learning*" New Delhi: Vikas Publishing House.

Chakroborti, M. (2006). "*Teacher Education Modern Trends*" New Delhi : Kanisha Publisher.

Darbyshire, P. (2005). Instructional Technologies : Cognitive Aspects of online Programs. singapour :IRM press.

Mujibul, H.S. (2004). *Technology in Teacher Education*. New Delhi: APH Publishing Corporation .

Khan, N. (2004). *Educational Technology*. New Delhi : Rajat Publishing.

Best, J.W. and kahn, J.V. (1998). *Research in Education.* (7th Ed.) New Delhi: Prentice Hall of India Private Ltd.

Kaushik, V.K. & Sharma, S.R. (1997). *The Essentials of Teaching & Learning* New Delhi: Anmol Publications Pvt. Ltd. pp.166-185.

Pagare, P.B. (2015). E-learning as a new dimension for improving quality of education, International Journal of Educational Administration and Management (A peer reviewed International Journal) ISSN No. 2348-9332Vol. II Number-1, pp. 305-309 New Delhi: APH Publishing Corporation.

Wiersma, W. (1991). *Research Methods in Education.* (Vth ed.) Boston : Allyn & Bacon.

Kothari, C.R. (1990). *Research methodology*. New Delhi : Wiley Eastern Ltd. Vikas Publishing House.

Pagare, P.B. (2015). Micro-teaching Skills for competency development of teacher *International Journal of Management and Social Science Research Review, E- ISSN – 2349-6746, ISSN* -2349-6738

E-learning as a new dimension for improving quality of education, International Journal of Educational Administration and Management (A peer reviewed International Journal) ISSN No. 2348-9332, Vol. II, Number-1, pp. 305-309, New Delhi: APH Publishing Corporation.

Blaxter, L., Ityghes, C., and Tight, M.(1986). *How to Research*. Buckingham : Open University Press.

Websites : http://www.worldwidelearn.com/elarning-essentials/elearning benefits.htm
http://www.sofweb.vic.edu.au/vinternet/research.htm

31

New Education Policy -2020: Impact on Social Sciences

Dr ParvatamVenkateshwar

Abstract

National Education Policy-2020 emphasised on providing a quality education which is beneficial to achieve the targeted economic growth in India. The new policy is aiming at achieve important aspects namely, highest quality, equity and integrity in the entire education system right from schooling to higher education. The New education policy announced by Government of India (NEP 2020) is a welcoming change and fresh news amidst all the negativities surrounding the world due to the challenges posed by Covid-19 pandemic. The existing education policy is concentrating majorly on theoretical aspects which lack the practical training among the students i.e. the major drawback for meeting the present global job opportunities. Therefore, the National education policy-2020 is to develop creativity, potentiality, skill besides analytical thinking which are needed in the global job market. Hence all the curriculum of social sciences should be redesigned and restructured based on the outcome of education. This paper also outlines the salient features of NEP and analyses how they would affect the existing education system.

Introduction

Higher education is an important factor in determining the economy, social status, technology adoption and healthy human behaviour in each country. It is the responsibility of the public education department of the country to improve the GER to include every citizen of the country in the higher education offers. The Indian National Education Policy 2020 is moving towards achieving such a goal by creating innovative policies to improve quality, attractiveness, and affordability by providing higher education to the private sector and at the same time increasing supply with strict controls to maintain quality. In every higher education institution, by promoting merit-based admissions with free-ships and scholarships, by continuing to monitor quality through biennial accreditation based on self-declaration of merit-based proven leaders and technology-based advancement in merit and research-based persistent performers and regulatory bodies as faculty. It is expected to meet its targets by 2030. All higher education institutions with the current designation of affiliated colleges may expand into multi-disciplinary autonomous colleges and confer degree authority in their name or become constitutional colleges in their affiliated universities. The impartial agency National Research Foundation funds innovative projects in the areas of priority sciences, applied sciences and social sciences and the humanities. The Higher Education (HE) system is transformed into a student centre with the freedom to choose core and allied subjects within a discipline. Faculty members also have the autonomy to choose the curriculum, methodology, teaching and evaluation models within a given policy framework. These transitions begin in the 2021-22 academic year and continue through the year 2030, where the first level transition is most visible.

The Union Government announced the new education policy on July 29, 2020. This is called NEP 2020. This is the NDA government's first major policy document on education. Historically, we have seen changes in the education system in India every 30 years. Based on the recommendations of Dr. Sarvepalli Radhakrishnan in 1948, based on the report of Kothari Commission in 1966, and in 1986, during the reign of Prime Minister Rajiv Gandhi, education policy was announced again. The Modi government has set up a committee chaired by former ISRO chairman Kasturi Rangan. On the recommendations of this committee central government announced the education policy. The Central Government has approved 67-page policy document prepared by the Ministry of Education based on the report given by this committee. The Prime Minister announced that this new policy on education will make our country a center of knowledge. But analyzing this new policy, there is no record of our country becoming a world leader in education as the government says. Any educational approach has some basic features. It appears in the ones that have come before. This is just how to achieve the Sustainable Development Goals by 2030. This policy only states how to enhance skills. This is a very vicious thing. Because that means the education policy must also confine to the constitutional objectives. However, PM Modi's statement did not state any constitutional objectives.

The centre suggested a major change in relation to school education. That change is for the last 30 years the policy of 10 plus 2 plus 3 has been going on in India. In contrast, the Modi government has announced a

5 plus, 3 plus, 3 plus 4 policy. That is to say, pre-primary education should also be brought into the field of education and inter (plus) should also be included in school education. However we invite both these. We have always wanted pre-primary education to be in public education. But the problem is that this new education system does not propose specific system for fulfilling pre-primary education. The Centre says that pre-primary education will be fulfilled through Anganwadi Centers. But the objectives of the Anganwadi Centers are different. Their main function is to provide nutritious food to children and mothers. It is not scientific to assign management of pre-primary education to centers that perform such massive functions. The primary purpose of education is to socialise and conquer culture. Education means uncovering the hidden intuition in human beings. Nature has imparted intuition to every human being.

NEP-2020: Excellence in education and Nation Building

'This approach deals with the creation, transmission, use, and uninterrupted spread of knowledge as part of continuous learning'. These very philosophical words are the last words in the latest copy of the education policy approved by the Indian Government.

- The Narendra Modi Government is reforming education policies **to make it relevant for modern firms to ensure this is new national educational policy 2020 and replaces after 34 years. The NEP 2020** multidisciplinary learning is the new forum of Indian education system under Modi government. No longer are children supposed to choose between science, arts or maths or sports as they can explore diverse interest under the NEP transform education NEP lay stress on how to think, it focus on making the youth force multipliers in Indian development journey. The Narendra Modi Government has given greater push to online learning like never before though Prime Minister Vidya online programme students can also seek clarity on the subject through visual media.
- The NEP aimed at ensuring universal access to quality education at all levels of schooling. It also focuses on new age. Skills as well as to provide enough room for students to learn at their own peace. The modi government remain committed to bring changes that ensure Indian pedagogy which reaches its foulest potential that is why NEP promotes learning mother tongue keeping education is more accessible multilingual.
- The NEP prepares youth to be solution oriented agile and mentally equipped. It enables them to handle real life solution. Higher

education remain a subject of commitment for the mode Government. The multiple exist and entry option makes students journey risk a worse and more unique. Education is not just about class room learning. It is also about gaining skills for life so that people can stand on their own feet. If necessary thus creating meaningful empowerment government is committed to bring an institutional change that enables Indian pedagogy to reach its fool lest potential. The new curriculum frame work and literacy aims for that every child attaining by the end of 2025. On the other hand the new NEP is one of the major factors in the grand exercise of nation building and assures the youth that the countries supports their aspirations and in this context prime minister Modi said that "New highlights to will be achieved in the future." A university in India is to set to revise its academic programmes and foster a research culture with student's centric initiatives. In Telangana state, Osmania university has embarked on 21 point action plan which will frame on serving its primary shareholders, students and research scholars and proposes to set up reading rooms, complex for students and corporate to interface with industries for recruitments, internship and workshops. On the other hand the administration more transparent, responsive and accountable.

Finally, the 21-point action plan includes a review and expanding of UG/PG courses and boost of employability and communication skills. Apart from streamlining admission and administrative system to support and advance the university vision and mission. Further focusing on the areas of recruitment and placing outstanding faculty for promoting higher quality of teaching and research which will effect on improved governance and development of enlightened.

Leadership for institutional autonomy and Performance based incentives and accreditation will be promoted. In general it is observed that NEP 2020 will generate excellence in education. Research will enhance the learning with higher order of thinking in the learner with skills and advanced knowledge which is the need of the hour. This National Education Policy was announced by the Union Ministry of Education on July 29, 2020 on the Department of Education website New National Education Policy Highlights are as follows:

Ensuring that school education is accessible to all at all levels from pre-primary level to 12th class; Quality care and quality education in early childhood for all children from 3 to 6 years of age; New type of curriculum in 5 + 3 + 3 + 4 system, system of teaching methods; Arts, Science,

Curriculum, extracurricular activities..., professional, academic subjects without any strict division; National level programme for the study of literacy and statistics with proper foundations; Multilingualism, focus on the study of Indian languages; mother tongue / native language / local language / regional language medium of instruction up to at least fifth grade, especially up to 8th grade or higher. Assessment Reforms - Board exams up to two times during the school year. A major test. Improvement tests if necessary.

Establishment of a new assessment center at the national level, Parakh-PARAKH (Talent Assessment, Review, Analysis, Knowledge for holistic personality development); Inclusive education on an equal basis - giving special priority to socially and economically disadvantaged groups (SEDGs); remote areas for opportunities, a separate sexual integration fund for groups, special education zone; Recruitment of teachers, a rigorous, transparent process for talent-based performance; Ensuring that all kinds of resources are available through school complexes and groups; Establishment of the Public School Standards Authority (PSSA). School education, opportunity for vocational education in the higher education system; increasing the gross enrolment ratio in higher education to 50 percent.

Multiple Opportunity Admission, Complete Multiple Curriculum Study with Exit Opportunities; Opportunity for the National Testing Agency (NTA) to conduct a joint entrance examination for admission in higher education institutions; Establishment of Academic Bank of Credit; Establishment of an educational and research system in universities that compares multiple curricula; Establishment of the National Research Foundation (NRF);'Simple but solid' control system.

Establishment of a single umbrella body by the Higher Education Commission of India (HECI) to make available access to the promotion of higher education, including teacher education, excluding medicine and law, Establishment of independent institutions on various issues. The Board of Universal Education to set standards, the Higher Education Grants Consulate for funding, the National Accreditation Council for National Recognition (NAC), and the National Council for Higher Education (NHERC) for regulatory matters. Expansion of the universal, distance education system is to increase the gross enrolment ratio (GER). Promoting education to the international level. The Professional education is an integral part of the higher education system. Providing opportunities for independent technical universities, universities of health sciences, law and agricultural universities, as well as other academic institutions to grow into multi-disciplinary institutions.

Teacher Education- Four year integrated stage with specialized subject study, specialised Bachelor's degree. National programme design for guidance, Establishment of National Education Technology Forum (NETF). Establishing the NTF as a platform for free exchange of views on the use of technology for the improvement of study, evaluation, planning, administration, etc. Integrating technology appropriately into all levels of education, Achieving 100% literacy among youth and adults, Establishment of multi-machinery systems with appropriate checks and balances to control higher education from becoming commercial.

Shaping educational institutions into non-profit organisations with uniform inspection standards. The Central Government and the States should work together to increase public investment in education to 6 percent of GDP as soon as possible. To further strengthen the Central Education Advisory Board for coordination to ensure full focus on quality education. Ministry of Education: It is desirable to rename the Ministry of Human Resources as the Ministry of Education so as to focus on education, study etc.

The National Education Policy 2020 has been finalised after the completion of a detailed consultation process with the States, Union Territories Governments, Authorities and all stakeholders. The National **Education Policy for the Year 2020 the Ministry of Education has informed all the States and Union territories that it must be implemented.** The Ministry of Education has organised a programme called 'Shikshak Parv' from September 8 to 25, 2020 to discuss the theme, implementation and suggestions of the National Education Policy.

The Ministry of Education also held a conference with the Governors on "The Role of National Education Policy in the Transformation of Higher Education". The meeting was attended by Governors of various states, Lieutenant Governors of Union Territories, Vice Chancellors of Universities in different States and other dignitaries. On this occasion, a positive and positive response was received from the stakeholders on the National Education Policy 2020.

The new national education system recognises the notion that vocational education is inferior to mainstream education. Therefore, the National Education Policy aims to dispel the current misconception of vocational education on a social level and to integrate vocational education courses with mainstream education courses. It also directed that all educational institutions should achieve this goal in a phased manner. To this end, secondary schools will have to work with industrial training institutes (ITIs), polytechnics and local industries. As part of this programme, skill labs will be set up in schools. The Skill Labs facility, which will be modelled on the Hub and Spoke, will be available to other schools as well.

Improving the quality of education at all levels, from primary schools to universities, is a continuous process. Many steps are being taken in this direction at present. A centrally sponsored scheme for comprehensive education for school education is being implemented. The scheme is being implemented with the objective of providing quality education on an equal basis at all levels of school education. The scheme states that 'school' is a process from preschool, primary, secondary, secondary and senior secondary education to higher education. Moreover, many schemes are being implemented in higher education as well. Rashtriya Uchchhita Shiksha Abhiyan (RUSA), Educational Research Activities Promotion Scheme (SPARC), World Class Programme on Education (GIAN), Research, Creative Technology Impact Programme (IMPRINT), Technical Education Quality Improvement Program (TEQIP), Active Study on Youth and Hope Study Webs (SWAYAM), National Digital Library Campus Liaison Programme, Uchatar Innovation Campaign, Unnat Bharat Abhiyan, Impact Research in Social Sciences (IMPRES .S), Atal Ranking Institutions on Creative Achievements (ARIIA), National Institutional Ranking System (NIRF) are being implemented to enhance the quality of higher education. The University Grants Commission (UGC) and the All India Council for Technical Education (AICTE) are also implementing various programmes to enhance the quality of higher education and technical education.

In addition to the centre in field of education, various states are also unequivocally endorsing the national education policy to significantly increase government investment. The Central and State Governments will work together to ensure that government investment in the education sector reaches the gross domestic product (GDP). Union Human Resources Development Former Minister Ramesh Pokhriyal Nishank said this in a written reply in the Lok Sabha sometime ago.

Strengthen pre-primary education system

Pre-primary education should also be part of education and a specialised system for its management should be developed. Trained teachers need to be set up. Without it is unlikely to run definitively. The 5 plus, 3 plus, 3 plus 4 approach should be implemented. The National Right to Education Act needs to be amended to make pre-primary education also part of the education sector. The National Right to Education Act stipulates that children between the ages of 6 and 14 must be educated. But the Modi government confined age under 3 to 18 years. Accordingly, the National Right to Education Act needs to be amended in Parliament to establish a special system for the administration of pre-primary education and the appointment of sensitive teachers. Only then will it have a chance to run successfully. Indicates several changes in relation to the field of higher education, these changes are also likely to lead to privatisation. For example, UGC and AICTE (All India Council for Technical Education) have been set up in the past to fund higher education. They have been funding the development of higher education for over 60 years. Donors to universities and colleges, but according to the new education policy, these will be abolished and a Higher Education Council will be set up. Its goal is not to fund universities and colleges, but only to control. This means that the higher education sector is already large-scale privatized and corporatised. To make this even bigger, the UGC is preparing to dissolve the AICTE and set up a Higher Education Council.

To sum up, in view of changing times and circumstances, the new education policy seems to be a very bold attempt being made by the PM Modi and his regime. Various institutional changes are included as part of the NEP 2020. Several educational reforms have been proposed and would be implemented throughout the country. While the policy is good theoretically, its implications after implementation may be appreciated in the days to come. In any case, focusing on more budgetary support to education will certainly help the education sector to develop better than before. Ultimately, the qualitative dimension of education is expected to be achieved with the implementation of this policy, perhaps.

References

1. Govt. of India. Report of the Education Commission (1964-66), Education and National Development, New Delhi. Ministry of Human Resource and Development1966, p.1.
2. Govt. of India. Draft National Education Policy 2019. Ministry of Human Resource Development, Govt. of India, 2019. p. 137.
3. Omvedt, G. Cultural Revolution in a Colonial Society: The Non-Brahmin Movement in Western India (1873-1930). Bombay. Scientific Socialist Education Trust, 1976.
4. NIEPA. Elementary Education in India: Analytical Tables 2016-17. New Delhi, p.76.

32

Flipped Classrooms as a Source of Advancing the Process of Teaching and Learning

Dr Rafic Taj. V

Abstract

We always aspire to have an entertaining/recreating environment around us, don't we? Learning environment also has no exception of it. Perpetually, efforts are rendered by concerned authority (Educators, Teachers, Policy Makers etc.) to make the learning more lively, jovial at the same time experiential. Advancement in Educational Technology has made this process of facilitating congenial atmosphere for learning more meaningful. Flip learning is one such strategy and a trend in the field of education which is facilitating active and participatory learning in the class room. So what is Flip learning? it is a type of blended learning where students are expected to be active participant in the process of teaching - learning by being instructed to have complete reading of the source (video/online lectures, digital resource, text reading etc...) shared or guided by the teacher. This paper is empherical in nature. The data is collected from 30 students studying in degree through a Questionnaire shared via Google forms. The findings of the study mostly reveal that flipped classrooms are welcomed by students as means of novel learning.

Keywords : Flipped classrooms, teaching- learning.

Introduction

We always aspire to have an entertaining/recreating environment around us, don't we? Learning environment also has no exception of it. Perpetually, efforts are rendered by concerned authority (Educators, Teachers, Policy Makers etc.) to make the learning more lively, jovial at the same time experiential. Advancement in Educational Technology has made this process of facilitating congenial atmosphere for learning more meaningful.

Flip learning is one such strategy and a trend in the field of education which is facilitating active and participatory learning in the class room. So what is Flip learning? it is a type of blended learning where students are expected to be active participant in the process of teaching - learning by being instructed to have complete reading of the source (video/online lectures, digital resource, text reading etc...) shared or guided by the teacher.

Jonathan Bergmann and Aaron Sams were the pioneers of flipped classrooms. They both were high school chemistry teachers. Significant relevance for flipping classes was aptly discussed by these personalities in their book Flip your classroom: Reach every student in every class every day (2012) as listed below:

- Flipping is very apt for today's students.
- Flipping keeps students engaged.
- Flipping assists slow learners.
- Flipping caters the need of students of all abilities.
- Flipping facilitates smooth learning with the provision of pause and rewind.
- Flipping increases student-teacher interaction.
- Flipping allows teachers to know their students better.
- Flipping increases student-student interaction.
- Flipping changes classroom management.
- Flipping changes the way we talk to parents.
- Flipping educate parents.

Steps to be followed for the implementation of Flipped Classroom

The 6-step guide to flipping your classroom by Jeff Dunn (2014) presented 6 easy steps for implementing flipped classroom. These steps should be followed by **review, revise and repeat.**

1. Plan: Figure out which lesson in particular you want to flip. Outline the key learning outcomes and a lesson plan.

2. Record: Instead of teaching this lesson in-person, make a video. A screencast works. Make sure it contains all the key elements you'd mention in the classroom.

In Bergmann and Sams' book (2012), they also pointed out that do not make a video just for the sake of making a video. Only do so when you feel these are appropriate and necessary. It all depends on the educational goal of your lesson. If making videos better facilitate your instructional goal, then go ahead.

3. Share: Send the video to your students. Make it engaging and clear. Explain that the video's content will be fully discussed in class.

4. Change: Now that your students have viewed your lesson, they're prepared to actually go more in-depth than ever before.

5. Group: An effective way to discuss the topic is to separate into groups where students are given a task to perform. Write a poem, a play, make a video, etc.

6. Regroup: Get the class back together to share the individual group's work with everyone. Ask questions, dive deeper than ever before.

Approaches flipped Class activities include:

Active learning - Allow students to apply concepts in class where they can ask peers or instructors for feedback and clarification.

Peer instruction - Students can teach each other by explaining concepts or working on small problems.

Collaborative learning - Collaborative learning activities could increase student engagement, enhance student understanding, and promote collective intelligence.

Problem-based learning - Class time can be spent working on problems that can last for the duration of a semester.

Discussions or debate - Give students the opportunity to articulate their thoughts on the spot and to develop their arguments in support of their opinions or claims.

Research Trends on Flipped Classroom

The impact of flipped classroom

The review suggested inconsistent findings regarding the effects of flipped classroom in student learning, with some suggesting benefits while others reporting negligible improvement over traditional teaching methods.

Perceptions of flipped classroom

"Students were generally satisfied with the approach, particularly the usefulness of the online modules, because of easy access to resources for self-paced learning" .

Attitude changes after using the flipped classroom

Positive changes were reported in a study. Studies have suggested that medical students reported increased enjoyment, decreased boredom, and greater task value in flipped classroom.

Knowledge, skills and behaviour changes with the flipped classroom curriculum.

Mixed results were detected regarding students' changes in knowledge and skills with the flipped classroom versus the traditional lecturing. Similar to student learning outcome, some studies found positive results while others suggesting no differences.

Objectives of the Study

1. To investigate the students' perception on flipped classes in understanding the concepts from Social Science course.

2. To study the impact of flipped classes on students in learning concepts in Social Science course.

Methodology

A survey method using the questionnaire is adopted to investigate the impact of flipped classes in learning and understanding the concepts in Social Science course.

Sample

Thirty students of III year degree from an unaided institution comprises the sample of the study.

Statistical technique used

Percentage analysis is used as a statistical technique to analyse the data collected.

Analysis and interpretation of data

Students' perception on flipped classes in understanding the concepts from Social Science course.

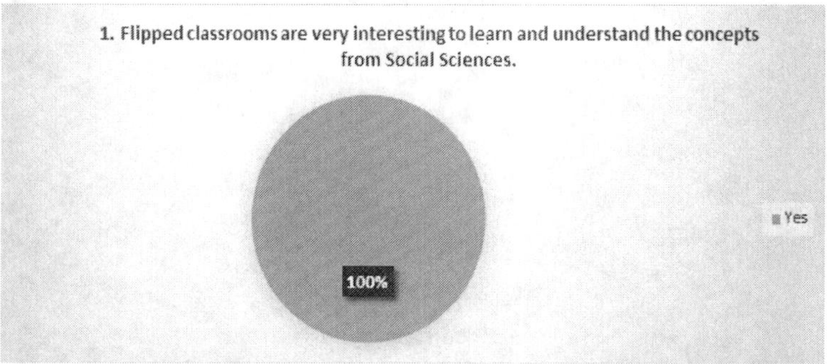
1. Flipped classrooms are very interesting to learn and understand the concepts from Social Sciences.
100%
Yes

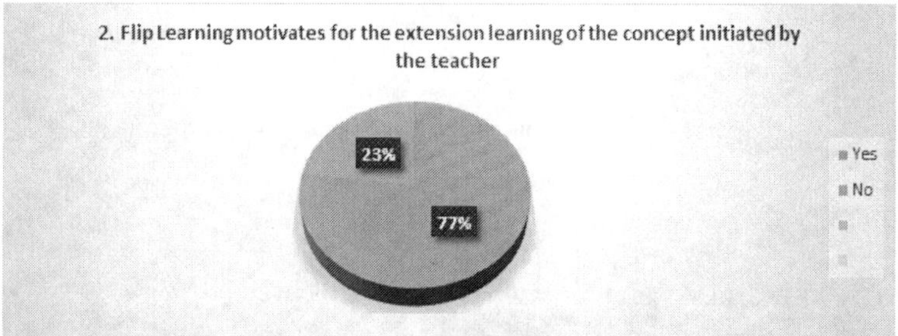
2. Flip Learning motivates for the extension learning of the concept initiated by the teacher
23%
77%
Yes
No

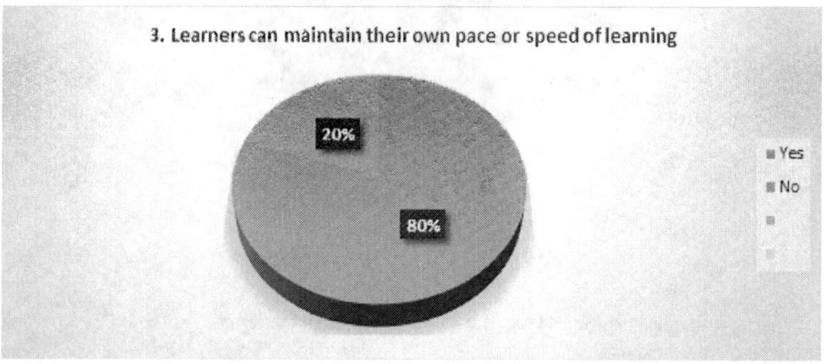
3. Learners can maintain their own pace or speed of learning
20%
80%
Yes
No

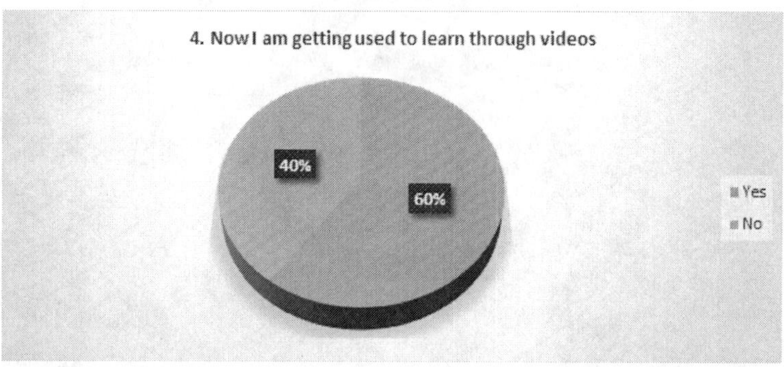
4. Now I am getting used to learn through videos
40%
60%
Yes
No

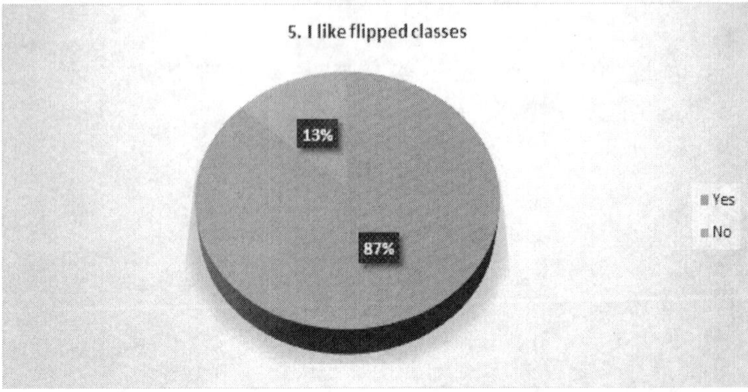
5. I like flipped classes
13%
87%
Yes
No

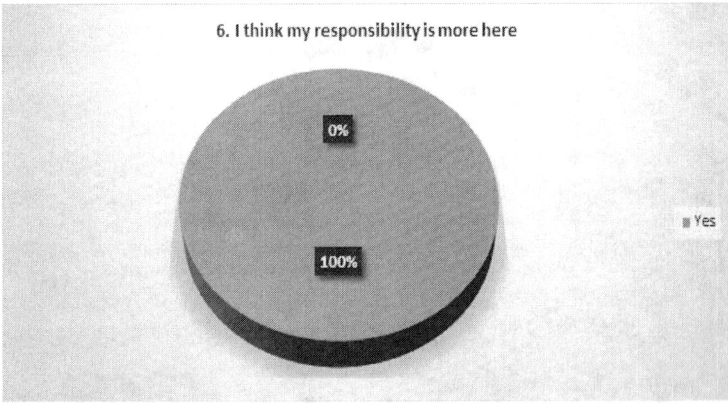
6. I think my responsibility is more here
0%
100%
Yes

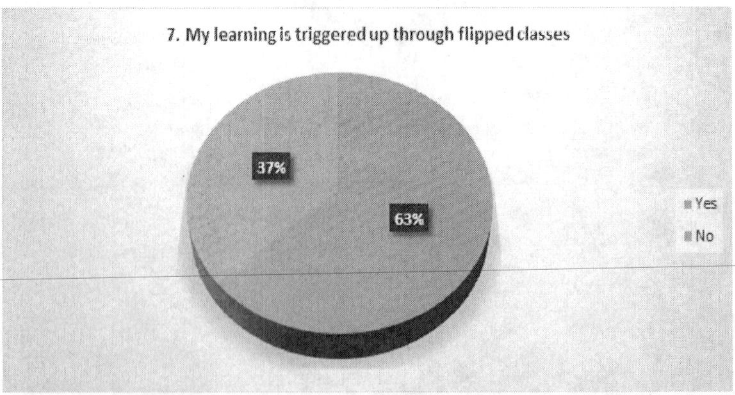
7. My learning is triggered up through flipped classes
37%
63%
Yes
No

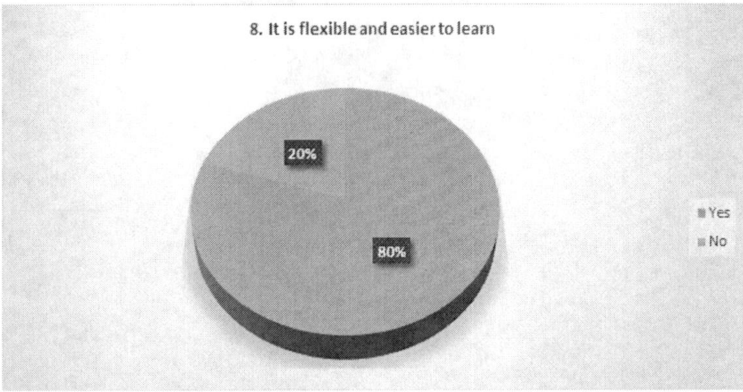
8. It is flexible and easier to learn
20%
80%
Yes
No

9. It is a kind of stress as assignments need to be attended mandatorily
30%
70%
Yes
No

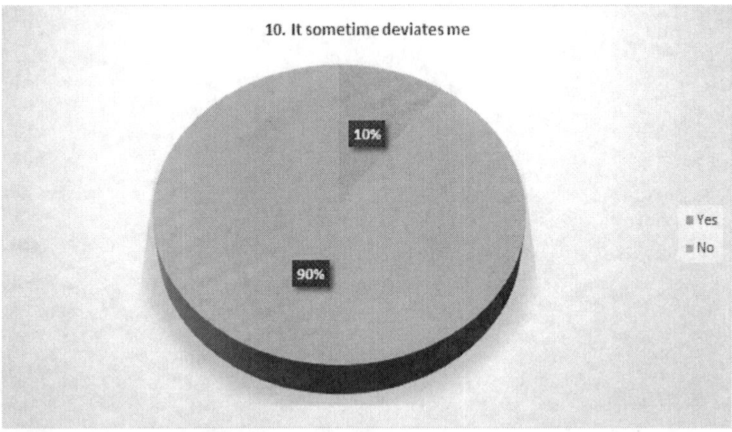
10. It sometime deviates me
10%
90%
Yes
No

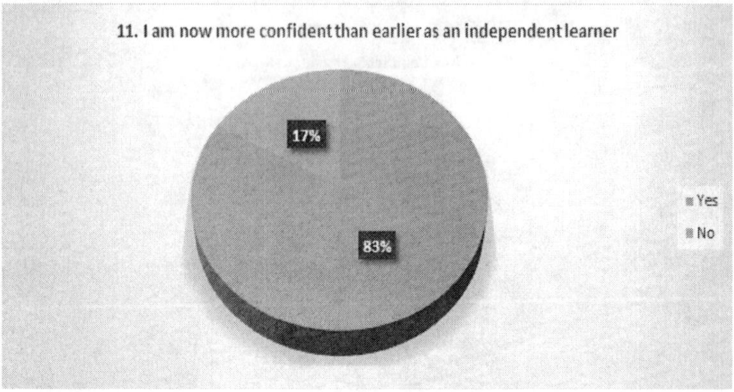
11. I am now more confident than earlier as an independent learner
17%
83%
Yes
No

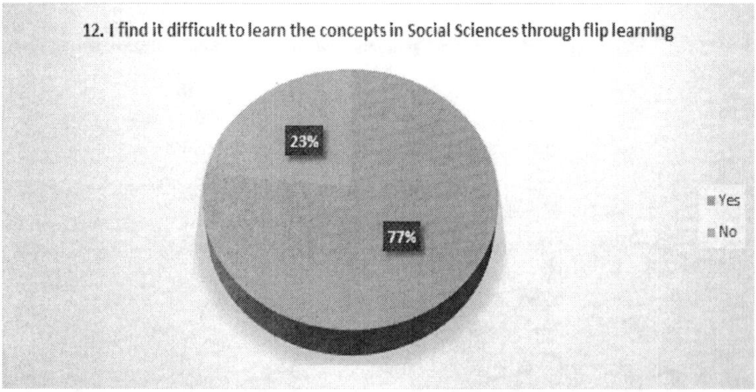
12. I find it difficult to learn the concepts in Social Sciences through flip learning
23%
77%
Yes
No

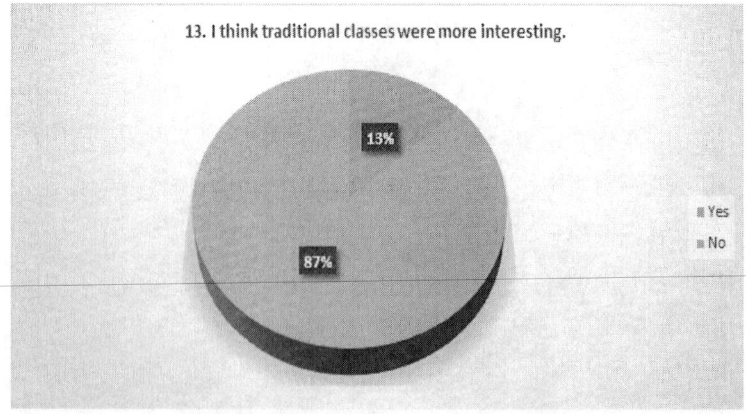
13. I think traditional classes were more interesting.
13%
87%
Yes
No

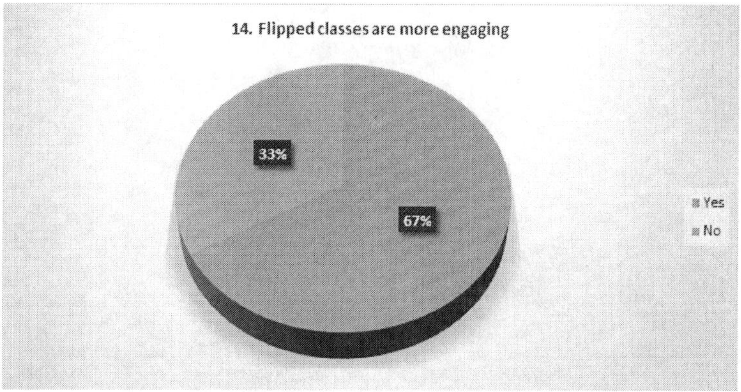
14. Flipped classes are more engaging
33%
67%
Yes
No

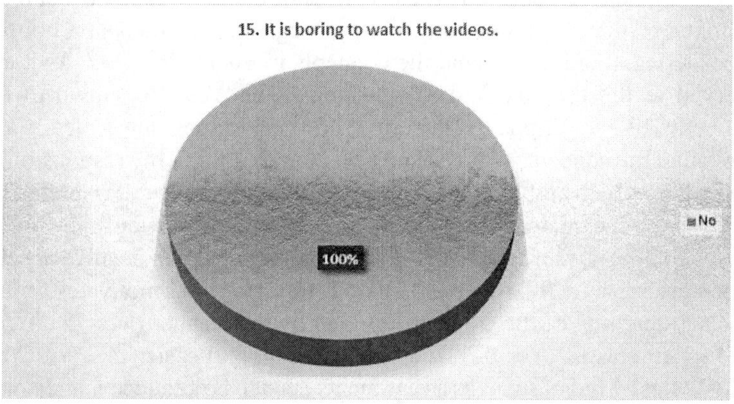
15. It is boring to watch the videos.
100%
No

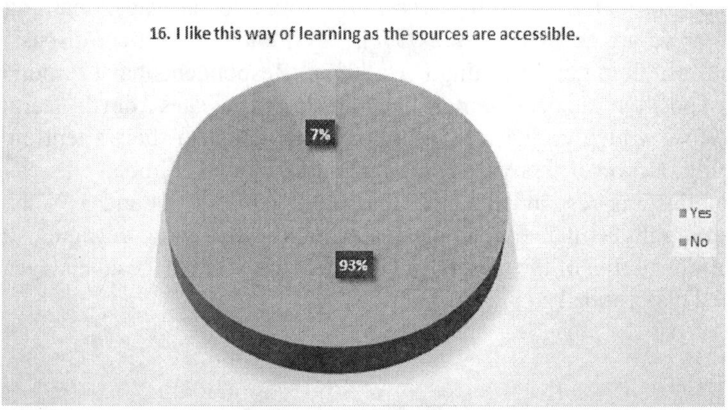
16. I like this way of learning as the sources are accessible.
7%
93%
Yes
No

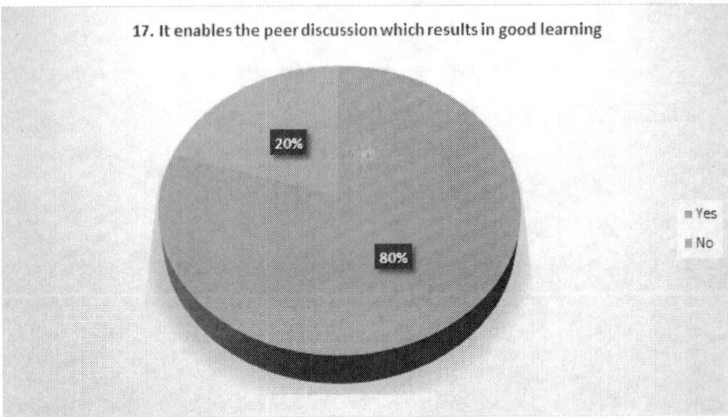

Investigators Observation

Through the present study the investigator could investigate that there are mixed responses on both positive and negative statements on Flipped classes to learn and understand the concepts in Social Sciences. As it can observed in the pie charts, 100% responses as 'Yes' are shown to the statements like 1. Flipped classrooms are very interesting to learn and understand the concepts from Social Sciences, 6. I think my responsibility is more here which highlight the fact that flipped classes are very interesting at the same time students feel that their responsibility is more in flipped classes. Similarly, more than 70% responses are gained on positive aspects flipped classes with the statements like 2. Flip Learning motivates for the extension learning of the concept initiated by the teacher (Yes-77%), 5. I like flipped classes (Yes-87%), 8. It is flexible and easier to learn (Yes-80%), 9. It is a kind of stress as assignments need to be attended mandatorily (Yes-70%), 11. I am now more confident than earlier as an independent learner (Yes-83%), 12. I find it difficult to learn the concepts in Social Sciences through flip learning (Yes-77%), 16. I like this way of learning as the sources are accessible (Yes-93%), 17. It enables the peer discussion which results in good learning (Yes-80%). Respondents have responded almost positively to the statement like Flip classes deviates from the learning (No-90%) which conveys that students can keep up their attention in learning. However there are some responses like 14. Flipped classes are more engaging respondents have responded 67% as yes and 33% as no which highlights that flipped classes should be still more engaging. It is the responsibility of the facilitator (Teacher) to optimize the advantages of flipped classrooms!

References

1. Awidi, I. T., and Paynter, M. (2019). The impact of a flipped classroom approach on student learning experience. Comput. Educ. 128, 269-283.
2. Chang, C. Y., Sung, H. Y., Guo, J. L., Chang, B. Y., and Kuo, F. . (2019). Effects of spherical video-based virtual reality on nursing students' learning performance in childbirth education training Interactive Learn. Environ 27, 1-17.
3. Chauhan, S. S. (2008). Innovations in Teaching Learning Process. UP: Vikas Publishing House Pvt. Ltd.
4. Kristen Purcell, Judy Buchanan And Linda Friedrich 2013. The Impact of Digital Tools on Student Writing and How Writing is taught in Schools. Pew Research centre Internet & Technology.
5. Learning: The Treasure within 1996.UNESCO publications Paris. ISBN: 92-3-103274-7.

33

Life Skills, Skill Development and Personality Development

Dr Sathyanarayana G.

Abstract

In the new millennium, education is undergoing a revolutionized change regarding science and technology, globalisation, privatisation, urbanisation, industrialisation, etc. They face many emerging issues such as Smartphone addition, global warming, drought, poverty, suicide, population explosion as well as other issues like alcoholism, drug abuse, sexual abuse, smoking, juvenile delinquency, anti-social acts, etc. that have an adverse effect on them and others too, to a large extent.

Life skills include psychosocial competencies and interpersonal skills that help people make informed decisions, solve problems, think critically and creatively, communicate effectively, build healthy relationships, empathise with others, and cope with managing their lives in a healthy and productive manner. The aggressive competition, unemployment, lack of job security, etc. are some of the major concerns for the educated and as a result, they are caught in the mad race. This new challenge requires immediate and effective responses from a socially responsible system of education. But in real scenario, most of them are unable to utilise their potential in an appropriate way due to lack of guidance and motivation. Social problems like alcoholism, drug abuse, sexual abuse, smoking, juvenile delinquency, anti-social acts, etc. have an adverse effect on them and others too, to a large extent.

This new challenge requires immediate and an effective response from a socially responsible system of education. Education, nowadays is very important, but the kind of education, to support and live life better is more important. 'Education' is important, but education to support and live life better is more important. It has been felt that life skills education bridges the gap between basic functioning and capabilities. It strengthens the ability of an individual to meet the needs and demands of the present society and helps in dealing with the above issues in a manner to get desired behaviour practical. Imparting life skill training through inculcating life skill education will help youth to overcome such difficulties in life. The present paper focuses on the importance of life skills education and the benefits of imparting life skill education in our curriculum i.e. developing social, emotional and thinking skills in students, as they are the important building blocks for a dynamic citizen, who can cope up with future challenges, and survive well. As personality development is totality of everything about the individual and research is one of aspects of education to be viewed as process or a tool for the development of personality.

Objectives

1. To Develop abilities and competence in young people as they face the realities of life.
2. To Assess the students behaviour change in the three areas- knowledge, attitude and skills.
3. To Enable individuals to translate knowledge, attitude and values into actual abilities.
4. To Assess the students physiological, psychological, psychosocial maturation and interpersonal skills.

Keywords: Skill, Life Skills, Skill Development and Personality Development.

Introduction

A skill is the ability of an individual to apply his/her mental and physical power to control the environment. It involves things like thinking, playing and implementation so as to solve social, political, economic and culture problems. These skills are the ability to understand one self, build sound relationships with others, survive under difficult circumstances, act responsibly and safely, and solve problems. It addresses the balance between knowledge, attitude and skills. No one has time for his/her 'self', to develop empathy with surrounding and to have harmony in society. Young mind is being considered, as the most productive members of the society, due to their physical and intellectual capability. Thus, the cardinal focus of Education, therefore, needs an extraordinary emphasis on developing such skills in students, as they are the important building blocks for a dynamic citizen, who can cope up with future challenges, and survive. Central Board of Secondary Education (CBSE) India has recognised this fact that it is necessary to develop scholastic as well as co-scholastic areas, and hence, has made life skill education as a compulsory element in its curriculum. It has been felt, that life skills education bridges the gap between basic functioning and capabilities. strengthens the ability of an individual to meet the needs and demands of the present society. Personality development encompasses the dynamic construction and deconstruction of integrative characteristics that distinguish an individual in terms of interpersonal behavioural traits. Personality development is ever-changing and subject to contextual factors and life-altering experiences. Personality development is also dimensional in description and subjective in nature. That is, personality development can be seen as a continuum varying in degrees of intensity and change. It is subjective in nature because its conceptualisation is rooted in social norms of expected behaviour, self-expression, and personal growth. The dominant viewpoint in personality psychology indicates that personality emerges early and continues to develop across one's lifespan. Adolescence is also the stage when young people extend their relationships beyond parents and family and are intensely influenced by their peers and the outside world.

Review of Literature

According to Albertyn *et al.* (2004) life skills training enhance critical thinking abilities, which further impacts were living life actively, being responsible in the job and in future planning too.

Ramesh and Farshad C. (2004) in his study proved the effectiveness of like skills training in increasing mental and physical health, pro-social behaviour and decreasing in behaviour. social problems and self-destructive behaviour.

Smith & *et al.*, (2004) noted significant improvement in interpersonal relationship and reduction in aggression and behaviour. problems.

Tuttle *et al.*, (2006), during their investigation, add the life skills to students' curriculum. The results of this study suggested the extraordinary capability of teens to positive promotion and flexibility.

Vranda and Rao (2011) proved that life skills training enhanced their psychosocial competencies.

Puspakumarag (2013) in his study showed that life skills training was effective in preventing a wide range of problems such as substance abuse, teenage pregnancies, violence Bullying and to promote self-confidence and self esteem among the adolescents.

Roodbari, Sahdipoor, and Ghale (2013) in their research showed that life skills training has a positive effect and improves social development, emotional and social adjustment, suggesting an increase in compatibility of children and public health. The present paper focuses on how enhancing social, emotional and thinking skills through life skills education, helps the twenty first century youngsters to achieve their goals strengthens the abilities to meet the needs and demands of the present society and be successful in life.

Life Skill Education

According to UNICEF, Life Skills are a behaviour. change or behaviour development approach designed to address balance of three areas: Knowledge, Attitude, Skills. The world bodies such as UNICEF, UNESCO, and WHO list the ten core Life Skills as:

1. Self-awareness, 2. Empathy, 3. Critical thinking, 4. Creative thinking, 5. Decision making, 6. Problem Solving, 7. Effective communication, 8. Interpersonal relationship, 9. Coping with stress, 10. Coping with emotion.

Need for Life Skills

As children develop, their life begins to change. Adolescents may develop a variety of life skills to prepare them to face challenges, take up family responsibility, make decisions and think about what they want to be in the future. Life skills education addresses these issues for the benefit of the individual and society at large. Life skills equip adolescents with knowledge and attitudes that should lead to the requirement behaviour. They reduce health risk and raise awareness on health and related behaviour. such as sexual abuse, drug abuse, violence, drunkenness, unwanted pregnancy, sexual transmitted infections (STIs) and HIV/AIDS. Life skills play a decisive role in helping to prevent these behaviour and enlightening teenagers about these challenges so that they can protect themselves.

Types of Life Skills

Individual Life Skills

The ability of a person to know and understand personal feelings, emotions, strengths, weaknesses as well as the position in life and society. It is also the ability of an individual to have a clear vision of self-identity of where he/she come from and culture which has shaped him/her.

The importance of Individual Life Skills

Individual skill is very important in building self-esteem and self-confidence as a person becomes aware of his/her own capabilities and position in the community. The more individual is aware of personal capabilities, the more capable he/she is of using those skills effectively and be able to make choices which are consistent with the opportunities available in the society which one lives. Individual life skills include self-awareness, ability to cope with stress, with emotions and assertiveness.

(a) Self-awareness

Awareness is the ability of knowing things. Thus, self-awareness is the ability of an individual to know himself or herself, his or her feelings, emotions, strengths and weaknesses. This skill enables a person to ask important questions about himself or herself.

(b) Copying with stress

Stress is a mental, emotional or physical tension or pressure. It can be caused by the events such as examinations, divorce, death of a family member or a friend or problems in the family. A person needs to develop skills that help him or her to cope with stress. Evaluate yourself.

(c) Copying with emotions

Emotions are strong feelings such as love, the desire to be accepted, fear, anger shyness and disgust. The ability to handle emotions enables a person to control his/her strong feelings and

(d) Assertiveness

Assertiveness is the ability of a person to know what he/she wants and why, and be able to take necessary steps to achieve it. An assertive person is able to express his or her opinions or desires strongly and with confidence. However, in achieving what he/she wants the person has to consider rights of others. Evaluate yourself; Let's say you are having a debate session in school. The motion is, 'Teachers should build laboratories for practical training in the school'.

Social Skills

This is the ability to understand and live in peace and harmony with others. These are skills for the development of positive interpersonal relationships with friends, family members, peers, people in authority and adults. Social life skills can be developed through the following:

(a) Building positive relationships with others

This is the ability of a person to meet and relate with others in various places such as schools, playing field and social gathering. Relationships can be between children and parents or students and teachers. They can also be between relatives, neighbours or peers. Being able to form healthy relationships enables one to know how to behave properly in each relationship.

(b) Peer resistance

Peer pressure is when one's peers/friends influence another person to do something. Our friends can influence us to do good or bad things. For example, positive peer pressure can lead to you to work harder in school and improve your grades. Negative peer pressure can cause you to engage in wrong activities, such as drug abusing and escaping from school. Such bad behaviour will get you into trouble with your teachers and parents. No one wants to have a friend who can lead one into problems. Peer resistance helps an individual to take control of him/herself by resisting negative influences from others.

(c) Empathy

This is the ability to understand other people's feelings and to feel concerned about their problems. When you empathize, you imagine yourself in the other people's situation. This skill enables us to share our friend's problems.

(d) Negotiation

This is the ability to agree on issues without undermining or going against one's principles. It is an important skill when disagreements occur. Negotiation skills build good understanding. Evaluate yourself. Imagine your friend wants you to discuss mathematics with him/her while you wanted to discuss civics. How would you negotiate with him/her so that both of you can agree?

(e) Effective communication

This is the ability of a person to communicate with people according to their mood, age and background. It includes speaking, reading, listening and writing skills. This skill is very important in maintaining good relationship with other people. Speaking correctly means saying what you want in a way that can be easily and clearly understood.

Effective decision-making skills

These skills enable a person to make good decisions. The following are the aspects of effective decision-making skills: Critical thinking, creative thinking, problem-solving and decision-making.

(a) Critical thinking

This is the ability of a person to develop a deep understanding of something. It helps a person to understand the environment in which he/she lives and problems which might prevent him or her from making proper decisions. Before making a decision, a critical thinker considers the advantages and disadvantages of various ways of doing something. Critical thinker helps a person to come up with ideas to solve problems.

(b) Creative thinking

This is the ability to think and come up with new ideas and ways of doing things. In life, creative thinking helps an individual to come up with solutions that other people had not thought of.

(c) Decision-making

This is the ability to make the best choice out of many available options. The choice is made after considering its results. In life, it is important to think about consequences before making a decision.

Sources of Life Skills

1. Family: Parents, guardians and other relatives are primary source from whom we learn different life skills.
2. Neighbours: We learn the different ways that people live from our neighbours. Good neighbours help us to behave well.
3. Friends: Friends helps us to acquire various life skills. Exchanging good ideas with friends help to mould us in to well-behaved individuals.
4. Schools: The good education we get at school enables us to develop skills for life.
5. Society: The way people live in the society allows an individual to learn what is expected of him/her and how he/she should behave in different circumstances.
6. Religion: Good religion teachings help to get skills which enable us to live harmoniously in society.

Life Skills in Students are as follows

Classroom Discussions: An activity, providing opportunities for students to learn and practice turning to one another in solving problems. Enables students to deepen their understanding of the topic and personalise their connection to it. Develops skills, in listening, assertiveness, and empathy.

Brainstorming: It allows students to generate ideas quickly and spontaneously.

Role Plays: Along with being a fun activity and involves whole class, to be active and participative, it also provides an excellent strategy for practicing skills; experiencing how one might handle a potential situation in real life; increasing empathy for others and their point of view; and increasing insight into own feelings.

Groups: Groups are helpful when the time is limited as it maximizes student input. Allows students interactions, allows to, know, one another better which in a way enhances team building and team work.

Educational Games and Simulations: It promotes fun, active learning, and rich discussion as participants work hard to prove their points or earn points. They require the combined use of knowledge, attitudes, and skills and allow students to test out assumptions and abilities in a relatively safe environment.

Analysis of Situation and Case Studies: It gives a chance, to analyze, explore, challenges, dilemmas and safely test solutions for; providing opportunities for working together in groups, sharing idea, new learning and gives insight and promotes sometimes to see things differently. Case studies are like powerful catalysts for thought and discussion. Engaging in this thinking process; students improve their own, critical thinking, decision-making skills. It also gives chance to confront with risks or any challenges and find ways to cope with it.

Story-Telling: Can help students think about local problems and develop critical thinking skills, creative skills to write stories, or interact to tell stories. 'Story-Telling' lends itself to draw analogies or make comparisons, help discover healthy solutions. It also enhances attention, concentration, listening skills and develops patience and endurance.

Debates: Provides opportunity to address a particular issue in depth and creatively. Health issues lend themselves well: students can debate, for instance, whether smoking should be ban in public places in a community. It allows students to defend a position that may mean a lot to them. It offers a chance to practice higher thinking skills.

Findings /Discussion

A relevant and proper implementation of life skill education is a need of an hour, for today's society. Imparting life skills education to the students, can be helpful as it specifically addresses the needs of children, helps in motivating, providing practical, cognitive, emotional, social and self-management skills for life adjustments, life skills education proves to be an effective approach in primary prevention education, as its more interactive, uses problem solving approach and is activities based. Hence, teacher and the taught both involves in learn and fun too.

On the whole, life skills education, have found to be an effective psychosocial intervention strategy for promoting positive social, and mental health of adolescents which plays an important role in all aspects such as strengthening coping strategies and developing self-confidence and emotional intelligence, as well as enhancing critical thinking, problem solving and decision-making skills has been well documented in the aforementioned studies.

Thus, there is, need and importance of life skills education to be integrated into the regular school curriculum and given on a daily basis by a life skills trainer/ teacher/counsellor to enhance the mental health of students, equip them with better adapted skills to face the challenges of changing life situations and empower them to become fully functioning contributors to the host society in particular and the world in general. In the light of above discussion, it could be concluded, that, Life skill education has its importance and significance in overall development of students, life skill education programme as a good supportive system for adolescents.

Future Implications

Although considerable progress has been made in the past decade, and in the present study too, to reflect, life skills education, as an effective mode of education, which does enhances social, emotional and thinking skills, and helps the twenty first century youngsters to achieve their goals, by strengthening their abilities to meet the needs and demands of the present society and be successful in life but still further empirical research is needed from future researchers, academicians and professionals in the related field to demonstrate robust findings.

Conclusion

There is more need of government intervention and policies to encourage these kind of courses in various sectors and raise the employability through various short term, long term and vocational courses. Although the need for skill development initiative is understood and realised by many sectors still there are few sectors where awareness needs to be created. Also ministry of skill development and entrepreneurship, National skill development council and sector skill councils are formulated still more work is to be done on identification of employability attributes, design and modify curricular course to cater the demand of the sector. If skilled can contribute to make the economy stronger instead of becoming the liability. The skill development will raise the efficiency level of the work force and raise the employability of youth, who otherwise feel alienated after being educated but not getting a job to earn.

References

1. Agrawal, J.C. (2003). Child Development and process of learning. New Delhi: Shipra publications.
2. Nair, M. (2005). Family Life & Life Skills Education for Adolescents. Abstract, University of Southampton.
3. Beron, R., Nyila R., B. Don B. Bharadwaj G. (2010). Social psychology. Pearsons publications Pvt. Ltd.
4. Mangal, S. K. (2010). Advanced educational psychology. New Delhi: Prentice Hall of India Pvt. Ltd.
5. Sidhu, Kulbir Sing (2011). Methodology of Research in Education, New Delhi: Sterling Publishers Pvt. Ltd.
6. Pillai, R. (2012). The importance of life skills education for children and adolescents Mind the young minds. Retrieved from https://sites.google.com/site/mind-theyoungminds/souvenir-cum-scientific-update
7. Bilohur, V. (2019). Formation and Development of Personality Established by Change and Growth. Humanities Bulletin of Zaporizhzhe State Engineering Academy, 76, 77-89.
8. Wrzus, Cornelia (2021). "Processes of personality development: An update of the TESSERA framework", The Handbook of Personality Dynamics and Processes, Elsevier, pp. 101-123, retrieved 2022-01-21.

34

Foreign Direct Investment and Role of Indian Higher Education System 2020

Dr Jaisheela. B

Abstract

India is the fastest developing country in international market has seen a shift in the education sector especially in higher education in past few decades. The transformation is major and visible. FDI is a buzzword in market. Foreign Direct Investment (FDI) has been a major non-debt financial resource for the economic development of India. Foreign investors invest in India to take advantage of relatively lower wages, special investment privileges like tax exemptions, etc. For a country where foreign investment is being made, it also means achieving technical know-how and generating employment. The present research paper discusses the transformation of education sector from black board to online method of education system in the higher education. It also discusses the introduction of FDI in higher education sector, the facts and issues relating to the same. Higher education is one such sector which witnessed transformation over decade.

Keyword : Investment, Higher Education, New Education Policy, Regulation.

Introduction

Education sectors in India especially higher educational institutions and universities are growing day by day and gaining lots of importance in the world and India as well. Education Sectors is likely to grow by the Gross Enrolment Ratio (GER) by 2020. Foreign Direct Investment up to 100 percent is allowed in most of the sectors more significantly. Thus the role of private sector in higher education has significantly increased in the last decade and the growth of this sector alone, estimates, to grow to US$ 70 billion by 2013 and US$ 115 billion by 2018. The study focuses on FDI and Role of Indian Higher Education System 2020 and evaluates the advantages and disadvantages of going in for FDI. Foreign Direct Investment has always been a matter of concern for India, when it comes to education sector 100 percent FDI is allowed by the Government but, besides its advantages, it has some limitations or disadvantages also. In this paper an attempt has been made to highlight the good and bad effects of FDI in Higher Education Sectors like Universities and Colleges.

In India education is the key factor to nation building process. Education is the major operating sector in the Indian economy as it stands as the major contributor of income to the economy. Contribution made by the education sector has rapidly increased during the past years. The scope of education and its advancement is mainly from the sources of higher education i.e., colleges and universities operating in large scale. Major participants of education sector are the top credited universities, which generate huge incomes and credibility to the nation by its high potential working patterns that deliver top quality education. These universities produce top quality potential youngsters who are the future of the economy. Enrollment into these universities is a matter of concern to the individuals as it involves a screening pattern which admits only top best candidates with high potential intelligence and competency. As understood by the fact enrollment into these universities is not an easy go, only high credentials candidate's make up to the top best universities. This becomes the major concern to the students and to overcome these complexities many choose to study abroad. Over the past decade, India's share of students enrolling abroad has increased rapidly. In order to arrest the flow of funds to foreign countries, it is feasible for the government to invite foreign universities for setting up their campuses in India.

Definitions of Foreign Direct Investment

- Foreign direct investment (FDI) is an investment in a business by an investor from another country for which the foreign investor has control over the company purchased.
- The Organisation of Economic Cooperation and Development (OECD) defines control as owning 10 percent or more of the business. Businesses that make foreign direct investments are often called multinational corporations (MNCs) or multinational enterprises (MNEs). A MNE may make a direct investment by creating a new foreign enterprise, which is called a green field investment, or by the acquisition of a foreign firm, either called an acquisition or brown field investment.

Review of Literature

Ms. Rida Shaikh and Prof. Ajay Shukla (2019) in their article discusses Foreign direct investment is the crucial factor for any economy growing towards development. Foreign direct investment enables the economy in balancing the need of finance with the inflow of funds generated through different sources of investment and paper aims at analyzing the need and effect of FDI in Indian higher education system. The study is based on secondary data. Data is collected through various sources such as referral books, articles, and journals.

T. Greeshma, S. Ujwala (2020) in their paper entitled "Role of FDI in Indian higher education sector" explained the problem of high competency can be over-casted by the foreign universities that deliver high quality education and feasible enrolment process. This paper aims at analyzing the need and effect of FDI in Indian higher education system.

Dr U. Y. Memon (2017) in this paper explained "FDI and Role of Indian Educational System", FDI may be associated with improved economic growth due to the influx of capital and increased tax revenues for the host country. Host countries often try to channel FDI investment into new infrastructure and other projects to boost development. Greater competition from new companies can lead to productivity gains and greater efficiency in the host country and it has been suggested that the application of a foreign entity's policies to a domestic subsidiary may improve corporate governance standards.

Bhavya Malhotra (2014) in this paper entitled "Foreign Direct Investment: Impact on Indian Economy", this research paper aims to examine the impact of FDI on the Indian economy, particularly after two decades of economic reforms, and analyzes the challenges to position itself favourably in the global competition for FDI. The paper provides the major policy implications from this analysis, besides drawing attention on the complexities in interpreting FDI data in India.

Sameera Sultana Bahmaida (2013) Study on Foreign Direct Investment [FDI] In Education, FDI explains about the net inflows of investment to acquire a management interest and also management control and profit sharing as a part of the national accounts of a country.

Objectives of the Study

1. To understand the post effect of FDI in Indian higher education system.
2. To know the regulatory framework of NEP in Higher Education.

Methodology

The study is based on secondary sources of data. The secondary data were collected from the various books, journals, annual reports and online and offline study materials related to present study. The main source of data is various Economic Surveys of India and Ministry of Commerce and Industry data, RBI bulletin, online data base of Indian Economy. Economic and Social Survey of Asia and the Pacific, United Nations, Asian Development Outlook, Country Reports on Economic Policy and Trade Practice-Bureau of Economic and Business Affairs, U.S. Department of State and from websites of World Bank, IMF, WTO, RBI, UNCTAD, EXIM Bank etc.

Understand the effect of post effect of FDI

Implementation and acceptance of foreign investment in higher education stands beneficial to the whole economy in many ways. Implication of foreign investment in the economy by allowing them to invest in the education sector results in growth of the economy by restraining the flow of funds. The first and foremost benefit of inviting foreign investment is the effect of retaining the flow of funds to the foreign countries, the host country or the origin country from where, most of the people are migrating will reduce gradually and this results in arresting the flow of funds to the foreign countries. By this, the flow of funds can be retained at least to some extent and the effect of FDI can be clearly understood with the below factors:

1. **Foreign universities enable's the country in creating new start-ups and also brings in huge foreign investment.**
2. Migration of potential youth can be reduced.
3. Retaining the flow of funds to foreign countries.
4. State of quality education at foreign universities can be experienced at their own place.
5. High chances of enrolment.
6. Development of greater work forces in the country.
7. Foreign universities help in the growth of the economy as it attracts foreign companies to set up their branches in the country.
8. Value for education in the India will increase with the inflow of foreign universities.
9. Job opportunities may gradually increase.
10. Creates employment as it resources various foreign company.
11. Development of potential youth with good technical skills.
12. Overall economy development.

FDI and Role of higher education in India 2020

As of 2020, India has over 1000 universities, with a break up of

54 Central Universities, 416 State Universities, 125 Deemed Universities, 361 Private Universities and 159 Institution of National Institutes of National Importance which include AIIMS, IIMs, IITs, IIITs, IISER and NITs among others. Other institutions include 52,627 colleges as government Degree Colleges, private colleges, standalone institutes and post-graduate research institutions, functioning under these universities as reported by the MHRD in 2020. Colleges may be Autonomous, i.e. empowered to examine their own degrees, up to Ph.D level in some cases, or non-autonomous, in which case their examinations are under the supervision of the university to which they are affiliated; in either case, however, degrees are awarded in the name of the university rather than the college.

Higher Education in India has evolved in distinct and divergent streams with each stream monitored by an apex body, indirectly controlled by the Ministry of Human Resource Development. The 433 universities/ institutions are mostly funded by the state governments. However, there are 44 important universities called Central universities, which are maintained by the Union Government and because of relatively large funding, they have an edge over the others.

Regulatory Framework of NEP 2020 in Higher Education System

Education Policy lays particular emphasis on the development of the creative potential of each individual. It is based on the principle that education must develop not only cognitive capacities - both the foundational capacities of literacy and numeracy and 'higher-order' cognitive capacities, such as critical thinking and problem solving - but also social, ethical, and emotional capacities and dispositions. Some of the key reforms introduced vide NEP 2020 in the Indian higher education system include:

1. Quality Universities and Colleges: NEP 2020 envisions to introduce certain key changes to the higher education system, which inter alia include :
   (a) Moving towards a higher educational system consisting of large, multi-disciplinary universities and colleges, with at least one in or near every district;
   (b) Moving towards a more multidisciplinary undergraduate education;
   (c) Moving towards faculty and institutional autonomy;
   (d) Re-vamping curriculum, pedagogy, assessment and student support for enhanced student experiences;

(e) Establishment of a National Research Foundation to fund outstanding peer-reviewed research and to actively seed research in universities and colleges;

(f) Governance of higher education institutions by highly qualified independent boards having academic and administrative autonomy; and

(g) Increased access, equity, and inclusion through a range of measures, including open schooling, online education and Open Distance Learning, keeping in view the needs of learners with disabilities and substantial increases in scholarships at private/philanthropic universities for disadvantaged and underprivileged students.

2. Institutional Restructuring and Consolidation: NEP 2020 intends to end the fragmentation of higher education by transforming higher education institutions into large multidisciplinary universities and colleges, each of which will aim to have 3,000 or more students. The idea is to build vibrant communities of scholars and peers, break down harmful silos, enable students to become well-rounded across disciplines (including artistic, creative and analytic subjects as well as sports), develop active research communities across disciplines (including cross-disciplinary approach) and increase resource efficiency, both material and human across higher education.

3. Shift Towards Holistic Education with less Rote Learning: NEP 2020 advocates for promotion of holistic arts education to ensure well rounded development of students. Departments in Languages, Literature, Music, Philosophy, Indology, Art, Dance, Theatre, Education, Mathematics, Statistics, Pure and Applied Sciences, Sociology, Economics, Sports and other such subjects needed for a multidisciplinary, stimulating Indian education and environment will be established and strengthened at higher education institutions across the country. Furthermore, to ensure that students actively engage with the practical side of their learning and improve their employability options, as part of holistic education, students will also be provided with opportunities for internships with local industry, businesses, artists, crafts persons, villages and local communities, etc., as well as research internships with faculty and researchers at their own or other higher education institutions or research-institutions.

4. Internationalisation: NEP 2020 focuses on promoting India as a global study destination providing premium education at affordable costs. It is thus intended that high performing Indian universities will be encouraged to set up campuses in other countries and similarly select universities will be permitted to operate in India. A legislative framework shall be formulated and introduced facilitating the entry of foreign universities in India, and such universities will be given special dispensation regarding regulatory, governance and content norms on par with other autonomous institutions within India. Additionally, research collaboration and students exchange programmes between the Indian institutions and global institutions will be promoted and the credits acquired in foreign universities will also be permitted to be counted for award of degree.
5. Teacher Education: Recognizing the importance of creating a team of teachers that will shape the next generation, NEP 2020 lays equal emphasis on revamping teacher education as well. To reach the levels of integrity and credibility required to restore the prestige of teaching profession, the regulatory system is empowered to phase out substandard and dysfunctional teacher education institutions that do not meet basic educational criteria. The teacher education needs to be conducted within composite multidisciplinary institutions having departments of psychology, philosophy, sociology, neuroscience, Indian languages, arts, history, and literature as well as various other specialised subjects such as science, mathematics, etc.
6. Professional Education: NEP 2020 envisages that professional education will become an integral part of the overall higher education and thus it must also significantly involve critical and interdisciplinary thinking and research. Thus, the practice of setting up stand-alone technical universities, health science universities, legal and agricultural universities or institutions in these fields shall be discouraged and all existing stand-alone professional education institutions will have to become multi-disciplinary institutions by 2030, either by opening new departments or by operating in clusters. The professional education standards, viz. technical, health and legal education are also proposed to be restructured to ensure that the education standards are globally competitive and adapt to the challenges evolving with time.

7. Promoting High Quality Research: Recognizing the importance of knowledge creation and research in growing and sustaining a large and vibrant economy and uplifting the society, NEP 2020 focuses on a comprehensive approach for transforming the quality and quantity of research in India. Thus, to focus on research and promote research culture in all higher education institutions in an interrelated and coordinated fashion, NEP 2020 provides for setting up of a National Research Foundation (NRF) which would bring a quantum jump in funding and support for research. The overarching goal of NRF shall be to enable a culture of research to permeate through universities and higher education institutions across India. In this regard, NRF shall inter alia provide a reliable base of merit-based peer-reviewed research funding, helping to develop a culture of research in the country through suitable incentives for and recognition of outstanding research. NRF shall also competitively fund research in all disciplines across the academic landscape viz. science, technology, social sciences, arts, and humanities.
8. Transforming Regulatory System of Higher Education: Presently, the mechanistic and disempowering nature of the regulatory system has been rife with very basic problems, such as heavy concentrations of power within a few bodies, conflicts of interest among these bodies and a resulting lack of accountability. Furthermore, India also has some of the toughest requirements in the world for setting up higher education institutions, which requirements are largely input-centric, focusing on land and space norms, endowment funds and their sources, etc.

In terms of NEP 2020, the fundamental design principles of an effective regulatory system will thus be:

(a) A clear separation of functions to enable adequate focus on each essential role while eliminating conflicts of interest;

(b) A single, empowered, responsive, but minimalistic regulatory authority to ensure basic regulatory requirements, such as financial probity and full public disclosure of finances, procedures, course and programme offerings, and educational outcomes, while otherwise empowering institutions to make their own decisions for the pursuit of excellence;

(c) Accreditation through the establishment of independent high-quality accrediting bodies, overseen by a meta-accreditor, as the basis of regulation; and

(d) Each body in the regulatory system run by Independent Boards consisting of persons having high expertise in the relevant areas along with integrity, commitment, and a demonstrated track record of public service.

Conclusion

In order to tackle this situation 100 percent FDI has been allowed by the Govt. but besides its advantages and it is having certain severe disadvantages which needs strict action on the part of Indian govt. A regulatory body should be framed otherwise India might face some bad consequences in context of culture and autonomy of foreign education providers.

References

1. Dr U. Y. Memon, "FDI and Role of Indian Educational System" , Pune Research Times an International Journal of Contemporary studies ISSN 2456-0960, Vol. 2, Issues 1, 2017.
2. Blomstrom, M., & Kokko, A. (2003). Human capital and inward FDI. Working Papers Series, No. 167, the European Institute of Japanese Studies (Stockholm School of Economics, Sweden).
3. Borensztein, E., De Gregorio, J., & Lee, J. (1998). How does foreign direct investment affect economic growth? Journal of International Economics, 45(1), 115-135.
4. D. H., Hasan, R., Lee, J.-W., Son, H., & Zhuang, J. (2010). Closing development gaps: challenges and policy options. Asian Development Review, 27(2), 1-28.
5. Carstensen, K., & Toubal, F. (2004). Foreign direct investment in central and eastern European countries: A dynamic panel analysis. Journal of Comparative Economics, 32(1), 3-22.
6. Cleeve, A. E., Debrah, Y., & Yiheyis, Z. (2015). Human capital and FDI inflow: An assessment of the African case. World Development, 74, 1-14.
7. T.Greeshma, S.Ujwala, "Role of FDI in Indian higher education sector", IOSR Journal of Business and Management (IOSR-JBM) e-ISSN: 2278-487X, p-ISSN: 2319-7668 pp. 31-36, 2020. www.iosrjournals.org..
8. Bhavya Malhotra. "Foreign Direct Investment: Impact on Indian Economy", Global Journal of Business Management and Information Technology. ISSN 2278-3679 Volume 4, Number 1 (2014), pp. 17-23 © Research India Publications. http://www.ripublication.com.
9. Sameera Sultana Bahmaida. Foreign Direct Investment [FDI] In Education, International Journal of Advanced Trends in Computer Science and Engineering, Vol.2 , No.1, pp. : 519 - 531 (2013) Special Issue of ICACSE 2013 - Held on 7-8 January, 2013 in Lords Institute of Engineering and Technology, Hyderabad, ISSN 2278-3091.
10. Cheng, K. L., & Kwan, K. Y. (2000). What are the determinants of the location of foreign direct investment? The Chinese experience. Journal of International Economics, 51(2), 379-400.

35

Evaluation and Assessment Teacher Education in India - A Critical Review

Kola Kiran Kumar

ABSTRACT

Quality and excellence in the education sector is one of the major initiatives of the Government of India in its Educational plans. To achieve the outcome of enhanced quality at all levels of Teacher education, Govt. of India has been focusing its attention on quality and excellence in higher education and as well as teacher education. Teacher quality has produced voluminous studies that line many a research library. Discussion on what it is, how it is developed, and its connection to student achievement have become the feature of educational slang in the twenty first century. Teacher quality and the strength of educators leadership are recognised as the greatest determinants of educational success. Quality teaching has a measurable impact on student outcomes. The teaching profession in India has much to celebrate. Our teachers and academic leaders are having a profound impact on our society. Teacher quality affects all stages of the teaching 'lifecycle, from attraction into the profession to ongoing development and retention in their own schools. These seek to look at teacher quality in away in which it brings: as a means to review how the terms excellence and quality are shaped by policy, identify how educators perceive teaching quality and to review how quality is cultivated in teachers. Within this scope, this research article provides an overview of teacher education and evaluation in India and lastly we discuss about issues and challenges in teacher education.

Keywords : Teacher Education, Educational System, Curricular Design, Educational Policy, Teacher Quality, Teacher Educator.

Statement of Problem

"The function of education is to teach one to think intensively and to think critically. Intelligence plus character that is the goal of true education."

Martin Luther King Jr.

The Parliament approves legislation on education and the Ministry of Education sets guidelines for all practical issues including teacher education, as well as being the main funder in the sector. In general, India does not experience shortages of school teachers but there are shortages in particular subject fields and locations, such as in the areas of mathematics, and science, especially in remote areas. Quality and excellence in the education sector is one of the major initiatives of the Government of India in its plans. To achieve the outcome of enhanced quality at all levels of education, Govt. of India has been focusing its attention on quality and excellence in higher education and teacher education. Management of teacher education is a difficult task because of the fact that there are large numbers of variables in teacher education programmes including variations in the purpose for which persons join teacher training courses of various levels. There are four types of teacher education institutions:

1. Government managed,
2. Examining body managed,
3. Government aided and privately managed and
4. Self-financed and privately managed.

University Grants Commission (UGC) is also involved with Departments of Teacher Education or Departments of Education in the Universities and Institutions Deemed to be Universities and Colleges of Teacher Education. Besides these, MHRD, there are also other ministries that have institutions which run teacher training programmes. Ministry of Women and Child Development has a large network of training of Anganwadi workers, who take care of pre-school component.

At the State level, the apex body that looks after teacher education is the Government Department of Education. In certain States, it is looked after by the Department of School Education. A few States have independent Directorates for Teacher education. In a few others, the Directorate and SCERT function under one Director. The teacher training institutions offering programmes for elementary and pre-school teachers are in many states under the control of the Department of School Education, whereas the teacher training institutions offering degree courses are under the Department of Education. In certain States all teacher education institutions are managed by the State government. In certain other States, majority of teacher training institutions are managed by private agencies under self-financed category. At the State levels, there are teacher training institutions being run by the Departments of Tribal Welfare and other administrative departments. Creation of separate cadre for teacher educators has been an important issue to be solved in many states.

Meaning of Teacher Education

Teacher education refers to the policies and procedures designed to equip teachers with the knowledge, attitudes, behaviours, and skills they require to perform their tasks effectively in the school and classroom. In early times, teachers were often scholars or clergymen who had no formal training in how to teach the subjects of their expertise. In fact, many believed that "teachers were born, not made." It was not until the emergence of pedagogy, the "art and science of teaching," as an accepted discipline that the training of teachers was considered important. Although there has been continued debate about whether teaching is a "science" that can be taught or whether one is "born" to be a teacher, it has generally been agreed, at least since the nineteenth century, that certain characteristics are needed to qualify a person as a teacher knowledge of the subject matter to be taught, knowledge of teaching methods, and practical experience in applying both. Most educational programmes for teachers today focus upon these points. However, the internal character of the individual is also an important aspect of teaching; whether that is something one is born with or can be taught, and what are the qualities that are needed for the role of teacher, are also a matter of debate.

Teacher quality and the strength of educators leadership are recognised as the greatest determinants of educational success. Quality teaching has a measurable impact on student outcomes. The teaching profession in India has much to celebrate. Our teachers and academic leaders are having a profound impact on our society. Teacher quality affects all stages of the teaching 'lifecycle, from attraction into the profession to ongoing development and retention in their own schools. To improve equity in educational outcomes, quality teachers must also work in schools where they are needed most including, remote and disadvantaged schools. Improving teacher and school leader quality requires action to: Attract the 'best and brightest' entrants to teaching; Train our future teachers through world-class pre-service education; Place quality teachers and school leaders in schools where they are needed most; Develop teachers skills and knowledge through ongoing professional learning; and Retain quality teachers and school leaders in our schools. Educational quality in developing countries has become a topic of intense interest, primarily because of countries' efforts to maintain quality or reverse the decline of quality in the context of quantitative expansion of educational provision. Many countries are simultaneously implementing reforms based on more active approaches to teaching and learning, further challenging education systems and, especially, teachers.

Quality of Education

Despite the importance of "quality" as the motivating factor for educational planning, approaches to quality can vary widely. In much of the literature, "quality" is used in a detached way, assuming consensus both on what the term means and on the desirability of the various educational aims and approaches promoted under the banner of quality. Whether explicit or implicit, a vision of educational quality is always embedded within countries' policies and programmes.

Harvey a familiar educationist provides a useful framework for thinking about quality by outlining five goals for education that define the vision of quality within individual systems. Education systems vary in emphasising a single vision or, more commonly, a mixture of the five goals:

1. Education quality as exceptionality: excellence is the vision that drives education, quality education is education that is exemplary; schools should maximize the pursuit of the highest potential in individual students.
2. Education quality as consistency: equality is the vision that drives education, quality requires equitable experiences, schools and classrooms should provide students with consistent experiences across the system.
3. Education quality as fitness-for-purpose: refinement and perfection in specific subject areas is the vision that shapes the system, quality is seen as preparing students for specific roles, instructional specialisation is emphasised.
4. Education quality as value for money: education reflects reasonable correspondence to individual and societal investments; quality is interpreted as the extent to which the system delivers value for money.
5. Education quality as transformative potential: social or personal change is the vision that drives education, quality education is a catalyst for positive changes in individuals and society, education promotes social change.

One way of looking at quality, prevalent in both the research literature and reports of programme implementation, concerns the relationship between different "inputs" and a measure of student performance, or "output." The outputs are usually students results on achievement tests, assessments, or end-of-cycle examinations. The inputs include a wide variety of factors: infrastructure and resources, quality of teaching environment, textbooks, teacher preparation, teacher salaries, supervision, attitudes and incentives, Educational Institutional climate, curriculum, student' physical well-being, and family and socioeconomic context. The another way of looking at quality involves measuring the efficiency of the system. Educational efficiency is measured internally by the rates of completion, dropout, and repetition. Efficiency is also measured externally by looking at the outcomes of education or the productivity of school leavers. This is measured according to, for example, wages or agricultural yields associated with an individual's or a community's level of schooling. This topic/ literature has a long history, primarily in educational economics, and has often used quantity of education as a proxy for quality. Studies of efficiency provide necessary information for planners, but this approach has relatively little explanatory power about what creates school quality without an accompanying analysis of the dynamics among the myriad school process factors that encourage students to stay in school and gain valuable knowledge and attitudes while there for studying. A more recently developed way of looking at quality focuses on the content, context, and relevance of education.

This approach to quality focuses on process within the educational institutions and classroom and relationships between the educators and the surrounding community. Greater attention is given to the ways in which inputs interact at the Institutional level to shape quality of learning, defined as the elements of knowledge and character that a society values in young peoples.

Role of Teachers in Promoting Culture and Quality

Good education is the result of the interaction of multiple factors, the most important of which is increasingly recognised to be quality teachers and teaching. The way teachers teach is of critical concern in any reform designed to improve quality. Teacher quality, teacher learning, and teacher improvement, therefore, are becoming the foci of researchers, policy makers, programme designers, implementers, and evaluators. In both developing and industrialised countries, teachers in the past were treated as semiskilled workers unable to make responsible decisions about their practice. They were required to follow instructional prescriptions and highly scripted and rigid teaching procedures. For their professional development, teachers received information on how to improve from "experts" in centralised workshops with little follow-up support at the institutional level.

Many educational systems are starting to advocate active-learning approaches for teachers as well and significant changes are taking place. If teachers are to become reflective practitioners who use active-learning approaches in their classrooms, where students learn through problem solving, critical dialogue, inquiry, and the use of higher-order thinking skills, teachers must learn and improve in professional development programmes that not only advocate but also use and model these methods.

The emphasis on teacher empowerment has grown from a variety of roots. The idea of reflective practice assumes that teachers are professionals capable of reflecting on the school and classroom situation and, thus, capable of making a large number of instructional and classroom management decisions. Even in circumstances where the level of teacher preparation is low, this perspective rejects the notion that teachers must work according to rigid prescriptions, incapable of independent decision-making. Although some challenge the notion that teachers in developing countries, with minimal preparation and minimal resources, can reflect on practice and make informed choices, the more widely held view is that the idea of "the teacher as professional" has reliably led to better teacher performance.

Action research plan is also closely related to teacher empowerment and has become an important component of what is considered good teacher development. Action or participatory research refers to teachers individually or in groups gathering and analyzing information in order to problem solve at the institutional level. In addition to mobilising teachers to study and reflect on their practice, action research advances the professionalisation of teachers by helping them develop and validate their knowledge. Action research often begins, in a teachers practice, as academic-based studies that are part of a preserves teacher education programme and continue as part of academic-based teacher professional development programmes.

Foundation for Teacher Development

As we have various research papers on this topic as “education quality” which demonstrates that there is a strong link between teacher professional development and quality. This is mainly because reforms leading to improved quality in preserves and in-services teacher education cannot succeed unless they are backed by on-going professional development and continuous teacher learning at the academic level. Teacher professional development ensures that theories acquired in initial preparation can be successfully implemented in practice. Quality in-services professional development, backed by a supportive academic community of practice, is essential to ensuring that reforms in teaching and learning reach the classroom, are correctly implemented in the classroom, and are sustained. Thus, this supports the important role that teacher learning plays in making the connection between theory and practice, and in improving education quality, by recognising and supporting the role of teachers as professionals capable of making sound decisions regarding classroom instruction and student learning.

Issues and Challenges in Teacher Education

An immense writing has appeared on educational quality in recent years, examining factors that help improve education and proposing ways to promote better learning in schools. The issue of quality has become critical in many countries. In countries like India where with constrained resources, the successful effort to increase access to basic education has often led to declining quality of education. In a search for the factors that promote quality, countries' programmes as well as the literature increasingly emphasize teachers, schools, societies and communities as the engines of quality, with teacher quality identified a primary focus.

The rapid changes in society led to teachers facing new and complex issues, resulting in changes in the area of teacher education. One of the most significant developments was the creation of Special education for children with special needs. For Special education teachers, learning how to effectively convey subject content is as important as learning this information. Special education teachers must be taught how information, especially more advanced and complex subject material, can be effectively taught to students in non-traditional ways. Special education teachers also often are required to study additional aspects of psychology and sociology.

Advances in technology have also posed an issue for future educators. Many educators have focused on ways to incorporate technology into the classroom. Television, computers, radio, and other forms of mass media are being utilised in an educational context, often in an attempt to involve the student actively in their own education. Hence, many teacher education programmes now include courses both in technology operation and how to use technology for education purposes. With the coming on of distance learning utilising mobile technologies and the internet understanding of technology or we can say e-learning has become crucial for new teachers in order to keep up with the knowledge and interests of their students in these delivery systems. The emergence of a networked knowledge economy presents both opportunities and challenges for teacher education. Used effectively, knowledge networks present opportunities for better informed and supported practice by education professionals and more authentic learning by students. The challenges include those identified above and, while much more research and development will be required to answer them.

As India's population or worldwide populations increasing which turn up to increasing demand for new teacher, while poverty, political instability, and other major issues have hindered governments around the world from meeting new educational demands. In some parts of the world, programmes have been initiated to draw new talent into teacher educational programmes. The UN's Millennium Development Project has eight established goals, one of which is to develop universal primary education in every country by the year 2019. Central Asia, Africa and Latin America are all target areas for this initiative. In order to help achieve this end, the UN has devoted resources and funds to helping improve educational infrastructure and to training more new teachers in targeted areas.

Summing up

Teacher education is a difficult assignment, especially at the present stage where teacher education programmes are being delivered by a large number of unaided private teacher education institutions. These institutions are also not sure of their tenure, as in near future; possibility of huge unemployment of trained persons may result in swinging fall. The surviving institutions can only be helped by appropriate authorities in improving quality of their academic management. This paper suggest an increase in responsibility for teachers but not an increase in authority: teachers are losing decision-making authority in the classroom. This research paper also indicates that a positive policy environment and ample support for growth are essential for creating and sustaining teacher quality. Government and educators will need to understand better the links between schooling and its social and cultural environment, the kind of socialisation and informal learning provided to children both before school entry and outside of the classroom and ways to develop more literate and encouraging environments in the family and the community surrounding the school. Although the task of recruiting for both miscellany and quality seems discouraging, several well documented and proven long-term strategies exist and but now we should support the creation of a stable pipeline for recruiting more and better qualified, diverse teachers. This article concluding with the words of APJ Abdul Kalam. "The purpose of education is to make good human beings with skill and expertise... Enlightened human beings can be created by teachers.

References

1. Dexter, S. L., Anderson, R. E., & Becker, H. J. (2019). Teachers' views of computers as catalysts for changes in their teaching practice. Journal of Research on Computing in Education, 31(3), 221-239.

2. Downes, S. (2016). Learning networks and connective knowledge [Electronic Version]. Instructional Technology Forum.
3. Elizabeth Leu & Alison Price. Quality of Education and Teacher Learning: A Review of the Literature (Available on www.ssrn.com).
4. Geoff Whitty.Quality Control in Teacher Education, British Journal of Educational Studies, Vol. 40, No. 1 (Feb., 1992), pp. 38-50, Published by: Blackwell Publishing.
5. Guidelines and Recommendations for Reorienting Teacher Education to Address Sustainability. Prepared by UNITWIN/UNESCO, October 2015.
6. Kothari, D. S. (1988). Chairman) Report of the Education Commission 1964-66. Govt. of India, New Delhi. Loughran, John. Developing A Pedagogy of Teacher Education: Understanding Teaching and Learning About Teaching. Routledge, 2019.
7. Prof. B. Wanjala Kerre, Science and Technology Teacher Education in Africa:Issues in the promotion of Scientific and Technological Literacy.
8. Rakes, G. C., Fields, V. S., & Cox, K. E. (2006). The Influence of Teachers' Technology Use on Instructional Practices. Journal of Research on Technology in Education, 38(4), 409-424.
9. Tisher, R. P., and Marvin Wideen. Research in Teacher Education: International Perspectives. Taylor & Francis, 2014. ISBN 1850007829.
10. Vappu Sunnari & Rauni Rasanen, Ethical Challenges for Teacher Education and Teaching:Special focus on gender and multicultural issues, OULU 2000.

36

Higher Education in the Wake of Covid-19 Pandemic: Challenges for the Higher Education in Hill areas in Uttarakhand and Himachal Pradesh

Dr Veerababu & Mahesh Naamani

Abstract

A new strain of coronavirus caused Covid-19 pandemic emergency on an unprecedented scale which was unheard of in the modern times. It didn't just cause a public health emergency but also challenged and negatively affected many sectors like economy, agriculture, health and specifically education sector. Almost overnight, schools and universities around the world were closed, affecting 1.57 billion students in 191 countries. This situation has significantly impacted both students and teachers equally. Universities worldwide have been forced rapidly to scale up online teaching. Apart from challenges of meeting new expenditures to transform physical classrooms into online setting, teaching professionals also faced the challenge of catching up with new technologies in teaching and pedagogy to stay relevant. In this context, the present study aims to bring out challenges faced by hill area students in Uttarakhand and Himachal Pradesh due to the lack of higher educational institutions in higher areas. First section of the study focuses on the disruption Covid-19 has caused to the higher education system in India and how it the entire community. Second section of the study brings out the issues of basic amenities like power supply, internet, poor road network, drinking water, health infrastructure, employment opportunities, shortage of doctors and non-availability of teachers. Moreover, this topic will look into how this issues holistically affecting the entire hill's economy and livelihood. Finally, the paper concludes by presenting an overall picture of issues associated with digital divide and deprivation. Further, we would like to give policy prescriptions for the decision-makers based on empirical research which also includes a way forward for higher education sector in India.

Keywords: Hill areas, Digital Divide, Higher Education.

Introduction

India is a diverse country, and we call it's a nation known for its beauty in diversity. When we think about the beauty of India, Hill stations strikes our mind. Most of the Indian could have visited hill states especially Uttarakhand and Himachal Pradesh. We deem this is renowned Holiday Spots for spending our Vacation with our families. Whenever you visit these hill stations, those mountains embrace you with love and great hospitality. Like our mother's love, the nature of hills is pristine. The flowers and snow greet us with affection. The soothing breeze from those hills pacify your pain. The sound of river flowing through the valleys is equivalent to meditation. Setting aside this beauty, if you approach these hills from the perspective of a researcher, the echoing pain and suffering of people is harsh reality of this topography. Today the ongoing pandemic crippled the higher education system of India. And specifically, the hill states are most affected one because the lack of proper infrastructure hit them hard. In this article, I am looking into two hill states Uttarakhand and Himachal Pradesh. The studies of 73 percent of the youth all over the world have been hampered due to the Corona epidemic. In India, since there is a severe disparity between different communities in terms of the availability of education, then the education of the youth has been disturbed the most. The main reason for this is that they have to work more at home. Especially in hilly areas, they have to go to distant forests to bring wood, grass etc., with this they have to go far for every small thing. And in return they do not even get money. Household incomes declined and economic challenges increased, due to which young boys and girls, especially in rural areas, dropped out of studies to take up small jobs to support their families.

Apart from this, another major reason for hindering education during the pandemic is the huge disparity in the availability of digital resources. There is a lot of inequality in India when it comes to having smartphones. The same situation is also in the case of internet facility. Because of this many students of India are facing the challenge of long term disruption in their education. Although schools have been opened in some areas, yet online education is being promoted more so that the crowd of students does not gather. The country has faced difficulties in adopting the online medium of education due to the huge gap in India's current digital infrastructure.

Students Migration

After all, how far will you fly, one day you will have to return to your abode, will you not? Today this feeling is clearly reflected in the mind and eyes of every old person in my village. His hopeless mind is holding a hope that at some point this escape will stop! Sometimes their children will return from the metropolis to the houses of those raw stones, which have now become a house! Today every house in the mountain is empty, only two old parents live in them. This migration in search of jobs and studies has emptied every village of the mountain. It has come to such an extent that a person is doomed to live in a village. There are schools but no children falling in them.

As soon as we are called a mountain, all those beautiful features come before us, which these mountains contain within them. Despite all the specialties, no one wants to live there today! Today, when we look at our past, we are proud that we are a small mountain in these beautiful valleys of mountains, on whose land the fruits of apricot, peach, pulam, bedu, and kafal will no longer ripen but instead of the luxuries of the metropolis. Only the seeds will burst. Now every house in every village on the mountain has become only for those old men who sweated their blood. From the high mountains made a house from stone pebbles so that in those luxurious shelters their coming generations could live without any problem. But where did they know that these generations would not like that luxurious home of the mountain and would like these narrow streets of the metropolis.

Livelihood Issues

There are at least 25-30 houses in each village, in which only 5-10 houses are lit every evening, the lights are on. The rest have big locks hanging. There are no children to play in the spacious courtyard of those luxurious houses. Old parents are sticking their children's gilli sticks, balls and bats to their chests like their capital, only in the hope that sometime their children will return to their house, and will play gilli-danda, ball-bat. The suffering of old people is brutal. When here only a few days when they return for a moment, just by sitting beside them for a moment, their eyes start shining, as if their eyes have been waiting for someone's return for centuries. If the condition of almost all the villages of India is looked into at the present time, then their day-to-day changing face will be accurately guessed. And the running life in it has brought a change in the whole life style. In today's time any person, if I am saying any person, then I am signing it to the youth who do not want to live in the village anymore. They are not liking the village now! Why come? It is believed by them that nothing is left in the villages. The search for a job and the desire to study is forcing a large group of youth to migrate from the villages to the metropolitan cities. Nobody wants to live in the villages anymore. The proof is that his house is in the city.

Due to this the population of the city is increasing day by day. And there is nothing left in the villages. Will be built, trees will be cut and there are many other aspects which will harm the environment. The average age of people living in cities is much less than the average age of people living in villages. The main reason for all this is environment. But do not know why still people are liking the urban life. If we keep money in the center of all these reasons, then this situation can be understood better. If a labourer works in the villages, then he gets a day's wage from one hundred rupees to one hundred and fifty rupees. The selfishness of earning more money pulls a labourer from village to city, in a way, selfishness is the main reason for migration. They are coming from the city to the city because they are looking for higher and better educational institutions which are not possible in the villages. India is a country of diversities, people of all kinds of traditions and cultures live in it and all these people

Rural Area Education Issues

India is absorbed in itself and is moving ahead. India is a country of villages and India lives in villages, this Mahatma Gandhi has said. Government should play a major role in getting rid of the situation of migration. All those facilities should be arranged in the villages, in the greed of which people from the villages are moving towards the city. There should be a higher educational institution within every five to six villages, from where young fellows studying should not have to wander here and there in search of employment. Truly, if India is to be saved, its beauty is to be preserved, then the villages have to be saved, migration has to be stopped, these people are the beauty of the village and in the beauty of the village lies the beauty of the country! The education of 73 percent of the youth all over the world has been hampered due to the Corona epidemic. In India, since there is a severe disparity between different communities in terms of the availability of education, then the education of the youth has been disturbed the most. The main reason for this is that they have to work more at home. They have to go to distant forests to bring wood, grass etc., with this they have to go far for every small thing. And in return they do not even get money. Household incomes declined and economic challenges increased, due to which young boys and girls, especially in rural areas, dropped out of studies to take up small jobs to support their families.

Apart from this, another major reason for hindering education during the pandemic is the huge disparity in the availability of digital resources. There is a lot of inequality in India when it comes to having smartphones. The same situation is also in the case of internet facility. Because of this many students of India are facing the challenge of long term disruption in their education. Although schools have been opened in some areas, yet online education is being promoted more so that the crowd of students does not gather. The country has faced difficulties in adopting the online medium of education due to the huge gap in the current digital infrastructure of India.

Without learning anything, the students going to the next class will not be right for their future. There is no doubt that the corona infection has affected every section of the state. This has affected not only tourism, industry and business, it has also had a negative impact on educational activities. The state government has closed schools and colleges in view of the increasing infection of Corona. The state government is constantly emphasising on online education. Online classes are being run for the students. The aim is that the students should not be deprived of education and their valuable years should not be wasted. This system was implemented in private and government schools since last year. Even in plain areas, children are still studying online, but in hilly areas, the situation is completely opposite. Due to lack of basic facilities, classes are not being conducted here. Due to this, children are also being forced to drop out of school. If seen, out of 13 districts in the state, nine districts come in hilly and four in plain area. The poor condition of communication services in the marginal areas is taking a toll on online classes during the Corona period.

Digital Divide

Digital discrimination, the increased burden of working without pay at home and the crisis of urgently dealing with the challenge of falling incomes for families have acted as a massive impediment to the education of the youth. There is a fear of increasing inequality going forward. This is likely to reduce the development of human capital and increase unemployment further. Due to lack of better internet facility and infrastructure, online education is already a problem in villages. In such a situation, this disease is becoming a curse for the students studying in hilly areas. In the state of Uttarakhand, where mobile network is always a problem due to the majority of the hills being hilly, it is becoming a difficult challenge for lakhs of students living in hilly areas to get education. Online education can never be a better option in these hilly areas. In the village, if someone has to talk on the phone, then he has to go four to five km up the mountain, even in the time of lockdown, children or their parents walk 4 to 5 km to download the study material. Had to go up the mountain so that the network could be found.

For studying in lockdown, students were given a new option in the form of online classes, in which the student can study at home, for which the student has a smart phone or laptop as well as the facility of a good net connection necessary. But here the question is whether the mountainous state, where the problem of poor mobile network is always there due to the hilly part of it, even today people have to walk many kilometers in search of mobile network to talk to the phone, whether in such a situation, can online education be a better option for lakhs of students living in the hilly areas of the state? Whereas the first condition for online class is good mobile network connectivity.

Online class acts as a discrimination among the students, on one hand there are students who have all the means to take online classes, while on the other hand there are students living in remote areas of the state who are unable to avail all the facilities used for online classes. Far away, the problem of digital divide arises among these students due to not getting equal facilities for all. It is true that due to the lack of resources in the state of Uttarakhand, a large number of students were deprived of online education, but this time the students studying in class 11 and 12 are being given tablets by the government so that they can be used for online education when needed. On the question of network connectivity, SP Semwal says that network connectivity is a big problem in hilly districts, due to this problem, many students are deprived of online education even after having smart phones, but the government is yet to solve this problem. There is no solution. The cities or towns of hilly districts are connected by roads, where internet facility is easily available, but in the marginal and remote areas of Chamoli, Rudraprayag, Uttarkashi, Tehri, Pithoragarh, Bageshwar and Champawat, the situation is completely different. The poor condition of communication services in the border areas is overshadowing the online classes during the Corona period. The online classes started during the Corona period in the state to keep the students' studies smooth are not being successful in the hilly areas. Due to lack of internet facility here, students and teachers are cut off from each other. This situation is worrying. This is not only affecting the education of the students, but this situation is also raising questions on the claims of the government regarding communication services in the hilly areas. Due to the interruption of the education of the children, many problems will arise in front of them. In hilly districts which are connected by roads, internet facility is easily available, but in the marginal and remote areas of Chamoli, Rudraprayag, Uttarkashi, Tehri, Pithoragarh, Bageshwar and Champawat, the situation is completely different. Here communication services have not come back on track so far. Due to the geographical location here, the mobile companies are pulling back in view of the cost of installing the tower. Along with this, there is also the problem of power supply in the marginal areas. For this reason, even if a mobile or laptop is taken in any way, then it is becoming a big challenge to charge it and get it repaired if it is damaged. The government should take quick steps in the direction of improving the communication system in the border areas, so that the students there can also get the benefit of online classes. Otherwise, they will be left behind by the students of the plains.

Policy Recommendations and Conclusion

According to FAO (Food and Agricultural Organisation) study, mountain people suffer from malnutrition and hunger due to inaccessibility and complexity of the mountain. We should extend the 'Special scholarship exam of North East Region' and 'Ishan Uday' Scholarship Scheme to the hill students as they are facing the same problems like their hill partners. In addition, we must provide special reservation to these students in higher education institutes of India as they face social handicap. Government should bring 'Special Developmental Zones' in hill areas to protect the fragile nature and develop industry to provide jobs. The infrastructure of road, rail and air should boosted with special attention in production zones based development. We must design special mountain specific courses to enhance their local knowledge and skills. Such course will help the marginalised section communities to empower themselves in their own locality itself. State and Central government should provide financial incentives and relaxations to unveil digital classrooms and starting business. Moreover Special disaster management and preparedness setup should set in every taluk to address any emergency situation. Today waste management is another substantial issue faced by mountain region. Here special task force should set up like 'Mizoram model' involving youth and private entities.

References

https://www.ilo.org/global/topics/youth-employment/publications/WCMS_753026/lang--en/index.htm

https://link.springer.com/article/10.1007/s41027-020-00291-w

http://lsi.gov.in:8081/jspui/bitstream/123456789/4809/1/44167_1961_CHA.pdf

https://himachalwatcher.com/2020/09/23/himachal-pradesh-report-on-plight-of-migrant-labourers-during-lockdown-in-state/

https://www.oecd.org/education/skills-beyond-school/AHELOFSReportVolume1.pdf

https://www.unicef.org/press-releases/schools-more-168-million-children-globally-have-been-completely-closed

https://www.moneycontrol.com/news/trends/current-affairs-trends/negative-covid-19-report-or-full-vaccination-must-for-visiting-himachal-pradesh-from-august-13-7313941.html

https://theprint.in/india/education/as-digital-divide-widens-india-risks-losing-a-generation-to-pandemic-disruption/568394/

https://www.borgenmagazine.com/digital-divide-in-india/

https://thewire.in/education/not-providing-gadgets-internet-to-poor-students-for-online-classes-is-digital-apartheid-delhi-hc

https://www.fao.org/english/newsroom/news/2002/6763-en.html

https://www.indiawaterportal.org/articles/problems-hill-states-and-hill-areas-and-ways-ensure-they-do-not-suffer-any-way-because

37

Equity and Inclusion in Higher Education

Monika

Abstract

Equity and inclusion both are the important aspects of the quality with special reference to educational outputs. The inclusion has two main features; to include all the sections of society and expected goals of education. First of all we have to understand the conceptual meaning of inclusion and equity to ensure quality output in higher education system in India. In higher education the role of equity and inclusion delineate the same importance because both are not be seen as separate policies where as inclusion helps in overcoming those barriers, which limited the presence of the participation and achievement of the learner and in the same side equity is about ensuring fairness, where the education of the learner is being seen as having equal importance. As we know that Indian higher education is the third largest in the world in term of the enrolment in higher education after United States and China. Throughout the expanse of higher education in India has gone throughout a phase of unprecedented expansion manifest by a huge increase in the numbers of students and institutions. With the expansion of the enrolment rates and institutions in higher education in India, it has not been appropriate with the growth of population and its diverse needs. There by, in addition to very low access to higher education in general, there are disparities between various marginalised social groups like schedule castes, schedule tribes , other backward classes, women's and Person with disabilities. For ensuring equity and inclusion in higher education there is need of broadening the concept of inclusion to reach all diverse students with their equal right and effective educational opportunities in higher education, it is very necessary to create safe and inclusive learning environment which are free from violence and discrimination of any kind and it is only possible through when we break the status of tokenisation. Hence, in higher education diverse settings the role of inclusion and equity are at the same level so, we can say that every learner matters equally. The present paper highlight the role of equity and inclusion in higher education and how it helps in ensuring the access to educational opportunities, avail additional resources, identifying the barriers, extra support, and flexibility in higher education system.

Keywords: Equity, Inclusion, Higher Education, Quality Education, Educational Opportunities.

Introduction

The idea of inclusive growth is based on the concept of equality of opportunity and Equality of opportunity demands that deserving students from all social groups are provided adequate opportunities for self-development. The main bases of exclusion in India are region, religion, caste, gender, economic disparities, and disabilities. Thus, strategies for achieving inclusive growth necessarily need to include affirmative policies targeting; socially disadvantaged, marginalised, economically poor, and people with disabilities. The progress made in any society needs to be assessed on the basis of the distribution of benefits among different social groups for assessing the inclusiveness of growth and development in that way equity and inclusion, meet the educational need with equitable provisions in an inclusive society in which all individuals rights can be recognised and protected.

The purpose of present paper is to highlight the role of equity and inclusion in higher education and how it helps in ensuring the access to educational opportunities, avail additional resources, identifying the barriers, extra support, and flexibility; While access to higher education has improved across all section of the population. Because of many reasons the underprivileged groups continue to lag behind in their access to core study programmes such as Science, Technology, Engineering and Mathematics etc. Furthermore, achievements in equity in access are overshadowed by the unfavourable conditions of progress and success faced by students from the disadvantaged groups inside the higher education institutions and campuses. The relative incompetence of institutional mechanisms to address diversity and discrimination results in uneven performance and poor academic achievement among the students from the disadvantaged groups.

Equity and inclusion in higher education

For any kind of accessible reading and writing material, it is important that the concept to be adopted is also inclusive. It means that the material must demonstrate diverse characters along with they must be relevant for children from diverse backgrounds. While developing any teaching learning material, we must think about all the children from different backgrounds;

with variations in their abilities, interests, socio-economic status, strength and access to use it and find it relevant. The attention and focus given by NEP; equity and inclusion in education is built on efforts and advocacy by state and national initiatives and other stakeholders in their relevant capacities to build a effective school system where children with different backgrounds learn together. "The global education development agenda reflected in the Goal 4 (SDG4) of the 2030 Agenda for Sustainable Development, adopted by India in 2015 - seeks to "ensure inclusive and equitable quality education and promote lifelong learning opportunities for all" by 2030". (NEP, 2020). National Education Policy 2020 also urges to ensure equity and inclusion, thereby rendering similar educational opportunities to all. In that way, if we want to ensure equity and inclusion in education, we have to focus on the main part of exercise that is practical implications of the policies and programmes.

Need of independent assessment in higher education

All these factor effects because of lack of evidences that we rarely evaluate the impact of current polices, programmes and this remains one of major challenge in the field of education of person with disability. It is liability of the government to do an independent assessment of all the schemes and programmes to inspect that there is no negative impact on person with disability and the needs of the person with disability properly met with same. Government should conduct a need assessment in every five year and formulate a plan for the conscription and training of teachers, parents, various stakeholders and care giver of person with disability and rights of person with disability should be included within all educational courses such as schools, colleges and universities. In the term of infrastructure there is need of mandatory accessibility norms as building follow the norms and guidelines which have been notify the government but after the construction it does not go with the norms it will be rejected. Hence, every new building must go with the norms that have been emphasis for making spaces accessible for person with disability.

Learning and Access is equally important in higher education

Most of the students with disability left the school because the lack of teacher. Acceptance of disabled children into their classroom sometimes mainstream teacher's complaint about the lack of resources, assistive aids, shortage of traning which place external burden on them. We don't forget that the learning and access is equally important if we want to achieve effective inclusion of disabilities so, there is need to understanding the learning level of the students. There are various studies talks about the mild, severe and moderate level of learning in which the student comes under severe and moderate level of learning never been enrolled in schools because they have least level of learning scale and the teachers unable to tackle with these level of learners. Hence, the result no. of disabled students left the schools or discontinues their education as because of lack of attention.

To promote equity and inclusion in higher education acceptance of diversities are necessary

India is a multi diverse nation having diversity in terms of race, ethnicity, gender, class, sexual orientation, economic status, disability, language and some political and religious beliefs. In simple words, we can say that diversity is everything that makes people different from each other. In the past, it mainly focused on strengthening inter-cultural tolerance but now in the present scenario, the term diversity emerged with the new ideas and as a result sense of inclusion has been developed. Inclusion not only means to include the people from marginalised sections but it is multidimensional philosophy grounded on the principles of social justice, equity and such a democracy where each and every citizen of the nation has the right to live with dignity. Hence, diversity is shifting the focus towards enriching human learning and experiences. In an increasingly complex and diverse society, the ability to connect the diverse peers with diverse backgrounds is invaluable. Certainly Inclusion ensures the value for enriching knowledge with the culmination of different thoughts. So, it is necessary to understand different perspectives and ideas of individual and it is only possible through education because it assists to magnify the position of inclusion in each and every domain of society. Through education we can identify the problems being faced by the individuals and will be able to facilitate them well. Education helps to create a link between individual and their needs/problems. Especially when we are talking about different disabilities in inclusive setup, the significance of education will be expand and with education, we are able to shape a better inclusive educational setup by knowing and respecting rights, laws and regulations for the student with different abilities.

Entrance into quality higher education can open a vast range of possibilities that can lift both individuals as well as communities out of the cycles of disadvantage. Accordingly, making quality higher education opportunities available to all individuals must be among the highest priorities. Policy envisions ensure the equitable access to quality education to all students in education system.

Due to the dynamic changes in higher education; there are many reasons for exclusion of deprived sections in education system. Whereas it should be common across schools in higher education sectors. Therefore, the approach to equity and inclusion must be the same. In addition, there must be continuity in across the stages to ensure sustainable reform. Hence, the policy initiatives required to congregate the goals of equity and inclusion in higher education.

Now, there are some facts of exclusion that are particular or more intense in higher education. For instance, lack of knowledge in higher education, economic opportunity cost of pursuing higher education, financial constraints, admission processes, poor employability potential of many higher education programmes, geographical and language barriers, and lack of suitable student support material.

There are some additional actions, for the purpose to specific to higher education goals that should be adopted by all higher educational institutes HEIs. Steps to be taken by the governments are:

- Allocate suitable Government funds in higher education.
- Set clear targets for higher GER for SEDGs.
- Enhance gender balance in admissions to HEIs.
- Enhance access by establishing more high-quality HEIs in desired districts and Special Education Zones containing larger numbers of SEDGs.
- Develop and support high-quality HEIs that teach in local/Indian languages or bilingually Provide more financial assistance and scholarships to SEDGs in both public and private.
- HEIs conduct outreach programmes on higher education opportunities and scholarships among SEDGs.
- Develop and support technology tools for better participation and learning outcomes. Steps to be taken by all HEIs.
- Mitigate opportunity costs and fees for pursuing higher education.
- Provide more financial assistance and scholarships to socio-economically disadvantaged students.
- Conduct outreach on higher education opportunities and scholarships.
- Make admissions processes more inclusive. Make curriculum more inclusive.
- Increase employability potential of higher education programmes.
- Develop more degree courses taught in Indian languages and bilingually.
- Ensure all buildings and facilities are wheelchair-accessible and disabled-friendly.

- Develop bridge courses for students that come from disadvantaged educational background.
- Provide socio-emotional and academic support and mentoring for all such students through suitable counselling and mentoring programmes.
- Ensure sensitisation of faculty, counsellor, and students on gender-identity issue and its inclusion in all aspects of the HEI, including curricula.
- Strictly enforce all no-discrimination and anti-harassment rules.
- Develop Institutional Development Plans that contain specific plans for action on increasing participation from SEDGs, including but not limited to the above items.

Conclusion

Undoubtedly, equity and inclusion in higher education ensure the access to educational opportunities, avail additional resources, identifying the barriers, extra support, and flexibility; while access to higher education has improved across all section of the population. Because of many reasons the underprivileged groups continue to lag behind in their access to core study programmes such as Science, Technology, Engineering and Mathematics etc. Furthermore, achievements in equity in access are overshadowed by the unfavourable conditions of progress and success faced by students from the disadvantaged groups inside the higher education institutions and campuses. Respect for diversities in higher education should be treated or welcomed at priority level.

References

Singh, A.K. (2022). NEP 2020: Vision and Pathways. Yojana, 66 (02), 9-12.

Rani.B.(2018). The Rights of Persons with Disabilities Act, 2016 Promoting Inclusive Education.

Singal, N. (2008) Working towards inclusion: Reflections from the Classroom Accepted 30 January 2008.

Singal, N. (2006). Inclusive education in India: International concept, national interpretation. International Journal of Disability, Development and Education, 53(3).

38

New Dimension in Higher Education in India

Dr Kandi Kamala

Abstract

Higher Education has an important role in the task of rebuilding a nation and it paves the way for overall development of a nation. The twentieth century has witnessed several revolutions like Green revolution, White revolution, I.T revolution, so on and so forth, taking human civilisation to new heights. At the start of twenty first century, we gave a lot of importance given to higher education. Every country realised the value of higher education and the benefits that accrue from it. "The social demands for higher education continue to increase. The inabilities of the state to support this growing demand result in new financing arrangements for higher education. The recent reforms in this area could be broadly divided into two categories: the privatisation of public institutions and the establishment of private institutions of higher education. Privatisation implies the application of market principles in the operation of public institutions, while ownership rests within the public domain. Promotion of the private sector implies the growth and expansion of the non-state sector in higher education, and very often this sector does not rely on state funding for its growth and expansion. Both of these measures have paved the way for market operations in higher education.

Keywords : Foreign Countries, Higher Education, Educational Quality, Access to Education.

Introduction

In his bestseller "The World is Flat": Thomas Friedman describes a world of shrinking trade impediments and expeditious technological advances which have led to revolutionary globalisation of industry. Domestic companies in India and other parts of the world are now able to compete on a level playing field with companies the world over. The *world has been flattened.* In today's world where there is neck-to-neck competition, education must be such that our graduates have a reasonable opportunity to achieve success. Education is important for the sustained growth of the nation. It is the foundation on which the development of every citizen and the nation as a whole is contingent.

The direct correlation between higher education and human resource development is an area of abundant research. Capacity building in the national context presupposes numerous resources of which human resource is the most important one. Developmental activities require a workforce that is proficient across a range of skills. With the emergence of LPG era, the value of education has multiplied leaps and bounds.

Globalisation and higher education: The Indian Scenario

Globalisation has changed the dynamics of economies and the politics of world nations. And policy formulation across the board is increasingly influenced by the factors of globalisation as the domestic markets protected so far opened up to completion from across the world.

The Indian higher education institutions have been undergoing transformation for the last 20 years under the influence of globalisation. Many new universities have been conceptualised and established to increase the reach of higher education throughout the country. The universities with stronger relationships with industry and the economy have adapted to changes arising due to globalisation and the ecosystem. Globalisation leads to many opportunities and also challenges in higher education in India.

Contemporary Issues in Higher Education in India

Shortcomings in Intuitional Capacity Expansion

The Gross Enrollment Ratio (GER) in higher education is only 27.1 percent in India as per the report of All-India Survey on Higher Education (AISHE) 2019-20, under the Ministry of Education. This ratio is quite low when compared to that of developed as well as developing countries.

Making higher education inclusive and equitable

The composition of students in higher education is not representative of the various sections of society. Merit should not be the exclusive domain of only the rich, wealthy, and elite which has increased after globalisation. Measures must be taken to ensure that the people untouched by the advances of technology and globalisation are also brought into the fold of higher education.

Ensuring quality and promoting excellence in HE

After globalisation, the higher education institutions are in competition not just with domestic institutions but with global institutions. Excellence in higher education has to be pursued to make the institutions globally competent and they have a lot to learn and implement from best practices across the world. Though the Government is consistently focusing on quality education still the UGC and our universities are not in a position to mark their place among the top universities of the world.

Expansion, excellence, and equity are interrelated any policy should address these 3E's.

Investment percentage of GDP

One of the reasons for lower quality not being able to attain a global level of excellence and also not being fully equitable is because of underinvestment in HE. In 1968 the Kothari commission has suggested 6% of GDP should be on HE. As per the Economic Survey 2019-20, the expenditure on education by the Center and the States as a proportion of the Gross Domestic Product (GDP) between 2014-15 to 2018-19 has been around 3%. National Education Policy, 2020 (NEP) reaffirms the recommendation of an increase in public investment on education to 6% of GDP, but this target has not been achieved till now.

Employability

Many a time, there is a long gestation period after graduation and before landing a good job. Sometimes people remain unemployed even after completing higher education because of lack of skills that are required for employment. The focus of education has to shift to skilling the students to make them industry ready and not just to impart knowledge.

Poor Infrastructure, Facilities, and Faculty shortages

Infrastructure particularly of public sector institutions suffers from poor facilities, faculty insufficiency, and the incapacity of the educational system to attract, retain and preserve well-qualified teachers have been posing challenges to quality education for many years. There are plenty of vacancies in higher education but still large numbers of NET/Ph.D. candidates remain unemployed.

Inadequate Research

Not much attention has been catered to research in higher education institutes. The quality of the research is getting compromised as the scholars are working either without fellowships or not getting their fellowships on time. Moreover, Indian higher education institutions are poorly tied with research centres and industries.

Poor Governance Structure

Excess-centralisation in decision-making, bureaucratic structures, and lack of accountability, transparency, and professionalism are some of the challenges faced by the Indian education system.

Companies Expectations from Universities

The author has interacted with HR and Managers (both from the technical and non-technical side) of different companies viz. Amazon, Google, Yash Technology Solutions, Sell Craft Global Solutions. They have responded to the questionnaire on varied aspects such as curriculum by the University, students' performance at campus placements, time period for providing training, percentage of the quality of students they are getting versus the quality of students they actually want, etc. On interacting with them it has been found that there is an immense gap between the skills required by them and skills possessed by the students. They got to spend most of their productive time training the unskilled freshers.

Other skills of high importance for employers: Oxford Economics Survey

Apart from the domain knowledge, there are other skills that are of high importance to employers for hiring a candidate as per the Oxford Economics Survey, refer Fig. 2 to 5. They included Communication Skills, Computer Skills, Numerical and logical ability, and behavioural traits like learning agility, adaptability, and interpersonal skills. From the figures, we can see that these skills which are so important for companies are necessary irrespective of the individual's field of study or course. However, most universities do not lay emphasis on these skills and there is an urgent need to redesign the curriculum, method of instruction, and evaluation to ensure that these skills are developed in students as part of regular instruction and also create extra-curricular opportunities for the inculcation of these skills.

Fig. 2: Skills in high demand over the next 5 to 10 years

Digital Skills				
Digital business skills	**Ability to work virtually**	**Understanding of corporate IT software and systems**	**Digital Design Skills**	**Ability to use social media**
50.6%	44.9%	40.1%	35.2%	29.3%

Source: Oxford Economics.

Fig. 3: Agile thinking skills				
Ability to consider and prepare for multiple scenarios	**Innovation**	**Dealing with complexity and ambiguity**	**Managing paradoxes and balancing opposing views**	**Ability to see the big picture**
54.8%	46.0%	42.9%	40.9%	15.3%

Source: Oxford Economics.

Fig. 4: Interpersonal and communication skills				
Co-creativity and brainstorming	**Relationship building with customers**	**Teaming**	**Collaboration**	**Oral and written communication**
48.3%	47.4%	44.9%	30.4%	29 %

Source: Oxford Economics.

Fig. 5: Global operating skills				
Ability to manage diverse employees	**Understanding international markets**	**Ability to work in multiple overseas locations**	**Foreign language skills**	**Cultural Skills**
49.1%	45.7%	37.5%	36.1%	31.5 %

Source: Oxford Economics.

Fig. 6: Employability Skills

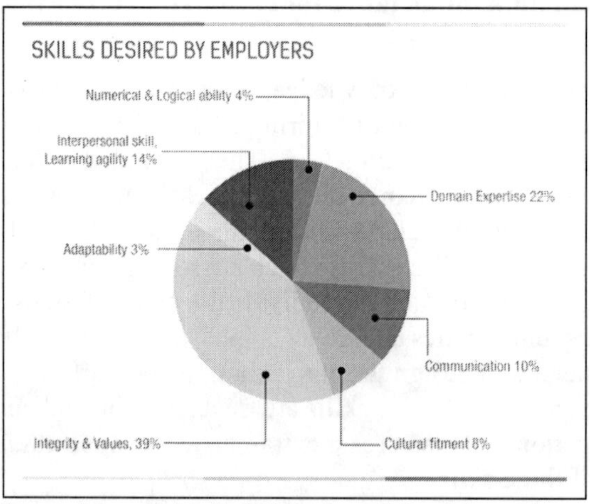

Source: Job-market-India-2015-an-essential-report.

From the graph above in Fig. 6, it can be seen that huge importance is given by industry to soft skills such as communication skills, interpersonal skills, etc which are given minimal importance in the current higher education institutes. Thrust must be given to these areas in higher education by making the courses more hands-on.

A student perspective on challenges faced during and after Covid

To understand the impact of Covid on the overall effectiveness of delivery of lectures, assignments, and activities in the effective delivery of education during and after Covid crisis, we have conducted a survey on students across different disciplines in Osmania university. We have delivered a short questionnaire to students and we have received a total of 184 valid responses. The questionnaire was sent in multiple methods such as SMS, WhatsApp, and paper-based. The results of the questionnaire are discussed in detail below.

1. Did the overall quality of education get adversely impacted due to Covid-19?
   We used a Likert scale of 5 with 5 being most negatively affected and 1 least affected. Of the 184 students, 17 percent chose 5 which is most negatively affected while 67 percent selected 4 which is negatively affected. A total of 154 i.e., 84 percent of the students feel that the quality of education has been adversely affected due to Covid-19. Nobody felt that Covid-19 has not affected education during Covid-19.

Fig. 7: Overall quality of education on Likert Scale

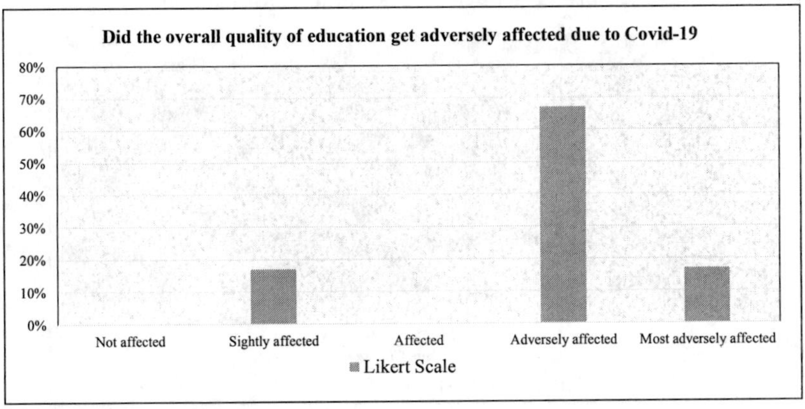

Source: Author.

2. "Which of the following are most affected during Covid-19?"
   For these 74 students, i.e., 40 percent of the students said that decreased access to university facilities was the most important factor that was affected followed by poor internet connectivity at 25 percent and insufficient interaction with faculty at 20 percent.

Fig. 8

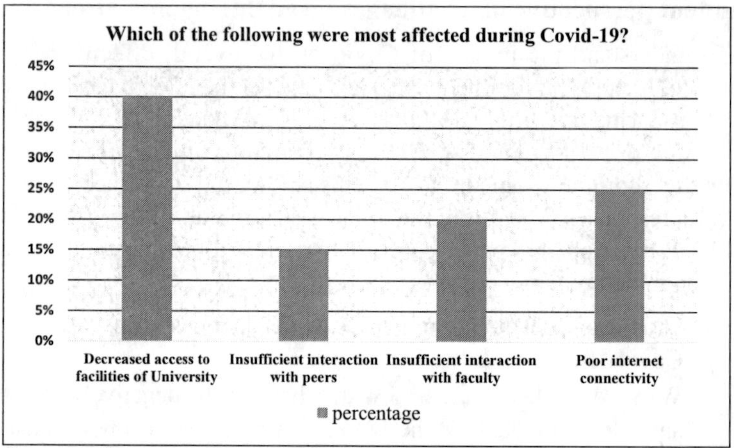

Source: Author.

3. "Do you prefer to have at least some classes online?"
   For this question, a whopping 83 percent, 153 students said yes.

Fig. 9

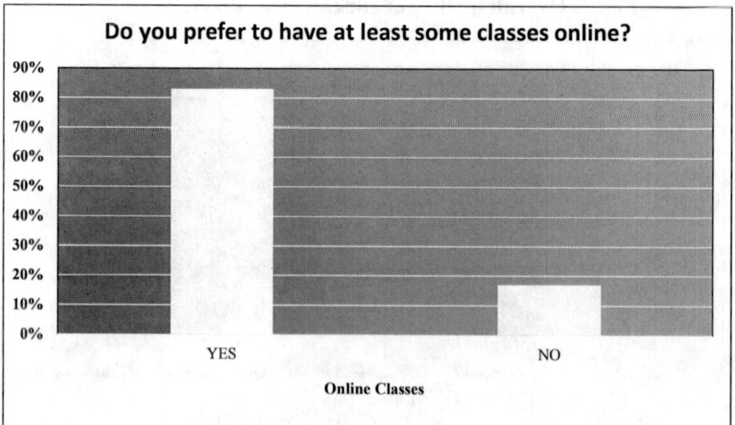

Source: Author.

4. On further asking "what percentage of the classes would you prefer online?" 17 percent of the students preferred to have 100 percent classes online while 33 percent preferred to have 70 percent classes online. So, a total of 50 percent i.e., 92 students preferred to have 70% or more classes online. Another 33 percent of the students preferred 50 percent classes online. Nobody wanted to have 100 percent in-classroom teaching.

Fig. 10

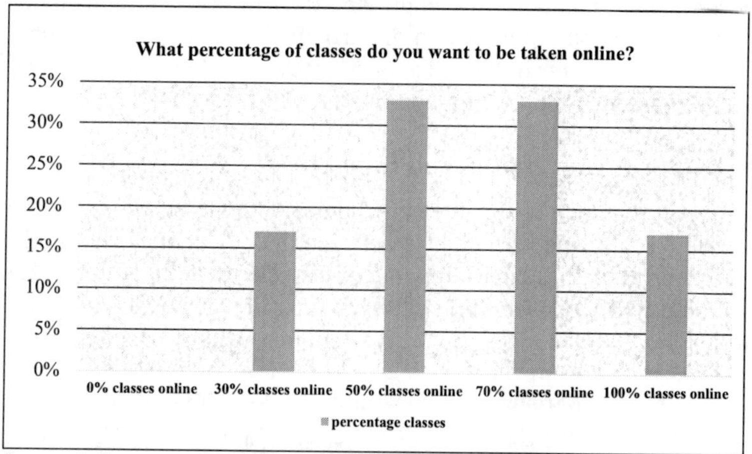

Source: Author.

Major Observations from the student survey

1. Students feel that overall education during Covid is adversely affected. They flagged lack of university facilities and poor internet connectivity as the main reasons.
2. From the above two questions it is clear that students on the one hand have overwhelmingly said that the education during Covid is adversely affected but on the other hand a vast majority still preferred the online mode of delivery of classes. This seems contradictory but the most reasonable explanation would be the flexibility of location and freedom to work while studying that online classes offer to be the reason for students preferring online classes while they do feel the shortcoming of lack of access to resources in the university such as the library, direct interaction with faculty, etc.

Need for foreign investment in Indian Higher Education

FDI in higher education will solve the problem of enrolment rate as we are in a situation of less supply high demand. Indian money and talent going abroad would be arrested to some extent. Infrastructure will improve in higher education will improve as the foreign universities will build their campuses as per international standards tried and tested in their countries. The ensuing competition would induce the homegrown Indian universities to become more competent by improving their infrastructure, method of imparting education, up-gradation of curriculum to keep abreast with the changing requirements of the industry. Moreover, FDI in education would generate immense employment opportunities.

Integration of Universities and Industries

By keeping in view, the intensified global knowledge economy, there is a need for strategic partnerships between the universities and industry that go beyond the customary funding of discrete research projects. Their partnership will work well when the research-driven university work in coordination with the innovation-driven environment of the company.

Fig. 11: Enrollment of Indian Students by fields of study

Field	Number ('000)	Total %
Arts	7,539	37
Science	3,790	19
Commerce & Management	3,571	18
Engineering & Technology	3,262	16
Education	733	4
Medicine	716	4
Law	373	2
Others	218	1
Agriculture	97	0
Veterinary Science	28	0
	20,327	100

Source: International Journal of Academic Research ISSN: 2348-7666; Vol.3, Issue-2(2), February 2016.

Attracting foreign universities to establish institutes in India

One of the recommendations of UGC is that foreign universities should be encouraged to offer their programmes in India. On behalf of GOI, there are several schemes which are offered by various regulatory bodies concerned with higher education. These schemes support the bilateral exchange of academic staff from India to foreign countries. Moreover, international institutions such as UNESCO, UNICEF, UNDP are also offering similar programmes. All these are aimed at bilateral transactions and aimed at Quality enhancement.

Global Initiatives for Academic Network (GAIN): Approved by Union Cabinet in Higher Education

Union Cabinet has approved a programme titled Global Initiative for Academic Networks (GIAN) in Higher Education aimed at tapping the talent pool of scientists and entrepreneurs internationally to encourage their collaboration with the institutes of Higher Education in India. GIAN will initially include the participation of foreign faculty in Institutes as Distinguished / Adjunct / Visiting faculty / Professors of Practice, etc., to participate in delivering Short or Semester-long Courses.

New Education Policy (NEP) 2020

The Government of India has come up with NEP with the aim to increase the Gross Enrolment Ratio in higher education from 26.3 percent (2018) to 50 percent by 2035 and increase public sector investment in the education sector to 6 percent of GDP.

Way Forward/ Suggestion

1. The States must come up with a new vision and programmes specifically addressing the needs of the State, its industry, economy, social setup.
2. Collaboration between higher institutes in India and abroad must be given more emphasis so as to enable the exchange of students, best practices, and knowledge sharing.
3. To enable diffusion of knowledge among research various research institutes in India, collaboration and inter-institutional research have to be encouraged to avoid reinventing the wheel, save resources, and achieve higher productivity and progress.
4. Government must promote an alliance between Indian higher education institutes and top international institutes and also generate liaisons between national research laboratories and research centres of top institutions for standard and synergic research.
5. There should be a multidisciplinary approach in higher education so that students develop rounded knowledge and personality.

6. Pedagogy must be improved through the following ways:
a. Increase the teacher training days and the frequency of training.
b. Establish teacher training institutes to cater to the existing and new faculty for training.
c. Collaborate with premier institutes in India such as the IITs and IIMs for teacher training.
7. Improving the quality of all Universities irrespective of Public or Private.
   (a) Stringent implementation of UGC norms will help improve the quality.
   (b) Many private institutes have mushroomed without basic infrastructure and facilities. These must be made to adhere to the norms failing which punitive measures need to be taken.
8. Need to create standard and qualitative education infrastructure to grab futuristic jobs.
9. Ensure that education policy is fully integrated into larger economic growth strategies.
   (a) Government should facilitate and enforce concrete integration of higher education with industry by making an internship mandatory. Incentives must be provided by the government to the industry for giving internships to students. This will boost the industry-higher education integration and will be a win-win as the industry can make a full-time offer to the interns and students can get real-life work experience for future job searches.
   (b) A percentage of classes conducted for the various higher education courses must be reserved for industry professions. This will not only foster stronger engagement of industry with higher education but also helps knowledge sharing on current issues faced in the industry and the best practices.
10. Move rapidly to develop new forms of digital and automation-enabled training programmes.
11. Develop and promote investment policies that encourage foreign direct investment and curtail long-term unemployment.

Conclusion

Higher education is the pipeline of manpower resources for all economic activity and the quality of output from the higher education institutions will determine the present and future economic growth and prosperity. It is indispensable that higher education has continuously evolve in tandem with the rapidly changing requirements of the industry in terms of knowledge and skill required. Indian higher education sector is fraught with many issues in terms of quality of education imparted, methodology of delivery, and the skills imparted. Apart from catering to industry, higher education also has to be accessible to all sections of society and to different geographies. Expansion of higher education sectors in terms of quality, as well as volume, is the need of the hour. While the government has made many efforts to expand the capacity of higher education such as attracting premier foreign higher education institutes, expanding Indian institutes and bringing about changes in UGC norms, etc, a lot more needs to be done to reform the higher education sector in India.

References

1. Kothari Commission, Vol.1, pp.1-287.
2. University Grants Commission Report, 2010.
3. Agarwal, 2006.
4. 'Social Infrastructure, Employment, and Human Development, Chapter 10, Economic Survey, 2019-20, Ministry of Finance.
5. Hanson, Melanie. "U.S. Public Education Spending Statistics" EducationData.org, August 2, 2021.
6. International Journal of Academic Research ISSN: 2348-7666; Vol.3, Issue-2(2), February 2016
7. John Handerson Moura Ar/global-talent-2021-52407222: Oxford Economics.

Weblog:

1. https://www.indiabudget.gov.in/budget2019-20/economicsurvey/
2. https://www.education.gov.in/en/aishe-report-1
3. https://www.indiabudget.gov.in/economicsurvey/doc/vol2chapter/echap10_vol2.pdf
4. http://www.skillsahead.net/job-market-india-2015-an-essential-report/
5. https://educationdata.org/public-education-spending-statistics)
6. http://iiti.ac.in/GIAN/
7. https://www.slideshare.net/JohnHandersonMouraAr/global-talent-2021-52407222

39

Status of Higher Education in India: E-Governance and Challenges

Dr M. Ramana

Abstract

In this paper, we explore the evolution of the Indian State's role in governance, and the implications this has for goal setting. We find that the Indian government's activist role in governance marked a change from the colonial period. This, we suggest, was not due to changes in the relative influence of different stakeholder groups. It was instead due to new national developmental goals, particularly industrialisation. The research study explain about the overview of higher education system plays an important key role in the country's overall development which includes creates income and employment development, empowerment of women, skill development, reduction of poverty, orientation programmes for weaker sections of peoples, rural development, new technology improvement, industrial, social, economic etc. Indian higher education system is one of the third biggest in the global level. The performance of Indian higher educational institutes namely colleges and universities in the present year is to deliver quality-based education systems in the field of education, research etc., to empower youth for self-sustainability. This research article relates the key importance and development that India is currently facing in higher education system and also relates many initiatives taken by the Union Government to meet those importance and development.

Keywords: *E-Governance, Higher Education, System of Higher Education, Importance, and Development.*

Introduction

The Higher Education system of India is today one of the furthermost growing sectors in the entire world. This datum has considerable development in the Higher Education Institution's setup of India in terms of quality and quantity. From the ancient period, India has rich practices of teaching-learning performs. Information was conserved and spread over oral tradition. Through the rule of the Mauryan dynasty, India succeeded with the foundation of institutions of learning. There stood universities like Taxila, Ujjain, Kanchi, and other institutions for medicine and education including astronomy and mathematics. Nalanda is now in eastern India and Taxila in Pakistan. Eastern India was popular by Buddhist universities and religious conclaves detained. Over the years subsequently, then the development of Indian Higher Education is occurred and flourished. Particularly in technical education IITs and IIM's have now marked their status amongst the superior Higher Education Institutions of the world.

E-Governance in Higher Education Institutions

E-governance can be defined as giving citizens the choice of when they access the government information and services as e-governance is a process of reforms in the way government works, share information and deliver services to external and internal clients for benefit of both government and citizens and business that they serve.

Traditional governance versus e-governance

Under traditional governance if citizens have to access to some information he/she was suppose to go to the particular department to seek that information. On the other side in e-governance now the scenario has been changed as government departments has come one step behind and information system are there so citizens can now use web service, web portals, or other media to get the information.

Pillars of e-governance:

- Process
- People
- Technology
- Resources

Objective of e-governance

- To deliver services to people in better way and that to in an affordable cost.
- To bring transparency and accountability.
- To empower people through information.
- To improve efficiency in government process.
- To improve interface with stake holders.

e-Governance initiative

A mission model project is an individual project within the national e-governance place that focuses on one aspect of the electronic governance such as banking, land records, and commercial taxes etc. Within NeGP "Mission Model" implies that project have clearly defined the outcomes, milestones, implementation, and timelines.

NeGP comprises of 31MMPs which are further categorised into states, central and integrated project, each state governments can also defines five MMPs specific to its individual need.

e-Governance in Higher Educational Institutions

Higher educational institutes develop the intellectual, capital, knowledge and innovations necessary for development of society capital such as good governance, rules, democracy and society.

Areas of Higher Educational Institutions for e-governance project:

- Interactive among faculty, school and departments.
- Integration of finance and account.
- Student enrolment and admission.
- Examination and certification.
- Research and development.
- Student placements.
- Enhancement of teaching skills of faculty.

MHRD and AICTE initiative

SWAYAM is the Indian electronic platform which proposes to offer courses from high school stage to post graduate stage in an interactive electronic platform covering all disciplines.

MOOC-Massive open online courses are available on all kind of subject. The purposes are to provide best quality education to more than three crore students across the country.

KYCP- Know your college portal was launched by the ministry of human resources development which promote and promise to be one stop shop for students and parents to know about various colleges in the country. The portal is updated with relevant information about every college. CBCS-Choice based credit system will enable students to take courses of their choice, learn at their own place, undergo additional courses and adopt an interdisciplinary approach to learning and all universities are in process to implement this system.

NIRF- National institutional ranking framework - In which each higher education is evaluated on five board parameter:

- Teaching
- Research
- Graduation outcomes
- Outreach inclusive nature.
- Public Perception.

GIAN - Global initiative for academic network

It was launched as an initiative to attract the best foreign academic to Indian universities of excellence. The programme has been launched to facilitate the partnership between higher education institutions of India and other foreign universities.

Role of e-governance in Higher education institution

1. Introduction of e-governance in education will empower the education system by providing new ways of communications between teacher to student, teacher ton their fellow teachers and between student to student.

2. E-governance can enhance and promote new methods of delivering the desired knowledge to students and will offer new insight to organise and deliver the requisite services.

3. Cost effective technology combined with the flexibility in learning and administration activities is essential to enhance efficiency as computer can be used for educational administrations.

4. The quality of our higher education system can be improved to make institutes really world class in fastest possible way.

Difference between E-government and E-governance

E-govt- The executive aim of the state, public administration in action arm of government, its application of ICT by govt. Agencies to improve efficiency, effectiveness, transparency and accountability in its entire activities.

Ex- Web portals of government agencies providing online services, UMANG portal of central government, paperless office, biometric attendance system, govt e-markets etc.

E-governance- It is the way government get its job done ways and processes by which government manages the affairs of state and nations and structure and process by which agendas are set, policies are formulated and its implementations.

It also the use of ICT in governance of a nation, as it helps in collaboration among multiple stakeholders, it also entails more efficient, effective, transparent and accountable governance model.

Ex- My govt portal, where in citizen participates in governance, online consultation and feedback by regulation, policy agencies, and parliamentary committee, social media PM interacting people on twitter online opinion poll.

Development of e-governance in India

- Department of electronics was set up in 1970.
- National information center was set up in 1977.
- NIC was able to connect all districts to New Delhi through VSAT terminal.
- 1984-89 Rajeev Gandhi gave big approval to computerisation and to use ICT in governance.
- 1990s-2000 Digitalisation of land records and other government records started, state wise area network (SWAN), e-governance in driving license, land registration and websites of government agencies were also done.
- 2000- IT act was there to do legal backing to digital signature, digital documents, and emails.
- 2006 National e governance plan was launched with 27 mission model project.
- 2008- Second administrative reforms commission titled promoting e-governance, the smart way forward launched the common service center.
- 2009 National unique identification project was launched (Aadhar).
- 2011-2012 NIC launched e-office, paperless office in central government ministries and agencies.
- 2014 My government. Portal was launched and national e-governance division under Ministry of electronics and IT launched several e-govt initiatives as UMANG (united mobile application for new age governance).
- 2015-2019 Digital India mission launched, direct benefit transfer scheme was launched, digital village etc.

40

New Education Policy 2020 Major Challenges

Dr. A. Madhuri

Abstract

The coverage that has stood out for introducing sweeping modifications in school and higher education is a boon for Telangana wherein it will improve getting to know effects, in particular for socially and economically prone college students it is important to understand the overall performance of Telangana in training. The overall performance grading index utilized by the ministry of education ranks Telangana at 17 out of the 37 states and Union territories in 2018-19. The huge-based totally metrics protected learning effects and high-quality, get entry to, equity, infrastructure and centers, and governance approaches. Telangana become ranked 30th in infrastructure and centers and 20th in access. it is for that reason vital for Telangana, that is financially properly endowed, to put in force the NEP. The NEP is familiar with the critical importance of exact exceptional childhood care and education (ECCE). specialists accept as true with that over 85 in line with cent of infant's cumulative mind development occurs prior to the age of six. through bringing ECCE to the centre of training with an explicit recognition on building foundational and numerical capabilities for every baby via give up of Grade 3, a quantum improvement in getting to know effects is anticipated. Telangana has at the least 10 districts with scheduled areas and kids belonging to Lambada, Koya, Gond, Yerukala, Chenchu and different groups will stand to gain. one of the motives for negative infrastructure and facilities of faculties is loss of budget with states. It also objectives to beautify get admission to by means of organising higher education institutes (HEI) in aspirational districts and unique schooling zones containing large numbers of social and economically deprived corporations. by way of 2030, the NEP targets to have at least one large multidisciplinary HEI in/close to every district. Aspirational districts in Telangana inclusive of Jayashankar Bhoopalpally, Kumarambheem Asifabad and Khammam will benefit. Telangana has a Gross Enrollment Ratio (GER) of 36.2 in keeping with cent. The NEP troubles a formidable name for boosting GER in higher training including vocational training to 50 according to cent via 2035.

Keywords: NEP.GER.HEI.GDP, RTE, MERUs

Introduction

The NEP stipulates the Centre and states work together to increase public investment in the education sector to six per cent of GDP. The Telangana state government's budget allocations to education for the 2020-21 fiscal saw a reduction from previous allocations. This is of major concern given that data recorded by the 2011 census shows Telangana's literacy rate as 66.4 per cent, much below the national average of 74.4 per cent. Lastly, the NEP has proposed sea changes in higher education that will better align with the needs of a changing employment market. Another striking example to improve equity is the attempt to include the mother tongue as the medium of both educational and vocational education. By including regional languages, in this case Telugu, as a medium of instruction, NEP 2020 strives to focus the child's energies on learning concepts rather than a new language. The NEP also acknowledges special mechanisms required to ensure that children belonging to tribal communities receive the benefits of these interventions. The decision to promote tribal languages will contribute to their educational empowerment.

Implementing NEP 2020 in Telangana State: Concerns and Challenges Implementing the NEP 2020 in Telangana involves ensuring the universal access to pre-primary to higher secondary education in the state. The new pedagogical and curricular structure of NEP 2020 has underscored the critical aspect of pre-primary education (for 3.6 years of age children) which has been undermined in the country for a long. Pre-primary and School Education Regarding this pre-primary education, universal provisioning of quality early childhood development, care and education is to be achieved by 2030. In this regard, more than 95 per cent of 3-6 years' age children (rural areas) in the Telangana state (as per the estimates of ASER 2018) are enrolled either in ICDS/Anganwadi centres (AWCs), in institutions for pre schooling or in any formal primary schools (govt. or private). But what percentage of them and to what extent they are imparted with pre-school curriculum (education) in these centres especially AWCs is a matter of concern. There are more than 35000 Anganwadi Centres across villages and habitations in the state and they are meant for providing all the ICDS or Anganwadi services. Although pre-school education (informal) is one among the six component package of ICDS/Anganwadi services, it appears that pre-school component is little neglected across ICDS centres not only in Telangana state but also all over the country. Around 70 per cent of children of 3-years age, 50 per cent of 4-years age and 20 per cent of 5- years age are enrolled in Anganwadi Centres.

If these centres are not able to provide comprehensive pre-school education for the holistic development of children, they would be deprived of it. Therefore, the mandate for the government of Telangana in implementing NEP 2020 is ensuring all the children in the age of 3 to 6 years not only access to pre-primary education but also to make them attend the same. It involves the implementation of National Curricular and Pedagogical Framework for Early Childhood Care and Education (NCPF-ECCE) Curriculum Framework across all the institutions (private and government including Anganwadi Centres) involving in imparting pre-primary education. Ensuring delivery of the services of pre-primary education for children in all these institutions with trained teachers and following norms would be a challenge. As a large chunk of children of pre-school age are enrolled in Anganwadi centres, training and capacity building of Anganwadi teachers along with equipping the centres with required materials is critical. Mobilisation of resources for these additional costs is another challenge for the state government. Further, the convergence across associated departments is also a major challenge as the planning and implementation of ECCE has to be carried out jointly by Ministries of Education, Health, Women & Child Development, and Tribal Affairs. School Education Telangana state is close to constitutional mandate of ensuring all the children of 6-14 years of age attend schools. Further, education is now a fundamental right of every child under Right to Education (RTE) Act 2009. Around 98 per cent of children in 6-14 years in the state are attending school.

Yet there is a gap, two per cent of children in this age-group are still remained out of school. The state government has a greater responsibility to ensure that right of every child in the state is realized by not only ensuring universal access itself but also attaining universal enrolment and attendance. Among the secondary school-age children (15- 17 years of age) the attendance rates in the state are more than 90 per cent. It is higher than national average and perhaps many other states. The mandate for the government of Telangana in implementing NEP 2020 is not only ensuring access to schooling along with attendance of all the children but also ensuring the delivery of quality education with improved learning-outcome to match with the expected outcome. First of all, in spite of high attendance rates the over-age and under-age children in different levels of education and in different grades / classes of school education (primary to higher secondary) is more prevalent in the state. As a result, the performance of Telangana state in the all India context in respect of net enrolment ratio (NER) by levels of school education (primary, middle, secondary and higher secondary) is little lagging behind when compared to its performance in respect of attendance rate among the children in the age group of 6-17 years which is appropriate for whole of school education. In this regard, streamlining enrolment and attendance of children in the state into the age-appropriate levels of education and age appropriate classes should be the major concern.

Most importantly integrating the whole of the school education system in the state is the need of the hour. Telangana and Andhra Pradesh are among the very few states in India maintaining separate administrative structures for both school educations up to low secondary and higher secondary (junior colleges) under collegiate education. Although the Telangana state has adopted the national strategy for school education i.e. Samagra Shiksha, it is yet to integrate junior colleges with school education. As NEP 2020 is concerned with the Foundational Literacy and Numeracy (FLN), it is definitely an urgent and necessary prerequisite to learning in the state as well as at the national level. Quality of education is cause of concern in the country and in Telangana state (see Reddy, 2019). ASER and NAS reports have shown the learning deficit or learning poverty (in World Bank terminology) in the school education. Primary education is an indispensable foundation for next levels of education and lifelong learning. In this stage, child acquires basic skills in numeracy and the necessary ability to read and write. As the surveys indicate many children are not able to demonstrate expected levels of learning outcomes / grade level competencies. In this regard, while implementing the NEP 2020, the Govt. of India is going to launch National Initiative for Proficiency in Reading with Understanding and Numeracy (NIP RUN) in a mission mode. It is important to identify and understand the extent of learning gaps and associated factors and to devise various strategies keeping in view the circumstances and diversities across districts in the state. Filling vacancies with qualified teachers is a part of the solution but beyond that the teachers' accountability and their training in accordance with requirement is critical in filling the gaps while attaining the expected learning outcomes.

Two examples one can cite is the performance in this respect is the schools under TSWREIS in Telangana state and also the public schools in Delhi. Scaling up the model performance and achievement of TSWREIS in Telangana, covering all the public institutions, is a challenging task for the government but not impossible. Initiatives with no major budget implications like active involvement of various stakeholders especially the school management committees (SMCs), parents and community which is critical in monitoring and tracking the students' progress in achieving expected learning-outcomes, and the required training and awareness drives are noteworthy in this context. To keep a regular check on education system, Govt. of India proposed in NEP 2020 to setup national assessment centre: Performance, Assessment, Review and Analysis of Knowledge for Holistic

Development (PARAKH). Also the World Bank is initiating a project for the purpose: Strengthening Teaching-Learning and Results for States (STARS). To tackle the learning losses due to school closures (like in the present Covid-19) or any emergency situation, the STARS project include a component: Contingency Emergency Response Component (CERC). The government of Telangana can take lead in this respect with developing its own strategies for improving the quality of education. Higher Education: General, Vocational, Technical and Professional as the NEP 2020 aims, implementing the policy in the state involves achieving the target 50% GER by 2035 with institutional restructuring and consolidation (a minimum of 3000 enrolments in each HEI), and transforming the state higher education system into a new and forward looking one with quality universities and colleges during the period of next 15 years.

The GER for higher education in Telangana state at present is 36% which is ten percentage points higher than national average. It appears to be that the Telangana state has an advantage of easily achieving the NEP 2020 target of 50% GER earlier than other states. However, increasing privatization of higher education, as it is seen, in the state has imperative for increasing private expenditure which has implications for affordability that may slow down the growth in enrolment and GER. In a study such a deceleration in growth of enrolment at the national. Consolidating the higher education institutions is a very big challenge not only in Telangana state but also across the country. There are almost 2000 HEIs along with more than 500 standalone institutions (such as polytechnics, teacher training institutes, diploma course level pharmacy and nursing colleges etc.,) in Telangana state. Keeping existing HEIs as they are and expanding their size to larger institutions, as envisaged in the policy, is not possible in near future. Many HEIs are sub-optimal in size and most of them do not have any prospects to grow large in size and the resources required.

Further, almost 80% of HEIs in the state are under private management, in most of the cases each entity (institution) has different individuals, trusts or organisations that are managing them. Bringing them together is also a difficult task. Although the acquisition and merger of the individual HEIs (in terms of their management) is facilitated and made possible, most of them (HEIs) are functioning in different locations. A large proportion of HEIs in the state are concentrated in and around capital city of Hyderabad or other major cities and district headquarters, but they are not located in geographical proximity. Geographical compactness of each of large HEIs is the underlying principle of consolidation proposed in the NEP 2020. Hence, making each of consolidated institutions (by management) as a single large HEI in one place (geographical location), is not possible through this acquisition and/or merger. One strategy could be facilitating expansion of selected potential institutions by consolidation while withdrawing/ closing down altogether the other institutions. Resources and catchment of closed institutions have to be diverted to those continue to exist.

Here the geographical distribution of HEIs in the state would be another major concern in the process. As NEP 2020 envisages consolidation is also involving with restructuring of the HEIs running a single programme, course or discipline institutions into multi-disciplinary ones along with restructuring of all these multi-disciplinary HEIs into universities of teaching and/or research and autonomous colleges. Except universities and some general education institutions (degree colleges) most of technical and professional HEIs in the state are specialized ones running single programmes. There are around 200 engineering colleges, 300 colleges for management courses, 200 B.Ed. colleges and 100 pharmacy colleges in the state. It may be said that nearly half of the HEIs in the state are of this nature (not of multi-disciplinary ones). Around 1050 are the degree colleges in the state, most of which run under-graduation programme with multiple courses in different disciplines (Science, Arts, Humanities and Computes). Most of colleges (HEIs) in the state are of affiliated nature. First of all, the government of Telangana has to mull its efforts streaming the B.Ed. programme into four years programme and making it as a part of university system, as envisaged in the NEP 2020. It means that all the individual B.Ed. colleges in the state may have to be closed down and ensuring a smooth transition from the present two-year course into a four-year one during the next couple of years. A thread connecting to the above is the setting up model Multi-disciplinary Education and Research Universities (MERUs) at least one for each district (as envisaged in the NEP 2020) and resource mobilization for the same is a great challenge in the state.

There are 33 districts in the state and hence that many model MERUs are to be setup in principle. But how it is dealt with, whether the existing institutions/universities in a district would be converted into model MERU for the district or altogether a new one would be set-up is an issue to be thought over. Again in the process of conversion issues like the required resource mobilization, management of public sector or private, or in public-private partnership (PPP) mode would crop up. Leaving it to any private initiatives have repercussions for growing private expenditure on education and affecting affordability especially in backward districts and for students belonging to economically backward classes in accessing educational opportunity in such premier institutions. Establishing so many model MERUs under public system would be burdensome for the state budget. Already existing higher education institutions under the public sector have been affected by financial crunch in state's higher education budget. Financing Education as the report of Analysis of Budgeted Expenditure on Education that compiled by Ministry of Education (MoE), Government of India, shows the expenditure on education in Telangana state comprises nearly 19.5 per cent of total budgeted expenditure of the state (Revenue Account) and 2.8 per cent of its Gross State Domestic Product (GSDP), for the year 2017-18. One must herein note that the report that is compiled by MoE (Govt. of India) covers more comprehensively all the expenditure on education across departments and ministries beyond the education department (see Motkuri and Revathi, Sep 2020). To compare with the other south Indian states, Kerala (4.2% of GSDP, 23.6% of State Budget) and Tamil Nadu (3% of GSDP, 25% of state Budget) along with Maharashtra (30% and 3% respectively) appears to have a better resource allocation for education than that of Telangana.

When budgets all the states are combined/aggregated (excluding Union Budget), the expenditure on education turns out to be 22.8% of total budget and 3.4% of GDP. Whereas at the national level, Centre (Union Govt.) and all the state governments together have spent 16% of the total budgeted expenditure of the country and 4.2% of GDP on education (see Motkuri and Revathi, Sep 2020). The government of Telangana needs to increase its resources allocation for educational development in the state. The Kothari Commission recommendation of 6% of GDP to be spent on education is applicable at the national as well at state level. The achievement of Government of Telangana is short of even the half-way mark in reaching goal of 6%. In this regard, as a short-term strategy it may have to increase the expenditure on education to at least 4% of GDP.

Conclusion

The new education policy has a laudable vision, but its influence will depend on whether it is able to effectively merge with the government's other policy initiatives Digital India, Skill India and the New Industrial Policy to name a few in order to effect a coherent reconstruction. For instance, policy linkages can ensure that education policy speaks to and learns from Skill India's experience in engaging more dynamically with the private sector to shape vocational education curricula in order to make it a success. This paper while analyzing the status of educational development in the Telangana state, critically examined the recent National Education Policy (2020) in general and its implementation process and challenges in the state of Telangana. The analysis brings out certain contradictions in the policy, issues and challenges in realizing aim of the policy. Overall, NEP 2020 although gauged to a greater extent the problems, issues, and challenges with respect educational development in the country, its approach and policy in addressing them would turns out to be challenging especially financial allocation.

Reference

1. Motkuri V. and Ravi C. (2013). Achieving Universal Literacy in Andhra Pradesh: Status and Prospects, Indian Journal of Human Development, Vol. 7(1).
2. Motkuri, V. (2004). Out-of-School Children: Child Labourers or Educationally Deprived?, Economic and Political Weekly (Commentary), Vol. 34 (38), 18 September.
3. Motkuri, V. (2005a) "On the Heterogeneities in the Incidence of Educational Deprivation of Children in Andhra.
4. Pradesh", in G. K. Karanth (ed.) Dimensions of Social Development: Status, Challenges and Prospects, Social and Economic Change Monograph Series 8, March, Institute for Social and Economic Change (ISEC), Bangalore, 2005.
5. Motkuri, V. (2005b). Educational Deprivation of Children in Andhra Pradesh: Associate Factors, Working Paper No. 251, Centre for Development Studies, Trivandrum.
6. Motkuri, V. (2006). Child Schooling in a Community in Transition: A Case of Scheduled Tribe in Andhra Pradesh, Journal of Educational Planning Administration, Vol. 20 (1), January.
7. Motkuri, V. (2007). "Telanganalo Prathamika Vidyaku Duramouthunna Chinnarulu" (Educationally Deprived.
8. Children in Telangana), in Telugu, in Sridhar Deshpande and Raghava (eds.) Telanganalo Chaduvu (Education in Telanagna), Telangana Intellectual Forum, Hyderabad.
9. Motkuri, V. (2008). Gender and Schooling Deprivation in Andhra Pradesh, The ICFAI Journal of Public Administration, Vol. 4 (1). Also, it appeared in A. V. Yadappanavar and Gyanmudra (eds.) Gender Issues in Education, National Institute of Rural Development (NIRD), Hyderabad.

41

Emerging Trends in Highere Education Technology Drive the Future of Education

Prof. C. R. Reddy

ABSTRACT

An individual possession of knowledge, skills and experience through education certainly transforms the nature's endowed resources as marketable products/services with 'economic value' is termed as human capital and knowledge economy. Enhance and enrich of human capital fillips nation's sound and health economy is the rationale of education. Education thrives to (a) educate, enlighten and encourage teaching, (b) input of understanding and (c) spirit and urge true facts. Education policy needs a clear-cut and transparency to lead in commercialisation and determination of values and proactive to the market logic. The great challenges accompany have been thoroughly exposed in recent periods through Covid-19 crisis. Interaction and integration with the economy of the rest of Worlds Counties, has now become a new emerging facet to bring out a unifying roof of the whole-teaching contents and methodology to attain the socio-economic development. To become a world-class academic institute heavily depends upon the committed faculty, quality infrastructures, supportive administration, and learning environment. Last but not least is the hardworking and brilliance or vividness is the foremost factor of promising among the young students. The corporate philanthropy to higher education is the call of the day to ensure trueness of education system for urging the prime goal of socio-economic development. This study focuses on the emerging trends in Indian higher education.

Key Words: Brilliance, Education, Human Capital, Knowledge Economy and Trend.

Description of topics or subjects that emerge or get more social attraction from the crowd over the past is termed as emerging trends. Higher education is a facilitating factor for learning or acquisition of knowledge, competitive skills, values, beliefs and habits through discussion, teaching, training and innovation. It promotes (a) industrial economy on its own right and (b) personnel for the rest of the economy of agriculture and subsidiary occupations for economic growth and development of nation. Education never stops and is lifelong students' learning always and also focuses on learning 'how to learn' and learning 'how to solve' problems. Learning is not only just in classroom but from projects, field study, interviewing experts and experiments and prototypes and in a variety of other ways. Knowledge is human capital and plays a key role in strengthening through available nature's endowed resources, in fact, a driving force in rapidly changing economy of the society.

Globalisation means integration of nation economy with the rest of the world countries economy and thus has become an emerging trend and encompassing mutual interest of nations towards the ultimate goal of socio-economic development by bringing under a unifying roof the whole teaching contents and methodology to attain the goal of high rise in living standard, improving health and envisioning higher education including technology advancement n an area of communication and computers which are the pillars of economic development. To make India power and shining thrust, globalisation of higher education has been a positive move in all the fronts of her economy. Therefore the academia would need to understand fully the facets of globalisation for better relations and more cordial harmony; what referred it as internationalisation of higher education.

A sound policy inscribes vision to achieve the intended objective of a concern/nation. Hence is the call of the day for 'healthy education policy.' The challenges of higher education confronting are commercialisation of education, obstacles in merit based admissions, deterioration in academic standards, encroachment in institutions and autonomy, teacher service conditions and education becomes subservient (Passive) to the advanced private sector market logic.

India is home to 1,000 universities and 40,000 colleges, the world's largest higher education system. Now, she sets to witness a major transformation in the space of higher education. Higher education system has been undergoing a tremendous change due to Covid-19 pandemic and the vital role of New Education Policy 2020 in shaping higher education. The upcoming trends in Indian higher education are highlighted below.

Curriculum Perspective: The curriculum, in the past, was more subjective with emphasis on the pre-defined content led to *monotonous coursework* with little or no scope to design on innovative thinking. Nevertheless, higher education will need space to motivate the students to utilize their creative abilities on the challenges of the society to invent means. Need to shift the focus on *how to think* instead of *what to think.*

The education programs were often all about imparting theoretical knowledge. But only textbook learning is not really fruitful to get a decent job. The colleges incorporate internships into their degree programmes and setting up for finding ways to start-ups.

Mobility: AS per All India Survey on higher education, Science, Technology, Engineering and Mathematics (STEMM) have become popular and increasingly gain more popularity among female students preferably than male students. Hence, need of focus on the studies of it in addition to the *mobility scheme* issues connected to the relocation of working women scientists. Foreign fellowship for women in Science, Technology, Engineering, Math and Medicine (STEMM) is another ways to allow women to participate in a research program in reputed universities in the US.

Private education: Did you know that one million students graduate 12th grade in India every year? This has led to an increased demand for educational institutions. Therefore, the private education sector will prosper or flourish. The private educational institutions often ties-up with businesses to allow the students get experiential learning. Such collaborations and constant effort to meet the old standards will enable private educational institutions to offer an incredible learning experience. BITS Pilani have even appeared in QS World Rankings 2022. Higher education can be expensive in private universities in India. So if you want to opt for higher study in India you can take an education loan. Also, taking a student loan enables you to fund your own education. Trend of privatisation is sadly noticed. The private sector involvement in promotion of higher education is to the extent of 60% which is a crashing radical change. Raising free structure is again a drawback. Resultantly, most of the students discontinue their studies as they cannot bare such fees.

Enrich student experience: Technological solution of AI is already integrated into the educational system and evolving to become more robust to meet the new requirements. An innovative learning content change how the coursework is to deliver making tracking students' progress super easy.

Assessment: Attention is moving from pen and paper assessments to online automation enabled assessments. Online proctored exam allow faculty to capture photos, and videos using a web camera. So, invigilators can examine if the right candidate is appearing for the exams and also eliminate instances where students may cheat.

Call for Artificial Intelligence: With AI research and development increasing at a rapid pace during the pandemic seem unfounded. AI is appearing seemingly everywhere in higher education areas like management systems, proctoring, grading, student information systems, library services and disability support. Today, AI technologies are almost every facet of students' lives and hence require the universities and colleges to rethink curriculums in supporting it. Recognition of uploading a photo on a social networking site is an example of application of AI. The intelligent digital personnel assistants like Siri, Google, Alexa are all powered by AI. It endeavours to simulate the natural intelligence of human beings into machines, thus making them behave intelligently. An intelligent machine is supposed to imitate some of the cognitive functions of human like learning, decision-making and problem solving.

Trend of students is 'how to learn to solve problem' instead of learning to memorise facts and figures. So this needs to completely re-imagine education and allow students to learn independently. Changes need at every level and have to infuse things like entrepreneurship into the curriculum which create students' own jobs.

Online Higher Education: Thanks to the pandemic, Institutes have been forced to choose online mode of instruction, but only colleges continue if willing this approach. Online education has existed before the pandemic as well and referred to as distance learning. Distance education is an example for online education. Owing to the increasing demand, higher education institutes create programs and complete online. Along with the online learning development, youth shows an interest in learning various types of languages.

Women Enrolment: India has the largest education system with the participation of women but relatively low. In 2018-19, the admission approximately 1.82 crore women enrolled for higher education which grew at an incredible 4.9 per cent CAGR to that of 2011-12 enrolment.

Emergence Foreign Education: Going abroad for (further) education is close to impossible. But being normal, the number of Indian students going for abroad studies will show no signs of slowing down. Earlier, the most preferred-countries were the US, Canada, Australia, and the UK. Now, considering the change in US immigration policies and Brexit, Indian students are expected to move to new destinations such as New Zealand, Ireland, Germany, France, Russia, etc.

Demand for International Course: The demand for colleges and universities providing international certification has witnessed a surge is a fact. Global courses from world-renowned universities like Harvard Business School and more to ensure our students learn and keep up with what taught across the globe.

Need of Skill Development: Skill development is key aspect for every individual to find decent jobs. The Indian Government is soon expected to increase skill development programmes to cater to 500 million individuals. It is also working on bringing in new skill centres, creating a National Policy on Skill Development and Entrepreneurship, making Amendments to the Apprentices Act and more.

The academia considers privatisation of higher education is very useful, in fact, less expensive. The underdeveloped countries like Bangladesh and development countries like the USA, Japan, Australia and many other have successfully switched over to privatisation of higher education with making it absurd. Can India be consider on these lines especially if money earned can 'plough back' into educational sector for its own sound and healthy improvement?

Entrepreneurship Education: Entrepreneurship education is more than just business, sometimes, labelled as venture creation programs. Teaching entrepreneurship is a similar way to other business degrees which makes distinction between the creativity and innovation aspects. Entrepreneurship is defined as the development of business acumen that can realize the full potential. Approach is to promote innovation or introduce new products, services, or markets in existing firms which is called corporate entrepreneurship. A recent approach involves creating charitable organizations which are designed to be self-supporting in addition to doing their good works and is usually called social entrepreneurship or social venturing. Entrepreneurship is being developed as a way of developing skills such as risk-taking and problem solving that facilitate achievement of life goals and in education. Whether start-up entrepreneurs or growing business owners, the challenge is much bigger than what we normally assume. It's critically important for us to know what we are getting into.

Entrepreneurship education programme promotes awareness among young women and men aged 15 to 24 years of the opportunities and challenges of business, entrepreneurship and self-employment. It helps them identify and work on some basic core entrepreneurial skills such as communication, negotiation and planning. Within the last decade, the programme has trained over 14,000 teachers and over 3 million young women and men to entrepreneurship.

Research: Research is a self-regulating and self-policing process wherein researchers conduct and present research without falsification and fabrication, giving credit to other scholars for their ideas when and where such credit is due. Research includes the aspects of competition including an emphasis on priority claims. Prestige has become associated with research excellence and high achievement. Hence, high quality of research is vital and as such it is equally important to conduct research in a culture which supports honesty and integrity to ensure the highest standards of ethical practice and behaviour.

The problem of scholarly wrongdoing is compounded in India due to rapid increase in the number of research publications in journals of dubious quality. It means research publications across the world have grown at a compounded annual growth rate of approximately 3 per cent over the two last centuries. This growth in research output has also been accompanied by a rise in poor-quality and predatory or greedy journals and lapses in ethical research practice.

Research misconduct is not uncommon because of ability to electronically scan documents and with the advances in machine learning and text analysis and data fabrication, falsification of results, mishandling of research subjects.

References

1. Adachi, C., & O'donnell, M. (2019). Degree Design thinking: integrated design frameworks for emerging online degrees in higher education. In y.w. Chew, k.m. Chan, & a. Alphonoso (eds.), *personalised learning. Diverse goals. One heart. Ascilite 2019 singapore* (pp. 349–353). Ascilite, singapore. [google scholar]
2. Arwu. (2019). Arwu world university rankings 2018. *Academic world rankings*. Retrieved from http://www.shanghairanking.com/arwu2018.html [google scholar]
3. Asfa-wossen, l. (2019, november 28). Where exactly are we with ai in higher education? *Study international*. Retrieved from https://www.studyinternational.com/news/ai-higher-education-2019/ [google scholar]
4. Australian research council. (2019). State of australian university research. *Era national report 2018-19*. Retrieved from https://dataportal.arc.gov.au/era/national report/2018/

Index

A

Aaron Sams, 278
Academic Achievement, 122
Academic achievement, 325
Academic Bank of Credit, 87, 118, 273
Academic Bodies, 112, 257
Academic community, 258
Academic Council, 257
Academic Council Meeting, 252
Academic Credit Banking System, 253
Academic information, 90
Academic leaders, 309
Academic learning, 256
Academic Networks, 339
Academic Reforms in Higher Education, 249
Academic Renewal Committee, 252
Academic spaces, 60
Academic spectrum, 70
Academic strengths, 236
Academic-based studies, 312
Academic-based teacher, 312
Account performance levels, 236
Adequate facilities, 103
Advanced education, 58
Advancement in Educational Technology, 277
Advantages and Disadvantages of Technology, 24
Advantages of internet-based learning, 137
Agra University Gaurav Shri Award, 108
Ali Yassin, 76
Aligarh University, 106
All India Council for Technical Education, 113, 276
All-India Survey on Higher Education, 331
Alumni associations, 71
Andhra Pradesh, 70, 165
Anganwadi Centers, 271
Anglo-Indian School, 36
APJ Abdul Kalam, 314
Art of Learning, 141
Artificial Intelligence, 103
Asia and the Pacific, 301
Asian Development Outlook, 301
Assertiveness, 292
Assessment Reforms, 273
Audio lessons, 50
Audio recordings, 155
Augmented Reality, 158, 159
Autocratic teaching strategies, 186
Autonomous committees, 233
Availability of student loan, 38
Ayushman Bharat, 166

B

Bageshwar, 321
Banaras Hindu University, 108
Bangalore, 108
Barriers to Critical Thinking, 177, 178, 179
Benaras University, 106

Benefits and Drawbacks, 70
Benefits and Risks of Media, 246
Benefits of Education Technology, 154
Bharat Jyoti Award, 108
Bharat mission, 170
Bhimrao Ramji Ambedkar, 193
Bhopal, 108
Biased Nature and Experiences, 178
Bibliometric technique, 77
Binding mechanism, 96
Board Exams, 117
Board of Examination, 36
Board of Universal Education, 273
Boards of Studies, 257
Bologna Process, 256
Bolsters Confidence, 242
Bricks-and-mortar, 60
British education, 173
British rule, 173
Building positive relationships, 292
Bureaucratic structures, 333

C

Capacity building, 331
Capital Grants, 111
Capital Works Programme, 111
Caste Disabilities Removal Act, 194, 197
Cell Phones, 209
Center for Skills, 133
Central Act, 106
Central Advisory Board of Education, 107, 119
Central Asia, 314
Central Board of School Education, 36
Central Board of Secondary Education, 38, 289
Central Universities, 106, 107, 230
Challenges before Educational Policies, 184
Challenges to the Higher Education, 140
Chamoli, 321
Chi-Square test, 70
Chief Information Officer, 62
Chief Technology Officer, 62
China, 98
Chinese travellers, 230
Choice Based Credit System, 259
Classroom Assessment Techniques, 179
Cloud Computing, 158
Collaborative learning techniques, 240
College governance, 112
College level assessments, 211
College of English Education, 230
College websites, 210, 213
Comfort situations, 63
Commerce and management, 33
Commissioner of Collegiate Education, 210
Committees of Courses, 253
Common Entrance Exam, 118
Common entrance exam, 149
Communication Skills, 333
Communicative Language Teaching, 44
Complete Multiple Curriculum, 273
Complete Multiple Curriculum Study, 273
Computer assisted learning, 263
Computer based education, 263
Computer Skills, 333
Computer technology, 27
Computers in teaching, 26
Concept of Equity, 130
Concept of Social Exclusion, 132
Conducts National Eligibility Test, 110
Conference Style Learning, 180
Connection problems, 25
Consolidated Fund of India, 110
Consortium of Educational Communication, 110
Constitutional values, 92

Coping with emotion, 291
Coping with stress, 291
Copying with emotions, 292
Copying with stress, 292
Corona epidemic, 319
Corona period, 320, 321
Corporate Social Responsibility, 232
Cost of higher education, 149
Country Reports on Economic Policy, 301
Course Era, 71
Course Management System, 49
Creating class websites and blogs, 23
Creative thinking, 291, 294
Credit Accumulation and Transfer System, 253
Credit framework, 251
Credit-based curriculum, 253
Critical Thinking, 175, 176, 178, 291
Cultural shift, 94
Current Enrollment, 35, 37
Current trends in the education industry, 116
Curriculum designers, 217
Curriculum Issues, 141
Curriculum planning, 258

D

Dalit candidates, 191
Dalit children, 195, 196
Dalit communities, 193
Dalit enrolment rates, 196
Dalit equality, 192
Dalit political activists, 193
Dalit population of India, 194
Daniel Markovits, 133
David Gordon, 132
Decision making, 291
Deemed Universities, 230, 302
Deemed-to-be University, 107
Degree Colleges, 302
Degree Colleges of Telangana, 44
Delhi University, 106
Demand for Open and Distance Learning, 103
Demographic Profile, 79
Developing countries, 76, 99, 229
Devi Ahilya University, 108
Device decisions, 157
Digital classrooms, 322
Digital Divide, 134, 320
Digital education, 134
Digital learning, 213
Digital learning tools, 154
Digital microphones in the classroom, 24
Digital schooling, 134
Digital technologies, 58
Digital University, 135
Directorate of Medical Education, 126
Disabled children, 326
Disadvantages of technology, 22
Distance Learning Institutions of India, 101
Distances and Disconnects, 140
District Primary Education Programme, 197
Downtrodden portion, 115
Dr. Bhushan Patwardhan, 109
Dr. Hari Singh Gour University, 108
Dr. Sarvepalli Radhakrishnan, 107, 270
Draft New Education Policy, 84
Drone Mentality, 177
Drop out rates, 152
Drug abuse, 291
Dynamic citizen, 289

E

E-courses in regional languages, 149
Early Childhood Care and Education, 164

Early childhood education, 149
Economic status, 327
Economically Disadvantaged Groups, 148
Economically poor, 325
Education at a glance, 132
Education Commission, 164
Education loans, 227
Education quality, 310, 312
Education Technology companies of India, 102, 226
Education-Based Development Programmes, 196
Educational Games and Simulations, 295
Educational Innovations, 166
Educational opportunities, 329
Educational process, 217
Educational quality, 309
Educational requirements, 59
Educational resources, 154
Educational Technology, 156, 166
Effective communication, 291, 293
Effective decision-making skills, 293
Effective governance and leadership, 149
Effective teaching, 27
Egocentric Nature, 177
Electronic devices, 95
Ellis and Goodyear, 61, 63
Emerging Technologies, 159
Employment opportunities, 212
English Language Context, 49
English Language Learning, 43
English Language Learning in Telangana, 45
English Language Learning Website, 46
English Language Teaching, 47
English proficiency index, 119
Enrolment in primary education, 197
Entrepreneur special courses, 75
Entrepreneurial opportunities, 76
Entrepreneurship educational workshops, 81
Environment Leadership Award, 108
Environmentalist of the Decade (Poorvanchal) Award, 108
Equitable and Global University, 133
Equitable Education, 148
Equity and equality, 130
Equity in Education, 191
Ethics in Profession, 143
European Credit Transfer System, 253, 255
Evaluation criteria, 238
Evaluation practices, 257
Examining body managed, 308
Experimental Learning, 161
Experimental study, 266
External distraction, 123

F

Fa-Hien, 230
Facebook live, 100
Factors affecting technology in education, 23
Faculty administrators, 232
FDI in education, 338
Female attendance, 198
Female Dalit enrolment rate, 195
Field trips, 160
Financial assistance, 328
Financial crisis, 52
Financial support, 149
Flexible spaces, 62
Flipped classrooms, 286
Food and Agricultural Organisation, 322
Foreign Direct Investment, 298, 300
Foreign education, 306
Foreign institutions, 89
Foreign investment, 301
Forum of Young Leaders, 199

Foundation for Teacher Development, 312
Freedom of choice, 232
Freeman and Greenacre, 238
Fundamental Duties, 92
Future Implications, 296
Future industry leaders, 54

G

Gamified Learning, 157
Gap in digital readiness, 136
Gaps in the literature, 69
Gender disparity, 35
Gender Gap Post-Pandemic, 134
General English textbook, 44
General mechanics, 239
Global citizenship, 220
Global Educational Standards, 219
Global Initiative for Academic Networks, 339
Global Standard Education, 219
Global student population, 99
Global warming, 288
Good religion teachings, 294
Google Chrome, 48
Google Class Room, 210
Google classroom, 44
Google Drive, 100, 224
Google Meet, 44, 46, 100, 210, 224
Google Plus groups, 243
Google site, 44, 45, 46, 48, 49
Governing Councils, 112
Government Degree Colleges, 43
Government Degree Colleges of Telangana, 45
Government managed, 308
Government training programmers, 75
Grade repetition, 152
Gram Panchayats, 121, 123
Gross Domestic Product, 170, 332
Gross Enrolment Ratio, 86, 94, 129, 148, 298, 331
Group Thinking, 177
Guwahati, 108

H

Hari Om Ashram Trust Awards, 109
Health Consciousness, 142
Health indicators, 202
Hernandez-Ramos, 26
High-tech training, 160
Higher dropout rates, 149
Higher Education, 47
Higher Education Commission of India, 86, 118, 273
Higher Education Council, 276
Higher Education Institutions, 85
Higher Education system, 121, 145
Higher educational institutions, 137
Himachal Pradesh, 317
Household incomes, 319
Household Social Consumption, 134
Huen Tsang, 230
Humanities and Liberal Arts and Sciences, 259
Hunter Commission, 230
Hybrid learning model, 119
Hybrid technology, 48
Hyderabad, 53, 108

I

Immanuel Kant, 131
Impact of flipped classroom, 279
Impact on facilities, 56
Impact on pedagogies, 56
Impact on students, 56
Implementation of NEP, 95
Implication of the study, 267
Importance of Technology in Education, 22

Inadequate Infrastructure and facilities, 149
Including tertiary education, 151
Inclusion in Education, 191
Income group, 36
Independent Boards, 306
Independent study, 62
Indian Caste system, 196
Indian Economic Survey, 30
Indian education system, 124
Indian educational institutions, 124
Indian Higher Education, 85, 203, 338
Indian Higher Education System, 298
Indian National Education Policy, 269
Indian Space Research Organisation, 84
India's education industry, 127
Individual Life Skills, 291
Industrial training institutes, 274
Information Communication Technology, 264
Inhabited Villages, 123
Institution of National Importance, 107
Institution under State Legislature Act, 107
Institutional autonomy, 272
Institutional Restructuring and Consolidation, 303
Institutions of National Importance, 106, 230
Inter University Centre, 110
International Commission, 150
International organisations, 123
International student movement, 227
Internet connectivity, 156
Internet facility, 319
Internet Live Stats, 57
Internet users, 57
Internship opportunities, 91
Interpersonal relationship, 291
Ishan Uday' Scholarship Scheme, 322

J

J.S. Verma Commission, 164
James Robson, 133
Jangaon, 204
Janta Curfew, 98, 221
Jean-Jacques Rousseau, 131
Jeremy Bentham, 131
John Dewey, 244
John Locke, 131
John Maynard Keynes, 115
John Stuart Mill, 131
Johnson Grammar, 53
Joint Information Systems Committee, 61
Jonathan Bergmann, 278
Junior Research Fellowship, 110

K

Kalaburagi, 230
Kanchipura, 230
Karimnagar, 204
Karl Marx, 131
Karnataka, 230
Kasturi Rangan, 270
Key student data, 157
Knowledge and Organisational performance, 133
Knowledge of Vedas, 173
Kothari Commission, 270, 332
Kothari Commission report, 92

L

Lack of guidance, 52
Language immersion, 160
Language Learning website, 45
Language Teaching and Learning, 47
Laptops and tablets, 158
Latest technology, 120
Latin America, 314
Leadership qualities in students, 54

Learn English, 49
Learner Centered Teaching, 53
Learning management systems, 243
Learning-curve, 245
Liberal education, 172
Lieutenant Governors of Union Territories, 274
Livelihood Issues, 318
Lomas and Oblinger, 61, 62
Love-hate relationship, 246
Low socioeconomic status, 63

M

Mahatma Gandhi, 319
Makes Better Citizens, 242
Management of Higher Education, 142
Mandal Praja Parishads, 121, 123
Massive Open Online Courses, 101, 225
Maulana Abul Kalam Azad, 108
Media Authority, 58
Media in the Classroom, 246
Medical and Engineering Education, 136
Medical incentives, 198
Members of Parliament, 96
Merit-based admissions, 97
Metropolitan cities, 318
Michael Bodekaer Jensen, 159
Michael Sandel, 133
Mid-Day meal, 172
Migrant students, 95
Millennial Development Goals, 218
Mobile companies, 321
Mobile network connectivity, 321
Modelling thinking behaviours, 181
Modern digital systems, 153
Modi government, 117
Multidisciplinary Education, 118
Multidisciplinary higher education institutions, 172
Multinational corporations, 299
Multinational enterprises, 299
Multiple Opportunity Admission, 273
Municipal Corporations, 121, 123
Municipalities, 121
Music videos, 244

N

Nagavi Vishwavidyalaya, 230
Nalanda, 230
Nation Builder Award, 108
National Accreditation Council, 118, 273
National and international agencies, 223
National Assessmen, 165
National Assessment and Accreditation Council, 108, 133
National Assessment Centre, 117
National Board of Accreditation, 185
National Certification Council, 86
National Council for Higher Education, 273
National Digital Library of India, 101, 226
National Digital Repository, 101
National Education Policy, 84, 89, 90, 92, 93, 94, 146, 164, 274, 326, 332
National Education Policy of India, 97
National Educational Alliance for Technology, 102, 226
National Educational Policy, 129
National Educational Technology Forum, 118
National governments, 151
National Higher Education Regulatory Council, 118
National Institutional Ranking System, 275
National integration, 83
National Knowledge Commission, 256
National Mission for Mentoring, 118
National Policy on Education, 230

National Qualifications Framework, 253
National Research Foundation, 86, 97, 118, 273, 303, 305
National Right to Education Act, 275
National skill, 296
National Testing Agency, 273
National Veda Vyas Sanskrit Awards, 109
Nationwide lockdown, 99
Navigation Support Documents, 43, 44
Negative Attitude of Parents, 149
Negotiation skills, 293
New Education Policy, 83, 84, 85, 90, 94, 339
Night classes, 199
North East Region, 322

O

Observation and Recommendation, 126
Online and digital education, 149
Online education, 69, 72, 223, 320
Online education in Telangana, 73
Online education settings, 157
Online governmental courses, 117
Online learning, 104, 146
Online lessons, 155
Online teaching, 55
Open and Distance Learner, 101, 149, 227
Open Distance Learning, 135, 303
Opening universities, 93
Oral communication, 188
Oral or written, 188
Ordinary Least Square Method, 30
Organisation of Economic Cooperation and Developme, 299
Organisational level, 57
Osmania University, 72, 272, 335
Overall management, 188

P

Pandemic crisis, 209
Pandemic scenario, 124
Pedagogical issues, 52, 54
Pedagogical Structure, 117
Peer resistance, 293
Perceptions of flipped classroom, 279
Periodicals, 205
Personality development, 289
Physical Fitness, 142
Political parties, 96
Popular media, 245
Population explosion, 288
Post-War Educational Development in India, 107
Pre-Pandemic Disparities, 122
Primary enrolment rates, 199
Private and government institutions, 136
Private colleges, 302
Private hospitals, 166
Private players, 166
Private schools account, 116
Private sectors, 167
Private Universities, 107, 230, 302
Privatisation of education, 88
Problem Solving, 291
Problems in Higher Education, 230
Prof Anita Rampal, 135
Professional development, 157
Professional Education, 30, 118, 304
Professional endeavours, 217
Professor Ved Prakash, 105
Programme designers, 311
Project Strategy, 187
Project-based Learning, 160
Promoting High Quality Research, 305
Provincial Act, 106
Public School Standards Authority, 273
Public-Private Divide, 136

Q

Quality education, 135, 185
Quality education, 151, 272
Quality Education and Learning Process, 185
Quality higher education, 327
Quality of Education, 156, 310, 341
Quality of higher education, 143, 144, 231
Quality teaching, 309
Quality Universities and Colleges, 302
Question-answering strategy, 187
Questions of equity, 137

R

Radhakrishnan Commission, 230
Raja Balwant Singh Shiksha Samman, 108
Rajiv Gandhi, 270
Ramesh and Farshad, 290
Random cluster sampling, 70
Rashtriya Uchchhita Shiksha Abhiyan, 275
Reader's Questions, 180
Reciprocal Peer Questioning, 179
Records of students, 156
Recurrent Grants, 111
Reference Books, 205
Reforms in Higher Education, 92
Research gap in literature, 78
Research Questions, 147
Research Trends on Flipped Classroom, 279
Research-Intensive Universities, 86
Residential Education Societies, 126
Restructuring of Syllabus, 141
Retention of special children, 151
Revenue Divisions, 121
Revenue Mandals, 122, 123
Revenue Villages, 122, 123
Right to Education Act, 93
Role of National Education Policy, 274
Rudraprayag, 321
Rural Area Education Issues, 319
Rural areas, 317

S

Sameera Sultana, 300
San Francisco, 240
Sanitation demands, 84
Sargent Report, 107
Sarv Shiksha Abhiyan, 170
Scheduled Caste, 148, 191, 231
Scheduled Tribe, 148, 191, 231
School Education, 308
School of Open Learning, 135
School systems, 157
School-based drug treatments, 198
Scientific and technological advances, 83
Scope for Private Institutions, 87
Search Engine Optimisation, 49
Secondary data collected, 78
Secondary Education Commission, 230
Security and privacy protection, 157
Selected Education Statistics, 30
Self-awareness, 291, 292
Self-financed and privately managed, 308
Sell Craft Global Solutions, 333
Serampore, 230
Sexual abuse, 291
Sexual orientation, 327
Sexual transmitted infections, 291
Sharma and Barret, 48
Shikshak Parv, 274
Shri Amit Khare, 109
Siddipet, 204
SMART Boards, 158
Smith and Toland, 239
Social Conditioning, 177

Social Exclusion, 191
Social media, 153
Social Sciences, 33, 286
Socially and Economically Disadvantaged Groups, 117
Socio-Economically Disadvantaged Groups, 129
South Africa, 251
Special Developmental Zones, 322
Special disaster management, 322
Special education, 313
Special Education Zones, 117, 328
Spontaneous Group Dialogue, 180
Standardized Credit System, 257
Standing Committees, 257
State levels, 308
State School Standards Authority, 118
State University, 107
Statement of the Problem, 147
Statistical technique, 280
Strategies to Promote Critical Thinking, 179
Student achievement, 238
Student centric learning, 54
Student Choice Credit System, 251
Student loan, 37
Student Survey, 49
Students and Faculty, 207
Students Enrolment due to poverty, 149
Students Migration, 317
Students with Special Needs, 148
Supreme Court ruling, 96
Sustainable Development Goals, 89, 129, 270
Swami Pranavananda Saraswati National Awards, 109
Syllabi and courses, 143

T

Takshashila, 230
Takshashila and Nalanda, 173
Tamil Nadu, 31, 36
Tea shops, 190
Teacher collaboration, 150
Teacher Education, 118, 304, 308
Teacher education institutions, 308
Teacher empowerment, 312
Teacher Survey, 49
Teacher-driven curriculum, 254
Teacher-student relationship, 211
Teachers Education Department, 126
Teaching, Learning and Evaluation, 204
Teaching profession, 150
Teaching strategy, 189
Teaching-Intensive Universities, 86
Technical and professional degree courses, 32
Technological developments, 143
Technology in education, 155
Technology portfolio, 159
Telangana educational system, 123
Telangana region, 123
Telangana state, 204, 272
Telangana State Council, 212
Telangana teaching resources, 70
Telegram, 224
Tertiary Level English Language Education, 44
Thinking Patterns, 177
Three-language formula, 96
Tool Used for data collection, 265
Tools of Technology in Education, 157
Traditional classroom, 156
Traditional classroom teaching, 48
Traditional educational approaches, 159
Traditional learning, 53
Traditional lecture, 26
Traditional methods, 27
Traditional mode of teaching, 187

Traditional organisational ideals, 249
Traditional paradigms, 102
Traditional pedagogical systems, 254
Traditional system, 124
Traditional teaching methods, 69, 70, 161
Trained teachers, 94
Training teachers, 151
Transfer students, 95
Transforming Regulatory System of Higher Education, 305
Tribal Welfare, 308
Type of Management, 37
Types of Technology used in the classroom, 23

U

U.P. Ratan Award, 108
Uchatar Innovation Campaign, 275
UG students of Telangana, 43
UGC Research awards, 109
UGC Website, 212
UN- General Secretary, 303
Un-inhabited Villages, 122
Unawareness of parents, 149
Undergraduate Programme, 250
Undergraduate programmes, 85
Unfinished learning, 53
Union Cabinet, 85
Union Government of India, 105
United Nations, 148, 301
Universities, 222
University autonomy, 111
University education, 228, 254
University Education Commission, 107
University education in India, 105
University entrance tests, 122
University graduates, 235
University Grants Commission, 101, 105, 106, 108, 109, 110, 275, 308
University Grants Commission Act, 257
University Grants Committee, 107
University leadership, 250
Unnat Bharat Abhiyan, 275
UN's Millennium Development Project, 314
Unwanted pregnancy, 291
Urban areas, 148
Urban Local Bodies, 84
Urban poor, 148
US and Canada, 139
Use of mobile devices, 23
Use of space in universities, 58
Use of technology in education, 149
Use Writing Assignments, 180
Useful digital tools, 154
Using Social Media, 245
Utilisation of Google sites, 49
Uttarakhand, 317, 320, 321
Uttarkashi, 321

V

Value Education, 143
Value of education, 31
Verbal communication, 187
Vice Chancellors of Universities, 274
Vice-Chancellor, 108
Video games, 153
Videoconferencing, 103
Vikramashila, 230
Village wells, 190
Villupuram, 30
Villupuram district, 31
Virtual careers, 160
Virtual class rooms, 209
Virtual Labs, 102, 226
Virtual learning culture, 99
Virtual platforms, 211
Virtual Reality, 158, 159

Virtual University of Pakistan, 60
Virtuous selection, 166
Vocational and academic study, 91
Vocational education, 85, 148
Vocational studies, 91
Vocational subjects, 84

W

Weekly progress reports, 237
Well-qualified teachers, 332
WhatsApp, 46, 100, 224
Work pressure, 178
World Bank, 197, 199, 301
World Commission for Environment and Development, 68
World Health Organisation, 98, 199, 221
Written dialogues, 180
Wuhan, 98

Y

Yash Technology Solutions, 333
Young Australians, 175
YouTube, 243
YouTube channel, 213
YouTube Live, 100, 210, 224

Z

Zero academic year, 51
Zero cost element, 68
Zoom App, 210